"Thoughtfully composed, oftentimes ocross superstar Brent Worrall offers the rea mina-tion of his own life, revealing a gritty an lream-come-true" moments, and shocking 3rent's autobiographical account is a bold a ΓORY over personal demons, and is a stunning and inspirational testament about the perseverance of the human spirt."

—Kevin G. Lefebvre, MA, RCC Psychotherapist

"Aspiring to achieve one's full potential through sport, regardless what form life's challenges might take. This is Paralympism - and this is Brent. Through a peer support connection, which is such a critical piece to rebuilding lives after a spinal cord injury, I have had the privilege of getting to know Brent and witness first hand how he has faced many adversities head on with his incredible tenacity, determination, strength and courage. With his love of sport and community, Brent has become a difference maker in the lives of those around him! Through very dark times you always found your way back to the light! What a powerful story and legacy you have created with your life's journey thus far, and I hope you continue to uncover and discover your true self."

—Sonja Gaudet, 3 Time Paralympic Gold Medalist

"Over the course of the 40 plus years that I've spent hanging around the sport of the motocross, very few people have inspired me the way Brent Worrall has. Through his determination to overcome adversity, I know that at times it has made me stop and remember that we should really only be living in the moment. I first met Brent just a day prior to his life altering accident at Walton Raceway in 2011. He had introduced himself and mentioned to me how much he enjoyed reading the Walton TransCan event program I had put together. He left a lasting impression on me that day and since then we have become good friends. In life, when you face the type of challenges that Brent has had to face since that fateful day in Walton, ON, you can either sink or swim. I think we can all agree that not only did Brent chose to swim, but has since swam as if he had been born in the water. Brent has also taught me that life is a gift and that we should cherish every good day we have, because you never quite know what is around the next corner, or over the next jump."

—Chris Pomeroy, Editor at *Motocross Performance Magazine*
and former top Pro National Motocross racer

MOTOCROSS
SAVED MY LIFE
FROM ITS DARKNESS

BRENT WORRALL

 FriesenPress

Suite 300 - 990 Fort St
Victoria, BC, V8V 3K2
Canada

www.friesenpress.com

ISBN
978-1-5255-5354-7 (Hardcover)
978-1-5255-5355-4 (Paperback)
978-1-5255-5356-1 (eBook)

1. BIOGRAPHY & AUTOBIOGRAPHY, PERSONAL MEMOIRS

Distributed to the trade by The Ingram Book Company

Table of Contents

I dedicate this book to my three incredibly brave, strong and loving children
Sonu, Sara and Nolan

Foreword

By Rick Hamer-Jackson

Brent Worrall was my first hero! When I was a young boy heading out to the motocross tracks around British Columbia and Washington State as a wide-eyed aspiring racer, Brent was the most badass mini cycle racer in Canada. When Brent, with his flaming-red afro, and his dad, Jim, a grizzled tough guy who looked like he ate nails for breakfast, showed up at the track, everybody knew they were there to kick ass! I wanted to be just like Brent from the moment I first saw him.

How quickly things change. This book tells the amazing story of a man who was living the dream life of a top racer who then virtually disappeared from the racing scene and all the friends that went with it, lost for the next twenty-five years in a seedy lifestyle of alcohol and drugs.

Unbelievably, Brent found the strength to make a comeback, returning to his beloved two-wheeled machines and piecing together lost relationships that his lifestyle had taken from him. The future couldn't have looked brighter until a devastating high-speed crash at a Canadian senior motocross championship in Ontario paralyzed him for life. Even then, there was no quit in him. From his wheelchair, Brent went on to become a champion yet again, this time as the top motocross media person in the country.

This is a gripping read that goes into incredible detail about how one person can go from the highest highs to the lowest lows over and over again, and still have the will to fight back. Here I sit, forty years after first meeting Brent, and he is still my hero, but now for entirely different reasons.

Introduction

Have you ever wanted to write a book? An in-depth introspective look back at your every move in this malady we call life? Putting each and every one of your highest chest-beating, flag-waving accomplishments on paper? What about the failures, gut-wrenching tragedies, and personal heartaches you have endured, realizing that something or someone has been lost or changed forever?

Maybe your story includes that time you were shot at in your crib as a baby. Or maybe you were nominated as your hometown's athlete of the year. What about that time you won a national title in your sport and then went on to finish in the top ten in the world in your age bracket? How about breaking the same leg five times in exactly the same spot, among countless other bones? Maybe you were so tired of being broken you said, "To hell with it," and decided to create your own excitement through a twenty-five-year career as a seemingly hopeless, depressed, and suicidal alcoholic, even lowering yourself to the point where you bought a can of Lysol to drink on a Grey Cup Sunday.

How about that time you got so tired of being sick and tired that you realized you were not a bad person trying to be good but a sick person who had a life-threatening disease and needed to get well? Slowly but surely, you made every effort to piece together the broken shards of your glass parachute. But once again, some ten years later, facing more seemingly insurmountable physical adversity, you left your body long enough to look everyone in the eye, all of them thinking you might die. Would it be a stretch to think such a thing could happen twice in the same year to the same person?

Well, all the above did happen, and it happened to me. I have survived a lot worse, much worse. My life hasn't all been blood and guts—there's been a lot of glory too—but right now, it's imperative that I tell you the story of how motocross saved my life...while the clock is still ticking.

1

Are We There Yet?

The year was 1966, and if the radio was on; it likely blasted songs by the Beatles, Frank Sinatra, Simon and Garfunkel, or Percy Sledge, bellowing out his brand-new hit, "When A Man Loves A Woman." That was the year I was welcomed into the world by my loving parents, James Robert and Donna Lynn Worrall.

I was born in the Chilliwack General Hospital on June 1, 1966, the son of a proud, burly logger and a highly intelligent, considerate, and caring bank clerk. I don't remember hearing any complaints about my head being too big or being born prematurely, so my entrance to the world must have been pretty normal.

The small farming community of Chilliwack, BC, an hour east of Vancouver, was home to about 15,000 people at the time. That relatively quiet and postcard-perfect town was my home for all my formative years, and then some. With its signature smell of fresh manure and the towering snow-capped mountains bookending the Fraser Valley, I certainly could have done worse.

While growing up our ancestry was never talked about or emphasized. However, over the years I have been able to fill in many of the glaring blanks and now know a lot more about where my journey began. To paint a vivid picture of the man I have become and to help provide some answers to the many choices I have made along the way, both good and bad (and trust me, there were way too many bad choices), it seems fitting to take a closer look at those who came before me.

On my father's side, my Great-grandfather Arthur Worrall, who was Anglican and born in Rochdale, England, landed in Canada in 1911. Souris, Manitoba, became the new home of eighteen-year-old Arthur and his wife, Elizabeth, who was merely sixteen. I can only imagine what life was like for them, enduring a new environment that included frigid winters on the barren prairies.

When World War I broke out in 1914, my great-grandfather went overseas and fought for our country alongside his eight brothers. Whether in Canada or during the war, survival was the order of the day. Pledging allegiance to and protecting our country's flag is a family trait that I have inherited. Being cut from the same cloth saved my life many times as my life's journey unfolded.

After the Great War, Arthur and Elizabeth had two children. In 1921 my grandfather, James Arthur Worrall, was born a year after his older sister and only sibling, Lillian. Unfortunately, I never took the opportunity to ask my grandfather what those days were like, and I can only imagine living through frigid six-month winters with no modern amenities.

Grandpa James served in World War II, during which he was stationed in England. As a kid I was intrigued by the thought of war. What did it mean to go to war? Why was my grandfather chosen, or did he choose to serve? Did he almost die in a battle? Was he responsible for anyone's death during the war? I was too afraid to ask, content with knowing that my grandpa was a hero of sorts. Such facts certainly gave me a better appreciation of those we were taught to be proud of, and to wear a poppy for on Remembrance Day. I remember staring proudly for what seemed an eternity at photos of him in uniform and his medals during a rare childhood visit. I also packed a book called *A Soldier's Story* to school with me, even though it wasn't part of our curriculum. I still have it. Was it an ominous warning or a preparation of sorts for my personal battles ahead?

While stationed overseas my grandfather courted and then married my grandma, Pearl Brenda Worrall. She hailed from the Berkshire Valley in jolly ol' England and was a nurse by profession. My father's parents were redheads, so I guess it's no mystery how I ended up with such a volatile red mop.

My dad, James Robert Worrall, was born on May 17, 1944, in Redding, England. When the war ended, my grandmother and grandpa parted for what was supposed to be a temporary period. My grandmother and my dad set sail for Canada to begin a new life. I'm sure it was an arduous journey for them both.

Their boat docked in Montreal. From there they headed west by train, settling in a small town called Bienfait in southeastern Saskatchewan, where they lived in a small, quaint, "Little House on The Prairie" abode with no running water.

Bienfait was tiny, and everyone knew everyone, but that didn't make it any easier, because my grandmother was never one to ask for handouts. She believed in earning things the old-fashioned way, through perseverance and hard work. She never owned a vehicle, and until the day she passed in 1987, she never had a drivers' licence or drove.

Grandma Pearl practiced as a nurse, so on most days, my dad was left to his own devices. As for schooling, Dad never excelled at that. In fact, some of his teachers claimed he had a learning disability and was unteachable. Later in life we discovered that Dad was colour blind, and I'm sure that affected him a lot in school. On the whole, however, Dad was sharp and just didn't like school. It was during those elementary years that he began to develop the kind of toughness and street smarts that typified him for the rest of his life.

When Dad was ten, they moved to Winnipeg and lived in a house across the street from the legislative buildings. Grandma nursed at the hospital, and Dad attended school.

In the big city, most of the kids had bicycles and other novelties, and my dad desperately wanted his own bike. However, my grandmother wouldn't buy him one, because she was always pinching pennies. With his dad still "missing in action," more figuratively than literally, Dad and Grandma had to live frugally. Soon my dad realized he would have to work to acquire the finer things he wanted.

His first job was a paper route, and it enabled him to buy the bicycle he craved. However, shortly after purchasing the bike from some locals at the city park, there was a knock at their door. The police were there to confiscate my dad's prized possession and return it to its rightful owner, because the bike was stolen. My dad loved that bike; it was his happiness and first real sanctuary of freedom. Heartbroken and angry, he got a broader sense of the "new rules" that he would begin to play by from that moment forward.

When Dad was twelve, he and Grandma left Winnipeg and headed farther west, settling in Chilliwack. Grandma continued to practice as an RN at the local hospital, and Dad carried on being his independent, resourceful, mischievous self. Much like everywhere else they had lived, Dad marched to his own beat. He was an active kid and, like most boys his age, loved ice hockey and anything with two wheels. Not long removed from the Great Depression, Grandma was still tight with their money, so Dad was never enrolled in hockey or any other organized sports.

My grandfather wasn't around, and didn't play any role in my father's upbringing. He had befriended "John Barleycorn" at a young age and was an alcoholic. He was also a compulsive gambler, and loved the ponies. Racetracks, bars, and bookies' lairs were his happy places.

When I quizzed Dad about that later in life, he told me he saw his dad only a few times during his childhood. One of those times was at Great-grandma Lillian's funeral in Manitoba. Dad was only about five years old, but he remembers his dad being there and, upon parting, saying, "I'll see you again real soon, son." However, Dad didn't see his father again for several years. By that time, Grandpa had moved to Vancouver, where he worked in the city's sanitation department. My grandpa was pretty much always AWOL, and not the military kind either.

The fact that my grandmother didn't put my dad in any type of sports or recreation didn't stop him from finding a way to be involved. In the 1940s, construction began on what became one of the town's most revered and iconic playgrounds, the Chilliwack Coliseum, though the Fraser Valley had a catastrophic flood in 1948 that hindered the rink's construction. Dad hung out there on a daily basis, and was spellbound with excitement by its enormity and grandeur. However, he knew that, short of divine intervention, there was no way his mother would sign him up for hockey.

The president of the Chilliwack minor hockey association, Ev Downey, had observed Dad's regular presence at the rink. One day shortly after the rink finally opened, he approached Dad and asked if he would be playing in the upcoming season. Feeling embarrassed I'm sure, Dad said it wasn't likely, because his mom wouldn't allow him to play.

Shortly thereafter, Ev contacted my grandma and volunteered to pay for Dad's enrolment. The organization also helped him acquire all the gear required to see him laced up and on the ice.

Dad loved hockey and for the first time in life felt like he was on a level playing field with other kids. At a young age, he was already of above-average height, and his arms were longer than most. Coupled with the grit he had obtained from his life journey thus far, he was a force to be reckoned with on the ice.

Hockey was not the only sport Dad took up. He also put his long arms to use in the boxing ring. He joined the Chilliwack Boxing Club and travelled to matches throughout the Lower Mainland. My dad was as tough as nails, and whether the gloves were on or off, he seldom lost a fight. As his old friends used to tell me, "Your dad is one tough SOB." That worked out in my favour later in life, because my high school principal knew my dad and his reputation.

By age fourteen, Dad left school permanently with a grade six education. He and Grandma lived in the west end of Chilliwack almost at the end of Wellington Avenue. One of the families that lived across the street were loggers by trade. Dad was curious about the work, because he knew loggers made the kind of money he desired. By the tender age of fourteen, my red-headed, freckle-faced father landed his first logging job, fittingly as a "whistle punk." A Whistle Punk In the days of logging with steam engines (steam donkeys), the whistle punk was a lumberjack who operated the signal wire running to a donkey engine whistle. From there he moved rapidly up the ranks to setting chokers on the rigging. Within two years, he was on a chainsaw and well on his way to carving out his lifelong career as a tree faller.

In 1963, his resourcefulness allowed him to purchase his first motorcycle, a 1962 BSA that he bought on Vancouver's rough-and-tumble East Side, and it was a beauty.

Later that year at a restaurant in downtown Chilliwack, my dad had what I deem the luckiest day of his life when he met a young waitress who was still in school. She was the most beautiful, caring, considerate, hardworking, and loving person on the face of the earth. That's right, it was my mother-to-be, Donna Lynn Champ.

Mom's Side of the Family and History

So, what about my mom's side? What traits did she and her family genetics equip this raring and ready newborn Gemini with to face the world?

My mother, Donna Lynn Worrall (nee Champ), was born in Vancouver at St. Paul's Hospital on December 6, 1945. You would have never known it if you were fortunate enough to have met my mom, but she had a rough childhood. However, as life moved forward, she always focused on the positive and was never one to complain. She met life's hardships with love and hard work. My mom was a believer no matter what came down the pike.

One of her strongest beliefs was that all good things could be attained if she put in a strong effort with a positive attitude. Mom was always good with numbers and never afraid to get her hands dirty. She had to be that way, because where she came from, things were unpleasant for many years. Some of the stories I have been told are soul-trembling head-shakers.

I can't remember how old I was when I first met my mom's dad, Grandpa Doug Champ, but we didn't see him much, and neither did she as a child.

My grandma, Jean McLeod (nee Gobee), was born on September 21, 1928, in Gods Lake Manitoba. Sometime in the late 1940s, she married Grandpa Doug, who she met in Winnipeg. Over the ensuing years, they had eight children, or so everyone thought (more on that later).

Much like my dad's father, Grandpa Doug was usually missing in action. I'm not just talking about weekend benders either. Yes, he liked to drink and gamble, but there was a lot more wrong with him than that. All my mom's surviving siblings have some pretty horrific stories about him. My mom didn't want to talk about it whenever I asked her. This a prime example of her staying focused on the future instead of looking back, always focused on the positive.

She was born in the middle of the eight children, as far as age goes. She was about five-foot-five and had brunette hair and beautiful eyes. Her youngest brother, who is and always will be my favourite uncle, Al Champ, has always been one of my few select "angels without wings." He has helped me connect the dots on most of the family's unspoken and unthinkable past truths. But were they unthinkable? Hold on to that thought for later. As they say, history can often repeat itself in tragic ways, as it did in my life. Unfortunately, I was cut from that genetic fabric. I'm not making excuses, but a lot like my mom and dad's childhood, my family life was pretty chaotic. Fortunately for me, I found some definitive answers and eventually parted ways with most of my demons.

My mom's parents also headed west and settled in Vancouver. They lived initially with Grandpa Doug's dad, who owned a fair bit of property, and the family was financially comfortable, at least for the time being.

One day at work, Grandpa Doug's dad, who worked in a grain elevator at BC Sugar, was struck in the head and knocked unconscious. He was checked out on site and medically cleared, and everyone assumed he was fine. However, that night, he passed away in his sleep.

Within short order everything he had owned was taken or repossessed. That presented huge complications for my grandma and grandpa and their children. His was the only family home they had known in their marriage's infancy.

Doug was never a responsible man, and most people I have asked said he was mentally immature. He was like a big kid, if you will, and responsibilities and managing finances were not his forte. However, he was never afraid to work, though surprisingly, that also proved to be problematic. You would think in that day and age, if a man was a hard worker, he would have no problems providing for a growing family. However, almost every time my grandmother became pregnant with one of their eight children, he would vanish. These were not just weekend benders either. Months and sometimes even years passed with no word from him. Each time he disappeared, the family was forced to relocate, under the watchful eye of social services.

Within a year or two of Doug's dad's passing, the family moved to Courtenay, on Vancouver Island. Once again it was hit and miss with Doug. My Uncle Al tells of the times that they had nothing in the fridge but a head of cabbage, which fed them for a week in the form of cabbage soup. They considered themselves lucky if they had a piece of cabbage in their portion.

My Uncle Larry recounts the pain of coming home from school on one occasion in his elementary years with a friend. The furniture they had purchased on credit was being repossessed as they entered the yard.

"Where's your furniture going?" his friend asked. "Are you guys moving?"

Sensing exactly what was going on, Uncle Larry thought up a quick response, in Grinch-like fashion. "They're taking it away to clean it," he said.

"Even your fridge?" his friend asked.

I can't imagine how awful they all must have felt. My grandfather was nowhere to be found, and my grandmother was left once again to face the financial music on her own.

The family left Courtney and moved to Chase River, also on the island. It was there in 1955 that Grandma was expecting their eighth child. She returned from the hospital a few days later with no child in her arms. She said there were serious complications, and the baby passed away at birth.

The family moved back to the mainland, to Rosedale, BC. Social services not only helped with support but also maintained a close eye on them, because they knew the kids needed more than was available to them. By then Grandpa Doug was back home and vowed he was a changed man and would do his best to be the father they all so desperately needed.

My Uncle Al says Grandma could detect when Grandpa Doug was getting antsy and about to bolt. She kept a watchful eye on him and would send one of the kids with him each time he left to run an errand. That was his style. He would leave for cigarettes, milk, or whatever, and not return. When he disappeared, he would head north and hide in a work camp, where he would make good money but never send even one red cent home for support. He gambled it all away, and when the work ran out, he came crawling back home to Grandma.

When he did it yet again in 1959, it was the last straw. Grandma had the doors bolted shut, and Grandpa banged for what seemed like hours, at least to the kids. They were instructed to hide and not make a sound. It's hard to imagine how those poor young children's hearts ached. Knowing now what my future held, I can't write that without tears of raw love and emotion running down my cheeks. It astounds me to see how solid each and every one of my aunts and uncles on my mom's side of the family are. If there were a picture in a dictionary under the term "Salt of the Earth," it could be of any one of my mom's brothers and sisters. I believe God never makes mistakes, least of all junk! To me there is no such thing.

That fateful day marked the last time any of the kids or my grandmother saw my grandpa until the late 1970s. My Uncle Mike (who sadly passed away in 1985 at the young age of thirty-eight due to heart disease) ran into him on a job site in White Rock, BC. Grandpa Doug and Mike got along quite well and reconciled their relationship somewhat. At one point, Grandpa Doug even moved in with Uncle Mike. Even though they were pretty much scarred for life, the rest of the kids seemed grateful to know their dad was still alive. I have never known any of my family to bear any types of grudges against anyone, and that in itself is quite cool.

Much later, around 2006, my Uncle Larry got a call from a man claiming to be his brother. It turns out that my grandmother had given birth to a son, James Champ, in September 1955 in Chase River. Social services had apprehended him at birth and put him in foster care, where he was later adopted out. My grandmother had been given an ultimatum to give him up or have her other eight children taken away. None of the siblings knew of that, or so we thought, but it turns out my mom's older sister, Aunt Cheryl, knew and was sworn to secrecy. His name was changed to Randall Barr, and he was adopted out to a lady who had two other adopted children.

At some point quite a few years later, his mom became ill and told the kids that they were all adopted. At first Randall thought it was okay, content with the only life he had ever known. Once again, that is a little heavy for me, and I'm fighting back tears as I'm writing this, though I'm not sure why, because it wasn't my life or reality, but his. However, my journey has made me an empathetic person and allowed me some deep emotional insights into what they all went through.

Randall's mom told him that he was "different." She said he wasn't put up for adoption but taken from a family who would have loved and cared for him as best they could.

I know I have not said it yet, because most of what I've said so far has been about what a shit my grandpa was, but Grandma Jean was another one of God's angels with invisible wings. She was soft, caring, and compassionate and always called a spade a spade. Later in life, as I got to know her better, she astounded me with her knowledge of current events, humour, and unconditional love. How could she not be such a person? She had survived things that would have finished most. Over and above all that, each of her children were walking, talking miracles, my mother included.

In 2005 Randall decided that he wanted to get in touch with the family that he had never known. He looked up the name Champ in the BC phone directory and within a few short calls got hold of my Uncle Larry, who then contacted Uncle Al and said, "We have a new brother!" I have a photo in the photos section of this book that shows the stark resemblance between the three of them.

James, who became a high school teacher in Quesnel, BC, is now an active member of our family. He was also present when I put a twenty-five-year vendetta to rest in his hometown in 2009. (I will go into some of those darker details a little later.)

My mom was a top student in school. She could learn anything she wanted when she wanted. A degree or diploma that would take most a long time to achieve, she could attain in short order.

In her graduation year, she met my father. I can't imagine how those two were attracted to each other. Both were strong-willed, smart, and determined to do better than their troubled, dysfunctional childhoods.

One day my dad walked into the restaurant she worked at after school in the "Five Corners" area of downtown Chilliwack and introduced himself. He had noticed my mom on one occasion shortly before that.

I should note that he had just finished a fifteen-month sentence in the Haney Correctional Institution. He and a friend had taken the law into their own hands and were charged with assault and battery after beating up a police officer, who had one of Chilliwack's most notorious reputations for being a bad cop. While in prison he met the leader of a certain motorcycle club. Despite his questionable affiliation, from that moment on, that man became a reliable and lifelong friend to my father.

When Dad left prison, he got on a Greyhound bus and, upon arriving back in Chilliwack, noticed my mom riding shotgun in his friend's car, which led to their first encounter in the restaurant.

Mom graduated the following year, and the next summer, the two were married in Chilliwack's United Church, with two of their best friends at the time, Sam and Jackie Douglas, at their side.

After their wedding in 1964, Mom started work at the Bank of Nova Scotia, and Dad continued his clear-cut path to logging greatness. I know that kind of talk may raise the ire of "tree huggers" nowadays, but that was the way it was back then.

South of the border, JFK was assassinated that year. Mom often recounted where she was and what she was doing when the news broke. She always paid attention to the state of the world.

When I was born in 1966, we lived in a small house on the east end of Spadina Avenue. In later years the house was converted into a dental lab, but the last time I went back there for a look, it was gone. Let's just say, "They paved paradise and put up a parking lot," although in this case, it was an apartment building.

Many things happened in that house that were more than a little eerie. First off, one night a bullet went through my bedroom window while I was asleep in my crib, and lodged in the wall. After a thorough investigation, it turned out that a local thug was firing randomly, and it was deemed accidental. Was I on a hit list already? No, but that would come later in my life. As far as I know, the trigger-happy person still lives in Chilliwack.

Within a few years of my birth, my mom and dad bought their first building lot. It was located three spaces from the south end of Bonavista Avenue on Fairfield Island adjacent to Hope Slough. The price was a mere $1,000. The house was built in short order by a family friend, Abe Dyck, and by age four, I had a new home.

My Uncle Al, who was still in high school, moved in with us and helped us with many things. He had his sights set on technical school after graduating. It felt good having him around, and he was with us for almost four years.

I'm not sure my sister, Kelly, can say the same thing. (I'm inserting a little private joke here.) I'm sure she knows what I'm talking about, because Uncle Al always saw to it that she finished any food he prepared for her. Kelly was a picky eater. In fact, she probably would have been happy on a steady diet of popcorn and fruit juice, but Uncle Al had other plans. In that regard, he was more militant than our parents. It never bothered me much, because, being Valley bred, I was a meat-and-potatoes kid from day one.

Kelly was born in 1970. It felt odd not having Mom at home when she went to the hospital to give birth to Kelly. Remember, it was 1970, and back then women spent a week or more in the hospital when they had a baby. With a new sister in the house, Uncle Al, and Dad seemingly always away in a logging camp, my mom soon proved to us all that she was also a good juggler. That was right around the time I went off to kindergarten to begin forging my own trickery.

3

Bonavista

Settled into our new family home just a stone's throw from Fairfield Islands, Hope Slough, and the Fraser River, my early years couldn't have been better. That rapidly developing part of Chilliwack had mostly been used for farming. Our street was one of about half a dozen within a radius of a few kilometres lined with brand-new homes. Ours was brown with three bedrooms upstairs and a full basement.

We played freely in our yard, and I could often be found outside exploring my limits on my bicycle. I was fascinated by life and its progression from a young age. I was on a need-to-know basis, and I needed to know pretty much everything. I loved the sights and sounds of airplanes flying overhead, especially the single-engine Cessnas. Speeding cars, motorcycles, I loved anything that went fast, with one exception: emergency vehicles and sirens. I hated them. If an ambulance, fire truck, police car, or anything that had a siren blaring came anywhere near, I would panic and cry uncontrollably. I often ran to my bedroom and slammed the door, sometimes even hiding under my bed. My parents consoled me and did the best they could to explain the nature of those sirens, but nothing helped.

After a year or two of that, my mom scheduled a doctor's appointment. Our family physician, Dr. Tam, was a unique character. A trip there always meant a long wait in the waiting room. Often, I saw him sitting in his office with his feet up, pondering his next move, while enjoying the last of his cigarette. It was the early 1970s, and smoking, even in a doctor's office, wasn't abnormal. I hated second-hand smoke. Both my parents smoked, as did most people back then. To me there was nothing worse than being trapped in the back seat of the family car when one or both of them lit up. Getting back to my trip to Dr. Tam, nothing revolutionary came out of it. Was my phobia part of some past-life regression? Overly sensitive ears? An ominous warning of what lay ahead?

Apart from my siren phobia, everything else in life was pretty normal. With most of my mom's brothers and sisters, as well as my grandparents, living within in close proximity, family was a big part of our life. Mom and Dad also had many friends and entertained often. My dad's best man at their wedding, Sam Douglas, was also his best friend. He and his wife, Jackie, lived in a big house at the foot of the Agassiz-Rosedale Bridge on the Cheam Indian Reserve. Sam was also the chief of the reserve and one of the kindest, happiest adults I knew.

One of our rituals was to spend Christmas Eve with them at their house. I think December 24 was Sam's birthday. Their two children, Lisa and Sammy, were my best friends. Lisa was my age, and Sammy was a couple of years younger, and they were like family to me. Dad worked with Sam in the bush. During their time off, they put in countless hours fishing on the Fraser River. We cut firewood with them and camped with them, and their family was a huge part of our lives.

By that point I was already proving to be quite an adrenaline junkie. I never felt different from my peers, but my actions often demonstrated that I was a daredevil in the making.

My dad reminded me of a time at around age four when I asked him what would happen if I rode my plastic toy tractor down the stairs of the Bonavista house to the basement. The steep set of wooden stairs led down to a frigid and unforgiving concrete floor. My dad replied that if I tried such a thing, I would likely get hurt.

Within a few seconds of him turning his back on me, I went for it. All Dad heard was thump, thump, thump, thump, and then nothing. I'm sure I was banged up, but when he ran down to pick me up, I told him that, despite his warning, I was fine. An early defiance of my father's authority? Not likely. I never went out of my way to do that, because I knew it usually came with a good whooping. If it was bad enough, he used a belt. My parents were kind and loving, but back then, that's how parents did things. I always respected and appreciated my parents.

We had great neighbours on Bonavista, the Dueck family on the north side of us and the Ballams to the south. They were polar opposites on many levels, but both had kids, who we played with. The Duecks were clean-cut and always went to church on Sunday. They had an incredible playhouse in their backyard, its blue siding matching the siding on their home. The Ballams were in the furniture business, and their boys, Mark and Jim, were a lot like me—hockey crazy. We played road hockey at every opportunity, and I was always Bobby Orr. The Boston Bruins were Stanley Cup champions at that time, and Bobby was my first bladed hero. I wore the big number four throughout my hockey career, even as a right winger. Many times, after summer games, we got to swim in the Ballams' pool.

Mark was a couple of years older than me, and I looked up to him. He was a big, burly kid who played defence and had his sights set on an NHL career. I'm grateful for the fond memories I have of the many great people who were part of our lives at that early stage. I did, however, carry a large cross for many years against organized religion after my one and only attempt at attending a Sunday school service.

As I mentioned, the Duecks went to church every Sunday. One day, being curious, I asked if I could go. They were more than happy to take me. Despite my curiosity, I felt uncomfortable when we arrived at the large church on Broadway Street, and that feeling continued throughout the lesson.

At one point I asked the teacher if I could be excused to use the bathroom. I had to pee badly and knew I couldn't hold it much longer. She said the lesson was almost over, and I would have to wait a few more minutes. Unable to hold it, I began to cry as I wet my pants. Man, was I ever upset, but more than anything, I was embarrassed and angrier than I had ever been before. Are you kidding me? What was wrong with that person? In my mind how could a loving, caring God have permitted that kind of embarrassment? There was no escape; every kid in the room of what seemed like 100 knew exactly what had happened to me. Making things worse was that Sunday school was before the main church service, and I had to sit through it in my soaked brown corduroy pants.

At that time religion, or even the word "God," wasn't often spoken of in my home. To me that was the norm, and so were my parents, but those religious people were no longer my kind of people. I thought for sure my father would have words with Mr. Dueck or the teacher after that incident. To my disappointment and surprise, no such luck. Shouldn't someone have been held accountable for a five-year-old's weak bladder or the Sunday school teacher's poor decision? I'm over it now, but that incident had a profound effect on my life.

We had a good-sized yard, and being a Gemini, I loved to play outside every chance I got. On many days my parents would get out of bed and find me playing in the sandbox in my pyjamas. I was smart enough to put on my rubber boots and even a jacket if it was raining or snowing. None of the elements ever stopped me from playing outside when I wanted to.

I'm not sure what I did to deserve it, but on one occasion my parents grounded me to my bedroom. They assumed I was playing quietly and taking the punishment until my mom came to tell me dinner was ready. She opened my door to find the bedroom window open and the curtains hanging outside. When she reached the window, she saw the top of my head peeking out of the sandbox. I had jumped out my second-floor window and went straight to one of my personal sanctuaries. Once there, I decided that if I used my dad's spade and dug a hole deep enough, I could hide in it, and no one would be any wiser to my whereabouts. I'm not sure what became of that, but I was proving at a young age that I had an unstoppable urge to test authority, not to mention the laws of gravity.

Strathcona Elementary, on the west side of Fairfield Island, welcomed this stout, somewhat portly, freckle-faced, blue-eyed redhead to his first day of school. Wearing a sweater, a pair of brown corduroy pants, and toting my Evel Knievel lunch kit, I was excited. Mrs. Logi was my teacher's name. Other than that, I can only remember sitting on a floor and not in a desk. I thought it was because we had yet to grow into our legs. I don't recall any reasons why my parents might have worried about my well-being at school. The teachers always had an abundance of positive comments about my demeanour, attitude, and efforts.

I enjoyed school, and I can't think of many days when I didn't want to go. However, my mom told a story of me being home sick one day watching *Sesame Street*. She was doing her thing in the kitchen when she heard me scream, "Look at that asshole on TV!" My mom was mortified and perplexed, wanting to know where I had learned such language, and why I was saying it. I looked at her square in the eye and said, "It's okay, Mom. The kids at school call me that all the time." Yes, I was learning fast.

For me school was about having fun with friends and experiencing new things. As far as the learning went, let's just say there were good days and bad days! The bad days usually landed me in Principal Huth's office. I never went out of my way to find trouble, or so I thought. Throughout most of my school years,

I had a wild mop of red hair. I was teased about it and often called "Ronald McDonald." It never bothered me though, and I thought we kids did a pretty good job of policing ourselves regarding such things.

Recess and lunch breaks always warranted ball hockey. When the bell went, it was a beeline to get out in front of the school, where the nets and sticks were kept in a bin. One day, for whatever reason, I ended up getting outside a little late. I got my hand on the last red stick at the same time as one of my classmates, Danny. He was a tough kid, not so much that he was a bully, but he came from a family who was not so well off, or so I thought. What other explanation did I have for the way he carried himself?

I stared him down, and neither of us would let go of the stick. The tug-of-war turned into a shoving match, and within a heartbeat, it was a full-on fistfight. One of the recess monitors intervened, breaking us up.

As we stood face to face after the fact, the monitor handed Danny the stick, saying I needed to learn how to share. Infuriated and still having a half mouthful of chewed crackers, which were intended to be my recess snack, I spit them in Danny's face. I remember thinking immediately that what I had done wasn't cool, but I needed to show someone how pissed I was. Lucky me—the duty teacher noticed and sent me right to Principle Huth's office, my first official trip there.

I sat in the corner for what seemed an eternity, awaiting my fate. I was pretty sure that no matter what the outcome of our meeting, my parents were going to hear about it. I usually did everything in my power to stay out of trouble at home. Remember, it was the 1970s, and I swear my dad only wore a belt so he could wield it in my direction, when needed. Mom was a lot kinder and more diplomatic, using things like black pepper on my tongue or washing my mouth out with soap if I used profanity. I knew the rules, and if I crossed the line, I accepted my punishment as the price for whatever adrenaline rush I was seeking.

When Principal Huth came into the office, I could tell he was somewhat rushed. He seemed shocked to see me sitting there, a forlorn look on my face. "Mr. Worrall, to what do we owe the pleasure of this rare visit today?" he asked.

First off, I liked Mr. Huth. He had the top position in our school, and over and above that, he got most of the cool points from me, because his son was on our town's Junior hockey team, the Chilliwack Bruins. His son's name is Gary Huth, and his nickname was "Huck." Our family went to games often, and I loved hockey and everything about it.

"I didn't give Danny the hockey stick," I replied. Strangely enough, I remember that encounter verbatim.

He looked at me and said, "Get back to your class, Brent, and play nice now."

That was it? No punishment? Was he going to find out that I didn't tell him the whole truth? Nothing else came of that incident, but to this day, I still feel slimy for spitting crackers in Danny's face. I also don't remember ever going without a hockey stick again in the schoolyard. Live and learn.

I played ice hockey in the same rink that my father so proudly watched being built, and also played in. My first year on the ice was 1972, as a "Peanut," at age six. I'm not sure of our team's name, but we had the coolest Boston Bruins-type uniforms. Wearing my number four proudly, I was always ready for the puck to drop.

My dad was one of our coaches, and so was one of his good buddies, John Archibald (father of NHLer David Archibald). I lived for hockey, whether it was on the ice, in the street, or in our schoolyard. It was also on television in our house. My mom was a devout Leafs fan and loved Darryl Sittler. Many others in our extended family cheered loudly for the Canadiens, but not me. I was a Bruins fan.

Like most kids early on, I had weak ankles, but I had a good, hard, accurate shot. Much of that was thanks to my father. Dad set me up in the basement and taught me the fine art of the wrist shot. No road hockey balls for that tutorial; we used real pucks. So, when I got a breakaway, it was often followed by a celebration with my teammates.

I'm not sure what the issue was, but in first grade I was having some problems with reading and math, and my teacher had planned a special test for me. My mom helped me at home with flash cards and told me that if I got a decent mark, she would buy me some of the hockey cards that all the other kids had. I passed the test and got a good follow-up report from my teacher.

Half a block away from Strathcona Elementary was a corner store, the Killarney Market. We loved that place, because they had a huge display case of candy. My mom took me there and asked the clerk for some packs of hockey cards. He reached up to the shelf beyond the counter, on which they kept the box, and pulled out the last two packs. That was it for that box, but surely he had another. No such luck. They were the last two packs of the first run he had ordered. I think the disappointment only settled in when I got home and realized how cool those cards were. I loved them so much, I wanted more.

As the school season wore on, my mom found more hockey cards. When my schoolwork slipped again, she knew exactly what to do. The bribe with cards to pull up my scholastic socks was on. It worked. I was never overly confident when it came to schoolwork—or most things, for that matter. I'm not sure what the deal was, but I was somewhat introverted and never felt that smart. I guess you could say I saved my best efforts and most of my energy for physical exertion, doing things that I enjoyed on my own terms.

With a new baby sister at home, again my mother was amazing. As a kid I was pretty much oblivious to the many hats she wore in our home. Mom was always upbeat and busy with something. She did all the cooking and cleaning and also worked at the Bank of Nova Scotia. She was creative, loved crafts, and was great with numbers. Dad, on the other hand, was pretty much a head-down, ass-up, hard-working bulldog. His job as a logger usually meant he spent time away from us in logging camps. My Uncle Al was also living with us at the time, and it certainly helped my parents. It also gave him the stability he needed to graduate and then get his electrical degree.

Life in the Bonavista house on Fairfield Island never seemed complicated, and if I had to use one word to define that stage, it would be fun, with a capital "F." On weekends, if we had nothing scheduled, we would go for long leisurely drives in the Fraser Valley. I'm sure things were pretty hectic at times for my mother, especially when Dad was away for work, but we kids never felt it.

In the early 1970s, we went through the infamous "Silver Thaw," where everything froze up with ice and snow. We were without power for days. It was eerie to be navigating the house via candlelight. Mom had a jigsaw puzzle set up in the basement, and with no power to watch *Sesame Street*, *Hockey Night in Canada*, or any of my other favourites, the puzzle looked like it could be fun. I still vaguely remember all the ornate buildings on the waterfront in the puzzle. I was a little slow at first, but eager, and I caught on quickly. I didn't build many puzzles in my life, but I did a few. That ice storm, like every other challenge we endured as a family, solidified our bond.

When Dad was away at work, Mom never let on that his job was as dangerous as it was. I never worried; heck, I was a kid, and worry wasn't part of my job description. All I knew was I wasn't even strong enough to pick up the chainsaw that Dad used daily. The chainsaws in Dad's era were archaic, to say the least. The bar on the saw, which housed the chain, was almost longer than I was tall.

What I did know was that they had clean, delicious clean fresh water up in the mountains where Dad worked. I knew that, because he would always stop at a fresh stream before departing for home and fill his Thermos with fresh, ice-cold run-off water for me. I loved it, and could often be found on the driveway, eagerly awaiting his return with that precious elixir.

When Dad came home from work, he always looked and smelled as if he had just run a marathon behind a wood chipper. I have fond memories of him coming home and telling us about his day while sipping a cold Pilsner on the porch. Dad loved his job, and it paid well. I know he made good money, but knowing my dad like I now do, I believe he just loved the fine art of falling trees. It was a science to him, and he was good at it.

Being a tree faller also came with the responsibility of fighting forest fires, if and when the need arose. In the early 1970s, there was a huge fire in the Boston Bar area of the Fraser Canyon, and Dad was called in to fight on the front lines. He stayed up there in a camp, and we didn't see him or hear from him until his two-week shift concluded.

One Sunday night while Dad was supposedly in the camp, my mom got a phone call from his co-worker's wife. She was calling to see if Dad was going to be okay and wondered what hospital he was in. My mom was aghast, knowing nothing of any incident involving my dad. Keep in mind that the fire season was huge, with a province-wide emergency declared. Adding to the confusion and lack of communication was the fact that it was 1972. There were no cell phones, computers, or any such modern means of communication. Even many of the landlines were compromised or out of order during the fire.

It turns out Dad was falling a snag (a dead, dried-out tree), and it contained a massive beehive. When the tree imploded upon hitting the ground, Dad was swarmed. Turns out he's highly allergic to bee stings. With no one around, and quickly falling into an anaphylactic coma, Dad was in grave danger!

One of his co-workers found him some time later, unconscious and with no pulse. He was rushed to the nearest hospital in Hope, BC, about an hour to the south. The accident occurred on Friday, and Mom received the call on Sunday night. Fortunately, Dad made a full recovery, and when he returned to work, Mom saw to it that he had medication to counteract any future bee stings.

To give you an idea of my dad's character, I don't think I ever saw him panic if a bee or a wasp landed on him. To me, that was weird, because they were potentially lethal to him. He always said, "The bees aren't bothering me, so why should I bother them?" Even though Dad got stung a couple more times, I'm sure his attitude toward these formidable foes helped.

Through all that, I, being a young student of life, always had a great teacher in my father. Most of what Dad has taught me can't be found by taking a course or reading a book. He often looked me straight in the eye and said, "Son, you are very lucky, because the school I graduated from is closed for good." Truer words can't be spoken. As much of a burly, take-your-lumps, suck-it-up, grin-and-bear-it type of individual my dad is on the exterior, his heart has always been one of the softest and most genuine I have ever known. For the most part, Dad was a man of few words, but he was always a thinker with a method to his madness.

Somewhere around the time Kelly was born, my dad bought his first dirt bike. I would stare at it in the garage for hours each day. It was an orange AJS (Alfred John Stephenson). He bought it from an old family friend, Vic Hudson, who had a dealership. Dad was never afraid to fire the bike up at home and head out for a rip down at the Fraser River, which was about a mile away on a paved road. The neighbours always looked the other way and never confronted the man who I would call the "alpha dog" of our first family neighbourhood.

Dad also loved old cars, and I always looked forward to rides in the rumble seat of our 1936 Ford Coupe. As time wore on, Dad outgrew the AJS or, as he says, "It was the worst motorcycle I ever owned." I joked often with him later in life that it wasn't the bike, but a case of operator abuse.

After the AJS, it was a white Yamaha YZ-360, bought from his good friend and 1970 Canadian National Motocross Champion Bob Mutch. Bob owned Capilano Motorcycles on Yale Road East, halfway between Rosedale and Chilliwack. We spent hour upon hour in that shop, and it soon became a home away from home.

Dad raced some motocross, but preferred cross-country racing. He felt safer in the bush than on the track. He wasn't afraid; he just knew he couldn't pack that massive chainsaw up and down mountainsides with his arm in plaster.

I loved being at the motorcycle shop, and was always in awe of the bikes, trophies, and pretty much everything motocross-related. Bob and Donna Mutch had two boys who quickly became close friends of mine. Robbie was my age, and his younger brother, Rodney, was a couple of years younger. At the tender age of six, Capilano Motorcycles became my new favourite place on Earth.

My mother had some concerns though, because one day my dad brought my sister home from the shop with a split forehead. She had been running around with Rodney, and together they unceremoniously went headlong into a stack of bikes. Kelly landed headfirst on the foot peg of a brand-new motocross bike. Ouch! Come on, sis, crashing was my job! Not to worry, because I would be back on top of the podium in that department sooner, rather than later. Kelly, who probably should have had stitches, was none the worse for wear after Dad took her across the street for some candy. I told you he was a quick thinker. He had to be, because soon he would have a whole lot more on his hands.

4

Two Wheels and a Heartbeat

In 1972, with Pierre Elliot Trudeau fearlessly leading our proud nation, it seemed that most people were content. I was restless in nature, though, and craved excitement. As reckless as I was, I never got hurt that much. But at age six, I guess I still bounced pretty well.

On one occasion though, after launching myself from the top of our fireplace mantel, I landed headfirst on the corner of our solid-oak coffee table. With blood everywhere, I was pretty lucky not to have lost an eye or split my skull wide open. I still bear a scar and a hole in my skull where the bridge of my nose meets my eye as a trophy. My parents have recounted many such stories, and they all pretty much validate my wild wide-open Gemini sign.

Our family bought eggs locally, just a few streets away, at a farmhouse on Fairfield Island. It was green and white with a long driveway. At the end of the driveway, just beyond the home, sat the barn that housed the chickens.

One day after a trip to the grocery store with Mom, we headed over there to grab some eggs before returning home. Quite often if we were in a hurry, Mom would leave Kelly and me in the car. Baby Kelly would be in the back in her car seat, and I would usually stand and watch from the front passenger seat. (There were no seatbelt laws in British Columbia at that time.) Mom must have been in a hurry, because she left our car running with us inside. She got out and had not quite reached the barn door when she turned back to look at the car. It's a good thing she did. She was horrified by what she saw next. I had ingeniously decided that if the car was still running, why not put it in gear and drive right up to the barn?

Mom claims that as she ran desperately to reach the car, some one hundred feet away, all she could see was me jumping up and down on the seat laughing my head off. Somehow, she managed to open the door and stop it before we all went through the chicken barn. It certainly was a good thing that I had not pulled my other prank of locking the door on her first.

At Capilano Motorcycles I was captivated by posters of motorcycle daredevil Evel Knievel. Whenever his name came up in conversation, I was enthralled. By that point Evel already had an illustrious career. In fact, a full-length motion picture called *Evel Knievel,* starring George Hamilton, had come out the year before. Eventually, my mother tracked down a copy of the iconic Evel Knievel wheelie poster. It was mounted over my bed throughout the rest of my childhood. That image of him flying fearlessly on the rear wheel of his Harley Davidson at high speed, wearing his signature patriotic red-white-and-blue uniform, serenaded me to sleep every night. Evel was quickly overtaking Bobby Orr as my biggest hero. No Batman or Superman for this kid; Evel was my "caped crusader."

One day in the early fall of 1972, my dad and I made our usual pilgrimage out Yale Road east to Capilano Motorcycles. Upon our arrival my dad and Bob showed me a bright-red motorcycle that was just my size. It was a 1970 Yamaha GT 60, not quite a motocross bike, but somewhat of an MX-Enduro Hybrid. I can't remember how I felt, but I know what happened next. Bob asked if I wanted to take it for a ride. I was excited; I had never ridden a motorcycle, and had only been a passenger on my dad's street and motocross bikes.

The shop was situated on a main road and secondary highway through the valley. The backside of the shop backed onto the same Hope Slough that our home was on, fifteen minutes to the west. Where was I going to ride it? Dad and Bob looked across the street at a large church that was situated across the way. "Let's try it over there," they said. Are you kidding me? A church! How fitting to get to ride a motorcycle for the first time at a place I detested. Well, I didn't detest church per se, but I was still raw from having pissed myself during Sunday school that spring, so it seemed like a fitting revenge.

The gravel parking lot was empty, because it wasn't a Sunday. The ride went well, and you could say I was a bit of a natural. I didn't fall, and I even figured out how to use the clutch to start and stop. Maybe it was just beginner's luck, but I could definitely ride a motorcycle.

After the ride we headed back to the shop. I'm not sure I was ready for what came next. My dad simply said, "Do you want it?" I'm sure I don't have to tell you what my answer was. Any kind of isolation or indifference to my peers I had felt up to that point was gone. That bright-red Yamaha, which seemed to have been built perfectly for me, was now my constant object of affection, my first "true love."

We loaded up the bike and took it home, where my mom and baby sister were waiting on the front porch. In no time flat, I was spinning laps in our front yard. Dad and Bob had rigged up a helmet for me that had a cool visor and a football placekicker-type cage on the front. Oddly enough, even as a professional racer, Bob wore the same setup. Other than that, it was runners, blue jeans, and a T-shirt. It was the 1970s, and pretty much every safety precaution had been taken, right?

I had a fall on our freshly paved asphalt driveway and bent the clutch lever quite badly. Not thinking anything of it, Dad straightened it out, and I was back in action in no time. What he failed to observe—or did and thought nothing of it—was that the knob on the end of the lever had broken off. It wasn't an issue, and the clutch still worked fine, though it was a half inch shorter.

I got braver with every ride and soon figured out how to get the front wheel up, where the grass met the edge of our driveway. Like my hero, Evel Knievel, I was doing wheelies on my own motorcycle, and I couldn't have been prouder.

Shortly thereafter my bravery proved costly when I took another spill while trying to navigate a sharp left turn to avoid the neighbours' fence. Bailing out, I dropped the bike, and when it landed, the sharp end of the broken clutch lever hit my foot. The lever pierced the canvas of my running shoe and was stuck deep inside. I don't remember if it hurt, but my mother, who was supportive and consenting to my new joy, suddenly had tangible reasons to worry.

Off to the doctor we went. After a few stitches and a tetanus shot, I was ready to ride again. Not so fast though. Dad had a quick remedy to prevent any further such injuries. We went to the Chilliwack Co-Op and got a pair of lace-up leather hiking boots. As for the bike, in MacGyver-like fashion, Dad used electrical tape to make a knob on the clutch lever in place of the one that had broken off. I was proudly back in action, and the new safety precautions only seemed to heighten my bravery.

Over the next year or so, life continued pretty much the same as it had. Riding dirt bikes was just for fun, and to me it was just that, FUN. Dad raced a couple of motocross races, and on the weekends that he didn't, we went out to watch races in Mission and Agassiz, at the old Stampeder track, among others. I also maintained my passion for ice hockey and road hockey; I never let up on that either. We kept our bikes outside in our open carport, and I don't ever even remember them being locked up. Economically, things were pretty strong all around, and the kind of crime that is rampant today was pretty much nonexistent. Dad continued to slug away in the bush, and Mom maintained her mastery of motherhood.

I loved going to town with my dad in his brown 1972 Ford 4x4. The truck was a climb to get in, but once inside, it was a man's office on wheels. It smelled like an oily gravel pit in the forest. A five-dollar bill seemed to go miles back then. On trips to town, it often bought him a box of Pilsner, gas for his truck, and even his cigarettes. I know I had my share of candy and junk food, too, but it wasn't my thing. As I said, I was a meat-and-potatoes kid. I never questioned any of it; it was just who my dad was, and I loved him more than anything. I loved my mother just as much, but in my young, impressionable mind, my dad was the best man on Earth.

Our friendships with the Douglas and Mutch families flourished. We also maintained a strong presence in our hockey and skating club community. I wasn't just a member of Chilliwack Minor Hockey, but also a member of the Kinsman Skating Club. While I'm at it, I might as well get the elephant out of the room and tell you that I also took piano lessons. That didn't last long, though. To this day, the only song I can play is the A&W root beer song, so I guess it wasn't a total loss.

Mom and Dad also had snowmobiles, and in the winter, they satisfied our off-road motorized needs. Much like the dirt bikes, they kept them in the carport and drove right out the driveway down the roads to wherever they wanted to go. The Fraser Valley had pretty mild winters, but living some seventy miles inland from the Pacific Ocean, we still got our share of snowstorms. Dad's was a 443 Yamaha, and Mom's was a smaller 292.

Later in life they asked me if I remembered the time Dad and Sam Douglas left the driveway to head out for a rip on Fairfield Island. After they blasted off and went to the end of Bonavista and around the block, Sam lost track of Dad.

He stopped to wait for him and, upon turning around, was mortified to see me hanging off the back of his sled. You guessed it, I had decided I was coming along and had bumper hitched a ride to Sam's sled. That's just the way I was. If I wanted in and someone didn't include me, I found my own way.

Christmas was always a special time in our home, thanks to the love and effort my mom and her mom, Grandma Jean, put into it. Every Christmas, the city of Chilliwack had a Santa Claus parade. I don't think we ever missed one. It was always an exciting way to set the tone for the big day.

One year on Christmas Eve, we were awoken by a loud knock on our bedroom door. Mom opened the door and, lo and behold, it was the big man himself, Santa Claus.

"Santa, I've been waiting for you all night," I proclaimed, wide-eyed. He gave me a candy cane, and told me to go back to sleep. He said if I had been good, he would be back later to bring gifts. It turns out "Santa" was a relative of our neighbours, the Ballams, who dressed up annually to greet kids like us. I always believed in Santa Claus no matter what the talk on the street was. (Evel Knievel was the one who changed that in 1976; more on that later.) With my mom having eight brothers and sisters, and all my grandparents back in our lives in some capacity, Christmas was an important time of year for the Worrall family. For us, Christmas was, and always will be about family.

Springtime usually meant family camping trips and motorcycle-riding season. Even though we were active on the ice, there were no other community sports for me. No baseball, no soccer, and no track and field.

For the first two years on my first bike, it was mostly trail riding along the Fraser riverbed, at the Douglas Reserve, or on our many camping trips. Dad continued to pursue his passion for cross-country racing, with the odd motocross race squeezed in. Race weekends usually entailed hitting the road in our loaded camper, bike trailer in tow. Many like-minded family friends often joined us. We frequented the Bachelor Heights area of Kamloops regularly. Even if there wasn't a race, we camped and rode in the hills in the McQueen Lake area for days on end. I credit that early tutorial of dealing with the kind of adversity the soft, hilly terrain provided to developing a skillset that I likely would not have found spinning laps on a motocross track.

The only thing I can remember not liking about those trips was having to go home and return to school. My friends at school all knew we had bikes, and that I rode. Even though I was unaware of it, it gave me a certain level of coolness with my peers, preventing harassment for my uncontrollably wild Ronald McDonald-like red hair.

In the spring of 1974, the "Broadstreet Bullies" (a.k.a. Philadelphia Flyers) became the first NHL expansion team to hoist the Stanley Cup. Early that same year, we received the tragic news of Tim Horton's passing in a car wreck on the QEW. I remember staring at his last hockey card, a 1973 green-bordered O-Pee-Chee, and wondering, why? I was an empathetic child, and internalized a lot of similar emotions. I'm not sure why I never asked many questions about such matters, but likely I didn't want to know the answers. Tim's passing was one of my first lessons about mortality.

That same year I raced in my first motocross event at a track just east of downtown Kamloops on Highway 1, where the Lafarge cement plant now sits. I was seven at the time, and I think competitors had to be at least eight. Fortunately, we still have some great 8 mm footage that my father took that day. I don't think my mom came along to the event; it was just Dad and me. Bob and Robbie Mutch were there too, with Bob being one of the fastest racers in Canada.

I lined up in the Schoolboy Class on my little 60 cc Enduro and did my best to follow in the wake of all the big bikes up the long starting stretch hill. I'm not sure how, but I managed to finish the race in one piece. My friend and growing nemesis, Robbie Mutch, finished much better on his brand-new silver first-edition Yamaha 80 cc motocross bike. He had an obvious advantage, with his dad being a former national champ and a Yamaha dealer. I don't remember the conversation, but apparently, my dad asked me if I was ready for the second race. In between races, I had already done some play riding with Robbie down below the track at the foot of the river. There was a little jump there, where we could get our wheels airborne, and we hit it repeatedly.

"No, I just want to go ride down by the river with Robbie," I replied. I'm not sure if Robbie raced in that moto, but I certainly didn't, because I was having more fun play riding. Even though most of these memories seem a lifetime away, I'm eternally grateful for the life into which I was born.

The balance of the 1974 race season saw me line up a few more times. The Agassiz motocross track was only a forty-five-minute drive from home. On many occasions, Dad and I went there to practice, so I could get a better feel for a motocross track. The Agassiz track, which is still in business today, operated under the CMA (Canadian Motorcycle Association) umbrella, the premier sanctioning body in Canadian motocross at the time.

I loved going to that track. It was always a fun drive, right from the time we left our driveway. Heading eastbound on Yale Road past our favourite motorcycle shop, coupled with the anticipation of the ride ahead, was the elixir of life for this seven-year-old. Where Yale Road met Highway 9, we turned left and then headed northbound. Shortly after that, high on the right side of the road, was Sam and Jackie Douglas's house. Highway 9 intersected what I had only ever known as "Sam's Reserve." In fact, it was the Cheam Reserve, and its people played a huge role in my upbringing.

Sam was the chief of the band, and we spent endless quality hours of my formative years there. Their two children, Lisa and Sammy, were my best friends. Many of those hours were spent on two wheels tearing up every inch of real estate and many gravel pits.

Once we breezed past the Douglas's, we crossed the seemingly gargantuan Agassiz-Rosedale Bridge. I loved crossing that bridge, high above the steady flow of the vast, chocolate-brown, west-flowing Fraser River. The bridge seemed as if it had been built by the Friendly Giant, with his Meccano set.

Once across the bridge, it was through the tiny community of Agassiz, and then north toward Harrison Lake. Just before the lake, we took another left turn due west onto a road that had many warning signs, signifying that we were approaching a maximum-security federal penitentiary. If I had to guess, the prison was less than a kilometre from the Agassiz track. I was always silent when we passed it, because I knew that on the other side of all the fences, walls, and barbed wire were some bad people. I don't think I asked many questions. Maybe I didn't want to know the answers. I'm not sure if it was for good behaviour or a work-release thing, but some of the inmates flagged our races.

Pulling into the front gate of the track was an incredible feeling. The bright banners that lined the first-turn wall berm. The announcer's tower. The starting line. And that rich, bright-red, vibrant one-of-a-kind Agassiz soil. To this day I have never seen anything like it. The track was situated at the foot of a shale mountain on a bench of dirt that had an amazing bright-red clay-like soil. It was primo, but when it rained, which it did often, let's just say, "Grease was the word."

That year I raced on the bright-red Yamaha 60 while wearing a Montreal Canadians Jersey with a big number "43" on the back made from hockey tape. I have no idea why I wore a Canadiens jersey, because I was a Bruins fan. Maybe I was saving my Bruins jersey for a finer occasion, like my wedding day. Maybe I took a bullet just to be certain that my jersey matched my bike and blinding-red hair. Was I that vain already? I thought that came later in life.

We have some great video of those race days. Part of the track had a hill and two straightaways that used the base of the mountain, where the track was located. One of the videos shows me coming down the backside, ripping down the hill in the smooth tracks the water truck had made. My dad always told me to pick smooth lines on the track, and to me, that was as smooth as it got.

On the other race day there, I launched the finish-line jump adjacent to the starting line and landed sideways. I ended up high-siding on the hard-packed concrete-like soil and sustained my first concussion after being knocked unconscious. I remember nothing of it, but our family video shows me standing beside side my bike in the pits with the handlebars bent down at a ninety-degree angle on the throttle side. My mom is standing beside me with a grave look of concern, and I'm playing into it. That is, until someone walks up and points at the bars and makes an "Ouch!" face. In the video, I just crack a smile and laugh. I had survived my first bad fall, and lived to do it again. Yes, I would do it many, many more times!

Racing and riding dirt bikes continued to be front and centre in my mind's eye. My parents always consented and participated in every way that they could to make it enjoyable. There was one golden rule, however: schooling. As long as I got decent grades, dirt bikes and racing was permitted. Academically, I was pretty average in elementary school. My letter grades were often high Cs and every now and again a little below. My mom put the most stock in my efforts though, as noted in the teachers' comments. I can't think of one teacher up to my graduation day who ever commented negatively on my persona, even when I was charged in high school with a heinous criminal offence that was raised to adult court (more on that later.) Even though I don't feel like I ever gave school 100 percent, I did pretty well. I had to; it was the proverbial hand that fed my motocross infatuation.

On September 8, 1974, my idol, Evel Knievel, attempted his ill-fated Snake River Canyon jump. I was intrigued but didn't know much about what happened. The thing that sticks out in my mind was people who said, "He's crazy." My parents never uttered those words though. Maybe because they knew I idolized him, or maybe not. My parents were non-judgmental people.

Another big event in the fall of 1974 was the sale of our Bonavista house. Up until the writing of this book, I never gave it a second thought. I guess my parents had dreams of moving up in the world. They purchased a building lot for $1,850 in a new high-end subdivision by the Chilliwack Airport, 8450 Hilton Drive, to be exact. There the plans were drawn up for a brand-new state-of-the-art split-level home with a twenty-by-forty-foot in-ground swimming pool.

After departing Bonavista, we moved temporarily to a farmhouse on Crescent Drive. We had more than an acre there. The property also backed onto the railway tracks, and I loved the sound of the train thundering past. It was a sweet package deal, because we had a huge fenced-in yard to rip up on our motorcycles. We also got a couple of cows, which did a good job of keeping the grass down. Or at least that's what I thought their purpose was.

One day Kelly decided she was going to show us her two-and-half-year-old climbing skills. She only managed to make it a few feet up the massive manure pile until she lost her boots to it. That stunt earned her the nickname "Kelly Kanure" (that was how she pronounced "manure"). Life just kept getting better. We were living the dream, until one day I woke up to a major catastrophe.

After school and pretty much every other day that I got the chance, I headed out to my own personal dirt bike track and rode until I ran out of gas. Quite often I left the bike parked there on the kickstand until my father came home. He would fill it up, so I could repeat my insatiable cycle of happiness. Each time that happened, Dad told me that I shouldn't leave the bike out in the field. He told me to push it into the barn, where the fuel was. Not thinking much of it, and knowing it was no fun pushing the bike that far, I ignored him.

One morning, like I did every single morning, I looked out my bedroom window to view my two-wheeled soul mate. There it was, just as I had left it, but something was missing: the seat. Had someone stolen it? Was my dad trying to teach me the fine art of how to use the foot pegs instead of sitting on my ass? No, none of the above. Our beloved cows had eaten it clean off, right down to the metal. I was devastated. The first thing I thought of was my dad's warning to push it into the shed. I don't think I ever disregarded a single word he advised toward my bike and its care after that.

As for the cows, let's just say that when they went to slaughter, I wasn't nearly as disappointed as Kelly. She was heartbroken, because they had become to her what my dirt bike was to me, her best friends. After Kelly found out where our dinners came from, I'm pretty sure it was many years before she ate beef again. Two valuable life lessons moving forward for us kids on Crescent Drive.

We made one more move caused by some building delays on our new home to a place just off of Brooks Avenue on Norman Crescent. It was on the backside of Robertson Annex Elementary, which we eventually attended. Our new home on Hilton Drive backed onto the same school. I'm sure my parents were getting excited, but as a kid who had never gone without a thing, it was all part of a great childhood journey. I must say though, I was getting excited knowing we would have our own swimming pool.

We were not able to attend Robertson Annex Elementary quite yet, because I was still only in third grade. We had to attend another school, the original Robertson Elementary, which housed grades one through four. That wasn't a problem though, because it was only about six blocks north toward Chilliwack's downtown core. It was also close to the old heritage railway station and our neighbourhood co-op. It was an old three-level schoolhouse that was built in 1921. Unlike the new, shiny, modern Strathcona Elementary I had previously attended, the building was a scholastic dinosaur. It had character, but it smelled old, and I was always cold in that building.

I don't have any bad memories of teachers or classmates. I pretty much did my own thing and got along with most people. My favourite parts of school were lunch and recess. I loved the swing set, and as soon as the buzzer went, I would race like a wild child to make sure I got a swing before others did.

Our third-grade class was up on the top floor, and it was two set of stairs and out the front door to get outside. The swings and playground apparatus were around the back of the building, so I had to hustle to get there. The kids on the ground floor had a clear advantage, and they often beat me to the swings. So, I devised a plan.

The first set of stairs facing the back of the building had two huge glass doors leading down the back directly to the play area. However, they were off limits to students unless there was a fire or a fire drill. They were marked with signs and likely even alarmed, and the teachers monitored them regularly. We all knew that opening those doors would mean serious punishment in the form of a pink slip from the principal.

One day I decided to crack the door open on a fake bathroom trip. I'm not sure if I had a plan in the form of an alibi if an alarm went off, but it was a chance I was willing to take. I had no choice; I couldn't stand watching the others swing when I wanted one so desperately.

My plan was failsafe at first; no alarm went off when I cracked the door, and no one was wiser to it. I was excited and couldn't wait to try it out. At this point, I should mention that the doors, installed in 1921, were wooden and ornate. They also had stained glass panes bordered by bevelled wood.

I couldn't wait for the 3:00 bell. It would be my acid test, my first real-life gate drop, if you will. The buzzer rang, and I was off like a rocket. I'm pretty sure I jumped the entire twelve or so stairs down to the landing, where the forbidden doors were located. Overzealous is an understatement. My forward momentum on the landing was way too much to stop me, and I lunged forward, out of control. I don't think any of the other kids were even at the top of the first stair when my well-structured plan became a bloody, unexplainable mess.

In an effort to open the door while falling face first into it at breakneck speed, my right arm broke through the largest pane of glass. My world was instantly silent, until some of the girls who, by that time, had made their way down the stairs started to scream. I looked down at my arm. Had I not seen large pieces of glass in it with blood spewing out, I would have continued on my way outside.

I think it was our principal, Mr. Stoudjestyk, who got to me first. In the nurse's room, they quickly wrapped my arm and then whisked me off to the hospital.

I don't remember any punishment resulting from that blunder. I'm pretty sure that when they asked me what happened, I told them I slipped and fell. Not quite a lie, was it?

I healed up pretty fast, like most kids do, and I don't believe that blunder even phased me. In fact, within a few short weeks, I was back in my happy place, pumping myself on the swing as high as I could go. Whenever the bell rang to call us back into class, it was always a personal challenge to see how high I could jump off the swings.

One day I didn't come off right away. Instead I continued until the school monitor pleaded that it was time to go back to class. With almost every other kid headed back in, I looked at her from afar and screamed, "I'm Evel Knievel!", then launched myself from as high as I had ever flown. Unfortunately, my rear end got hung up in the seat, and instead of landing on my feet, I was a human lawn dart, landing headfirst, though I used my arm to cushion my fall. It broke instantly. I don't remember who, what, when, or how, but the next thing I knew, I had my first plaster cast on my right arm. I was eight years old and had my first real adrenaline-rush-related trophy. I don't remember how long I had to wear the cast, but once again, I had survived another error in judgement. No, Evel didn't make me do it, but he was my hero, and I know he would have been proud.

5

8450 Hilton Drive

In 1976 we moved into our brand-new, posh home on Chilliwack's Hilton Drive. Situated in the northeast corner of the circular subdivision, the setting was pristine, and I'm sure it was envied by many. The house had many new bells and whistles that we kids had never seen before, not even on television. It even had a full unfinished basement, which was perfect for indoor ball hockey.

As for the yard, all that mattered to us kids was the twenty-by-forty-foot in-ground swimming pool. It was fully equipped with a slide and a diving board. We even had a special sauna room and a change room. The yard was fully fenced with a six-foot high perimeter wall that bordered our fortress.

Behind us was the pathway that led to a bridge that crossed a small creek to the school we would attend that coming year, Robertson Annex Elementary. The subdivision out front, circular in fashion, wasn't a thoroughfare, so our many road hockey games and BMX bike-jumping sessions were never a burden to anyone. In fact, most of the largest traffic issues on our streets were on motocross race weekends. Our home was often the scene of a pool party before or after each race.

After one Agassiz race, trucks, trailers, motorhomes, and every other race-related vehicle imaginable lined our entire neighbourhood. It was on that weekend that our friend and top-level expert racer, Larry Mackenzie, brought his unicycle into our backyard. He rode it like a circus clown on the pool deck. I was astounded when my dad climbed aboard and had no problem riding it. It was a unicycle; where in the world had my dad learned to do that? I don't think I even asked him. All I remember thinking was, *If that old bugger can do it, so can I.*

Larry had no problem leaving the contraption with me until the following race weekend to see if I could master it. It took a bit longer than a week, but I eventually figured it out. Shortly after that I got my own unicycle, and it turned out to be one of the best cardiovascular, balance, brain, and abdominal muscle workouts I know. It also became one of my passions for releasing endorphins while doing something extremely fun. I eventually owned three different unicycles. One of them was a full six-foot-tall circus-style model. I loved riding it to school, even in high school. I never cared what anyone thought. It was who I was, and that was all that mattered to me.

I have many other memories associated with our pool parties, and they were not always positive ones. On one occasion our neighbour, who had bark mulch in his front yard instead of grass, was unhappy to find empty beer bottles buried neck deep in his front yard. I think it bothered him a lot more than it bothered my dad, who never put much stock in what our neighbours thought of him. He never went out of his way to make trouble, but if someone poked their nose where they shouldn't, they usually regretted it.

It was on Hilton Drive that we kids started to form some solid lifelong friendships with many of our peers, including the Dedels, the Velonises, and the Maiers, to name a few. Our Hilton drive friends included Rudy and Marianne Dyck, along with their sons, Robbie and Greg. Rudy owned Chilliwack Leisure World, and we bought our campers from him. His father, Abe, was a carpenter by trade, a nice man who built our first two homes.

My mom had not yet returned to the workforce since Kelly's birth. Some days I would return home from school to find our house full of schoolkids making or building some sort of craft. Mom always had an incredible amount of energy and selflessness for kids—anyone's kids. My friend George Velonis, who had immigrated from Greece in around grade three, still credits my mother's volunteer tutoring (she knew he was struggling) to helping him pass into the next grade.

As I said, I don't remember not liking school, but I was a bit put out early in elementary school when my teachers forced me to write with my right hand rather than my left, which I felt more comfortable with. I can't remember how things ended up, but I still write with my right hand today. I loved to draw motorcycles or hockey players in my notebooks. I always drew with my left hand and still do.

To me, school was just part and parcel of being a kid. I never fussed much about the learning aspect, but around grade five or six, I started to realize that I had a phenomenal memory. When it came to historical dates, names of geographical places, world news or leaders, or sporting event results, you can bet I remembered the answer. Often after a verbal lecture or an assigned reading project, we would be quizzed verbally in class. More times than not, my hand was the first one up. Surprisingly, my friends didn't give me a hard time about that. I was by no stretch a class geek or a chess club kid. I was a fiery redhead who loved two-wheeled action and ice hockey more than anything on Earth. By age ten, my developing personality had already become clumsily confident and outgoing.

Being a Gemini born on June 1, birthday parties on Hilton Drive were always a hit with my friends. My mom often made an awesome chocolate cake that looked like a motocross track, complete with bikes. With the swimming pool being the ultimate draw, it's safe to say that every kid attending Robertson Elementary knew to whom the large brown home that backed onto the schoolyard belonged. I spent my fair share of time in the water but never considered myself a good swimmer. I liked the water, but swimming end to end was never in my wheelhouse of pool fun. Diving off the board, on the other hand, usually kept me hopping.

Most parties that started in the backyard usually ended up on the streets, with all of us jumping BMX bikes or playing road hockey. We had two large BMX ramps that my dad had constructed out of plywood and two-by-fours. They were huge and heavy, and yes, they were a hazard to many. After all, Evel Knievel was my hero and the king of ramp-to-ramp jumping. After a few mishaps with some of my friends, my parents decided that maybe the ramps shouldn't be placed so far apart. For the most part, I was okay, because I could jump a pretty sizeable gap. I took my share of headers, but I don't remember breaking any bones on my bicycle. I guess I was saving the best crashes for my motocross bike.

By 1976 we were living life to the fullest. Everything seemed to be getting bigger and better. We were always up to something sports related, but our family life was starting to revolve around motocross and off-road racing. I add in off-road racing, because Dad still had a hankering for cross-country racing—a long, arduous, and physically demanding type of motorcycle race over mountainous or desert-type terrain. Even though it was physically demanding, Dad felt he would be putting himself at more risk of being injured on a motocross track. I can't argue pro or con or give any advice on safety, for that matter. Remember, it was the 1970s, and safety for me meant runners tied up, jeans buckled, and T-shirt tucked in.

Dad did have one huge problem with the cross-country racing scene though. Unlike a motocross track, cross-country tracks were not lined with fences and banners. Instead, they were marked with different coloured ribbons. Yes, that's it, just small ribbons tied to trees, stakes, rocks, cacti, whatever. Dad's problem was that he was colour blind. That created a significant problem, because some of the colours were used to signify dangerous obstacles. I have no idea how he did it, but my dad was smart beyond words when it came to having a sixth sense on a motorcycle.

One thing I remember him teaching me about that type of racing was to look for people. I had no idea what the heck he was talking about. Look for people? He explained that the average person who came out to watch one of those events would stand where they thought something exciting was going to happen. With human nature being what it is, I soon figured out that where people were gathered was a good place to slow down and look twice before leaping. These cross-country races were for big bikes only, and for good reason.

In 1976, we went down to the biggest desert races in the northwest, the Mattawa 100. Not far from Wenatchee, Washington, Mattawa is in a desert-like area. We had teamed up with the Mutches, and Bob's Winnebago was our home for the weekend. I don't remember a lot about the race, but one of the boys who came down with us, Jordan Sinclair, who was around fifteen or sixteen, competed in the event.

Late in the day, the race had to be called, because a fire broke out in the desert, and it was a huge safety concern for all the riders. When the sun went down, Jordan still had not returned. His bike had broken down, and he was trapped with smoke and fire surrounding him. Late that night, he was found and was returned safely to our camp. It was a big deal to me, because I had never seen such concern for a human life due to something I loved, racing.

I also remember my mother exclaiming how thankful she was that I wasn't racing cross-country races—not yet anyway. Her days of worrying would come soon, though. I'm pretty sure my dad took it all in stride. If he was worried, it was never in his character to show it. Mom got served a double dose of "what-for" that weekend, because Kelly's four-letter-word vocabulary increased exponentially after the Mattawa 100.

With the outdoor racing season in high gear, 1976 marked the first year we hit almost every motocross race in British Columbia. Once again, the tracks in Agassiz, Mission, and Aldergrove (Little Rock Raceway, RIP Walt Levy) saw most of the action. One-off races also took place in the northern parts of the province and on Vancouver Island. We also started racing every Thursday night during the summers at Hannegan Speedway in Bellingham, Washington. Hannegan was amazing, and I was impressed with the racing scene south of the border. They took things to the next level, and the grounds were well-kept.

Hannegan had three racetracks. First was an oval for flat-track racing. Some call it dirt-track racing, but I will always call it "flat-tracking." The main motocross track for the big bikes circumnavigated the flat track and had a big jump that launched riders over it into the infield, where the finish flag was located. For smaller riders there was a mini-bike track. These races were held on Thursday nights between 5:00 and 9:00 p.m. just before the sun went down. I could hardly contain myself at school on race days, knowing I was heading racing. On the flip side, I always felt a little sluggish getting out of bed on Friday mornings. The only thing that kept me motivated was knowing it was Friday, and that meant only two more sleeps until we were racing or riding somewhere on Sunday. At that time, life couldn't have been better for this ten-year-old.

Hannegan Speedway also had incredible trophies. They were huge and amazing in all their shining glory when the outdoor trophy room opened for presentation. I had not won a trophy yet, and was starting to think it might never happen.

My dad always walked the track with me and pointed out lines that I could use to help improve my speed and endurance. He would take me to a spot on the track and show me exactly what he meant. He would also point out things as other riders went by to illustrate what he was talking about. I was still on Yamahas in 1976, the only brand I had known to date. The 1976 YZ-80 was my second full-size 80 cc bike. I'm not sure why, but our beloved dealer, Capilano Motorcycles, had closed its doors. Bob had gotten into the RV business, among other things, some good and some not so good. Bob was still one of Dad's good friends, and we saw the Mutch family often.

Bob bought some property in the Ryder Lake area in Chilliwack, and immediately built another track. I ended up T-boning Robbie on that track when he stopped at a corner and turned around, coming at me from another direction. It was an accident and no one's fault—unlike the time Robbie was poking fun at me outside his dad's shop, and I turned and dropped him to the ground with one punch to the jaw. Robbie's father recounted that story many times. Bob had a distinct laugh. He would often laugh and say, "Robbie had it coming," and he did. I was tired of him thinking he could push me around whenever he felt like it. It has never been in my nature to initiate physical aggression unless absolutely needed. On that day there were a ton of people at the shop, because the annual boat races were passing by behind it. From that day forward, Robbie never attempted to push me around. We did, however, fight again in Calgary, at Race City Speedway, in 1989. I will tell that story a little later.

The new Yamaha dealer in Chilliwack was Cross Country Motors. The shop was in a huge building, where the CN railway tracks crossed Yale Road. Owned by the Peters family, the shop became our new hangout and Cross Country Motors my new sponsor. The Peters family was new to motorcycles and were quite religious. However, several of the staff and mechanics from Capilano moved to the new dealership, so it wasn't a total culture shock for us.

The owner's son, Wally Peters, who was around twenty-two, became a good friend and mentor to me. He was calm, easygoing, and methodical. Wally never seemed to get too ramped up about anything. He always spoke like a gentleman, and never used profanity. That was a good fit for me, because I was always hell-bent and ready for whatever chaos lay ahead. The Peters family also bought the old Mutch farm track, which was on forty acres between Yale Road East and Little Mountain Elementary School. We burned many tanks of gas on that track together. Wally was a weekend warrior junior-class rider and was okay with that. At ten years of age, I recognized several traits in him that I had admired immensely.

I just learned recently of Wally's untimely passing quite a few years back. Wally, I may have been too young to tell you this or even understand what I was sensing, but your mentorship and the times we spent together helped me with many things, including letting go of a deep dark hatred toward organized religion. Today I believe God works through people, and I'm thankful he put you in my path. RIP, old friend, you are missed.

Until that point, I had predominantly raced against older, stronger riders. We had no 60 cc bike classes yet, and if someone raced an 80 cc, like I did, he had to line up against kids who were as old as sixteen. Nevertheless, it was in 1976 at Hannegan Speedway that I got a "holeshot" (first racer to the first corner) and never looked back. Well, that's not totally true, because one of the things I did often was turn around and look back. Dad hated it! He would show me video that he had taken, and sure enough, there I was ripping it up with my head on a swivel. "Looking back at what?" he would ask. "Everyone has passed you. You're last, so go!"

On that night I felt the wheel of the rider behind me more than once trying to open the proverbial door, which I kept slamming in his face. I don't think I ever knew his name, but he was a big tall kid with number 103 on his bike wearing the ugliest face mask I have ever seen on a gold helmet. He got a wheel in on me on the last lap. Unfortunately, he just beat me to the finish line. I was beat but I was okay with that. I knew I had run an almost perfect race and come up just short to a rider who was at least four years older than me. I also knew that one of those beautiful, highly coveted Hannegan Speedway trophies would soon have a new home—mine!

My dad never seemed to change pace when he was happy, mad, sad, or whatever. However, when I won my first trophy, Dad said I had done well, and that he was proud of me. I didn't hear him say that often, but when he did, I knew damn well he meant it. The trophy was a combination of gold, wood, and marble with a huge "1976" on it. I must have looked at it all the way home. It put a huge smile on my face when Dad was asked by the US Customs official at the Sumas border crossing if we were bringing anything home from the USA. Dad responded with a smile and pointed at me, beaming with my trophy.

We got home at around 9:30 p.m., our house being only about an hour from Hannegan Speedway. Mom wasn't home yet, because she had something on the go with my sister on most Thursday evenings, likely swimming. Unlike me, Kelly loved to swim and had joined the Spartan Swim Club at Canadian Forces Base Chilliwack. I was a little bummed that no one was home to see my first motocross racing trophy, but Dad quickly came up with a plan. He knew Mom and Kelly would be home any time, so he told me to lie on the couch with a blanket. "When Mom comes in, tell her you're not feeling well, and need a glass of milk." He placed my trophy in the fridge behind the milk carton. I will never forget the look of concern on Mom's face turning to excitement when she grabbed the milk. It was only a trophy, but it was my first, and to see my family celebrate what was truly a family effort gave me great satisfaction. Mentally, I was beginning to fill our home with trophies. I wanted more; I wanted to win. Yes, riding and racing was fun, but now that I knew I could win, that's all I wanted to do every time I lined up.

By the fall of 1976, the end of our outdoor race season, I had accumulated a half dozen or so trophies. I was so proud of my collection, and I knew the story behind each. I often closed my bedroom door and cranked the music on my new record player to my favourite single, Manfred Man's "Blinded By The Light." It became a ritual of sorts in the morning before school and upon returning home. It was always a great jam session with my trophies and my loud music.

That winter also marked the first year we ventured south on weekends and raced in AMA (American Motorcycle Association) races. These races, like most in the US, had many more riders than our local races. The riders down there were fast and seemed to be ahead of the game in the R&D (research and development) department. Dad knew that, which is why we went. There were many wet, soggy, muddy events at places like Startup Raceway Park, Seattle International Raceways, Puyallup, Spanaway, Woodland, Monroe, Washington, and so on. The races were held mostly on Sundays, but some were full weekend events.

One of Dad's moto buddies was none other than "Bouncing Bob" Henrikson. He was the father of one of the riders I raced with, Lorne, who was a couple of years older than me. The Henriksons lived just off the 176th Street exit in Surrey, beside Highway 1. Many days we were up at 3:00 a.m. on Saturday or Sunday morning to make the trek from Chilliwack to pick up Lorne and Bob. From there it was off to a track south of Seattle. As a kid I never batted an eye. It was who we were and what we did. Dad reminds me of a time that I wanted to go to a race when I was just seven. He told me that if I went to sleep and woke him in the morning, we would go. No alarm clocks were set, but I was punctual in waking him up to go racing, and he honoured his commitment.

That winter, though, I noticed things were starting to change in some regards. Dad seemed to be growing a little more accustomed to the racing schedule and scene. Mom, who was usually with us at the races, wasn't always there anymore. Her involvement with Kelly's swimming and skating took priority on weekends. It was especially notable in the winter months, because that is when the swim club and skating clubs practiced and competed.

Dad, who I knew to have a beer or two or three or four when he felt like it, seemed to me to be drinking more often. Sometimes driving home from a long day, I would tell him that I was thirsty, and he would hand me his stubby bottle of Old Style Pilsner. I often took a drink, but I hated the taste of beer.

We had a camper on the back of our truck, and we towed the bikes on a trailer. It was a ritual for Lorne and me or whoever else was travelling south with us to ride in the camper. When we got a few minutes from the border crossing, Dad would pull over and tell us to lie still behind the curtains. It's funny now looking back on it. Why the heck was he hiding us? I knew I was having a "bad hair life," but come on, we were just kids. Nothing ever came of that, and Dad always handled the border as he believed he was supposed to. His only advice to me in that regard was to answer their questions but not to volunteer anything. I think lying beneath all that was Dad's assault charges, for which he had done time. Back then it was definitely a lot easier to cross the border, but Dad didn't want to take any chances on not getting us to the races. He always got us there. It wasn't always in the same vehicle, but we always made it in one piece. Home? That was a different story.

Our first stop across the border was at the gas station, and it wasn't always for gas! I remember the back of the camper door opening and two flats of Coors were thrown in. That was usually followed by, "Get back to sleep! We'll be at the track in a few hours." After a long day of racing, it would be another five or six hours before we were back home in Chilliwack late on Sunday night. As for all that beer, it was never a problem, because it was usually gone by the time we crossed back into Canada.

On one occasion we returned home to get a phone call from a racing colleague to notify that we had left our dog at the track, but he was with him, safe and okay. Beer may have been involved in that incident.

One of the highlights of the winter of 1976 was making our second consecutive trip to the AMA's Trans-AMA event at Puyallup Raceway Park in southwestern Washington. The Trans-AMA series pitted the fastest European and world-renowned riders on a grand stage against the fastest in the USA, right in Uncle Sam's backyard. The Puyallup track was predominantly sand-based, long, and flowed well. I was spellbound with how many people lined the sidelines to watch in the cold wintery rain. In the years that we attended, that event attracted 30,0000–40,000 spectators each year. With its large geographical draw, the Pacific Northwest was a motocross hotbed.

Heading into that series, Roger DeCoster had just been crowned 500 cc World Champion by winning 7 out of 12 events. The Belgian, known simply as "The Man," was one of many riders who lined up at the event with nothing short of rock star status in the motocross world. He was lined up against my newest two-wheeled hero, the fast, young, wild, up-and-coming Bob "Hurricane" Hannah. I can't remember a lot about the results on that day, but what I do remember will stay with me for a lifetime.

On race day, we woke up early and headed down to the hotel's restaurant for breakfast. I gagged on the smoke when I walked in, because back then people could still smoke in restaurants. (In my early teens, we found out after a couple of sudden asthma attacks, that I'm highly allergic to cigarette smoke.)

We were not seated for more than a minute or two when my dad looked over to the next table, and then nudged me. "There's Roger DeCoster and his 'dentist,'" he said. Roger was seated across the table from his Team Suzuki teammate, Gerrit Wolsink. The Dutch racer, who was a licensed dentist, was also a five-time winner of the United States World Grand Prix, which was held annually at Carlsbad Raceway.

Dad told me to go over there and sit beside him, and tell him who I was. Without needing any other encouragement, I moved in. Before a word even came out of Roger's mouth, he greeted my approach with a welcome smile. I introduced myself and told him I was a huge fan of his accomplishments. I was a little starstruck to be sitting at the same table as the baddest, fastest, and, in my opinion, the most methodical rider in the world. That day I cheered loud and proud for Roger, and I still have a photograph that my dad took of him and his growing nemesis, Bob Hannah. That year Roger won his fourth consecutive Trans-AMA Series.

In 2014, I caught up with Roger again at the Anaheim Supercross and interviewed him for the *Canadian Moto Show*. I talked with him at great length about the day I met him, and what it meant to me moving forward. I was also astounded by his great recollection of our encounter in Puyallup, which now seems a few lifetimes away. Roger De Coster, you will always be "The Man" in my books, not just for what you accomplished on the motocross track, but also for how you handled yourself as a professional human being, and the way you treated me.

With the disco movement in full swing and the Montreal Canadians sweeping the Boston Bruins in four games to win the Stanley Cup, 1977 was another great year of firsts for the Worrall family. On June 1, I turned eleven, and my body was changing quickly. Still not quite out of my baby fat, it seemed like I was growing hair everywhere. The year started off on a bad foot—literally—because

I broke my right foot and ankle late that winter playing ball hockey. It wasn't a big deal at the time, but it was the first of five breaks of that same ankle. None the wiser, I did what any kid would do and put it in the rearview mirror. I'm not sure I even missed a motocross race, because it happened in between winter and summer racing. I did, however, miss some hockey, which was soon to become a common theme in my life—hurt on my dirt bike, and unable to play hockey as a result. I always signed up and played, but when it came to the rep teams, the coaches knew there would be a time when they would have to do without my reliably accurate shot. It didn't bother me at first, but I began to regret it later. I loved motocross, and I loved ice hockey. Hockey was more all-inclusive in the sense that all my friends played. I could interact with them on the same level, unlike moto, and they all knew the rules and the who's who of the sport. Moto was different. Most of my friends knew of my accomplishments and that I rode a badass dirt bike, but for the most part, that's where it ended. These two sports were the fabric of my existence, and I needed them both constantly.

On the racetrack, I was consistently finishing in the top five at the provincial level. Many of the faster riders had a few years on me. It never stopped me from being the fastest eleven-year-old I could be each and every weekend.

In 1977, Dad decided to enter another cross-country race in Salmon Arm, BC. As usual, we packed up the family racing rig and headed to the Shuswap. We also took my bike along, so I could do some free riding.

Upon arrival in Salmon Arm, Dad informed me that I would be racing the event alongside him on my own bike! What was he talking about? How could I even compete on my 80 cc motorcycle or even finish a full cross-country race? The Salmon Arm area, unlike most of the cross-country races we had been to, had a heavily treed landscape. The rocks were pretty massive in spots as well. Once I realized what was happening, I felt calm and confident that my dad knew what he was doing—or so I hoped.

When we went to the starting line, 200 bikes were ready for the Le Mans-style start (meaning a dead engine and running to the motorcycle to start it when the green flag waved). I'm sure my bike got a few indifferent looks, but I don't remember anyone saying anything.

That race was no easy task, because my father had to dismount and help lift my bike over several obstacles. He also had to walk my bike up many of the steep and, by that time, blown-apart hillsides. Back in the pits before we finished the final leg, the word was out that my dad was a madman and that we had no hope of finishing. Over eight hours later, after collecting all the necessary checkpoint markers, we crossed the finish line. It was an incredible accomplishment, and to this day, the ribbon I got for finishing is one of my most-prized trophies. My dad always had a method to his madness, and in that case, going from that race to a motocross track was like dropping the medicine ball and picking up a basketball.

That season was also the first year we travelled east to the biggest national motocross event in our country, which was held at the Blackfoot Motocross Park in Calgary, Alberta. It was 1977, and the iconic motocross track in the heart of Calgary's industrial area was already in full swing. Instead of towing a trailer, Dad mounted my motorcycle on our truck's front bumper. He wasn't racing, so the trailer wasn't needed.

My dad's father, my Grandpa James, lived in Edmonton at the time. We planned to visit him and his wife, Edith, the week before our big race. Prior to that trek, I had only met him once or twice. My mom and dad never talked about him much, and if they did, I must have tuned it out, because he wasn't an active part of our life. It was a long drive, but it was worth it. I liked my grandpa, who was always kind and generous with us kids. His home was well decorated, with all his plaques and medals displayed proudly. I assume they were from the war, but as a kid, I was good with just knowing that my grandpa was a badass of sorts.

We were fortunate enough to be in Edmonton when the famous Klondike Days were on, and we got to go to that as well. Dad and Grandpa even played the ponies one night at Northlands Park. My grandpa always seemed to know a guy who knew a guy who had a horse, if you know what I mean. I took it all in stride, but was I getting a sneak peek at the "hand" I was unknowingly holding in life.

We left Edmonton, not realizing it would be the last time that we saw my grandfather's Edmonton home. Finally, it was time to head down to Calgary to our biggest race of the season. Even though we had a camper and were prepared to stay at the track, if needed, we bunked down for the weekend at the Blackfoot Inn.

We had not been in our room more than a few minutes when we heard a commotion outside. A pedestrian had been struck and killed, and it was a mess. Once again, as with most things of that nature, my parents didn't have a lot of answers for the many questions that I wondered, about but never asked.

As for the race, I'm not even sure how I placed. The track was insanely gnarly compared to most that I had ridden up to that point. The elevation changes on the hard-packed soil were like riding a roller coaster. We have some great video footage from that event, and I'm so thankful for that. The winner of the 80 cc national championship was Roger Bellerose, whose father was also a motocross champ.

After the event I had a greater appreciation for where I was at in terms of skill and what I needed to work on if I was going to achieve my ultimate goal of winning a national title. I had a lot of work to do, and things were changing quickly.

Taking on the World

With the price of fuel being just under twenty cents a litre and movies like *Grease* and *Saturday Night Fever* topping the box office, 1978 proved to be a breakout year for my family and me. Economically speaking, as a nation we were still in great shape. Pierre Elliot Trudeau was still holding the federal leadership conch, and our premier in British Columbia was none other than Bill Bennet. Our dollar continued to trade strongly against the US greenback, even well above par, and that boded well for us. That April, we had our sights set on our first World Mini Grand Prix in Orange County, California. The track was nestled in the scenic Trabuco Canyon knee-high into the Santa Ana Mountains. With some local races under my belt already that season, including my ten-race undefeated Puyallup Winter Series Championship, this seventh grader was ready.

With our trusty camper loaded high above our mean and somewhat stoic-looking brown Ford 4x4 pickup, off we went. We towed an open trailer with two 1978 YZ-80s, which proudly sported my newest assigned racing number, seven. That was the first race year for me with the upside-down hockey stick. That number stayed with me for the balance of my well-decorated mini cycle career. We had a full load, which included my two best childhood friends, Lisa and Sammy Douglas. Not only were we headed to the biggest motocross race in the world for my age category, we also planned to play tourist in southern California for the first time. All four of us kids were elated to be able to hit the local tourist hotspots, including Disneyland, Knott's Berry Farm, and Universal

Studios. Lisa, Sammy, Kelly, and I rode the entire way to California in the back of the camper, even at the border crossing!

On the way down, about a day away from our destination, my parents decided we needed a hotel room to clean up. It was in Stockton, California. I remember the owner of the motel backing my dad right up to the rear of his office door to ensure my two motorcycles would be safe. I had two bikes on board, because I would be racing the 80 cc stock and modified classes.

We woke up early the next morning to discover one of the bikes was gone. It had been stolen. I believe that if not for the fact that he would get locked up and not get us to the race, my father would have beaten the whereabouts of my missing modified YZ-80 out of the motel owner. Instead, he called the police and made a trip to the Stockton police station, where we went through the usual BS protocol. Then one of the officers took Dad aside and gave him directions to a local riverside riding spot, but I can assure you it was a needle in a proverbial haystack to find that bike. Knowing that, we didn't stick around Stockton long.

That season we had the two bikes. We bought one, and the other was provided by my sponsor, Cross Country Motors. It was the latter bike that was stolen. I know my dad didn't look forward to having to explain what had happened. I was a little bummed that I would have to ride my bone stock bike in the modified class. There were some seriously fast 80 cc motorcycles in southern California in 1978, and DG was king of almost every aftermarket part you can think of. Their team, managed by none other than Harry Klemm (DG's race team manager) boasted talent like Chris Heisser and Ted Brady, among others. Almost every other mini cycle prodigy of the time attended the race, including A.J. Whiting, Brian Myserscough, Erik Kehoe, George Holland, Louie Franco, Ron Lechien (who I would lock horns with in the nine-to-eleven-year-old class), and the eventual Yamaha Race of Champions winner, sixteen-year-old Jeff Ward. The Race of Champions that "Wardy" won was his last small-bike race.

Getting to the event was no easy task, because there were quite a few detours due to catastrophic mudslides earlier that spring. In fact, had the race been scheduled even a week earlier, it probably wouldn't have happened.

Upon our arrival at the track, the damage the rains had caused was evident, but the sun was out in full southern California style. Pitted at the top of the hill just a few short feet outside the long, sweeping, left-handed first corner, we were set.

It was there that we met our first-ever southern California friends: Jerry Marcell and his son, Taylor, who was a year or two older than me. Jerry, who worked as an R&D engineer for Kawasaki USA, always had a huge smile on his face. Taylor was a typical blond-haired California kid who spoke a type of slang that I didn't quite understand. We became friends pretty much instantly. It was cool to have someone show me around the amazing state-of-the-art track.

The venue had several full-sized tracks, a skateboard circuit, a BMX track, and an area devoted to hang gliding. The track itself was hard-packed, which was my forte. In the motocross world, we call that kind of hard pack "blue groove," because the soil becomes so compacted that the tires actually stick to it when the brakes are applied or the throttle is twisted hard. One of my fondest memories of the facility was high above it at one of the tracks that wasn't being used that weekend. Taylor called it the Tony D. track, named for 1977 250 cc United States National Champ, Tony Distefano. Ironically, Tony now lives in a wheelchair too.

I raced two classes, with three races for each class. I raced the 80 cc 9–11-year-old stock class as well as the 80 cc 9–11-year-old modified class (meaning the bikes had engine work done to make them run faster). The starting line was at the bottom of the entrance hill, and it had the first real steel starting gate I ever lined up behind.

I wore a jersey that had a huge Canadian maple leaf on it instead of my brand. From a family with a rich military history, I have always been proud of my country and what our flag represents. After the event concluded, I exchanged the jersey for one of Taylor's Kawasaki jerseys.

When the full gate of thirty riders dropped on my first race, I got a great start. I think I was second to the first turn, right behind eleven-year-old Ron Lechien. I loved that high-speed, sweeping, left-hand first corner.

Afterwards Taylor's dad smiled and complimented me, saying, "Just like a flat tracker." Over and above being a top-shelf human being and one of Team Kawasaki USA's best innovators, Jerry was also a highly accomplished flat-track racer. I think back to that moment like many others in my life; you just never know when you may be experiencing or on the verge of something that will shape your life, decisions, and confidence forever. Jerry, I know you have passed on now, old friend, but on behalf of my family and me, I thank you for everything you did for us.

Thanks to Jerry, I got to tour the Kawasaki R&D plant, and hit up a race at the legendary Orange County International Raceway (OCIR) the following week. That night at the OCIR, the first person Taylor introduced me to was Warren Reid, one of the fastest 125 cc racers in the world. Until then I had only seen him in *Motocross Action*, *Dirt Bike* magazine, and the weekly *Cycle News*.

As the four-day event wore on, I had great success in the stock-bike class and finished third overall. It was an incredible accomplishment, because I was racing with the best nine- to eleven-year-old riders in the world. The trophy I have from that event is still the heaviest one that I have ever been awarded. The event gave me a ton of confidence. Though I was somewhat satisfied, I wanted more.

On the final day of the event, the Yamaha Race of Champions was held. Twenty of the fastest mini cycle riders from every NMA district in the United States were selected, as well as the Australian, Canadian, Mexican, and British champions. Jeff Ward, who was already racing in the bigger bike classes, also lined up on a brand-new stock 1978 80 cc machine, which was the type used for the event. The brand-new motorcycles, numbered one through twenty, were kept in a compound and were completely bone stock, so no rider would have any type of mechanical advantage. The other thing to keep in mind is that the 80 cc bikes back then were about as big as today's 65 cc motorcycles. Each racer drew a number from a pot, and the number they got was the bike they rode for that race, changing bikes with each race to keep things as fair as possible. National Mini Cycle Association (NMA) mechanics were in the compound to help with handlebar and lever position setups according to each rider's preference. They were also responsible for breaking in the bikes. The only downside to that day and that weekend (mostly for my younger sister) was that it was Easter Sunday, and the Easter Bunny totally forgot about us! I'm not sure how my mom and dad smoothed that one over, but Kelly still recalls it as the day that she stopped believing in the Easter Bunny.

To be trackside watching the likes of Jeff Ward and the rest of the fastest sixteen-year-old-and-under riders on the planet was awe-inspiring. One of the riders who competed in that race was Bremerton, Washington's "Flying" Phil Larson. Phil, who had won the Washington NMA districts championship, was already a gorilla-sized kid. I have no idea how the frames on the bikes used in that event, which were already notorious for breaking, didn't implode under him. I'm not sure where Phil finished, but he was always in the top five in that event. I even got to meet him at one point. The Larsons also became good family friends. Jeff Ward pretty much destroyed the field, and my final and long-lasting thought of that event was, *I need to win the Canadian title, so I can be invited to the Race of Champions representing Canada!*

On a sad note, that facility closed its doors in September of that year when the owner died in a horrific air disaster in San Diego on September 25, 1978, when Pacific Southwest Airlines flight PSA-182, a Boeing 727, collided with a privately-owned Cessna. The airliner hit the ground in the heart of San Diego just north of the intersection of Dwight and Nile, killing all 135 passengers and 7 people on the ground. At the time, it was the worst airline disaster in US history. I have researched many things writing this book, but never knew of that tragic event's connection to the racing world until now. I also learned that where that track used to be now sits the ritzy Cota De Gaza gated community, which is home to *The Real Housewives of Orange County*.

After the races we hit all the above-mentioned tourist traps, which was cool. However, it wasn't nearly as cool as dirt bike racing. I wasn't fond of standing in line for almost an hour or more to get on Space Mountain, which had opened that year at Disneyland.

Throughout the balance of the year in Canada, things on the track continued to improve. I was racing with riders as old as sixteen. A top-five finish was a good weekend, but I wanted more.

Off the track and in school, I was becoming well known for the motocrosser I was becoming. On a social level, I had many neighbourhood friends, and I think it's important to mention a few of them here, because they played a major role in my life moving forward. I mentioned the Velonises and the Dycks earlier, but there were more. The Maier family was headed by Al, a licenced chiropractor, and his wife, "Toots." They had three kids close to my age: Dean, Cynthia, and Shannon. It was handy having a chiropractor as a friend and neighbour, because my increasingly barbaric lifestyle required many visits.

The other family of significance was the Dedels. Ed, an industrial appliance and refrigeration aficionado, and his wife, Evelyn, had three boys: Allan, John, and Howard. Howard was my age, and we did many things together, some good and some bad.

One time I heard some of my schoolmates talking about the things they had pinched (stolen) from the nearby co-op store. Wanting to fit in with my peers, one day Howard and I went in together, and I filled my overalls with pens, pencils, erasers, a small notebook, and pretty much anything else I could steal.

We left the store and went back to my bedroom in the Hilton Drive house and closed the door. We proceeded to write down in our brand-new notepads what we had just done.

At that moment my father opened the door to tell me dinner would soon be ready. Panicked, I tried to hide the evidence under my bed. My dad sensed something was up and reached under the bed to see what I was trying to hide. He opened the notebook and read the first line I had written: "Today my friend Howard and I stole some goods for the first time." Let me tell you, that is no way to start a bestseller. I thought my dad was going to lose it on both of us. Unfortunately, that didn't happen, and I think it would have been a whole lot easier to deal with than what happened next.

Dad sent Howard home and then told my mother what was up. It was the first time my dad took charge of something in my character that he knew would be toxic to my development.

The next day my mother and I had a date with the co-op store manager. I was afraid, because my parents told me that he might call the police. My fear was legitimate, because many things had been stolen from that store, and they needed to set an example to deter others.

As we sat across the desk from the manager, who seemed to be a droid-like being in a suit, my hands were cold and clammy. My blood drew in like a cat that had just broken through the ice on a freshly frozen pond. I produced from the bag I held between my trembling knees what I had stolen from the store. It seemed to take forever to get a response out of him, and I took that to mean things were not going to work out in my favour. Part of me thought it was only pencils and erasers, for crying out loud. However, the other part of me, the part with the proper moral fibre I had been raised with, knew it was dead wrong.

After pondering for a while, he looked at my mother and asked if stealing had been a problem in my past. She told him it wasn't, that I was a good kid and so far, had been honest with most things. Looking at me like a judge, he told me that he never wanted to see me in his store again without my parents. He also told my mom that she should keep an eye on me, because dishonesty could turn out to be a problem later in life. That statement bothered me, but little did I realize how true his words would become.

As the 1970s wound down, I was on a collision course with puberty and many more life changes. Hockey season ended with a bang. That being my final season as a Pee Wee, I was on Chilliwack's top rep team. Our hometown hosted its annual Chilliwack Pee Wee Jamboree. The tournament had always been graced with some of the most talented hockey players and teams from across the continent. The tournament also had a serious "it" factor in terms of how well it was attended and supported by the community. It was almost a given that if you were lucky enough to be on one of the Chilliwack teams, the coliseum, which held 2,500 people, would be full to the rafters.

I worked my ass off on and off the ice. I was on the ice at least five times a week. We usually played twice a week (a home game and a road game) plus two 5:00 a.m. practices. Over and above that was drop-in hockey, public skating, road hockey, hockey at school, hockey on TV, and hockey card hockey. Sometimes I think I was a little like Happy Gilmore in that I was already becoming a talented motocrosser but instead fancied a career on the ice.

We made the B final of the jamboree. The building was packed, and the energy was electric. It seemed like every time I touched or got near the puck, the crowd buzzed with excitement. Late in the second period, we scored a goal over a sprawled-out goaltender as I was being pushed onto my back. The last thing I saw before I was mauled in a dog pile by my teammates was the puck ripple the top right corner of the mesh. I was a little taller than average, but I had great puck sense and a hard shot. That goal put us on even terms at 2–2, but we still came up a goal short to a team out of Seattle. For me there has never been any glory in losing, but we were proud of our accomplishments. Our coaches, Greg Reid and Jim Beck, deserve much credit for their tireless efforts. Both former top-level players, they loved making us the best we could be. I hated them at every 5:00 a.m. practice, but what they were doing worked. They were the first guys outside of my dad who had a profound mentorship effect on me pertaining to something I loved.

February 1979 also saw my first Supercross as an amateur in the Seattle Kingdome. It was the second year in a row that we had attended the event, the previous year as spectators. For me at twelve years old, Supercross (stadium motorcycle racing) was off-the-charts cool. For the pro races, which ran on Friday and Saturday nights, to have over 50,000 ravenous spectators each night was commonplace. With the strong smell of two-stroke exhaust hovering above the cool track in the same building in which the NFL's Seattle Seahawks played, it was an exhilarating experience.

It was also the first time that I had the pleasure to hear the voice of track announcer Larry "Super Mouth" Huffman. He instantly became my announcing idol. When I visualized myself on a breakaway, skating in over the blue line and the late Danny Gallivan on the mic saying, "…and Worrall gingerly skates in over the blue line and lets go a cannonading drive," Huffman was every bit of that and more. The riders were the show up to that point, but when Supercross was born in 1972, Huffman was definitely the show maker. I bet Huffman could have made a dog show exciting. The fact I have to back that up is in 1994, Miller Lite ran a Weiner Dog Winter Nationals commercial that aired during the Olympics, the World Series, and the Super Bowl, using Huffman. He also played announcer roles on many shows that I watched growing up, including *CHIPs*, *Fantasy Island*, *Knight Rider*, and *Miami Vice*.

Of the many Seattle Supercrosses I attended, 1979 was the most memorable for a few reasons. By that time, Bob "Hurricane" Hannah had already inched ahead of Roger De Coster as my newest motocross hero. He got the win on Saturday night, and I also got to meet him after the event. Also making the event special for me was Gresham, Oregon's Rick "the Lumberjack" Burgett. He was the 1978 500 cc AMA National Champion, but more importantly, he always took time for me. Whether it was at a Trans-AMA race, a national, or a Supercross event, Rick always showed me around his pits and signed a jersey for me.

On that night in 1979, he had gone down hard and taken a handlebar to the chest. When I got around to seeing him, he had a big smile on his face as he signed right above the hole in the jersey the handlebar had made. It was becoming evident to me that the real winners in life and my great sports were the ones who showed their human side. Even though Rick does not live far away from me geographically, it has been many years since I've seen him. Lumberjack, you are on my bucket list of people I need to see before the checkers wave. My dad always told me that you were as tough as nails, and a winner. I remember you more as the guy who made me feel like a winner. Thanks for that, old friend.

Those were positive memories, but I have a couple of others that are a bit haunting. First off, that was the first year I got to witness a guy who went by the nickname "Wheelie King," Doug Domokos. He could wheelie a motorcycle over and around anything! It was awe inspiring to see him navigate a full-on, whooped-out, technical Supercross track while cultivating it with his green rear fender. How was it even possible? His bike was always on the rear wheel, so much so that the numbers mounted on the side number plates were stuck on at a forty-five-degree angle, so when he was upright, they were legible. After the event and seeing Doug a few more times live, my appetite for riding on my rear wheel as well as on my unicycle increased tenfold. Sadly and tragically, Doug died in an ultralight plane crash in Murrieta, California, in November 2000. RIP, Wheelie King. Thanks for the incredible memories. You left us way too soon.

One other rider out of the Pacific Northwest I grew fond of was Auburn, Washington's Pat Jacobsen. On many of our winter races south, I couldn't help but be overwhelmed with how fast and talented he was on a motorcycle. Pat, who got a late start in racing at around age fourteen or fifteen, quickly made a name for himself as "The Next One." Pat was humble and always had time to talk to younger riders.

In the winter of 1978 at Startup Raceway Park in Washington State, the racetrack was a wet, blown apart, muddy, deplorable mess. However, motocross goes ahead 99.9 percent of the time, rain or shine. I had just completed my race and quickly put on what was supposed to be my clean and dry moto two rain jacket. My mom and dad asked what I was doing, because my next race was still a couple of hours away. I told them that the pros were on the line, and I wanted to head down onto the track to watch Pat.

The start-up track had a huge infield jump that was similar to Unadilla's "Gravity Cavity." I knew the track was a mess, but I wanted to be at that spot and watch Pat air it out. My parents didn't balk and sent me off with my rain jacket and an umbrella. Pat didn't disappoint as he came around that section in first place. He also hit that jump with the style, authority, and airtime that screamed, "What rain?" Pat was a true professional, I couldn't wait to see more great things from him on our sport's grandest stage. I knew Pat was a winner and going places, and hopefully, he would get noticed soon.

That April we went back to California for the World Mini Grand Prix. For the first time ever, the race was held at the legendary Saddleback Raceway Park in Orange County. My parents had also decided that we needed to upgrade our racing rig from our customary truck and camper to a full-sized motorhome, which we bought from our friend Rudy Dyck at Chilliwack Leisure World. Now we could travel the continent in style.

On that trip I learned what an awning was the hard way. Just into the mountains before Valencia's Six Flags Magic Mountain, we hit a huge windstorm.

If you have ever driven that stretch of Interstate 5, you likely are familiar with the boisterous and brazen Santa Ana Winds. All I heard from my "crow's nest" (overhead bunk) was a crash and a bang. The commotion was followed by more than a few expletives from my father in the driver's seat. He quickly pulled over to assess the situation.

"So much for our awning," he said a few minutes later.

"What's an awning?" I asked.

"It doesn't matter," my dad said. "We don't have one anymore."

That's the way my dad was. He didn't bother my sister or me with things that we didn't need to worry about. In an effort to balance things out, I know my mom always worried double. It's okay, Mom. Looking back now, your concerns were always legitimate, and without that, this survival story would likely be a lot shorter.

7

The Global Plot Thickens

Pulling into Saddleback Park for the first time was like a dream come true, an iconic motocross track that I had only ever seen in magazines. We were finally there, and it was everything I expected it to be and more. As we drove through the area that would be our pit for the next two weeks, everywhere I looked, I was in awe.

We arrived on a Tuesday, some ten days before the world championships started. An AMA 125 cc/250 cc National was also scheduled at the track for that weekend. In addition to getting in some early seat time on that unique, technical, and hard-packed surface, we planned to take in the national event, too. It was such an exciting time to be able to watch those I idolized rip up the same track on which I would be racing.

When we arrived, riders were out on the track practicing, and many others were already pitted for the week all over the vast, hilly, multi-use facility. When we finally parked, just below our motorhome was the same rider who had won the previous year's Yamaha Race of Champions, Jeff Ward. He was loading a KX-125 into the back of his Toyota pickup. Jeff was short in stature. His truck, which was a 4x4, obviously had a lift kit, and it was a tall order for him to get his bike into it. When he got the bike halfway up the plank, I thought there was no way he was going to make it. I thought he'd drop the bike or someone would jump in assist him. No way! Even though he stopped for half a second to hop into the truck box while continuing to push, it was no problem for him at all. In my eyes the "Teenie Meanie," as he was called at one point on his way up through the ranks, had become a serious badass. I also learned never to underestimate a championship motocrosser.

The World Mini Grand Prix that year saw me lined up in the twelve-to-sixteen-year-old expert class. Yes, I was still just twelve. It was going to be interesting, to say the least. That race was the biggest event of its kind. Long before Ponca City and Loretta Lynn's National, it was the annual event in which all racers and the industry put the most stock. My dad always preached that in this sport, and anywhere else in life, you were only as good the company you kept. That "stick with the winners" approach helped with many things in my formative years. Sadly, before the midpoint of the next decade, I sought many of what I would call "lower companions." For the moment, however, let me press on with the segment of my life that I believe is responsible for helping me cheat death more than a few times. I was learning not just life lessons, but also gaining a glimpse into what my future would hold.

Before we knew it, the weekend arrived, and the gate was about to drop on the 1979 125 cc and 250 cc Nationals. The sun was out, and unlike the previous year with all the mudslides, I don't remember even a drop of rain. That was fine by me, because the predominantly wet west coast climate back home had its share of mud races. Even though I was a decent mud rider (heck, living in BC, I had to be), I hated riding in it. I didn't mind getting dirty or anything like that, but I wanted to go as fast as possible in every race. A muddy track took away from that and hampered my ability to jump some of the larger jumps. I loved to go fast and fly as far as I could on every jump. Throughout my racing career, my father never encouraged me in that regard. He never pressured me into doing any jumps or obstacles I wasn't comfortable with. In fact, he often scolded me, saying, "If your wheels are in the air, there's no horsepower making traction with the ground." In an era where most dads were trackside waving for their sons to go faster, my dad would point his index finger at his head encouraging me to use mine. It usually centred me, my dad's way of letting me know I had things under control.

On the weekend of the nationals, Dad and I spent the better part of two days walking the perimeter of the track watching the best grown men in the sport go faster than we had ever seen. (I have included a cool photo in the photo section of this book that I found on the Internet, of me standing trackside halfway up Banzai Hill on that day.)

The riders lined up behind the same steel gate that I would. The starting stretch was a long uphill haul of hard-packed soil covered with bits of compacted aggregate. Like most motocross tracks, a good start at Saddleback was a must.

The track and starting line were wide and fair, but there was one glaring difference between that race and mine. Prior to each race, the soil was cultivated and tilled up to a foot deep in most spots. Then water was added, so the first riders around the track were actually blazing trail in the form of flattening and creating the race lines. As long as we stayed between the track markers, which were as far as twenty to thirty feet apart, there were no rules regarding which part we used. The freshly tilled soil was cultivated out of hard-packed clay, which created large, hard, heavy "landmines." When a race went, most riders following the leaders ended up on the path of least resistance. It was usually the shortest distance between two points in order to prevent another rider from cutting inside of them. If none of that makes any sense to you, then let me put it this way: better to be a trailblazer than a follower.

The 250 cc class was dominated by the top 250 cc rider in 1979, wearing the big number one from his previous year's title, Bob "Hurricane" Hannah. Hailing from Carson City, Nevada, he was the man to beat. I remember cutting out my own trademark Bob Hannah lightning bolts from self-adhering Mactac to apply to my own bikes and helmet. Hannah wasn't just a winner on the track; he was also a straight shooter who always took time for his fans. That wasn't always the case; riders of his calibre were hard to get close to. The pit area for the pros was highly secured and safeguarded. I'm not sure how he did it, but Dad always found a way in. Even at the Supercross races, somehow, he always wound up in the press box. We knew better than to go looking for him, because he was likely somewhere we couldn't get to anyway.

At the top of Saddleback's starting stretch was a sharp 180-degree left-hand corner that led to the legendary Banzai Hill. It was a ten-storey drop of clay, rock, shale, and grass. Grass? Perplexed? How does grass stay on a motocross track with bikes chewing it up with knobby tires? No, the answer is not them flying over it. That hill was only used for the biggest events with the most skilled riders. Hurricane Hannah didn't disappoint, and he won both 250 cc races day. He had some good battles early on with Marty Tripes, who rode a Honda and wore number fourteen. I give Marty full credit, because when he pressed Hannah for the first twenty plus minutes of the forty-minute-plus, two-lap race, his alternate line choices were impressive. In this sport you need to get creative at times to make a pass if the guy in front of you is occupying the race line (the fastest section of the track for that section). Tripes finished two and two on the day for second overall.

Not lost in all that, my attention quickly turned to another rider. I'm not sure what happened in the first race, but in the second race, number forty-two, riding a Maico, was insanely fast. Not only that he was the only one of forty riders to jump almost from the top of Banzai Hill to the bottom. He was my newest hero, Forrest Hill, California's own, Danny "Magoo" Chandler. A redhead like me, Danny was slight in stature but rode a dirt bike like a gorilla. Once my eyes caught that, their focus remained on his red-and-orange bike.

It wasn't just Banzai Hill, but on other parts of the track as well, that Danny was absolutely fearless. He was creative in the sense that he visualized and did things on the motorcycle that no one else had thought of, or had the "nads" to do. Sadly, Danny was cut down in the heat of the battle, breaking his neck in France at a Supercross-style event in 1985. Danny lived the rest of his life in a wheelchair, until his passing in 2010 at age fifty. It still brings a tear to my eye reading through Danny's long list of accomplishments, and knowing how hard he worked to give back while living the type of life that no one wants to be confronted with. RIP, Danny. There will never be another one half as good as you!

The 125 cc class went to Yamaha's Broc Glover. He won both races quite handily. The rider I had my eyes on was my Pacific Northwest hero, Patrick Jacobson, who rode a yellow Suzuki and wore his customary bright-red R&R Bellevue Suzuki jersey. I was excited to see him finish in thirteenth place in the first race. In the second race, Pat got a much better start and finished fourth. He was on decent equipment from his dealer, but it wasn't a patch on what the factory guys were riding. Overall for the day, he came in seventh. I was excited for Pat, because I knew many eyes were on him, which could make life a whole lot better for him quickly.

After the national ended, the focus was back on the World Mini Grand Prix that I would race. With two bikes in tow again, it would be two classes, the twelve-to-sixteen-year-old stock and modified expert classes. My equipment was pretty decent, because Cross Country Motors and Yamaha were on board. Keep in mind that we were in the epicentre of the motocross world in southern California, where almost every racer, big and small, had bells and whistles that we had never seen.

My results on the track were not great. On a gate of thirty plus riders, I finished mid-pack in both classes. I did get to spend the better part of the week leading up to the event with my newfound friend, Costa Mesa's Taylor Marcell, who I had met the previous year. Thanks to Taylor I was able to get a tour of the 700-acre facility that only a local was capable of.

At one point, we headed to the far north part of the facility, close to where the famous Matterhorn Hillclimb was. On the way back, he pulled over by one of the pits at track number two. He smiled, and said hi to an older guy sitting comfortably in a lawn chair. The grizzled, bearded fellow smiled and returned the greeting. Taylor looked at me and said, "Brent, meet Rex Staten." Are you kidding me? Rex was a serious badass in the motocross world! My dad talked about him often, and was a huge fan. We had watched Rex race in Puyallup a few years before on an AMF Harley Davidson, of all things. His teammate on that occasion was Marty Tripes. Believe it or not, Harley Davidson fielded a motocross team back then. Now that I had met him face to face while he was taking a breather after pounding laps in the searing heat, he became one of my favourites.

Even though the event wasn't the most successful for me in the results column, it was a great learning experience. In motocross, there's no such thing as a natural when it comes to learning how to win. It's a process, a form of alchemy that can't be completed without putting in a certain amount of time.

After watching Ontario's Jeff Sutherland represent Canada at that year's Race of Champions, all I wanted was to be in that race.

That summer our bike dealer fell on hard times. The overhead in the huge building, coupled with a string of break-ins and thefts, left them in financial hardship. It was all a little over my head, and I never put much stock in it. However, I ended up getting a Suzuki deal for the upcoming Canadian nationals, which were held that August in Aldergrove, BC. I had been on Yamahas up to that point, but Suzukis had a lot more low-end horsepower (needed for good starts and quick acceleration). My dad tried everything in his arsenal to make the Yamaha faster. He even shaved the flywheel down. That ended badly on the starting line at Hannegan Speedway one night. The flywheel blew clean out of my engine on the starting line, hitting the rider next to me in the leg and ripping his pants. (I can only imagine what that poor kid thought.) Taurus Chuck was the dealer's name, and he was new to the sport, or at least to us. A mothership of a shop in the heart of Surrey's Newton District, Taurus Cycle, fielded a huge race team that season and a couple of others before closing their doors.

Just before the big race in Aldergrove, I received some terrible news, the impact of which continued to grow throughout that year and beyond. Our Pacific Northwest hero, Pat Jacobson, had been paralyzed in a first-turn crash in Texas. By that point, Pat had been signed by Suzuki USA to ride their factory bike. It was the racing opportunity of a lifetime. When I got the news, it felt like something inside me died. I'm not sure why, because at age twelve, I didn't know much about the nature of that type of injury. I knew it was bad though, and the meaning of that would only intensify in the fall of that racing season.

Our national competition at Little Rock Raceway that August was packed with racers and spectators from far and wide. At the gate on a new tricked-out Suzuki, I wanted to win badly. Winning that race, the Canadian national championship for racers under sixteen, meant an invite to represent Canada in the world championships. It was a huge deal.

Despite my high hopes, the weekend was a disappointment. I ended up tenth overall. One could argue that a top-ten finish at any national championship is a great result, but I wasn't happy. I felt awkward on the bike, which I had only ridden a few times, including two Thursday-night Hannegan Speedway races. The day was blistering hot, and I also felt a bit out of shape. It's hard to believe that a thirteen-year-old (I became a teenager that year on June 1) could feel that way. Motocross requires top physical conditioning, because it's one of the most physically demanding sports on Earth. Once again, we were learning, and my parents were always positive and in for the long haul. However, this sport, even with support, be it financial or otherwise, is excruciatingly taxing on a family. I never saw that aspect until years later, because it was the only life I had ever known. The rider who won my class on that day and stamped his ticket to the following year's Race of Champions was Abbottsford, BC's Al "Too Trick" Dyck. Al may have been the only exception to the above-mentioned "natural" rule. He won the event in only his second year of racing!

As summer wore down, there was another monumental change on our family's horizon. My parents sold our dream home, and to this day, I'm not sure why. If I do the math, I'm sure the expensive, wide-open racing lifestyle we were leading was the reason. But once again I was a kid, and on a need-to-know basis. We bought a place on Clare Avenue back on Chilliwack's Fairfield Island, where we had built our first home, near the east end of the street adjoining my first elementary school. The house was a typical late-1970s split-level with two huge cherry trees in the front yard. It didn't have a pool, but that didn't bother me, because swimming wasn't my thing. The house was only about a mile away from the Fraser River, which was my motocross playground throughout the winter months. I would also be attending a new school, my first year of high school. I was thirteen years old and headed into eighth grade. It was a cool fit for me, because I would be reunited with many of my friends from grades one through three.

Home life was also starting to feel different. My dad was drinking regularly, and it was no longer just beer. He had a hankering for whiskey, and on many weekends, he didn't even come home. I'm not sure if it was just because I was a teen, but I noticed a difference in my dad's sense of patience. I didn't like it, and neither did my mom. I remember going to a race on a Sunday morning that year, and him looking at me and asking, "Who the hell shit in my mouth?" I knew better than to become a second victim of his hangover by responding.

Around the first or second week of September, my dad told me that they were having a benefit race for Pat Jacobson in his home state of Washington at the Spanaway track. Pat was going to be there, and so were his Team Suzuki teammates in a show of support. It sounded cool, and I couldn't wait to go.

When we got there, it was the usual protocol, as far as racing goes. The event atmosphere, on the other hand, started out somber but amped up when Pat arrived. I will never forget the many thoughts that raced through my head seeing someone I looked up to, in a wheelchair. I know it happens every now and again, and in today's era, seemingly more times than not, but I never cor-related the love of what I was doing with a life-changing injury like paralysis. I wasn't scared, but for the first time, I was aware of how dangerous our sport was. Seeing Pat do wheelies in his wheelchair had everyone cheering. I knew he appreciated every minute of it, but I also sensed that the man that I, and the entire Pacific Northwest, had come to love was now looking at the world in a much different light.

The two Team Suzuki riders who showed up were Darrell Shultz and Scott Gillman. I was disappointed that Mark Barnett and Kent Howerton weren't there. However, their national series had just concluded a couple of weeks before, and I believe injuries were a factor. Seeing Shultz pretty much destroy the field was impressive. Darrell finished seventh overall that year in the 500 cc AMA class. Another cool fact is that the rider I had met that spring at Saddleback, and cheered for at the Trans-AMA races, Rex Staten, was fifth overall in that years 500 cc series.

As the day wore down and my races were completed, the last race of the day was the 500 cc pro class. Standing a few short feet away from Shultz railing the 180-degree steep turns against the local pros was so cool. After that race, being at the Suzuki truck with Pat, Darrell, and the rest of his team has stayed with me for my entire life. I have had some interaction with Pat on social media but have not seen him face to face since that day. I hope to be able to hand Pat a copy of this book and tell him how knowing him affected my life in such a positive manner. I still have the photo Darrell "Shu Ain't Scared" signed for me that day. I have many signed photos and have met many famous people, including Wayne Gretzky, Mike Tyson, and Rick Hansen, and I even saw Terry Fox on his Marathon of Hope. All those moments played a huge role in my life and in motivating me at some point in my journey. Because of his solid and genuine character at that poignant event, my signed Darrell Shultz picture and the memory of that event will be forever etched in with my favourites. To everyone who was there that weekend, thank you all for the fortitude, strength, and understanding that you sent home with me. I was going to need it.

The Golden Ticket

I always loved the fall, because it meant I would soon be back on the ice playing hockey. The fall of 1979 was also my first year of high school as I headed into grade eight at Chilliwack Junior High. The school was large, archaic, and always smelled like primitive janitorial cleaning ingredients. As a "Gummer" (what eighth graders were called), I was happy to be reunited with my old friend Mark Ballam (who lived next door to us on Bonavista). Mark was in grade nine, and I hung out with him daily. He was a towering, buff, and burly fourteen-year-old who probably weighed 180 pounds. I was of average height and weight for my age.

High school was an entirely new deal. It meant many more students and dealing with more than one teacher. Those aspects were never a problem for me, because I was easygoing, and not too difficult to get along with. My problem was focus. I have never been diagnosed, but I'm pretty sure I have ADD, and maybe even bipolar disorder.

In that new setting, I was easily distracted by the many new ways of my world. Things were happening quickly. Things that used to be monitored regularly in regard to curriculum were now left up to me. Unlike elementary school, where most work was done in class, I had a lot of homework. That was a huge problem, because my life outside of school was so full.

Every lunch hour Mark and I walked into town. We ended up at either the bakery to grab a half dozen long johns or at the 7-11 for a submarine sandwich. On one occasion I walked out of the 7-11 to find Mark standing out front with a beer in his hand. Several other kids were also out front, and Mark had a serious look on his face. I looked at him and said, "Where'd you get the beer?"

"My friend gave it to me," he replied. I didn't think it was odd, because Mark was popular in town as a member of the Junior A hockey team.

"Well, give me a drink then," I said.

Straight-faced, he handed me the stubby bottle of Pilsner (just like my dad often did if I was parched on a hot day, and no other drinks were available). Without hesitation, I began to guzzle, but I noted almost immediately that it was warm, stale, and gross. I quickly spit it out, half through my mouth and half through my nostrils in a gargling upchuck fashion. Mark and a few others began laughing profusely.

"You idiot," he said. "I found it beside the building on the ground. It could be piss for all I know."

I'm not sure that it was, but who knows? All I wonder about now is why it was so important for me to have that drink. Was I predisposed toward alcoholism or just trying to be one of the boys? Sadly, both answers fit.

I always took my books home and had every intention of getting my homework done, but more times than not, I didn't. My life was wide open, and there was never enough time in the day to do the many things I wanted to do. I was either riding my dirt bike at the river, on the ice somewhere, or at a Junior A or Canucks hockey game. That fall Mark had made the Chilliwack Colts Junior A team. I was at every game and practice. I even went to the road games, mostly travelling with his parents while he rode on the team bus. Yes, I still wanted to be a world champion motocrosser, but when hockey season started, that sport got most of my attention. The Colts were not a great bunch that year, and I told myself that would change when I made the team in a year or two.

That hockey season was also the first time the world had its eyes blown wide open by a player that my grandfather had told me about a year prior, Wayne Gretzky. I idolized Wayne, and I look forward to telling you in a few chapters about the day I got to meet him at the Stanley Cup finals in 1987.

For me that year, it was the Chilliwack Bantam rep team, playing alongside most of the same teammates I had played with since my Atom years. Two of them were identical twin brothers, Dale and Darcy Frey. Those guys were a hoot. We were always up to something together, and more times than not, it was mischievous. They had migrated west from Elmira, Ontario, and were from a solid family. Their parents, Ken and Sandy, always looked out for me when I was around. My parents did the same with Dale and Darcy. The twins continued to play a huge part in my pre-adult and early adult life. I must warn you though, a lot of it wasn't good, at least for me anyway. The Frey boys always said, "Worrall, you're crazy!" They also said that if there was something that no one was crazy enough to do, "Worrall would do it." I didn't think of it as a bad thing. It was just my way of earning a reputation as a badass, I guess.

Right around the time the Iranian students stormed the US embassy in Tehran, taking more than sixty hostages, I got my first high school report card. It was awful. For the first time in my life, my best mark was a C-, and that was in physical education. How could that be? I was fit and loved sports. The problem was, I was starting to get acne, and sweat added to my floral-red complexion, making it worse. How was I ever going to land a girlfriend looking like a Dominoes flyer? In all seriousness, the worst part about the report card was the teachers' comments regarding my efforts, which they said were non-existent.

That day after school, I did like I did every other day and went to Mark's house. He showed his parents his report card, and then his dad, Jim, asked how I did. I'm pretty sure I lied and said I did okay. Mark knew otherwise, having seen my report card, and he knew full well that my parents were going to be livid.

No longer able to prolong the inevitable, at around dinner time, I headed home. I thought for sure I was going to lose something, but I didn't know what. My dad had slapped me upside the head a few times in my day, but it had been a while. I had outgrown the belt, but I wasn't afraid in the physical sense. I was most afraid of losing my motorcycle until I could prove I had righted my academic ship. My mind was racing; what was next? How had almost three months gone by with me disregarding the only thing that my parents had ever wholeheartedly asked me to do: to put in effort at school? They had always told me that was the only prerequisite for them to keep supporting my love of motocross.

That night, after what seemed an eternity, my parents came up with a solution. I was allowed to keep my dirt bikes, and it would be business as usual with hockey. However, I could no longer hang out with Mark after school or go to his games or practices on weekdays. I also had to agree to show my mom my homework assignments before and after completion. They also concurred that if my next report card showed as much as one D, I would be off dirt bikes altogether. That was serious business, because my heart was still set on being the best our country ever had on the motocross track.

I managed to turn things around quickly. Like most things throughout my life, when I put my heart and soul into it, good things happened. As bad as that experience was at the time, it was a valuable and timely life lesson, because 1980 would be a big year for my family and me.

That year started off with a bang in terms of hockey; not so much for me but for the hockey world as a whole. The Olympics were held in Lake Placid, New York, and everyone knew the superpower team from the Soviet Union was the team to beat. I will never forget leaping off my basement couch on Clare Avenue when Mike Eruzione scored the game-winning goal against their Cold War rivals from the USSR. It was incredible to see the drive, determination, perseverance, and self-confidence that the US team had. Mentored by the late Herb Brooks, the Boston University graduate Eruzione galvanized the nation and the entire hockey world by pulling off the improbable. It became known as the "Miracle on Ice," even though I, like most fans, started out skeptical. But it happened, and it gave me tangible proof to keep believing and fighting. It was David defeating Goliath, and next to the Ayatollah Khomeini, the Russians were public enemy number one! That US team continued to galvanize their nation and the hockey world by defeating the Finnish squad 4–2 in the gold medal game. In the words of the man who called the game, Al Michaels, "Do you believe in miracles?" I certainly did then.

We had big plans for the upcoming racing season, because the motocross nationals were slated for August in Notre-Dame-de-la-Salette, Quebec. I needed to get nothing less than an overall win to be invited to the following year's Yamaha Race of Champions, representing Canada.

That winter we went back to Yamaha. Thanks to Yamaha Motor Canada and our good friend Bob Work (team manager at the time), I became the first 80 cc rider in Canada signed to a factory team contract. Bob ("Bo," as he was known in the motocross community) was pretty laid back. But when it came to on-track talent, he always managed to sniff out the diamonds in the rough. That was the same year that, after his second-place overall finish the previous year to Stan Currington in our 500 cc national class, the legendary Ross "Rollerball" Pederson began riding for Yamaha Motor Canada. I can't tell you how awestruck I was to be a teammate to a rider who was well on his way to becoming a legend.

We went to Richmond to sign the contract and pick up the bikes and all the bells and whistles that came with it. They hooked me up with the same gear their factory riders were wearing that year. The term "trick" is used often in this sport, and when I tell you the stuff we wore that year was, I mean it even in the literal sense. Yamaha had their own signature brand called Tric, and indeed it was. The jerseys (racing shirts) had my name and number on the back, along with the names of our sponsors, with the likes of Bel-Ray, Dunlop, and Champion Spark Plugs on the front. The pants were made from a new breathable, high-tech material to help dissipate heat. They even had my name, across the backside and down the legs. Bob pointed us toward a place by the Vancouver International Airport called the Iona Peninsula. There was a great sand-based practice facility there. It being February, almost every member of Team Yamaha was there breaking in their new equipment for the upcoming season. My teammates, so to speak, included Terry Hofoss, Kevin Ferguson, Tim Krogh, Ross Pederson, Al Logue, Mike Harnden, Scotty Lockhart, and others.

Yamaha's support gave me a ton of confidence. I remember Bob saying as we departed Iona that day, "We believe in you, Brent, and we know you're going to do us proud by winning the schoolboy title this year." Pressure? Maybe a little, but even before those words were spoken, I believed I could win that year.

The season started off on the west coast in early March, and I don't think I lost more than a moto or two that spring.

I turned fourteen that June. At home life was regimented around motocross and school. I was doing fairly well in school and ran a C+ average. That kept my parents happy, but truthfully, I was still only giving it about a 75 percent effort.

I was on the bike five days a week and, for the first time, training off the motorcycle. I would start by riding my unicycle to school, and then home at the end of the day, about a ten-kilometre round trip. After school, after riding or working on the bikes, I would go for a five to eight-kilometre run around Fairfield Island. That was life-changing for me, because I became addicted not only to the adrenaline rush I got on my dirt bike but also to the "runner's high." Still to this day, at the age of fifty-three, if I can't get on my hand cycle and pump out a good, long endorphin release, I become restless, irritable, and discontented. I'm a Gemini, and my sign needs to be constantly in motion. Yes, the wheelchair makes it tough, but it has not slowed me down.

That year Canada got a new prime minister, Joe Clark. The 1979 election campaign saw Clark make promises to cut taxes to boost the falling economy. However, once in office, his minority government proposed a budget designed to curb inflation by slowing economic activity. The Clark government also proposed an eighteen-cent-per-gallon tax increase on gasoline to offset a budgetary deficit. Needless to say, the seemingly "Average Joe," who was the youngest prime minister elected up to that point, didn't stay in office long. By March 3 he was out.

Quite frankly, it likely wouldn't have mattered if it was the Sultan of Brunei ruling our country at that time. Canada was in the way of the heavily falling financial dominoes to the south. Through all that, my parents, much like they had always done, never worried us kids with money issues. I knew what to ask and when to ask it. Be it right or wrong, that's the way it was in my house. I did a lot of research on my own though, watching the eleven o'clock news every night. It has always been important for me to have my index finger pressed tightly on the pulse of the world.

Spring quickly moved into summer, and with it came a CMA Schoolboy BC Provincial Championship. The series was made up of eight or nine rounds of racing. We loaded up our motorhome and spent all of August on the road, the focal point being the Canadian national championship in Quebec. I had never been east of Calgary or Edmonton before.

Our first stop of note was the tiny town of Bienfait, Saskatchewan, where my father was raised. Incredibly, the little old house was still there. I remember thinking how long and desolate the roads and even the driveways looked. It certainly gave me a greater appreciation for the life into which I had been born. We also stopped in Winnipeg and viewed his former home there, which was still intact, right across the street from Memorial Park beside the Manitoba legislative building. My dad never said much when he showed us those spots, but I could see his internal motor was fully engaged. That's the way my dad was. He didn't say much about his feelings. I always respected that, because I knew those memories were associated with a lot of pain. I have always hated seeing a loved one suffer.

We planned on racing the support class at the famous St. Gabriel National a couple of weeks before my big race. What an incredible natural terrain track that was. It was located in a farmland area, and it was world class with loamy soil and lots of elevation changes in the form of ravines and valleys. We were set up in the pits with some of our BC racing friends, including Wally Levy, Rick Sheren, "Captain Marvel" (the late Marv Cross), Gary Chubey, Larry Mackenzie, and others. Also out east with us in his own truck and camper, was our good friend Roger Jansen. Roger was an intermediate-calibre racer and an all-around good guy and good friend. I would guess Roger was around thirty years old at the time, and his mentorship helped me a lot. He called himself my trainer, and I guess he was. Roger was married to Kyle Beaton's Aunt Linda, who followed us to our big race as well.

I couldn't wait to hit the St. Gabriel track. I got some pretty incredible airtime launching off some of the biggest hills my 80 cc motorcycle had ever seen. I went one and one, winning both races that day by a considerable margin over some of the best from Quebec.

After the second race, I was just getting my bike back on the stand back at the pits when the referee approached my father. "Are you the father of number seven?" he asked (my racing number). To this day Dad recounts his thoughts before opening his mouth: *What the hell have you done now, kid?* When my father acknowledged who he was, the referee asked him to produce my birth certificate, because a protest had been launched questioning my age. It's funny, because people could race that class up to age sixteen, and I was only fourteen. But I was pretty big for my age, and I also had a full beard, so full, in fact, that my nickname at school was "Grizz," short for Grizzly Adams. My dad got my mom to show him my birth certificate, which, fortunately, we had brought along in case of such an incident.

The track that would host the national championship, which I so badly wanted to win to stamp my ticket to the Yamaha Race of Champions the following year, was cool as well. The serene valley setting, just fifty kilometres north of Gatineau, was alongside a river. Many of my BC racing colleagues had made the journey east in search of Canadian moto glory. A couple of my rivals included Terry Sabat and the late Bobby James (who, unfortunately, took his own life later on). I never put much stock in who was there, because there would be many new fast guys I had never seen before. Ontario has always bred fast motocrossers. Three that I can remember are Randy Ford, Glen Caley, and Frank Watts. The local Quebecers buzzed about their own hopefuls, Stephane Mallet and Miguel Duhamel, a soon-to-be-famous AMA Superbike racer, and the son of legendary Canadian road racer Yvon Duhamel. Yvon made the number seventeen recognizable as a member of the powerful Kawasaki road-racing team. Miguel was also the younger brother of another accomplished motocross and road racer, Mario Duhamel.

Both men stood beside me on the line with Miguel prior to moto one. I won't say I was intimidated, but it was cool to be in their presence.

At first glance, the track layout looked fast and like it would flow well, suiting my aggressive, wide-open riding style. The soil was fairly firm hard-packed clay, which I liked. The start was at the bottom of the valley and went straight up a long hill. At the top of the hill was a right-hand corner that sent riders back down toward the river.

The weather up to race day, Sunday, had been beautiful and sunny, so we were prepared for dry, hard-packed conditions in terms of suspension and tires. Then, in the early hours on Sunday morning, sleeping in the top bunk of our motorhome, I was rudely awakened by the sound of torrential rain pounding, as if it were machine gun fire penetrating our aluminum roof. I kept it to myself, but I was certainly not happy. I had my heart set on a dry race. I had won many races in the mud, but I never felt as comfortable.

Dad and I walked the track that morning, as we did before every race. I always took his advice, if he offered it, on the things he saw. By that point, though, I was pretty independent in that regard. But similar to a golfer trusting his caddy's advice, I always trusted my dad. Walking the track that day was no fun at all. Our rubber boots were absolute gumbo. At the bottom of the track, which went up a steep hill, we couldn't even make it up on foot. Dunlop was our tire sponsor, and we went with what we had in that regard. Dad let out a little air but not too much, because I weighed about 145 pounds and didn't want to risk a pinch flat.

Lined up for moto one, with my dad and Roger Jansen at my side holding umbrellas over my head, it was go time. I got a great start, and I led to the first turn and through the first half lap. When we got into that bottom section, which was pretty much as muddy as the adjacent river bottom, I stalled my bike. A few riders got by me, and there was no way I would be able to catch the winner, Honda-mounted Glen Caley. I fought back hard, but finished about fifteen seconds off his pace.

Back at the pits, my family was happy with my result, but I certainly wasn't. It was a feeling that I had not experienced all season. I would not call it losing, because, in my opinion, there's no such thing. I had just been used to having my way out west with most fields of riders. I also found out later that day that my dad had been struck by lightning while standing trackside holding an umbrella during moto one! Incredibly, he was okay, but the digital watch he wore never worked again.

Now I was faced with having to win the second race outright to take the overall Canadian national championship and receive my invitation to the biggest race in the world. Many people came by between races and congratulated me on a great moto one. Some of the support systems of the other riders even claimed there wasn't anything wrong with second place. I'm not sure I even acknowledged such remarks, because they infuriated me.

My dad and Roger made some adjustments to my bike, which included stiffening the suspension for better traction. My mom and sister kept me calm and fed between races. I don't remember interacting with anyone. Dad took me back out to the track to show me some of the areas in between the track markers that were still unused by other riders. In fact, those areas still had grass on them.

We headed to the line for moto two, and I looked no one in the eye. In staging and on the line before the gate dropped, I buried my head in my crossbar pad. I told myself repeatedly that I was the fastest rider in the country, and no one was going to steal my opportunity to be the best. By the time the thirty-second board went up, the sun came out. The rain had let up about an hour or two before.

When we got to the first turn, I led the pack by a narrow margin. Within a lap I was starting to break away from everyone. In a couple of sections, I could see the other riders in my peripheral vision. About fifteen minutes into the twenty-minute plus, two-lap moto, I was out front by about fifteen seconds. I was astounded at how many people trackside were waving their arms in encouragement. Some of them were so loud that when I geared down for corners, I could hear them. One girl in a green T-shirt was actually right on the track in front of me! I saw her yelling "Go!" and signalling with her hand to gun it. It turns out she was the sister of a rider I was racing against from Ontario. In the same way that many cheered against me in BC, because they were tired of seeing the same person win, I think she wanted to see someone finally beat Glen Caley, the Ontario rider behind me, who had pretty much dominated the province like I had done out west. All that motivated me to go even faster. I already had a sizeable lead though, and maybe I should have run a little more conservative.

It's a good thing I didn't. With three laps to go in a dogleg downhill section, on one of those slick grass lines that Dad pointed out, I hit the front brake too hard and went down. The bike landed on top of me, and gas was pouring out the overflow of the carburetor and all over me. I was in shock. What the heck had just happened? Quickly remounting my stalled bike, I kicked for all I was worth to restart the engine. That awful dead, drowning sound you hear when a motorcycle's top end is flooded with fuel incensed me! By that time, Caley had gone past me. As I kicked and kicked, all I could see was him disappearing out of sight, sucking my title hopes in his wake. No sooner did he reach the bottom of the hill and the river section than my bike finally started. I don't remember being exhausted or winded, which I must have been. Adrenaline kicked in like I have never experienced since. All I remember thinking is, *I will not be beat today*. I had about ten seconds to make up, and I made up most of it in that lap. I passed Glen and then shortly after got the white flag, signalling one lap to go. As I passed my dad and the mechanics' area, he did what he always did—pointed his index finger at his head, encouraging to use mine. It worked, because I crossed the finish line some five to ten seconds ahead of the second-place rider. For the first time in my life, I felt like a winner. I had accomplished what I had set out to do. I had won many races up to that point, but that was the one I wanted most. Now I had my golden ticket to the Yamaha Race of Champions!

9

"Give That Boy Some Freedom"

With the biggest race of my motocross life to that point now in the books, many exciting things were happening. I had achieved what I had set out to do in winning the Canadian national title, so what was next? I would certainly do everything in my power to be prepared for the big race, which would be held the following April in California. But I was just a kid, and I needed to soak up the moment a little, right? I knew that once I returned to Chilliwack, with the start of school and all, my life would be regimented once again. At that point I don't think I ever regretted any choices I or my family made on behalf of my racing. It had just been a lot of fun. But with success in anything, be it sport or otherwise, sacrifices are a necessity.

On the way back from Quebec, we visited Niagara Falls. Seeing the water cascading over the falls was certainly the strongest force of nature I had ever witnessed. We headed back toward Thunder Bay, with Labour Day weekend approaching. My parents only took me out of school for motocross if it was an absolute must. We drove home in tandem with Roger and Linda. I loved riding in Roger's truck. He was a great human being and had an amazingly loud stereo. I loved loud music more than anything, and Roger made many A&B Sound treks upon my request. Roger was such a good mentor to me. Where my dad was sometimes stoic and silent, Roger always took the time to explain things. Dad was a great teacher, but Roger was an outside influence that I viewed from a different angle.

As we approached Thunder Bay, I was back riding in the motorhome up in the top bunk. I saw signs saying that Thunder Bay wasn't far away. No sooner had I climbed down than my dad started to slow down, right on Highway 17. It was eerie; neither of my parents said a word. We noticed a police-like procession with flashing lights everywhere. Moments later we saw a huge sign that said, "Marathon of Hope." As my dad pulled the motorhome right up beside Terry Fox, Dad honked, something my old man would do. As I leaned out the window over Mom's lap to get a glimpse of that relative unknown (at least to me), Terry glanced over his shoulder. When we made eye contact, everything stopped! I don't know why, but in that moment, the look on Terry's face told a dark yet determined truth. His cheeks bright red, his hair matted and soaked, I could tell he was uncomfortable and in pain. My thoughts raced, but I was silent. I had many questions inside. What did this mean? Would he succeed? Why was he doing it? To me it looked like many things, but fun certainly was not one of them.

Afterwards my parents filled me in as best they could on Terry and his situation, including his goal of running across our great nation in the hopes of raising a dollar of awareness for cancer research for each Canadian citizen. Now I know a lot more about why time stood still on that day and why it was so important to me. (I promise you, many more dots will be connected as my story unfolds.) I never did speak with Terry, but the 3,339 miles he ran in those 143 days and seeing the look on his face just days before his Marathon of Hope ended speaks to me daily.

Back at school in grade nine, I was in a good space—positive, confident, and upbeat about my future in motocross and life in general. I looked forward to the school year, and there was no way I was going to let it start like the previous one. As you can imagine, pretty much everyone in my school and in the valley town of Chilliwack knew Brent Worrall, the motocrosser. Many articles and photos ran in our local paper, and I was often interviewed on the radio. Heck, even my teachers knew of my motocross accomplishments. I had one teacher come up to me and say, "Hey, I saw you on TV." He added that it wasn't fair that I got to be on TV, because he made more money than me. I'm still not sure what he meant. He was right though; it was cool to be on CKVU-TV.

All the attention added extra pressure for me to perform academically. I figured each teacher knew enough to know that accomplishing what I had on two wheels took some brain power, but maybe they didn't. The bottom line is they expected good things, as did my parents, and so did I. I started to harness the power of visualization. However, even though I could visualize the successful outcome,

I was often short on legwork. Having a positive attitude and being somewhat popular amongst my peers and teachers was a good way to start the year, though.

As our racing season wore down, so did my bikes and my body. The two Y-Z 80s, which had countless hours on them, were completely worn out and ready to be sold. The problem was, there was still four months until the new year and new bikes. For the next racing season, I would be on 125 ccs, much bigger bikes. Canadian national 125 cc champ and my good friend at the time, Terry Hofoss, with the approval of Yamaha Motor Canada, lent me his 125 cc bike to practice on that fall.

During the third week of September, while practicing at the river, I noticed a pretty girl on a horse. At first, I thought she was just passing by at the end of Young Road, where it meets the mighty Fraser River. Thinking nothing of it, I continued to burn laps on a corner track I had laid out. I had been dropped off there by my uncle, because my parents were out of town for one of Kelly's swim meets. Before you get all wound up, saying, "Hey, someone should have been there watching you," I agree with you 100 percent. But it was a different era. My dad smoked in our vehicles, I jumped twenty-foot gap jumps on my BMX bike on paved roads without a helmet, and just four short years before (1976), it became mandatory to wear seatbelts in vehicles.

After pounding out lap after lap, I pulled over to take a quick breather. Looking up I was surprised to see a dark-haired, horse-riding beauty watching intently. I said hello when I recognized her from school. Her name was Sherry Dewan, and she was a competitive and highly decorated horse rider. We didn't chat long, and then she headed down the gravel road.

I went back to doing my thing on my bike, carving the corners deeper and deeper. After another session, I pulled off and saw Sherry blaze by again. I waited for a bit and then decided to take off after her. She had almost disappeared, and I was more focused on that than I was with the lay of the land that I was ripping up. Without any warning, somewhere in the midst of fourth gear, I hit the butt end of two-foot-high log, which was camouflaged amongst the surrounding rocks, sand, and river rubbish. I was on the ground rolling around in pain before I even knew what hit me. I realized instantly that my leg was broken badly.

As fate would have it, at that moment Sherry turned around to see what had become of me. She didn't stop at the sight of me lying there, because I sat up quickly to act as if I was okay. However, just then, my uncle came back to check on me. I was still sitting on the ground, but fortunately, the bright-yellow YZ-125 and my racing apparel was visible from the gravel road. As soon as Uncle Al pulled up, I said, "Load the bike, and let's go to the hospital. My leg is broken."

Sure enough, it was broken at the ankle and just above in three places on the tibia and fibula bones. At that point in the season, it didn't bother me much that I would miss any motocross action. Apart from winter racing, riding, and training, the season was over. The thing that bugged me most was that it was hockey season, and I would be sidelined for the first two months of it.

When I returned to school in plaster and on crutches, one of the first people to greet me was Sherry. She apologized for not stopping. "I thought you were faking it to get me to stop," she said. It's a good thing that wasn't my strategy, because it wouldn't have worked! Sherry and I became good friends, and over the following two years, she travelled to many races with our family. Her brother, Randy, passed away a number of years ago in prison. He was also a motocrosser. RIP, old friend. Thanks for always looking out for me as a kid. I know you are still missed by many.

Grade nine saw me raise my academic game considerably. I think my parents were a little shocked to see my worst grade was a C+ in my weakest subject, math. I remember thinking that the key to scholastic success was to apply myself and put in a decent effort. It may sound funny now, but that was news to me back then.

When my leg healed up around November, the push was on to get back on the bike. It was only about five months until the World Mini GP that coming April. Another big racing change was also coming up for me in the upcoming year. I would be racing bigger bikes and on a Yamaha 125 cc for the Canadian racing season. Yamaha Motor Canada had lent me a pre-production 1981 YZ-80 to prepare for the World Mini GP. GA Checkpoint Yamaha in Port Moody, thanks to Gord Aulenbach, provided me with the bike.

As far as hockey goes, I managed to earn my way back onto our town's Bantam rep team. It hurts my funny bone to look back now and laugh at the massive head of hockey hair I was rocking at the time. That was the way I rolled. I loved the "hair metal" of the era, and I was a product of my environment. My friends poked fun at my out-of-control red afro.

Speaking of friends, I didn't have many. A lot of people knew who I was, but I never let anyone in too close. Looking back now, I'm not sure why. Maybe it was because of the way we lived. We were pretty much always on the road travelling to practice or racing our dirt bikes. Over and above that, my dad always had me in our shop working on the motorcycles. I got on well with my school and hockey friends, but that's where it stopped. It was probably a good thing for me at that point, because most of the extra-circular stuff at that age included drinking, smoking dope, or trying whatever else the peer pressure of the time dictated. It didn't bother me (yet), because I was focused on being an athlete and, more importantly, world motocross champion.

I spent the remainder of the winter pounding the heck out of what little life was left in Terry Hofoss's 1980 air-cooled 125 cc at the river. That winter we didn't travel south much to race. I'm sure the change in the financial landscape of our country played a big part. Ronald Reagan was elected president of the United States on November 4, with more than 50 percent of the popular vote over Jimmy Carter. The Democrats had initiated steep domestic spending cuts in response to the Federal Reserve's new disinflationary monetary policy. Reagan, a Californian, seemed like a likeable choice when elected. The former movie star turned politician also had the tension-filled Iranian crisis that had plagued Jimmy Carter's administration to thank for his popular vote. It's fitting here to add that my dad also preached that if it happens or is popular in the USA, it's coming to Canada; it just takes a little longer. He was right, especially when I look back to all those highfalutin mini bikes I battled at my first World Mini Grand Prix. At any rate, the freewheeling, carefree, flower child times of the 1970s had become a fleeting memory.

With the New Year upon us, I keep my scholastic throttle red-lined and continued to perform well academically. I rode the brand-new 1981 Yamaha 125 cc a fair bit at the river before the season opener in Mission, BC, that March. Seeing as I had moved up from the smaller bikes, my father pleaded with the CMA to let me race in the senior class (now called intermediate), to no avail. They said I first had to win three races to permit advancement, proving I belonged. I won the first race, both motos, with familiar ease, as I had done the previous year on 80 cc bikes.

We had only three short weeks to be in California for the Race of Champions, but tragedy struck our family hard. My dad's best friend and my trainer, Roger Jansen, had a brain aneurysm as a result of drinking some whiskey that he and my father had made. Roger went into a coma, and shortly thereafter, was pronounced brain dead.

Roger's death confused and angered me to the point where I went deep inside my mind and soul to protect myself. Within a day or two of Roger's death, it was Monday, March 30, and I needed to get to school. For the first time in a long time, I didn't want to go, but I forced myself. Showing up late and walking through the front doors, I heard on my headphones that Ronald Reagan had been shot! I always had my portable boom box in tow with headphones on, because music was my off-bike sanctuary. On the road, it also allowed me to tune in to the many Vancouver Canuck hockey games that I wanted to watch but couldn't.

I stopped in my tracks at the bottom of the stairs in the lobby that went up to the second floor and backed up against the wall. No one was in sight. I had missed the final bell and was late. For the first time that I can remember, I was overwhelmed with emotions. What was the world coming to?

No sooner had all that happened than Sherry Dewan walked up to me. She had good radar and could see I was upset. "It's Roger, isn't it?" she said. Sherry had been to many races with me and knew Roger as well. Everyone liked Roger, and now, in an instant, he was gone! I responded with a yes, and she did what she could to console me. Being right in the lobby of my high school, I buckled down and kept most of it inside. Off to class I went, but I don't remember much about the next week leading up to Roger's funeral. For the first time ever, I was numb with raw emotion, so much so that I didn't even think much about the world championship race, which was less than two weeks away. I had been thinking about that race every day for four years straight! I never even wondered if we were still going. The only thing that mattered was my dad and Roger's family.

My dad never showed any emotion other than anger. When Roger died, I know he was heartbroken, but he never shed a tear, at least not that I saw. To put that in perspective, one time in the shop he was trying to start my bike. I laughed at him for kicking and kicking, saying, "There's no f*****g spark!" He burnt me a look that I knew better than respond to, but I did anyway. Dumbass that I was, I started laughing louder. Without looking at me, Dad pulled the spark plug out of my bike and held it out to me. "You wanna know what spark is? Hold that." He had me hold the plug, which was still plugged into its housing against the base of the bike's cylinder, while he kicked it over. I swear to God my afro grew eight sizes that moment when the electricity from my motorcycle went through my body. I can't help but laugh now writing that, but my dad was a real prick at times. Sadly, I loved every minute of it and would not have been raised any other way.

Roger's passing was the first time Dad took me aside to explain his death as best he could. He told me that we would attend the funeral, and three days after that, we would head to the world championships. He did his best to explain that Roger's death was an accident, but pointed out that he believed the moonshine-like whiskey they had made was responsible. I'm not sure what the medical examiner's outcome was, but my father immediately put the plug in his own jug, and he quit drinking cold turkey. It's been thirty-eight years now, and I still believe the world would be a much better place with Roger in it. RIP, number eighty-seven, and thank you for your selfless role in my childhood. I can't wait to see you again one day.

After the funeral we had a ton of work to do to get ready to hit the road. I had not even been near my bike in two weeks, and we were headed to the biggest race of my life. In addition, I had been riding the 125 cc bike for the last couple of weeks before departing, but I was going to climb back onto the 1981 80 cc bike in order to get re-accustomed to it. That never happened. My dad gave me a list of things I was responsible to put in our trailer while he and Mom packed our house on wheels. Dad also did an oil change on the motorhome.

We hit the road Sunday afternoon and hoped to get well south of Seattle on day one. When I climbed into the motorhome to leave, for the first time in my life, I was heading to a race completely exhausted—physically, mentally, and emotionally. Damn, how did that happen? I was only fourteen, for crying out loud.

Once we crossed the border, I fell asleep in the top bunk. The next thing I remember was waking up to the smell of toxic smoke. My parents had pulled over just outside of Olympia, Washington, and our motorhome looked like it was on fire under the hood. It turns out my dad had not put enough oil in the engine when he did his oil change, and the motor blew up.

Silently fearing the worst of watching my dad explode or take his anger out in some irrational way, I was worried. I was also worried that my dream of racing in the Race of Champions was in jeopardy.

We ended up having the motorhome towed to an auto dealer and slept in it there. Although I was completely worn out, I couldn't sleep a wink. What was next? Where would we go, and how would we get there?

Finally, around noon the next day, we got the prognosis we feared. Thankfully, my parents had figured that might be the case with the motorhome, so through the night, they had come up a plan. It wasn't fancy, but it worked. It was a long metallic-blue Ford Econoline van from a rental agency. I can't tell you how tight it was in that van once we hit the road to Saddleback Park, but off the four of us went—Mom, Dad, Kelly, and me—packed in with enough crap to industrialize a third-world country. We drove steadily and had only one night in a motel, which Dad insisted we pack everything into, bike included.

We pulled into Saddleback Park early Wednesday afternoon, as planned. Once there, pulling in behind the starting gate area and looking over my right shoulder to Banzai and Webco Hill, everything in life seemed okay again. My big race was the following weekend, but first it was the AMA 125/250 cc national championship race. It was incredible to be trackside once again watching my hero, Bob "Hurricane" Hannah, defeat his nemesis, Suzuki's Kent Howerton. Hannah, who was coming off a serious leg injury the previous season, on a bike he deemed "a tub of shit" (because it was considerably heavier than Howerton's factory Suzuki), bested his foe on that day! I have wanted many things in my life, but I will be eternally grateful for being trackside for what was arguably the fiercest, hardest-fought, all-out war between two riders in our sport's history! The fact that they were doing it on the track where I would represent my country had me amped up and ready for the following week.

With the World Mini Grand Prix being held over the course of three full days of racing, the gate couldn't drop soon enough for me. I raced my bone-stock and almost brand-new bike in the stock and modified classes. I battled hard near the front of the pack in all six races. None of them mattered to me. They were more of a preparation for the big race on Sunday, the Yamaha Race of Champions. I would be pitted against nineteen of the fastest riders aged sixteen years and under in the world.

They had us in a fenced-off compound with the brand-new bikes that we would ride. Fans gathered in large numbers on the sidelines to get a look at the best of the best, just as I had so enviously done for the previous three years. We were all given matching gear to wear as well as a silky suede disco-like DG jacket. After some words for the television cameras and a group photo, we drew numbers. The number that we drew corresponded with the bike we would ride for moto one. We would draw a new number and ride a different bike in each of the three races. That was designed to keep things as fair as possible. Each bike was brand new and just broken in prior to the race.

The race was a dream come true. There I was, where I felt I belonged, with the best of the best. I wasn't at all nervous. I drew bike number fifteen for the first moto. The bikes were managed by NMA mechanics who oversaw any changes that needed to be made, such as handlebar, clutch, and brake lever positioning. That was done in between in each of the three motos, because we rode a different bike for each race.

For moto one, I lined up to the left of centre. It was a good, long uphill haul to the first left-hand corner before descending downhill. When the gate dropped, I got a good jump and was fourth or fifth to corner one. The race was led by Arizona's Troy Blake. The pace on that freshly and deeply tilled hard-packed track was incredibly fast, the fastest I had experienced. After lap one, I was seventh and had a pretty good gap over the balance of the field.

I had no idea where I would stack up against any of these lightning-fast guys. I felt comfortable with my pace and could tell by the sideline signals from my dad that to stay upright and maintain that position for moto one would create a great outcome, but I was hoping to be in the top ten overall. Up to that point, no Canadian had done that in that race.

After the moto I felt relieved not only to have it in the books but also knowing that my speed was on point, especially given everything we had been through in the past few weeks. All the front-running racing I had done the previous year created a sixth sense on that day.

Back in the compound for moto two, we went to change bikes and have the usual setup done, under my dad's watchful eye. It drove him nuts that he wasn't allowed to operate the wrenches.

My start in moto two wasn't quite as good, but I was still inside the top ten coming out of turn one. On lap two on the bottom side of the track, I launched an outside line to make a pass into eighth place. When I landed the motorcycle bottomed out the front suspension, and my handlebars slipped right down to where they almost rested on the gas tank! I didn't panic and just told myself that I would have to make do. Riding a motorcycle almost as fast as it can go is virtually impossible. However, in that race, we were all literally stretching the throttle cables to make those bikes go faster. Now I was confronted with getting the best result I could on a bike whose handlebars were in an awkward and compromising position. I placed eleventh in that moto, but it could have been worse. I minimized the damage and didn't crash, which was a good thing.

For the final moto, I got another great start, but guess what? The same thing happened, and the handlebars slipped down to the gas tank. I don't even think it upset me; I just continued racing the way I had in the previous moto. I ended up placing tenth, even though it could have been better if the bars had stayed where they were supposed to be. I was pretty happy with that result. I had achieved a great result in a race that I had worked toward for so many of my formative years. I ended up getting tenth overall out of twenty based on my 7–11–10 moto finishes. I don't think it ever felt so good to be a Canadian competing with the world's best. It was truly a team effort, and to be able to share it with my dear mother, father, and sister still gets me a little emotional.

On a sad note, I got word a few years back that the guy who won the race, Tempe, Arizona's Troy Blake, had passed away. I have heard from a few who were close to him that, much like me, he struggled with some demons after he was out of the sports spotlight. Rest in peace, Troy. You will always be gold in my memory bank!

10

The Big League

Returning from California, it was full speed ahead into the 1981 racing season. That spring also saw the powerhouse New York Islanders crowned as Stanley Cup Champions for the second straight year. I liked the Islanders, because they had a diverse cast of unique and hardworking characters. But for me, although hockey was always on my mind, it would have to wait until the following winter.

Back on the new Yamaha 125 cc bike, on which I had already won the first race of the year, I won my next two consecutive races. When I lined up in that class, I expected to win, because I felt I was faster than all of them. Perhaps I was a bit arrogant, but in motocross, confidence is a huge part of the winning formula. That win allowed me to move from the junior class to the senior class (which is now called intermediate here in Canada). It was a relief to be promoted to the next level so quickly. I had my sights set on the top level, sooner rather than later.

I loved the new first-ever water-cooled 125 cc Yamaha bike. I felt great on it, and in no time flat I was riding it for all it was worth. The bike was the traditional Yamaha yellow, and I wore the colourful kit that GA Checkpoint provided.

My first senior-level race was at the sand-based Mission Raceway track. The track had just been relocated a year or two before from its previous drag-strip track circuit to where it sits today. That track, unlike the current one, had many hard-packed dirt sections, one of which was a massive dirt jump that must have been thirty to forty feet high. The jump was located after 200 feet of straightaway outside the first turn. There was no way a rider could air out that jump beyond the downslope, because the bottom was flat and full-on sand.

When the gate dropped on my first senior race (which was a provincial championship race), I got the holeshot (first to and around the corner one). Racing toward that massive mound to stay ahead of the rest of the field, I shot off its face like a cannon. I can't imagine what my fellow competitors or the fans who lined the track thought when I flew through the air. I landed flat about twenty feet beyond the mound and bottomed out hard in the sand. Miraculously, I managed to stay on my bike. As the foot pegs bottomed out though, my right foot pancaked forward beneath the motorcycle, and I experienced the all-too-familiar agony of knowing that my right leg was badly broken at and above my ankle. I don't even remember being pissed. I just thought, *I'm going to keep riding until I can't take the pain anymore!*

I stayed on the bike and finished fourth, although I did pull over to the sidelines a few laps in to let my dad know my leg was broken. By the time the moto ended, the pain was still there, but it wasn't as bad, because my motocross boot prevented the inevitable swelling. In the pits, after I explained to my dad what was going on, his first response was, "Don't take that boot off." Looking back now I question that move, but at the time it made perfect sense to me.

That was a provincial championship race, one of about five that year. I wanted to win the title badly. I also needed a good showing, because I hoped to be promoted to the expert class (now called pro) in time to head east for the first 125 cc Canadian national event.

The doctor casted me up and warned that if I didn't let it heal properly and broke it again, I could be in serious trouble. I never put much stock in that, because I always healed. After all, that's what we motocrossers do; we heal up when we get hurt.

The injury also didn't deter me from staying focused and doing well at school. By that point, my grades were as much a part of my winning formula as anything. Doing well and succeeding on and off the track made me feel good about myself.

Within four weeks of wearing a plaster cast up to my knee, it was pretty much falling apart, so my dad cut it off. We never went to the doctor for his opinion. We gauged our progress on how I felt. Yes, it was still painful, but I wanted to ride and race my dirt bike.

I ended up finishing the provincial championship in second place, Richard Szabo was the eventual winner. The big question now was, would the CMA permit me to move to the expert class, so I could travel to the nationals?

The question was put to a panel, and they voted against me by one vote! I was gutted. I don't remember crying over much at that stage in life, but that hurt. I was fast, and I knew I was ready to compete with the best in our country on a 125 cc bike. Here's why. Back in 1981 the experts and seniors raced on the track at the same time. However, they did two gate drops, allowing the experts to go first. After the experts had cleared a few corners safely (about thirty seconds ahead), the senior gate dropped. On most occasions by mid-moto I caught up to the expert pack and finished well inside the top five. On two occasions I even finished second to Yamaha factory rider Rob Van Diemen. Either way, moving to the expert class would have to wait until the following year. I still believe I was at the fastest I have ever been on a motorcycle that year.

One of those race-day Sundays was June 28, 1981. The race was in Aldergrove, and we left our house at about 6:30 a.m. to make the forty-minute trek. Just as we approached the railway crossing on Yale Road, we heard on the radio that Terry Fox had passed away a few hours earlier. Once again, I didn't show any emotion to my father and just internalized what was happening. I don't think we said more than five words to each other the rest of the way to the track. I was shocked, to say the least. How was that possible? The determined look of pain and perseverance that we had seen on Terry's face just the summer before was now gone. I didn't know a lot about cancer, but it felt so wrong!

When we pulled into Little Rock Raceway, we pitted with the usual suspects. One of them, who I had grown up admiring for his raw speed and wildness as a person, was "Captain Marvel," the late Marv Cross. Marvel's nickname for me "Wart." I'm not sure I liked it, but what the heck, I came by it honestly. Back then almost everyone in the world smoked, or so it seemed. Somehow at one of the races along the way, Marvel accidentally burned me with his cigarette. It was at a riders' meeting, and as he stood beside me, his lit cigarette burned the top of my hand. It left a nasty blister that Marvel called the "Wart," so I was stuck with it. Anyway, when I got out of our truck, the first person I saw that day was Marvel. I told him that Terry Fox had passed away. Marvel stopped in his tracks and looked at me and said, "Damn it, Wart, I thought they were going to save him." I'm not sure I said it at the time, but yes, I thought so, too.

That year, I was nominated by the Chilliwack Parks and Recreation staff for Chilliwack's "Athlete of the Year." It was a real honour for me at fifteen years of age. I also received letters of praise from members of Parliament, including one from the House of Commons in Ottawa. To open that up and see it embossed on our highest government's letterhead was impressive. I also won a Max award for our sport's excellence, which was awarded at a gala dinner that fall in Toronto. I received a few other awards and nominations, too, but those were the big ones. The collision course I was on for a derelict and vagrant lifestyle in the unforeseen years ahead caused me to lose track of many such treasures. Miraculously, some of those items found their way back to me. But trust me, if they had any monetary value, they often found new homes in order to fund my habits.

That fall, I started grade ten and also made more new beginnings in my young life. I had loved to draw in my school notebooks for as long as I can remember. I would either draw hockey goalies or dirt bikes, the two things I loved and lived for. I took my first art class in grade ten and loved the creative aspect of it. It was new, it was fun, and I got a top letter grade in the first semester. I also parlayed my creativity into writing and suddenly became a hit with my English teacher, Mr. Hawkins. He was a cool dude and, like me, an LA Dodgers fan. It didn't look good at first, but after losing the first two games of the 1981 World Series, our Dodgers came back and did the unthinkable by beating the Yankees for the next four games. That etched them in my memory forever, because they, like me, never gave up on their dreams of becoming champions.

Something else new and overpowering happened in that class. You guessed it, for the first time in my life, I was in love. I had courted Sherry for a couple of years prior, but in the end, we were more good friends than anything. The new object of my affection was Andrea. She was a gentle, petite, pretty, short-haired brunette with braces and big, beautiful, brown eyes. She instantly became everything to me. I was young and in love for the first time in my life. That period also saw me come of age. I was a man now, or so I thought.

When the calendar flipped over to 1982, I also went through a motorcycle brand change. One of the guys I had grown up racing with, Abbottsford's Ken Enns, owned Abbottsford Kawasaki. Ken was a great guy, a family man who was always positive, smiling, and upbeat. I liked that in people, because I was also a positive person. My good racing friend, Wally Levy, who had mentored me somewhat while he was a lad, also rode for Kawasaki Canada out of Ken's shop. Wally also had me help him teach his motocross schools during my last couple of seasons on small bikes. It was a good fit for him, because he could stand trackside and point out to the students what I was doing and how I was doing it. I take pride in knowing I was the first small-bike racer to attempt his late father Walt Levy's brand-new "camel back" double jump at the Aldergrove track in 1979. What great memories those motocross schools were. They were not just one- or two-day events either. They were full-on one-week stays at the Levy household on 264th Street, only a few blocks from the family-owned Little Rock Raceway. The schools also included dietary and maintenance seminars along with dry-land training, ughhh. Wally, I can't thank you, your late parents Walt and Afke, and your brothers and sisters enough for everything you sacrificed for me. Because of you I have some of the most valuable memories one could ever want. Wally, my man, that sure sucked when that poor lad broke his femur on the top of the Diamond Head jump. I can't remember his name, but I will never forget his screams while I drove your van with you and him in the back trying to keep his leg stable.

Speaking of which, my driving was pretty good for a thirteen-year-old (which is how old I was at the time of the Diamond Head incident). Heck, it had to be.

One night in 1979, Dad and I drove from Chilliwack to Vancouver, where we met up with Terry Hofoss and his dad, so Terry and I could watch Wayne Gretzky and the Edmonton Oilers for the first time. While Terry and I took in the game, our dads went across the street to the pub and drank their faces off for four hours.

After the game ended, we dropped Terry and his dad back at home. Then we headed across the Port Mann Bridge toward Chilliwack, some sixty-five miles away. Just as we past the 176th Street exit on Highway 1, we saw flashing red-and-blue lights everywhere. Dad pulled over and went through the usual licence and registration protocol. The officer looked at me and then looked back at Dad and asked him how much he had had to drink. I had seen that movie many times before with my dad. I was damn tired of it, and I just hoped we would make it home, because I had school the next day.

After what seemed like forever, the officer looked back at me and asked if I had anything to drink. I told him I hadn't, and the officer looked at my dad and said, "I think you should let him drive home." Are you kidding me? I was only 13 years old. In the officer's defence, I had a huge set of lamb chops and a full red beard. I was also fit and of above-average height. I didn't analyze it too much, because before I knew it, my dad got out and was trying to open the passenger door, which I had locked. We were in our black Ford van, and I had driven it quite bit already. Maybe my dad was prepping me for a scenario like that. At any rate, I drove down Highway 1 for about fifteen minutes until my dad said, "Okay, it's safe now. Pull over." I did as I was told, and he kicked my ass out of the driver's seat and drove the rest of the way home. Thank God, Roger's passing marked my dad's last drink, because things were getting ugly in regard to his habit. We didn't tell my mom about that part of our night when she asked how the game was.

The year 1982 started out with a wild first ride on the brand-new Kawasaki 125 cc bike. The race season had not yet begun, and we had two brand-new KX-125s in the garage. It was different, because they were green and, in my opinion, not very attractive. But as they say, "Beauty is in the eye of the beholder." The bikes even had the side number plates as part of the rear fender panel. Yuck.

One cold February weekend, the same week we picked up the bikes, my parents went down south for a swim meet with my sister. That was becoming more commonplace, because Kelly had joined the elite Hyack Swim Club out of New Westminster, BC. It was an arduous 2.5-hour round trip to and from New West, but my mom and sister did it five times a week for the first year. This is where I get a failing grade as big brother, because I knew little about my sister's swimming. I knew she was good and had the ribbons and medals to prove it, but I only went to a handful of meets.

Dad gave me strict instructions regarding the bikes that weekend. He told me to ride one of them on Saturday and break it in and then do the same to the other bike on Sunday. He also gave me the usual, "Clean them up, tighten everything, and take the owner's manual to bed with you." That sounded like a perfect plan when I added in the company of my girlfriend, Andrea.

The weather that weekend wasn't particularly warm. It was about a five or ten-minute ride to the river at the end of Young Road on the bike (depending if I rode side saddle or just pinned it). The police patrolled Young Street regularly for such violators. I knew a few people had called in complaints, so even though I had never been caught, I was always on the lookout for the "fuzz."

We geared up, me in my moto gear and Andrea in my Kawasaki jacket and Bel-Ray hat, on backwards. I rode the bike for a bit, and then we headed over to Gill Road, another hot spot amongst two-wheeled outdoorsman and pretty much every other hell-bent Road Warrior wannabe.

About two hours into that endeavour, I realized we were getting low on fuel. Andrea climbed back aboard, and away we went. I elected for a different route home, southbound on McDonald Road. The road was long, about half a mile, and lined on both sides with residential housing. About halfway down the road and approaching us quickly was a police car. As the officer passed, she looked me in the eye. That was all I needed to know that she was about to go into full U-turn mode.

I'm not sure why, because I knew it was the wrong thing to do, but I told Andrea to hold on tight. In no time flat, I had the KX-125 through the gears and going as fast as I could. As I approached Bryce Road, I slowed enough to look over my left shoulder. The cop was still there! I had a choice of going left or right on Bryce and caught a huge break by going right. To the right was a traffic-calming concrete divider to prevent cars from entering, but I squeaked my bike through. Glancing over my shoulder at the stopped police car, I knew I was clear. I hit the throttle so hard that the hat Andrea was wearing fell off. *No problem*, I thought. *We'll get another one.*

Once I swept around the next long corner, an opening for the pathway that went into Strathcona School appeared. I blazed across the schoolyard to the opposite pathway that came out on my street, Clare Avenue. Adrenaline had obliterated my fear of being caught. It was exciting to defy authority, which was weird for me. I had always respected authority, especially when it came to dirt bikes. Even though my dad hung with many untrained two-wheeled yard apes at times, he always told me to be respectful of people and laws regarding bikes. He said that the connection I make with someone might be the only impression they ever get of a motocrosser. Good point, Dad. The school you went to may be closed for good, but you did learn a thing or two.

By the time I reached our house, I was in fifth gear and flying. I started to apply the brakes while cutting across my neighbour's yard. Needless to say, it left a twenty-foot skid mark that was a few inches deep. I took the bike around the back of the house and quickly covered it with a tarp under the sundeck. Then we went inside and peeked out the windows to see if anyone was any wiser to what had just happened. I had a feeling that somehow that officer would make her way down our street.

Sure enough, about thirty minutes later, the cruiser crept by our house. By that time, my neighbour was out in his yard addressing my landscaping "improvements." The first time the officer drove by, he didn't even give her a look. I figured for sure that we were off the hook. But a few minutes later, the cop came back. She stopped in front of our neighbour's house, which belonged to the Long family. I couldn't hear the exchange, but it ended with the police officer walking around to our backyard. Damn, I knew I was busted, but I was determined to beat it.

When the doorbell rang, I didn't answer it, but I had a sick feeling inside. I wasn't afraid to answer to the authorities. I was afraid of having to deal with my dad's wrath. I was getting too big for corporal punishment, so I knew something had to give.

After a couple of hours passed, I figured it was safe to go outside and bring the bike into the garage. I never washed it, just wiped down everything as best I could. I certainly didn't want to be caught red-handed in my wash station, which was at the end of my driveway. That was Saturday, and I still had to clean and service the bike plus get back to the river with the other one on Sunday.

My parents returned home on Sunday night, as expected. I don't remember it being an issue, but when Dad asked how it went with the new bikes, I told an outright lie. That was big, because I don't remember ever lying to my dad about anything. Maybe I was lucky enough to know, that I would have to face severe consequences if I did. Also, the scare I got from stealing from the co-op a few years earlier helped a lot. In my heart, I have always believed, that if you do something wrong, the powers that be always have a way of balancing things out. In other words, I believe in karma, big time. No, not an eye-for-an-eye thing. Heck, that would leave us all blind. Due to the good moral fibre with which I was raised, it was more of a sense that I would always be looked after as long as I did the right things. My belief may be a little like a lost boy whistling in the dark in the hope of fending off demons, but it hasn't let me down yet. However, in one year's time, those silent voices would begin screaming louder than ever.

That Monday after school, I went over to Andrea's house to study, or so my story went. I went there, because I was afraid the police officer who failed to catch me in the act would return to our home. At around 6:00 p.m. my dad showed up at Andrea's house. He told me that I needed to come home, because someone was there and wanted to see me. We got into my dad's truck, and he never said a word, and neither did I.

At home, there she was, parked in our driveway, which was quite long, right up against our garage doors. I knew I was busted. She gave her proverbial "You should have stopped. You should have slowed down when you saw me. Do you know it's a federal offence to flee from law enforcement?" And then, to my great surprise, she handed me the Bel-Ray hat that Andrea was wearing. I think I stopped breathing momentarily, because I realized how dangerous and stupid it was to put my first love in danger!

She didn't press charges, just gave me a stern warning. However, if I was caught riding on the road again, my bike would be confiscated. As for my dad, all he said was, "You heard her. Smarten up." Despite that incident, I continued to ride my bike to the river but always side saddle, with both legs on one side of the bike, because it was easier to jump off if law enforcement appeared.

The spring of 1982 turned into heartbreak for the talented up-and-coming Edmonton Oilers. They looked to be in position to dethrone the Islanders. To put that in perspective, the Oilers won the Smythe Division that season with 111 points, some 38 points ahead of the second-place Vancouver Canucks, in what is now called the "Miracle on Manchester Street." That series saw the Oilers bow out to the last team to clinch a playoff spot that year, the Los Angeles Kings. Though much more powerful and somewhat cocky, the Oilers were defeated by the Kings in five games. The Miracle on Manchester refers to game three in Tinseltown, where the Kings did the unthinkable by erasing a five-goal deficit and winning in overtime. Kings owner Jerry Buss (who also owned the LA Lakers) left the building after the second period, fearing that the writing was on the wall for his team's demise. Once again, I was astounded! How could the Kings be so resilient in the face of certain defeat? This was my kind of team, until, of course, they lost to our own Vancouver Canucks!

The Canucks went on to the Stanley Cup final after "towel power" was born in Chicago in 1982. It was a result of bad officiating in that series between the Blackhawks and the Canucks, and spearheaded by the always clever Roger Neilson (who was behind the bench after Coach/GM Harry Neale was suspended). When the series headed back to Vancouver, every single one of the over 16,000 fans in attendance were waving a white towel as if their lives depended on it. Despite their incredible blue-collar work ethic, coupled with the brilliant goaltending of "King" Richard Brodeur, the Canucks succumbed in a four straight games to the ever-powerful New York Islanders. The fact that the Canucks even made it that far was a miracle in itself. Despite the loss, I admired the fact that the Canucks never gave up and fought their way to the final.

The 1982 racing season wasn't a great one for me. It had its moments though. Starting out locally at the provincial level, I struggled to get used to the green contraption I was riding. It felt much heavier than the previous year's Yamaha.

It probably wasn't; it was more a matter of comfort, suspension settings, and general bike geometry. If you are not from the motocross world, it's kind of like comparing car brands. Some things are similar, but when you're reaching speeds of over fifty miles per hour on rough, rugged, ungroomed tracks in the hot sun, such differences matter!

I was top five in each race in the expert class when the provincial series ended. However, I had lost considerable ground on a couple of the other faster riders that I had battled with the previous year. That frustrated me to no end. I just couldn't manage the top-level speed on that bike, and I knew it.

I have since joked with him on a live episode of my *Canadian Moto Show*, but I took my frustration out on one particular rider. The race was in Aldergrove at Little Rock. It was the first 125 cc expert moto of the day. I got a mid-pack start and worked my way up to fifth. On the last lap, with less than a quarter of a lap to go, Rob Van Diemen's big brother, Rick, passed me. There was a big jump that led into the finish line, a 180-degree right hander. After I landed that jump, I thought, *There's no way you're beating me, Van Diemen!* As he applied his brakes hard on the inside line, I followed but didn't apply any brakes at all. I braced myself for the impending impact. Bang! I hit poor Rick in the same manner that I knew Bob Hannah wanted to hit his foe, Kent Howerton, the year before at Saddleback. Upon impact, I knew I had made a serious mistake. The Van Diemen boys, from Keremeos, BC, were tough-as-nails turkey farmers. They were fit and buff, so I knew I would soon be answering some serious questions—that is, if he didn't knock me out first.

Sure enough, after the race it wasn't long before Rick found my pit area. He was fuming and aggressive. I was calm even though I felt like he could drop me with one punch at any second. For whatever reason, my blatant attempt to put him through the outer perimeter fence gave me a spark! I was honest with him and admitted it wasn't a safe or a smart pass attempt (an understatement). Rick accepted my apology, but he said if he ever felt my wheel on him again, he would retaliate. I thought that was fair enough. Rick and I never became close friends, but after that race, that incident, like most racing incidents, never gained any traction. However, it did give me a better understanding of what playing in the big leagues with the big boys was like.

To give you a better picture of that era, even though we had referees, riders pretty much policed themselves. When we went to the starting line, we all knew who was tougher than who, and we kept note of that. On that day, apparently, I dropped my notebook. What would I have done if someone hit me like that? I'm not sure I can answer that, because I don't think I was ever hit that aggressively by another rider.

I turned sixteen on June 1 and was excited to be of age to get my driver's licence. My dad had bought me a pickup truck. It was a 1967 Ford half-ton. Sky blue in colour, it had a "three on the tree" transmission. He bought it off our old carpenter friend, Abe Dyck, who had built our first two new homes. It had only been driven from job to job and was in great mechanical shape, a steal at $500. It tormented me in our driveway for about a month before I could drive it.

I got a job at a local autobody shop, where I was hired by Tommy Thompson to do after-school clean-up and yard chores. I couldn't wait to let him see my truck, because I wanted to get a new paint job. The truck's paint was kind of flat, and it had a few dings from being a work truck. I'm not sure how many hours he quoted me, but I couldn't wait to get it done. Once painted, the truck looked incredible, and I loved it. Some white-spoke mag wheels spiced it up nicely. It was a game-changer for me, because now I could get to and from anywhere I wanted or needed to be.

That year being a bit of a learning curve, I didn't head back east to contest all the pro nationals. Instead, I joined the series when it came to Edmonton's Antler Lake Motocross Track. Oddly enough, not going didn't bother me as much as it had the year before. I knew I wasn't ready, and I didn't like the Kawasakis at all. I also had a new toy (my truck), a girlfriend, and many places to go and people to see, or so I thought.

My mom's dad, Grandpa Doug, who I didn't know that well even though he now resided in Chilliwack, passed away right after my birthday. He was in his mid-sixties and had a lot of hard miles on him. I never saw him in action, and only remember him showing up at our house every now and again when I was a child. He was always smiling and seemed to be in good spirits. I know that my dear mom and most of her brothers and sisters still bore deep scars from their traumatic upbringing though.

His wife held a funeral service at their house. Not even an hour into it, my dad looked at me and said, "Grab your keys. Let's go get your driver's licence." Things were a little different back then. I had my learner's permit, and after a couple of weeks, I could take my road test. I must say my dad caught me off guard. He knew it, too. He hit me out of left field with that, so I wouldn't have time to stress about the test. I drove us down there, and within the hour, we were back at my grandfather's wake, my driver's licence in hand. Dad, your methods were unorthodox, but they worked well with me.

One of the highlights of the year came at the first ever Arenacross/Supercross held in British Columbia, the Cowichan Valley Supercross. It was held in the Vancouver Island town of Duncan, in the hockey arena, with a motocross track built right on the concrete floor. The event created a lot of excitement in the town and in the motocross community. I was excited too. It was an opportunity to mix my two favourite sports, motocross and hockey, for the first time.

When I got there, everything felt small and tight. Walking the track prior to the race, I noted how high the dirt was banked against the hockey boards. The track was all blinged out in banners and hay bales, awaiting the large crowds that were sure to come.

That night was the pinnacle of the reset button that I seemed to hit after the Van Diemen incident a couple of months before. I liked the idea of being pitted in our motorhome in the downtown hockey arena parking lot. It was a great way to interact with the many fans, most of whom were new to moto.

That night I did something that I had not done since my days on 80 cc bikes: I got the holeshot in my qualifier and won it handily. The track was tight, and the loose dirt on the surface wore down to the concrete quickly. None of that bothered me. I rode mistake free, and it had been a while since I had done that.

I had a repeat performance in the main event. I was first to the first turn, and the only bikes I saw were "lappers" (riders who were a lap behind me). When the checkered flag was waved in the direction of my high-flying number twenty-one bike, I felt like I was back where I belonged, on top. Sharing that victory with my family and my sponsor, Ken, was a special moment for me. It certainly gave me some much-needed confidence to head to the Edmonton nationals. It's cool to note that the home of one of my best indoor races is now home to the world's largest hockey stick. Was I another Happy Gilmore, who should have been a hockey player? Spoiler alert: my motocross racing career was about to start looking like Happy Gilmore toughening up for hockey season.

11

A National Crisis

Now that I was rolling independently with my own set of wheels, life couldn't have been better, or so I thought. With 1982 wearing down and our economy continuing to trend down as well, money seemed to be on everyone's minds. Maybe it was just the age I was at, but there never seemed to be enough to go around. In terms of employment, my dad's logging gigs close to home had slowly disappeared. Now he had to start making lengthy treks and stays in logging camps up north. Mom, who was working as a legal assistant, also underwent some major changes. Kelly, who was swimming in the New Westminster-based Hyack Swim Club full time, needed to be there in the water twice a day. That was virtually impossible, because it was a 2.5-hour round trip from our home in Chilliwack on a good day. My mom decided to apply for a legal assistant job in New West and got it. My parents also rented a fourteenth-floor apartment in downtown New West. If I had to guess, that rent likely cost more than the mortgage on our home, but that's who my parents were. They did everything necessary to keep us kids competitive in our respective sports.

Incidentally, Kelly did have a dirt bike, a Honda Mr-50, but it wasn't her thing. In her defence, female racers were few and far between. Walt Levy had a ladies' class race one day at the Aldergrove track for some of the girls who were family members of riders. I was so excited to be trackside cheering on my sister. She was the smallest one out there, and so was her bike. It was kind of like the Hare and the Tortoise story. The other gals all had 80 cc bikes or bigger. Kelly's "alchemy" was something that I could have noted a time or two. She stayed upright and was consistent throughout the race. I don't even know that she took the bike out of the second gear. All I know is at the end of the day, my little sister was my big racing hero.

That fall was my first hockey season with my own wheels. I easily made it to half of the Canucks home games that year. It's incredible to think that I could put $10 of fuel in my truck and buy an upper-blue ticket at the Pacific Coliseum for $6. A $20 bill would get me that and my Vancouver Canucks NHL Hockey Happy Meal. I loved sitting beside or right behind iconic Canucks announcer Jim Robson and Howie Meeker's play-by-play booth.

My allegiance to rock'n'roll music was as strong as ever. I attended many rock concerts during that time. I loved AC/DC, Van Halen, Molly Hatchet, and the "Ten Fingers of Doom," "Mr. Wango Tango," Ted Nugent. If they or any of my other favourites played in Vancouver, there was a good chance that I was there. My parents never blinked an eye. It was my money, which I earned at the body shop and delivering pizzas on weekends. I would tell them where I was going and roughly when I would be home. As long as my report cards were good, my parents were okay with that. They had no reason not to be, though it was the big city, and I often went alone. I took Andrea whenever I could, but if she wasn't allowed to go or I was short on dough, I'd go on my own. Attending NHL hockey games was a family tradition, though my parents stopped purchasing season tickets a couple of years prior. Gee, I wonder why?

The fall saw me snake-bitten once again on the injury front. If you've been paying attention, the smart money would be on a broken right tibia fibula, just above the ankle. If that was your guess, unfortunately, you are painfully correct. What the heck was going on? I couldn't catch a break come hockey season. In my final year of Minor Hockey, when all my friends and teammates were being scouted for Junior, I was out of action once again. Thinking back on it now, I guess my Higher Power (whom I had not yet made contact with) was steering me toward motocross as a career choice.

I'm happy I brought the Higher Power thing up now. No, it's not a religious term by any means in my vocabulary. It's a spiritual term that I use for the driver of my "bus," which holds the committee of demons in my head in check, who don't often play well with others. I will expand on that a little more in the next chapter.

Back in school things were still going well. In fact, I even got a top letter grade in English during the first semester. Maybe the little things along the way prepare us for something bigger in our journey. In my case, even though I couldn't see it, I owe a lot of my passion for writing and baseball, among other things, to Mr. Hawkins, my high school English teacher. He was a real dude who knew how to keep me intrigued. I believe that is what my dad lacked in school, teachers who were able to hold his interest. My dad is no dummy, and he has more street smarts than any other man I know.

The fall and winter of that year weren't great. For the first time in my life, or so it seemed, all my friends were doing cool stuff, and I was parked. It hurt inside, and I hated it. Also, for the first time I was a little envious of friends who boasted about partying on the weekends. Partying was not my thing. It contradicted everything that I believed in about being an athlete. I never went to parties. It even reached the point where my friends stopped inviting me, because they knew I wasn't into it. I didn't have any use for drinking, smoking, or anything like that, but I was feeling left out socially.

A lot of my Fairfield Island friends hung out at the Fraser River, sturgeon fishing while drinking beer and smoking weed. I spent many hours at the river, but to me it was all about becoming a world motocross champion, not a sturgeon slayer. Yes, I had other aspirations in my own country as well as Supercross, but the world was calling. After all, Berkley, California's "Bad" Brad Lackey had just been crowned the first American rider to win the 500 cc world championship. Lackey had finished second overall in the championship two times prior, but he had his share of bad luck along the way. So much so that he was nicknamed "Bad Luckey." It took him ten years to accomplish the win, but if Brad could do it, so could I. That 1982 500 cc world championship was Lackey's swan song, because his sponsor, Suzuki, scaled back their program. Lackey wound up retiring on top. Nice work, Brad. My dad always said you were a badass. The fact that no other American has equalled or bested your feat proves it.

No sooner had I and my colleagues grown accustomed to green (the colour of the Kawasakis I rode in 1982), I was seeing red. The dawn of 1983 saw me riding R&M motocross Specialties' Hondas out of Vancouver. I can't thank Rick Sheren and his father enough for their support. The Sherens, who were originally from California, brought "factory" to Canadian motocross. (I should also mention that, while in California, the Sherens also started the Ricky's restaurant chain.) The bikes we raced were good stock, but many aftermarket parts were available in the USA that we couldn't get in Canada. Rick and his family changed that forever. We were now able to get any aftermarket parts and accessories we wanted right at home. Unlike the previous year, I loved my new two-wheeled platform. The geometry of the Honda suited my riding style well. I had a brand-new 125 cc bike as well as a new 250 cc.

I'm not sure how the financing shook down, but I know my dad's father bought the 250 cc for me. He was also living in Chilliwack, though we never saw him much. It was no fault of ours, because my grandfather continued to drink regularly. My dad, who had quit drinking when Roger died, wanted no part of my drunken grandpa. I can't blame him. I loved my grandpa, but when he drank, he certainly had a Jekyll and Hyde personality. Every now and again, he would show up in the middle of the night, pissed out of his mind, and my dad would let him have it. Even though my dad always reacted with anger, I know he loved his dad dearly. Those wounds were deep though. Unfortunately, I soon pushed the boundaries on behalf of our family to an all-time low.

I did not ride a motorcycle until mid-January 1983. I had been off bikes altogether for two and half months. By then, from about halfway to the ankle from my knee, my leg was a massive ball of scar tissue. It had been badly broken four times, and I walked with a permanent limp. It always hurt and made a loud clacking sound when I walked the halls of my school. My friends took it all in stride, because that's who I was. I went along with it, but being hurt all the time was starting to wear on me. My doctor, who had seen his share of misfortune, questioned my parents' and my sanity. His concerns were legitimate, but we were in too deep to back out now. That year was going to be a break-out one for me; I could just feel it.

We had to get to work though, because the first national that year for 250 cc bikes was in Ulverton, Quebec. The 125 cc series started the following week at St. Gabriel. I rode the bikes a fair bit at the river, but once I got comfortable on them, Dad shut the river riding down. The sand base and fine gravel was tough on the bikes, and Dad didn't want me to wear them out prematurely. I know my parents' resources were pretty tapped, and we had to be proactive. I also believe Dad was starting to think the river was bad luck for me, because I had broken my leg three out of four times there.

We hit a few races in the south, and before we knew it, the racing season at home was upon us. I had good speed on the 125 and competed in the top five provincially. The 250 was a bit bigger and heavier, but I also started the year off well on it. My CMA racing number for the season was twenty-one. I liked the number, but I wasn't superstitious. Black cats crossing my path, walking under ladders, Friday the thirteenth, none of that ever got as much as raised eyebrow from me, though maybe they should have. I can take some consolation in knowing that it's too late to change what is written. Besides, the ride I'm going to take you on through the rest of this story would not be nearly as exciting, would it?

In April at one of the BC championship races in Agassiz, I landed hard on my 125 cc bike and jammed my wrist. I never crashed, just landed with the suspension totally collapsed on that track's signature hard-packed and unforgiving red soil. I finished the moto, but within moments of doing so, I knew something was wrong. An X-ray of my left wrist revealed a large fracture in the radius. To say I was gutted is a huge understatement. Why now? My doctor gave his usual warnings about my infatuation with dirt bikes. He also said that the scaphoid bone which was also fractured, would likely take many months to heal properly. That wasn't what I wanted to hear. He put me in a new type of high-tech fibreglass cast to keep it immobilized.

The injury presented me with a huge problem. The nationals were in June, just two and half months away. Was there enough time to heal and be ready? To my disappointment, the answer to that question would have to wait. I thought I was a somewhat patient individual, but my chronic injuries were changing that rapidly.

My mom and sister carried on in New Westminster and came back home to Chilliwack on non-swim meet weekends. Dad continued to slug away in the bush, and I continued doing as well as I could at school. Within a month, the pain in my wrist was subsiding, and the cast had just become unwanted baggage. I went a week without it but steered clear of my doctor, because I knew he would not approve.

At about the six-week mark, my dad asked me how strong it felt. I was honest with him and said that even though bearing a load wasn't a huge problem, bending it hurt quite a bit. He pointed out that it was my left wrist and that the throttle wasn't on that side of the handlebars. Yes, my dad was the eternal optimist when it came to my health. He had to be, because if I listened to my doctor from day one, I'd likely be a retired professional golfer today. Dad rigged up some exercises, where he tied a paint can to some rope with a wood dowel handlebar. He also got me a grip-strengthening device. Was it going to work and have me strong enough to race a 250 cc motorcycle at the opening round of the 1983 pro motocross national series? Once again, only the increasingly unpopular Father Time knew that answer. For the record, that SOB has been off my Christmas list ever since.

I got back on the bike a few weeks before the series started. I was still uncertain if I would be going. I raced two consecutive weeks on Thursday night at Hannegan Speedway, just outside of Bellingham. I loved that track. It was fast, it had decent soil, and there were always lots of fast racers there. What I didn't love was that all the confidence and speed I had built up earlier that year was gone.

One of the riders I had banged bars with down there on smaller bikes put a wheel in on me on one of those nights. You could say I was at fault, because I had failed to protect the better part of the inside line. Hannegan had many 180-degree bowl turns, and when I started to tire late in the race, it was easier to blaze the outside of the turn. The rider who put the wheel in on me was Rick Albee (who I had stayed with from time to time at his house in Bellingham). I had to check up and grabbed too much front brake. I thought for sure I was headed to the ground face first with my fragile wrist. Thank God I saved it. However, that incensed me! I lost it and went after Albee for all I was worth.

I set him up in the same fashion I did Van Diemen the year before. I'm not sure Rick knew I was on him within the lap, but maybe he did. In a right-hand corner, he went wide, leaving it open for me to get my revenge. What was I thinking? We were battling for fifth place in a race that meant nothing (to me anyway). It was supposed to be a tune-up test for my wrist, not two-wheeled warfare. Nevertheless, I hit Rick so hard that he flew right over the berm and disappeared into the long-festering Hannegan weeds.

Soon after that I got the white flag, followed by checkers. I headed back to the pits, took my helmet off, and sat in my chair. Dad came back and asked how I felt. I told him I was okay, which was a lie. I hated myself inside. I felt lethargic on my bike and had just about sent someone who had been my friend for years to the hospital.

"What happened to Albee?" Dad asked. "Did he go down?"

I looked at my dad and nodded. "Yes, he did."

No sooner were the words out of my mouth than Rick showed up, fuming. He had grown into a pretty big kid, and, unlike me, he loved weight training. As I said, Rick and I had been good friends at one point. I even spent a week at his house one summer. I don't remember much of it though, because a rope swing we had built in the woods broke, and I was knocked out. It was a bad one. After two days of not knowing where I was or who anyone was, my dad had to come down to Bellingham and bring me home to my doctor.

I'm not sure how long our exchange lasted, but it wasn't pretty. My dad stayed out of it and let Rick and me sort it out. The thing that bothered me most about that incident, much like the one with Rick Van Diemen, was that my frustration had led me to try to take those guys out. I don't think I have seen Rick since that day at the iconic Hannegan Speedway, which is still run by the Mt. Baker Motorcycle Club. Rick, I hope you're well, old friend. A special thanks to you and your family for helping me out during my formative years.

That Hannegan race was the last time I rode my motorcycle before I headed to Quebec the following week. But this trip was going to be different, much different. Both my parents were staying home. At just seventeen years of age, I would be driving across the country with a racing colleague named Mike Boyce. Mike was around twenty-five years old and a native of Dryden, Ontario. He had recently transplanted to the west and was also an expert-class 250 cc racer. We also brought along a friend of Mike's, Brian Gauley, who Mike worked with at the shipyards in North Vancouver. Brian was from Lachute, Quebec. He would provide us with some local knowledge as well as a place to stay at his parents' home.

We set out in a big white cube van with large Honda Canada logos on each side. We were styling. This was it, the day I thought would never come. I was headed across our beautiful country again to race in the pro national series, which hit most provinces in an east-to-west sequence. We planned to drive to Dryden and then duck down into the United States via the Duluth truck crossing. The price of fuel in 1983 was skyrocketing compared to the year or two before, and the cube van was a fuel pig. My mom had taken the initiative to have a letter notarized stating that it was okay for me to travel across border without them. My dad gave us only one set of instructions: "Whatever you guys do, don't try to cross the border late at night." I never thought anything of it, and apparently, neither did Mike.

Our journey across the prairies was pretty mundane. We slept in the back of the van with the bikes. I didn't sleep well, although that wasn't new to me. For reasons unknown to me, and which I had kept it to myself for a long time, my heart would often ache and race at night with bad tachycardia. It seemed like there was no reason for it, because I was as fit as a fiddle (or so I thought). I might have mentioned it to my mom, but I don't remember. I do know that I didn't want anything more to do with doctors or medical issues. I just wanted to live like a normal kid and race dirt bikes.

We stayed in Dryden for a couple of nights with Mike's mom. I would like to say that Dryden was a nice town, but that would be a lie. Dryden is a mill town, and it sure smelled like one. I don't mean to be ungrateful though, because that stop allowed us to sleep in beds for the first time in a few nights.

We pulled out of Dryden early the next afternoon. We wanted to go to Thunder Bay and check out the track, where we would race in four weeks' time. We had to get a move on though, because we had a seven-hour drive to the border. From there our plan was to drive into Minnesota and Wisconsin. In Wisconsin we planned to take a ferry across lake Michigan and then back up into Canada over the Ambassador Bridge from Detroit.

Of course, we ended up staying at the Thunder Bay track way too long and were in jeopardy of having to cross the border at night. Dad knew a thing or two about how the world worked, and in that case, he was spot on.

It was after midnight when we approached the crossing, and there was no lineup. It was interesting to watch Mike field the questions from the customs official. I had never witnessed anyone other than my dad do that. The official asked Mike if he would pull the van up in front of a large vacant bay. I sensed instantly that we were in trouble.

At first they moved us into a room and asked us a few more questions. I thought it was strange, because none of us looked like bandits. I couldn't help but think about how often my father, who was covered in prison tattoos from his ankles to his eyeballs, evaded the fate we were facing. Why was it happening? We were completely innocent.

The three customs officials proceeded to remove everything from our van. To put that in perspective, we had three dirt bikes, replacement parts, and food and clothing for three individuals, who planned to be on the road for two months. They made a huge mess. It didn't stop there though. Once they had everything out of the van, they began removing light covers, door panels, you name it. Through it all I never worried about our well-being, because I knew we had nothing to hide. The two guys who I was travelling with were salt-of-the-earth individuals, and I trusted them. My biggest concern was if we were ever going to get everything back together and on to our destination. The process took hours!

Finally, shortly before dawn, we were on the road again. The ferry out of Milwaukee was scheduled to leave at noon that day. Sensing we would get hung up in St. Paul and Minneapolis traffic, we pulled over to get an hour or so of sleep before moving on.

We stopped at a bike shop in Minnesota, and after that it was my turn again to drive. We all took turns behind the wheel. That time though, Brian and Mike went to sleep. The van didn't have a radio or stereo in it, but I had my trusty boom box. At that time Golden Earring's "Twilight Zone" had just come out, and I loved that tune. With my travel mates asleep, it was just me, my music, and the open road of I-94.

A while into the four-hour drive to the ferry, the batteries in my music maker died. Just outside of Madison, Wisconsin, I was starting to flag, and I was having a hard time staying awake. That stretch of highway is fairly forgiving, but it's a four-lane divided highway and quite busy. Then the inevitable happened: I fell asleep and drove off the highway at sixty miles per hour. All I remember is waking up and the "road" feeling rougher than any motocross track I had ever been on. Thankfully, there was a sixty-foot grass median off the highway.

The boys awoke instantly, and we all got out and assessed the damages. We were all okay, but the van's wheel alignment was a little messed up. Mike took over the driving duties after I fielded a couple of questions from a state trooper, who had pulled over when he saw the van off the highway.

With Mike at the wheel, we made it by the skin of our teeth to what we thought was the last ferry across lake Michigan. We were in luck, no cars, no lineup nothing. When we pulled up to the kiosk though, it was closed. We tracked down a janitorial employee, who told us the ferry was closed until 5:00 p.m. the next day for unscheduled maintenance. Another delay we certainly didn't need.

We quickly decided that it would be best to drive down to Chicago and around Lake Michigan. I liked the idea, because I had always wanted see Chicago. The big cities that housed the professional sports teams I cheered for were always on my radar. What an adventure it was turning out to be.

Within an hour of leaving Milwaukee, I couldn't believe how many vehicles were on the many different freeways going in seemingly every direction. In the passenger seat, I sat with my disposable Kodak camera in hand, ready to capture the images of a world that was travelling at a pace that I had never seen.

An orange Corvette convertible with a male African American driver, who wore a matching orange leather jacket, was my first "victim." Let's just say that when I encouraged Mike to speed up beside him so I could take his picture, he was anything but thrilled. His single-digit flightless bird gesture was all I needed to see to know that I was overstepping a boundary. Mike and Brian quickly looked the other way as I learned another valuable life lesson.

Michigan was up next. Seeing the Motor City of Detroit and the Joe Louis Arena, home of the Red Wings, from Ambassador Bridge was exciting. I don't remember the three of us even worrying about crossing the border. The sun was still up, and we all realized that the border guards in Duluth were just dicks. Ambassador Bridge was quite archaic, but I loved the view it gave back into Detroit as well as into the Canadian side of Windsor, Ontario.

That was a Thursday, and our plan was to go to Mike's sister's place in Toronto to spend a couple of days to recuperate. After that we would head to Quebec to spend the week before our first national event of the year.

Mike's sister lived in Whitby, which is a suburb of Toronto. While there I experienced the midsummer Southwestern Ontario humidity for the first time. Even though I liked the heat, I soon discovered that humidity isn't my thing.

During our first night there, I woke up in the middle of the night with one of my tachycardia episodes, and that one scared me. It was painful. Mike's sister helped me through it and woke up her husband, who happened to be a top cardiologist in Toronto. They immediately had me in and checked out. I was afraid—not of dying or anything like that, because that has never been a real fear of mine. My fear was that my parents would find out and that I would not be able to race in the nationals, which started in just over a week's time.

After a few days, it was determined that my tachycardia was as a result of a heart valve that was failing to close properly. It turns out I was born that way. Oddly enough, just a few years ago, I found out that my sister had similar tachycardia problems. They discovered she was born with an extra heart valve, which was surgically removed in a dicey operation in 2016.

We eventually made it to Quebec for the opening round of the 1983 national series. I will never forget how surreal it was to crest the hillside against which the Ulverton track was perched. We parked and pitted down below by the river. Many others from BC had also made the trek, and it was nice to interact with some familiar faces. It was also a little daunting to see so many racers who I had never seen before. I started to get a bit nervous, but once I hit the track, that feeling went away.

Practice went well, but I certainly missed having my dad there. In fact, because Mike was racing, too, I didn't have anyone at the starting line with me for the opening-round gate drop. To put that race in perspective, I was lined up with the likes of multi-time Canadian National Champ Ross "Rollerball" Pederson and the rest of the best racers in our country. Yamaha Motor Canada had also brought in Jeff Surwall, fresh off his Florida winter series victory. Surwall was a sand specialist but also a good all-around rider who had finished eighth overall at the Hangtown National the year before. Jeff was considered to be one of the twenty fastest riders in North America. Current MRC referee Paul Kingsley rode the rather archaic KTM. To say the KTM was a stone at that time is a huge understatement. Paul's brother, John, was Yamaha Motor Canada's team manager and desperately wanted to beat the current champ, Pederson, who was riding for Team Suzuki.

The Ulverton track, which has seen national racing action as recently as a couple of years ago, has not changed much at all. Built on flowing farmland, the track has great scenery and elevation changes. It also has soil that becomes dry and floury throughout the race day if not watered properly. When a motocross track like Ulverton gets rough, it's as rough as hell.

That day was a scorcher. It seemed like the only portion of the track that got any watering was the long uphill starting section and descent out of the first corner. In the opening moto, I got a horrible start and finished outside of the top twenty of forty riders. Not bad, but I didn't like how uncomfortable I felt out there. I knew I was riding over my head (meaning I was pressing out of my comfort zone to keep up with riders ahead of me). I wanted to be in the top twenty, because that's where I needed to finish to score national points.

Moto two was even worse. The track was way rougher, and my start wasn't good at all. On the first lap, down below in the section by the river, I was mid-pack and couldn't see anything. I sensed the bikes beside, behind, and in front of me, but I couldn't see five feet in front of me. No sooner than midway down that full-on, fifth-gear, balls-out straight, my front end dropped into a dust disguised hole that I swear was made by a land mine. My handlebars wobbled from side to side for what seemed like forever. Somehow, I saved it. I'm sure I still have imprints of those Oakley handgrips permanently embossed in my palms from the death grip I had on the bike in that moment.

I didn't realize it immediately, but by the time the checkered flag waved, my previously broken left wrist was in a world of hurt. But at the end of the day, even though I wasn't happy with the result, I was happy to have finished my first 250 cc pro national in one piece.

From Ulverton we headed back to Brian's parents' house in Lachute, Quebec. The following Sunday, I raced the 125 cc at the prestigious St. Gabriel De Brandon track. Once again, St. Gabriel (which I had raced at in 1980 on a smaller bike) was an incredible natural-terrain track. It had big jumps, which I loved, and decent soil. In addition, the best motocross fans in our country are from Quebec. I was excited.

Back on the 125 cc bike for that event, I felt great during practice. It gave me the confidence that I was lacking the week before. In moto one I got a great start. In fact, I was almost first out of the first turn but got pushed a little wide. I got shuffled back a bit by some of the faster riders, but was holding my own in the top fifteen out of forty. More importantly, I felt better, stronger, and more confident with every lap. It had been a while since I had strung anything that positive together under top-level racing conditions. These national motos were 30 minutes plus two laps for the 125 cc bikes and 40 minutes plus two laps for 250 cc bikes. So, when I say motocross is the most physically demanding sport in the world, I mean it.

I got the mid-moto signal (two rolled up flags crossed) when apparently my moto guardians (if there is such a thing) took a timeout without notifying me. I crested the finish-line jump at St. Gabriel on the far outside left line with a little too much speed. As I became airborne, I knew I was sending it, but I didn't worry too much about it. The landing was flat, and the 125's suspension worked well for me. The fact that I had outjumped every other rider was a problem, because I landed hard in one of the deep bomb holes on the track. From flying proudly through the air on that fourth-gear, three-quarter-throttle jump, I bottomed out so hard that it almost stopped me dead in my tracks. When the rear suspension was completely flattened, my right foot came off the foot peg, and it buckled with my already-broken-four-times leg and ankle beneath it. Once again, I never fell off the motorcycle, but the instant agony was unmistakeable. Damn, some thirty-five years later, that moment still brings a tear to my eye.

I rode straight to the pits, hopped off my bike, and sat in a lawn chair. My leg was broken, and I knew it. I was devastated. All I wanted was to be the motocross champion that I knew I could be. From that moment forward on our trek to the Joliette Hospital, half an hour away, I started to block things out as a way to preserve my sanity. I could no longer stand being broken; it was ripping me apart inside. Through it all though, I never wondered, why me? I never felt like a victim, just unlucky.

We were at the hospital for hours. If I had dropped dead in that moment and went to hell, it would not have surprised me if hell turned out to be a hospital. One of the biggest stumbling blocks was finding a doctor who spoke English. Finally, one gave us the news that we feared. My right leg was broken just above the ankle. Despite my heartache, once again there was somewhat of a silver lining. Brian's mom (who we were staying with in Lachute) worked at Dorval Airport. The next morning she took me to work with her and helped me book a flight back home. What was next? Was my dream of becoming a motocross champion gone forever, or would there be a miracle in my near future?

My parents, James and Donna Worrall, Merritt, BC

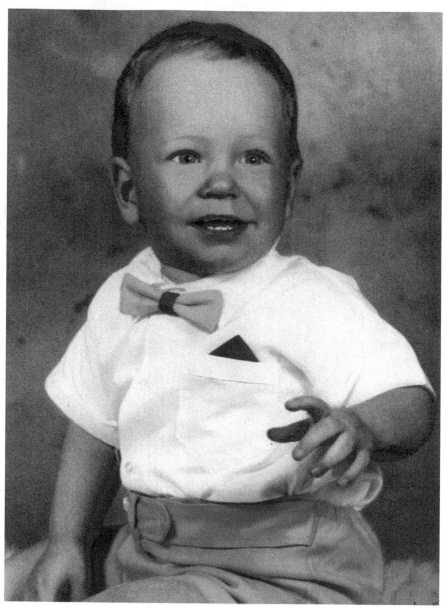

Mom always had a knack for keeping me sharp.

Grandpa James Arthur Worrall with Lisa Douglas and me

Uncle Al was a big part of my upbringing.

A proud father and me outside our Spadina Avenue home.

Grandma Pearl Worrall and me. Yes, she was a redhead too.

1973 Chilliwack Minor Hockey, me in front of Dad (coach) on the left side

1974 Logan Lake with Bob and Robbie Mutch

My sister, Kelly, was always keen to help her big brother.

Mom, Kelly, and me with the number 104 bike,
which I wore proudly for my idol of that era, Roger DeCoster

A motocross-themed birthday at our Hilton Drive home

Puyallup Winter Series victory photo that ran in the *Chilliwack Progress* in 1978

Hockey has always been a huge part of my life.

Looks like we are off to support my sister's dreams of becoming the next Karen Magnussen.

Backyard birthday pool party with friends on Hilton Drive

1978 holeshot at Mission Raceway

Escape County, former home of the 1978 World Mini Grand Prix.
Today it's home to the *Real Housewives of Orange County*.

A solid start leading moto one at the 1978 World Mini Grand Prix

Startup Washington, Winter Series, the first season that I wore what became my signature number seven

1979 Aldergrove Canadian National.
Canadian motocross legend Al Dyck was the winner that day.

AWAITING THE SHOT — Brent Worrall of the Chilliwack B's waits for the point shot with Eastside's Sean Baker lying on the ice during their jamboree encounter on Friday.

Chilliwack Pee Wee Jamboree 1978

Notre Dame de la Salette 1980 Canadian National

Dad and Roger celebrating with the newly crowned national champion

Holding my hand-carved plaque on the top step of the podium

I always loved ice hockey and for many years had the Ogie Oglethorpe hair to prove it.

Jim and Donna Worrall, 1981

Yamaha Race of Champions group photo, Saddleback Park 1981

The rider to my left, Troy Blake, was the overall winner of the 1981 ROC.
RIP, old friend

HOUSE OF COMMONS
CANADA

Ottawa, Canada
April 7, 1981

Dear Brent:

It was a pleasure for me to hear of your outstanding accomplishments in the field of motocross racing.

My understanding is that you are now the Canadian Champion in the 80 cc. class of motocross racing, the British Columbia Champion, winner of the B.C. points award, and recipient of the MAX award, and that you will be competing at Saddleback, California, in the World Mini Grand Prix later this month.

Your success is not only an honour to you, but to the community you represent, and I do want to congratulate you on the skill and perseverance you have shown in achieving such unqualified success in this your chosen form of competitive sport, at this stage of your life.

With my best wishes to you now, and in the future, I am,

Yours very sincerely,

Alex B. Patterson, M.P.
Fraser Valley East

I have lost many things over the years but still have a few treasured gems.

209 CORBOULD ST. S., CHILLIWACK, B.C. V2P 4A6 TELEPHONE 792-2737

EVERGREEN HALL • EXHIBITION GROUNDS • AG-REC CENTRE • CHILLIWACK COLISEUM • CHILLIWACK ARMOURIES • LIVESTOCK CENTRE • PARKS

File #106 110

May 8, 1981

Mr. Brent Worrall
46268 Clare Ave.
Chilliwack, B. C.

Dear Brent:

It is our pleasure to inform you that you were nominated,
along with several other members of our community, as "Athlete
of the Year" for 1980.

A Mr. Eric Larsson was finally selected for this honour, but
we can assure you the Chilliwack Parks and Recreation Committee and
the Ag Hall Committee had a very difficult task in the selection of
the winner.

You should be proud of your outstanding accomplishments in
Motorcross Racing along with your involvement with soccer and hockey,
and we extend our heartiest congratulations to you in all your
future endeavours.

Yours truly,

Geoff Clark
Parks and Recreation
Committee Chairman

GC/dp

I was honoured to be nominated for Chilliwack's Athlete of the Year,
for the sport of motocross.

This photo was taken just days before Roger passed away.
After that my dad put a permanent plug in the whiskey jug.

The Costa Mesa Kid, Taylor Marcell, at Saddleback Park in 1979, Banzai Hill in the background

Worrall wins national title

Chilliwack has a national champion.

Brent Worrall of Fairfield Island nailed down the national motocross motorcycle racing championships for school-going juniors at Notre Dame de Sallette in Quebec.

Fourteen-year-old Brent, who has been racing for four years, won the B.C. championship by achieving the highest point standing in an eight-race series in April, May and June.

Winning the Canadian championship entitles him to take his Yamaha 80 to California next April, where he will represent Canada in the world mini-motocross grand prix, called "The International Race of Champions."

More information on Worrall is on Page 5B.

NATIONAL CHAMPION — Brent Worrall, 14, of Fairfield Island holds a carving and the award plaque he won in Quebec by beating all other Canadian motocross drivers in his class. Behind him are a few of almost 200 trophies he has won in four years of MX racing.

Chilliwack Progress from 1980

Standing on Banzai Hill watching the 1979 125 cc/250 cc Pro National
(Denison Design photo)

Inventing the scrub up in the Tamihi Creek area of the Fraser Valley,
November 1983

Graduation, Chilliwack Senior Secondary 1984

Grandpa James Arthur Worrall in Reno, Nevada

Kelly, my sister, wins the first ladies' race held at Little Rock Raceway.
(Other girls left to right: Betty Levy, Tracy Henrikson, and Janna Fownes)

Grandma Pearl, Kelly, and me at Heathrow Airport shortly after the
Boy George incident - 1984

12

Hero to Zero

There I sat, perched on a firm-bottomed leather chair in Dorval International Airport, my broken right leg aloft on the adjacent seat and bridged by one of my crutches. Now what? I had no idea what would happen next. All I knew was that I had put an incredible amount of time, energy, effort, and love into my passion for racing motorcycles. It was to the point where motocross racing defined me. Every person in my life, be it family or friend, knew me as Brent Worrall, the motocrosser. Now there I was, watching hordes of people on early Monday morning with places to go and people to see. My leg hurt, but it hadn't stopped hurting since the last break. I felt vacant, derelict, and empty. All I could think about was what my doctor's prognosis would be. Not once did the thought of giving up my passion enter my mind, though. But I was gravely concerned that my doctor, or possibly my family, might try to persuade me otherwise.

As we were called to board the plane, I grabbed my carry-on bag. The swelling was pretty bad when I got on board, and the stewardess helped me elevate my foot on another seat. Once we were airborne and headed for Vancouver and the seatbelt sign was off, she brought me ice regularly.

Throughout the flight, my mind raced uncontrollably, but more than anything, I was angry. Up to that point, I believed I was easygoing and didn't anger easily. I'm not saying I turned into the Tasmanian Devil or anything like that, but something in my life was different. I wasn't yet a full-on hell-bent rebel without a cause, but it was coming.

Somewhere over the prairies, I dug out the newspaper that Brian's mom had so thoughtfully given me. It was a Montreal-based tabloid. I had taken French in school and liked it, my motive being a belief that Quebec would play a big role in my racing future. I never read a word of that paper. I just combed through the photos and then stopped at my favourite part of any newspaper, the sports section. To me sports is a universal language in which I have always considered myself well-versed. You will never guess what the front page of that newspaper's sports section showed: a half-page photo of the first corner of my second moto start from the day before at St. Gabriel. My number twenty-one R&M motocross Specialties Honda was grouped tightly in the top five rounding the first corner. It was an incredible photo. It captured everything in that moment and froze it in time. I was stunned. I quickly looked for an article that supported the photo, but there wasn't one, just a quick blurb below the picture. It didn't bother me though, because suddenly all my anger, frustration, and pain were gone. The sight of my bike grouped in the top five with the best in our country temporarily took it all away.

Landing in Vancouver and being picked up at the airport by my dad wasn't so exciting. The reality of where I was at once again hurt more than ever. My dad and I had many different kinds of road trips together. Some included a ton of dialogue and mentorship while others didn't see two words spoken. That ride home from Vancouver was the latter. Not at all worried about my bikes or any of my belongings with Mike and Brian back east, I did my best to stay positive. I had so many things to be grateful for. My family and friends, whether I realized it or not, always valued Brent Worrall the person, not just the motocrosser. I felt lower than I ever had to that point, but I knew I had to fight to make the best of it.

I had a doctor's appointment that Friday, and he sent me in for more X-rays. I had to wait until the following week to get the results.

On Tuesday morning, we got a call from my doctor's office. Trust me, when the doctor calls and says he wants to see you, it's never good. My doctor, who was of Japanese descent, had a pretty good poker face, but he often joked and kidded around. Not on that trip though. When he called my parents and me into his office, I'm not sure any of us were ready for what happened next.

He placed the X-rays in the light holder and then grabbed his pointer. Before he could say a word, I saw all the white calcified scar tissue. It was massive. *Man, I hope I can still walk when I get old*, I thought. No, at the time, that was no "standing joke;" I was legitimately concerned. Then Doctor Tam told us that he saw no indications of any new breaks! He did point out that my ankle was badly sprained and that the calcification scars were likely what the doctors in Montreal thought were breaks. *Are you kidding me?* I thought. *This is the luckiest day of my life. I can race again, and soon.*

Not quite. In fact, he booked an appointment to have my leg immobilized and set in a fibreglass cast. I wasn't happy with that decision, though he said I would only have to wear it for a few weeks. There I went again, from hopeful to full-on bummed. My mom and dad never blinked an eye. I know they were worried about my future with my seriously messed-up right leg. Dr. Tam also sent me to a cardiologist to address my tachycardia and mitral valve. Later that summer we confirmed that my heart's mitral valve wasn't closing properly. There is no real cure for it; it's just the way I was born.

It only took a few days at home for my father and me to decide to remove the leg cast. I wasn't sure if it felt any better or worse—that is, until I put weight on it. I sucked it up and told my dad it felt fine. I love that word, FINE (Fucked Up, Insecure, Neurotic, and Emotional). If you know my dad by now, we were good to go, right?

The next round of the 125 cc Canadian nationals was the following weekend in Thunder Bay. Mike would be there with our bikes, because he was continuing to race the series. I had been to the Thunder Bay track on our trek out east and desperately wanted to race it. It had incredibly firm and tractable soil with lots of big bumps and elevation changes. My mom got on the horn with the travel agent, and once again, I was airborne. Mike picked me up at the airport, and off to the track we went. How crazy my roller coaster ride of a life had become, but I loved the racing and travelling. It was and always will be the best escape from reality that I have experienced.

It felt so good to see my motorcycles and my race crew again. I'm not sure if it was adrenaline or a sheer desire to block it out mentally, but my leg felt okay. However, I was glad we had walked the Thunder Bay track when we were there the month before. The feeling of being back on that starting line at the top of the hill was amazing. I didn't even care about the results. Just being there was a huge victory. I needed it, because I was starting to feel somewhat defective, inside and out.

The 1983 Honda I was riding had a clutch pin issue, and sure enough, mine let go in moto one. I was in a position to score my first national points, but it wasn't meant to be. In between motos, the Honda Canada guys helped repair my bike. It was a known issue to them, and I'm thankful for their help. It allowed me to line up in moto two and finish the day on a positive note. In the second race of the day, I placed twenty-third out of forty. Not great but not bad for a kid who couldn't go a moto without breaking something or someone. When we pulled out of Thunder Bay to head west for the sands of Austin, Manitoba, I felt like a winner.

Austin was another out-of-this-world experience. You may have heard about that track. The only thing I can say is what I experienced. Before the racing started, albeit fun and fast looking, the track also looked quite easy. So much so that, upon walking the long back straightaway, I laughed to myself, thinking how my 125 cc bike would be in fifth gear and wide open before even hitting mid-stretch. Two laps into practice, though, much like a modern-day Gopher Dunes, in short order, that track resembled the Colossus roller coaster at Six Flags Magic Mountain. That proved to be one of the most physically gruelling events I ever raced on a hot and nasty summer day.

Despite his hopes, Yamaha's Jeff Surwall, the sand specialist, I believe, didn't get the best of Rollerball on that day. That was no real surprise to me, because the longer, rougher, and tougher a race was, the better Ross Pederson was. I might add that Ross was my second-favourite Canadian motocross racing professional. The top spot went to the late Bill McLean. Bill was the first Canadian pro I ever looked up to. Much like Ross, he wasn't just a workhorse but also a meticulous individual at the track. From around the time I was eight years old, I noticed how Bill handled himself on race days. It was certainly different than most. RIP, Bill.

With the national series over, something new and cool was on the horizon for our sport in Canada. We had already had a few Supercross races in the east, thanks to the likes of our good friend Carl Bastedo. But now for the first time in the west at Calgary's MacMahon Stadium, the stage was set for a Supercross on August 25th. In case you don't know, a Supercross is a motocross race in a closed or open stadium venue. It is high energy and has lots of big jumps. It is also unique to our sport in the sense that, unlike most outdoor motocross tracks, you can see pretty much every square inch of the track from your seat. I always loved and excelled at tight-track racing, whether it was Supercross or Arenacross.

My mom and dad, along with my girlfriend, Andrea, made the trek to Calgary. Once there we pitted in our motorhome right outside the Calgary Stampeders' dressing room at the south end of the stadium. Man, I was amped up for that one, taking in the sights and smells of the track, filled with fresh clay and lined with banners and advertisement as the 46,000 empty seats awaited the showdown.

The day before the race, the Stampeders had a practice on their practice field adjacent to the stadium. Being a chronic sports buff, I knew almost all of them. After practice, a bunch of them came over to my pit to chat about motocross. That interaction has stuck with me ever since. The lineman I was talking to, who was flanked by many teammates, was also in the process of eating donuts. He had a whole box in his hand and was putting them back like mad. After I explained the nature of our sport and shared a few other stories, he told me that maybe he should take up motocross when he retired from pro football. As soon as that came out, he and his teammates and everyone else broke into a deafening crescendo of laughter. Now whenever I see a box of donuts, it reminds me of the first-ever Calgary Supercross.

The race was well attended in the seats and on the track. By the time the gate dropped for the night show, the track was hard-packed, baked, and dry, so much so that if someone had added water to it, it would have been like watering polished concrete and slicker than whale shit!

Some heavy hitters from the US were on the program for that race, including Jim Holley, Donnie Cantaloupi, and 1982 500 cc world champ Brad Lackey. I liked the track and felt good on it. Jumps were my thing, and that track had some huge booters! The roost (aggregate off the rear tires of the bikes in front of me) was piercingly painful.

Unfortunately, in my semi I collided with a rider in the air and landed off the track on a hay bale. My right foot was the first thing that hit the unforgiving MacMahon Stadium floor. Despite the pain, I was able to get up and finish the moto. Although I ran a solid race, that mistake cost me a trip to the LCQ (last-chance qualifier), where, back in these days, only the winner made it to the main event.

Back in the pits after the moto, for the first time that I can remember, I heeded my mother's pleading not to race in the LCQ. My decision surprised me, but I knew my leg needed to heal. At that junction, in my head, I was starting to give up. Later I came to realize, through making some serious mistakes, that the definition of insanity is doing the same thing over and over, expecting different results. That's what I was doing, and I hated it. But I was tired of struggling and being broken. Maybe I should have been a hockey player. I didn't know anything other than that, for all intents and purposes, racing season was over, or was it?

With summer drawing to a close, it was time to head back to school for my graduation year. My courses were a good balance of academics and electives. As for hockey, I got yet another late start to the season. I wasn't happy about that. I had to let my fall job at the body shop go, too, but I continued delivering pizzas on weekends. Our good friends from our Hilton Drive neighbourhood, the Velonises, owned the Pizza Factory in Chilliwack. John, I can't thank you enough, old friend, for your mentorship and patience with me.

I guess now is as good as time as any to tell the story about that house I almost drove into at five years old (when my mom left the car running to go in and get eggs, and I put the vehicle in gear, heading straight for the barn). One night I was sent out to that same house on Fairfield Island for a delivery. It was late, close to 2:00 a.m. I banged on the door but got no answer. I had two pizzas in my hand, and I knew John would be pissed if I came back with them. I drove down the road to the Killarney Market and called him from a payphone.

"Did you try the door?" he asked.

I was perplexed. I told him that I wasn't going into someone's house if they weren't answering their door. Then I hung up and drove back to the house. I walked around to the back and, through the side window, saw someone passed out on the couch. I couldn't tell if he was big, small, or anything like that; I just knew I was uncomfortable with trying to open the door, which was likely locked.

Taking a deep breath, I turned the handle, and the door opened. Rather than yell, "Pizza guy's here," I crept to the edge of the living room, though I wasn't sure what to do next. I didn't want to startle what I guessed was a mid-thirties male. Then I noticed a twenty-dollar bill on the coffee table. The order was for around $18. I decided to put the pizza down and take the money. I thought for sure that the cracking and popping of my messed-up right leg would wake him up. It didn't, and I left a little unsure of what had just happened. The payoff came the next day, when the guy who had ordered the pizzas called to let us know he was thankful we had taken the initiative to do what I did.

My final year in high school was laid back and much different than I expected. Things weren't as regimented as they had been to that point. I knew that no matter what the rest of the years showed, my marks would leave a lasting impression on that segment of my life. I wasn't sure if I wanted to go to university. I had taken a forestry course in grade eleven, and I had seriously considered taking the post-secondary version of that course at BCIT (British Columbia Institute of Technology). I thought it would be a good fit, because I had pretty much grown up in the bush in a logging family. I wasn't sure what I wanted to pursue as a career other than motocross. Not too worried about what I would do or where I would go after graduation, I continued to do the best I could.

In September, it was announced that there was going to be a first-ever Supercross race in Vancouver at BC Place stadium. At the time I didn't think much of it. My bikes had been parked since we had returned from Calgary in August. There they sat in our shop, still dirty and unloved. That wasn't like me at all. Something was different; I didn't even want to see a dirt bike at that point.

Two more weeks went by, and that pattern continued. Then one day after school, I pulled my 250 out of the shop and parked it under the huge cherry tree in our front yard. I loved that 1983 CR 250. It was fun to ride and had tons of horsepower. The entire setup was on point. The thing I loved most about that bike was that my grandfather had bought it for me. Yes, by then Grandpa had a few bucks. Why wouldn't he? He was a frugal SOB who always pinched pennies. He had done well on some of his pensions, but he also had some gigs on the side taking bets and loan sharking at local bars. My grandpa loved his money, and we all knew it, even though he never bought my father a bicycle when he so desperately wanted one as a child.

I got the bike looking clean and new again. It certainly felt better to have it looking the way I liked it. I still had no real desire to climb on it though; I just wanted to be healthy. I also knew that other than the upcoming Supercross race in Vancouver (in which I had no intention of riding), my season was over. I should add that, unlike other years, I wasn't even anticipating the following year's action. It was a strange feeling.

That day when my dad came home, he noticed the bike back in the shop and the makeover I had given it. We hung out in our basement shop and talked about a few things. It was light chatter, but I was always wary in conversations with my dad, because he didn't say a lot.

After about fifteen minutes, he asked if I felt like racing at BC Place. It was just two weeks away, and the entries had to be in. That race was gathering a lot of anticipation and excitement. Many entries were coming in from far and wide. Funny thing is, when Dad asked me, I didn't even have to think about my response. It was an instant yes! I had gone over a month without riding a motorcycle, but that didn't bother me. In fact, before October 25, 1983, the night of the first-ever Vancouver Supercross, I rode my bike only once—at the Fraser River at the end of Chilliwack's Young Road. We filled the gas tank in the shop, and Dad instructed me to just go down there and burn it all. That's all he said. Nothing fancy, just ride, brake, and corner. Dad never worried about jumps, because I needed no encouragement, practice, or anything like that with those. The air was my safe haven. The ground, on the other hand, has been having its way with me for years.

The dirt they brought into BC Place that night was decent but a little heavy. It would provide us with a technical track. I had been to many big races up to that point, but that one was special. All my family and friends who knew Brent Worrall, the motocrosser, would have a great opportunity to see a big race.

We pitted in the north end of the stadium under some folded-back grandstand chairs. From there we had a decent view of the venue, which was beginning to fill. The stadium holds 60,000 people at full capacity, but on that night, I believe the announced attendance was around 25,000. Pretty solid numbers for a first go at Supercross.

That night on the racetrack wasn't going well for me. In my qualifier I got a great start but crashed a couple of laps in. That meant a trip to the semi-final, where I had to finish in the top five to make it to the final, which was a gate of twenty riders. That didn't happen, because I made another mistake and fell. I was uninjured in both incidents and, thankfully, didn't aggravate my right leg. But it meant I had one shot to make the main event in what was pretty much a home race for me.

I went to the line for the LCQ knowing I had to win. I don't remember feeling any type of pressure or nerves. To me it was just for fun. To sit there on the line looking out toward that first right-hand corner at the end of the long starting straight put a huge smile on my face. Why wouldn't it? We were racing in a brand-new state-of-the-art stadium that had just opened that spring. I had been there on opening night with 59,999 others watching my Vancouver Whitecaps defeat the Seattle Sounders of the NASL 3–0. Peter Beardsley, who eventually moved on to Newcastle in the English Premier League, scored all three goals that night. I told you I was a sports buff!

When the five-second board went sideways, I was ready! The gate dropped, and I was gone. I didn't see any other tires, wheels, or fenders on either side of me. I rounded the first corner first and led early. To my surprise, coming around the starting stretch to complete the first lap, I got some hand signals from my dad. He was never big on chalkboards or any of that; he just used his hands. His usual routine was to point his index finger at his head to encourage me to use mine. That time though, he held his arms apart to indicate that I had a bit of a gap lead. LCQs are usually short. I believe that one was six laps. Seeing that signal from Dad encouraged me.

As I rounded each of the 180-degree turns, I tried to get a peek at how close the next pursuer was. I saw no one. No sooner had I done that than I ended up a little sideways through the "whoops" and had to chop the throttle. Losing all my momentum and RPMs, the back end of my bike bucked sideways. I came to a complete stop and almost high-sided. I didn't though, and my bike stayed running. I got back up to speed just in time. The second-place rider put a wheel inside me in the next right-hand corner. Even though I had made a gaff on the whoops, I was surprised to see him so close. It was bike 101, a Suzuki ridden by Nanaimo, BC's Ken Gregory. That incensed me! There was no way I was letting him by. I had less than half a lap to go to collect the checkered flag. When the flag waved, I was exhausted but relieved to have stamped my ticket to the main event. If I didn't make the main event in those races, I wouldn't receive a paycheck.

Within seconds of the race being over, I was interviewed trackside on the stadium's big screen. About halfway through the interview, I looked up into the stands and saw myself on the Big Screen. That victory ranks right up there with some of the best I had, because I got to share that great event with so many who had never seen me race.

I had only a bit of time to prepare for the twenty-lap main event. Another complication of winning the LCQ is that I got the last starting line gate pick. I lined up in the last spot on the far outside. It was to be my fourth race of the night—another reason why it would have been best to get through to the main race in my first qualifier. The gate hadn't even dropped, and I was tired. I wasn't afraid or worried of anything bad happening. I just told myself to go out there and have fun! That was easy; Supercross was always fun.

The thirty-second board went up, and shortly after that the gate was on the ground. I got a great jump. I was on the far outside and had more distance to travel on the first turn than the riders inside of me. I got to the first corner somewhere in the top twelve. I rode that main event as good as I had ridden a motorcycle since the World Mini Grand Prix two years earlier. Finishing fourteenth out of twenty riders that night felt like I had just won the lottery, considering the year I had survived. I would also like to note that my pay for that race was $475. Is it just me or has our sport's purse money not kept up with the times? As far as risk versus reward goes, passion has nothing to do with money, does it?

I rode my 250 one last time that November at Tamihi Creek just outside Chilliwack. It was just a fun ride with some friends from school. They told me there were some big jumps up there, and I could likely jump some vehicles if I was into it. Not knowing what to expect other than fun in the dirt with some of my school friends (which I had never done up to that point), I was in. What a blast it was to go out and rip shit up Road Warrior style. Bikes, dune buggies, and off-road vehicles were everywhere up there. I quickly laid out a motocross track, but it was a struggle to keep everyone going in the same direction. Fearing I would run headlong into someone wearing an open face helmet with no goggles, I gave up on the moto idea and scoped out the jumps.

I found one massive hit with about a fifteen-foot jump face that went straight up. There was no downward landing, just the flat of the gravel pit to absorb the impact. The first time I hit it, I flew a long, long way. One of my friends who came out that day was Ken Downing, who was twenty-three. I had started to hang out with him quite regularly. He had his camera along and got some great shots of me jumping vehicles and anybody who was stupid enough to stand below. Unfortunately, I lost or sold most of my treasured belongings in subsequent years, including those photos. However, just this past winter, I was going through some old hockey programs with my friend, Brent Carlson, and one of those photos fell out. I'm not sure how it got there, but it was a nice surprise. (I've included that photo in the first photo section of this book.) That day was significant for me, because it turned out to be the last time I would ride a motorcycle for twenty years.

As the fall wound down, I was getting restless. I played some Church League hockey that Fall, but had a hard time getting a skate on my right foot. Through all the abuse, my right foot and ankle had grown in size permanently, so much so that at one point when I bought shoes, I had to sneak a ten and a half in the box for my right foot, even though my left foot was only nine and a half. It definitely wasn't an honest approach, and I'm sure it messed with the store's inventory, but I was doing what I felt was required to survive.

That Fall, I started attending as many Vancouver Canucks and New Westminster Bruins games as possible. I attended some of those games with friends, and before long, that entailed us picking up some beer for the trip. I had not drunk anything up to that point, so I felt like I had some catching up to do.

I was cautious at first, or so I thought. We had double time-blocks in our house construction class at school, and the afternoon portion meant we were on a job site somewhere. Along with a few of my mates, which included the Frey boys, Dale and Darcy, we would pound back three or four beers over the course of our lunch break, then show up at the site with a pretty good blaze on. It was such an escape from all that ailed my body and still-developing brain, a euphoria like nothing I had experienced. It felt good, and I was hooked instantly.

I didn't get hangovers at first, because I was usually sober by the time school ended for the day. That Christmas for the first time in my life it was more about getting away to parties with friends than it was about family. It was a big change, because Christmas had always meant only one thing to me: family!

In early 1984, the high-flying Edmonton Oilers were having an incredible season, eventually taking down the four-time reigning Stanley Cup Champion New York Islanders in five games. Before that happened, though, the "Great One," Wayne Gretzky, was in the midst of the longest consecutive scoring streak in NHL history. Wayne had gone an unheard of fifty-one consecutive games with at least one point. However, on January 29, 1984, the Los Angeles Kings and goaltender Rogie Vachon put a stop to that at Northlands Coliseum. I watched that game in my bedroom with Andrea.

After the game we had a disagreement about something. For reasons I still don't understand, I sent her home and told her I didn't want to continue our relationship. I didn't really want her to go away; I was just pissed off. Whatever the reason, I carried on, thinking she would come back or make an effort to reconcile our differences. A few weeks went by, and it never happened. I kept it to myself, but it hurt inside, and I knew I had made a huge mistake. I was still convinced we were meant to be together, and everything would work out eventually.

Within a week or two of that, my parents called me upstairs to the kitchen table to talk. We didn't have many round-table discussions like that as a family, but that one had been coming for a while. I still get a little bit bent when I think about that day. The conversation started out based around school (which was still going pretty well). Then it turned to general chatter about life, love, and the pursuit of happiness, relationships, and so on. I know my parents sensed that things were starting to deteriorate a little in my approach to life. I wanted no part in that talk, though. Yes, I was reeling from the decision I had made to end my relationship with someone for whom I cared dearly, but in my mind it was no one else's business, and I would handle it on my own. The problem was, I wasn't handling anything. I was burying my emotions as deep as possible. I just wanted to escape. Where? I didn't know. I was just restless, irritable, and discontented.

My dad asked what I had planned for the upcoming racing season. I had no resumes out, and I had not so much as looked at my bike since the previous November. I paused for a second and then looked at my parents and said, "To hell with it. I don't want to race anymore. I just want to go hang out with my friends and be a normal kid."

Silence followed my declaration. What had I said? Did I even mean it? Heck, I didn't know what I wanted. I just didn't want to be broken anymore!

That spring my metalwork teacher convinced me to try out for our school's rugby team. Rugby was one sport I didn't know a lot about. I knew it was a physical game though, and I liked that aspect of it. Mr. Robinson was convinced that I was the "hooker" his team needed.

The sport turned out to be invigorating and a lot of fun. We got to travel throughout the valley and into Vancouver to compete. One of our last games of the season was in Abbottsford. I drove there and took a few of the boys with me. After the game we decided to grab a case of beer and head back to Chilliwack.

After driving around town and pounding through the first case, we decided it was time to get some more. After a quick stop at the Royal Hotel, we went up to a house on Little Mountain that we had been working on in our construction class. That is where things went sideways big time!

We were smart enough to know that driving around town at age seventeen almost completely hammered wasn't a good idea, but that is where our intelligence ended. It was a clear, picture-perfect, moonlit night. We grabbed our beer and started climbing around in the house, which was just beyond the framing stage. One of the guys said he was heading out back for a piss break.

Some time went by, and he never returned. We called his name, with no response. We headed into the backyard to look for him. Nothing. The house backed onto to the Anglican Odd Fellows Cemetery. As we headed up that dark, damp, eerie, piercingly silent hillside, I hesitated. Even though I had no idea how bad that situation was about to become, I had some serious reservations. Then our lost mate screamed out from the top of the hillside, appearing only as a silhouette standing stoically beside a massive tombstone. When we reached him, we all gathered our breath and our thoughts. Thoughts? Four grade twelve boys almost a dozen beer later in the middle of the night in a cemetery thinking? Clearly, we were not!

I'm not sure who did what first, but I remember our lost mate on his hands and knees reading a tombstone when one of the others pushed the massive ten-footer over. Are you kidding me! Did that just happen? Topping it off, it almost landed right on my friend. That thing was so heavy, it must have sunk a foot into the ground. After seeing that I headed up to the top of the cemetery, where an old oak tree was, and sat beside it. Down below the guys carried on making a mess. How did something so innocent go so haywire so quickly?

The next thing I did is something that I didn't do often (because of my Sunday School incident): I prayed. I knew what they were doing was wrong on so many levels, and I wanted it to end. I looked up at the moon and said, "God, if you're out there, please see to it that we don't get away with this." I may have been a lot of things at that time, but every shred of moral fibre I was raised with wanted to make it right.

Within moments of me uttering that prayer, a set of headlights turned into the cemetery parking lot. Someone got out with a flashlight and walked around for what seemed like an eternity. Then he walked over to where my car was parked. (I was driving my mom's Toyota Corolla that night.) Once there, he took down the licence plate number. My teammates were also in hiding while that was happening. The entire time, I sensed we were about to be in more trouble than we had ever experienced in our lives.

When the vehicle drove away, we made our way back to my car and drove home. I don't remember much about the next day at school. I was pretty hungover and feeling raw inside about what had happened. I consoled myself with the fact that I didn't do any damage to the cemetery property. It was the others who had acted so stupidly. In my heart, I knew that to be true. I was a motocross racer who had been nominated for that town's athlete of the year just two years earlier. I wasn't a vandal or a grave robber.

Around 6:00 p.m. that night, there was a knock at our door. It was the police. They wanted to talk to the owner of the orange Toyota Corolla that had been in the vicinity of the Anglican cemetery the night before. My dad told the officer that he owned the car, but I had been driving it.

"Son, would you please go get me your boots," the officer said.

I went to the bottom of our basement stairs and came back with my dad's shoes. I didn't even get a chance to present them to the officer before my dad bellowed, "What the hell are you doing? Those are my shoes." I guess there were boot marks everywhere at the cemetery on the over forty gravestones that got overturned or kicked over. Once I got the officer the shoes I was wearing, I thought that maybe I didn't have to worry after all, because I had not participated in the vandalism. Once he took my shoes, the officer asked me about a 1,500-pound cross that was missing from the cemetery. Now I was confused. We didn't take it, I swear. I will give my dad credit on that one. He looked at the cop and said, "A fifteen-hundred-pound cross in that thing?" He pointed at the Corolla. The officer acknowledged that it would be highly unlikely that we could have got it in there.

The Crown put their case together, and it was decided that we be raised to adult court. Being just a month away from my eighteenth birthday, and given the nature of the crime, it didn't surprise me. The lawyer my mom had worked for in Chilliwack before moving to New West represented me, though he warned me before our first court date that the Crown was looking to make examples of us. Over the years, lots of incidents had occurred at that cemetery, so much so that the person who came up that night to check on us was the groundskeeper doing a random check.

When our case was heard, the courtroom was full. I was able to take the stand in my own defence and told it exactly the way it happened. I spoke on my behalf only. When asked what I saw in regard to the others, I said little, noting that it was dark, and I was drunk.

When we returned to the courthouse for sentencing, my lawyer gave me a heads-up that we were all going to be punished equally. I was disappointed. I didn't want a criminal record at seventeen years of age. I didn't think I had done anything to warrant that.

When the judge read the sentences, I was last. Maybe it was an alphabetical thing. I can recall the judge's verdict verbatim. I don't know how he was able to read it in its entirety while looking me in the eye. "Mr. Worrall, I find you guilty of willful damage over five thousand dollars. Even though you and your colleagues have sworn in court that you didn't participate in any acts of vandalism, I find you equally guilty as charged. Your engineering of that entire trip facilitating the damages incurred makes you the accessory that instigated that entire debacle."

The courtroom was silent. I couldn't argue a word the judge said. He was right; I was guilty and had hopefully learned a valuable life lesson. Then he read out the punishment. "I order you to pay restitution of five thousand dollars to repair the damaged headstones. You will also be required to do a hundred and fifty hours of community service at the Anglican Odd Fellows Cemetery. After that you will report to a parole officer for one year."

Even though I believed the punishment fit the crime, working the first five weeks of that summer vacation digging graves with a shovel was one of the most humbling things I have ever had to do. I didn't mess around and took what I was doing seriously. I got along well with the groundskeeper and the others with whom I had to work. But where was I headed? The headlines of our town's newspaper, which had only ever boasted about my accomplishments, now had a front-page spread that read "Graveyard Vandals Sentenced." Because we were sentenced in adult court, the article was accompanied with our names and photos. Everywhere I went—my neighbourhood, the shopping mall, school, wherever—I got the gears from those who had read the news. I know I deserved it, but it didn't make it any easier. How had I gone from hero to zero so quickly? What was next? Would life get better or worse?

13

Forging the Weapon of Destruction

As my final year of high school wound down, most of my fellow students were focused on the upcoming graduation ceremony. Even though my marks were good, I wasn't too excited about grad. I still felt like a loser due to the cemetery incident. I also knew that soon after graduation I would be on that mountainside putting in my time digging graves. I was also still not over my decision to end my relationship with Andrea. Making things worse, I caught wind that she had a new boyfriend. Why had I been so stupid? Did I still have a chance? I had so many questions for which I had no answers. I'm embarrassed to admit it, but sometimes I prayed that the SOB who was dating Andrea would die.

I attended the graduation ceremony at my high school, but I left as soon as I got my diploma. My parents didn't attend, nor did anyone else from my family. I was okay with that. I just wanted that chapter of my life closed.

I also went to the after-grad party. It was down at Island 22 on Fairfield Island, not far from my home, at the same spot where I had been riding my dirt bikes for years. I headed out there with my friend, Ken, who was also graduating. Yes, the same Ken with whom I had traveled to many hockey games. He had come back to school at age twenty-three. Even though I never got ID'd or carded, I liked hanging out with the older crowd. It seemed like there was less drama and hassle. The way I have lived my life may contradict it, but I have always hated drama. Ken was a good dude, and we partied a lot together. Was I just making up for lost time, or was my genetic predisposition for alcoholism already shifting up a gear or two?

Our beer of choice was O'Keefe's Extra Old Stock. We called it "high test," because it was 5.65 percent alcohol. As some of my American friends say, Canadian beer is pure moonshine. I was about four or five beers in as we headed out to the after-grad party. It was a pretty safe venue, and most parents seemed to know what was going on. I don't think mine did, but that's only because I never saw them much anymore. My mom and sister were in New West pretty much full time by then, and my dad was usually away in a logging camp. But even if things were different, I probably wouldn't have told them anyway. I knew there would be booze there and plenty of it. I liked that, but I also knew my parents didn't approve of drinking. It seemed that no one approved of my drinking from day one, no one except for the committee of demons in my head.

Several cars lined both sides of the gravel road on the way to the party site. We had to park and walk for a ways. We had not walked far when I pointed at something in the distance. Not realizing we had just approached a cattle guard, I tripped and fell onto it face first. Everything went black for a moment. I didn't lose consciousness, but it was close! I collected myself, got up, and dusted myself off. My foot had slipped on the first bar, and my face was the first thing to hit the last one. My lip felt like a soccer ball, but other than that, I was okay, or so I thought.

Ken looked at me and started laughing. He wouldn't stop! I started laughing too. What was so funny? Yes, I had fallen, but there was a problem. After finally wiping the tears of laughter away, Ken said, "Brent, your two front teeth are gone." That's when I stopped laughing. As quickly as I could, I looked at my face in a vehicle's side mirror. Sure enough, my two front teeth were broken off just below the gum line. Damn, I was starting to look as ugly on the outside as I felt on the inside.

I dusted myself off, and we carried on to the party. I don't remember a lot about that night, but here is what I do remember. The army camp at CFB Chilliwack had lent our grad class some massive tents for shelter. We also had a grad car that our class had purchased. Tons of people were at the party. I recognized most of them, but I was never fussy about who I drank with.

Early into the night, I fell dangerously close to the fire. While lying there on the ground, I passed out. Some of my friends, noting that my face was starting to turn a few different shades of red from the heat, moved me into one of the large tents to sleep off my drunkenness.

At around 2:30 a.m. I awoke as I was being dragged out of the tent feet first. The tent was on fire, and someone was pulling me to safety. I remember looking up, regaining focus, knowing full well how lucky I was, but I don't remember driving home or anything else after that.

The next day at around 4:00 p.m., the police were at my doorstep. Someone had mentioned my name as the guy who was pulled out of the burning tent. In addition, throughout the night, all the army's tents had been torched, along with our grad car. I didn't have any of the answers the police were looking for. All I cared about was getting back to bed to execute that banger of a hangover that had every fibre of my body scratching life's chalkboard.

When I arrived at the cemetery to do my first day of community service, the greenskeeper, who I knew from court and had seen around town, greeted me. Then he introduced me to the two guys who worked there on yard maintenance full time. Before he showed me around, he told me that the others were going to be starting their hours the following day. Then he asked me why I wasn't going to the funeral. I didn't know what he was talking about. He informed me that one of my mates from elementary school had perished the previous week on a motorcycle. I took the memo (figuratively) and headed for the funeral.

The next day marked my first official day of work service, which saw my fellow guilty cronies and me cutting grass and digging graves with a shovel every weekday for a month straight. It was incredibly hard physically, because the holes had to be a full six feet deep. We also had to insulate the hole with a solid concrete liner to house the casket. It was messed up. I was eighteen and had better things to do, such as finding a real job, because my dreams of becoming a world motocross champion were fading quickly. In fact, the only time I even thought about motocross was when someone brought it up. That was almost every time I ran into someone, because that's who I had become, Brent Worrall, motocross racer. I was starting to despise running into people, because I didn't want to confront the topic at all.

I completed my work service and was commended for my efforts. I have never been afraid of hard work. Busting my hump as hard as I could was my way of showing that I genuinely felt bad about my part in what had happened.

When that was complete, my dad's mom, my Grandma Pearl, took Kelly and me to England for three weeks. She had retired, and that was her dream, to take us grandkids back to the homeland. I had never been there, and it was a good time for me to get away and connect with my heritage. Still eighteen, I was under the UK's legal drinking age, but that didn't stop me. I filled my gullet as often as I could to numb the constant dialogue of negativity from the committee in my head.

Landing at Heathrow Airport was pretty surreal. When we cleared customs, screaming fans were everywhere. What for, us? I knew better; something else had to be up. I continued to walk casually with Kelly beside me. When we finally reached all the people, it got worse. I turned to the right to check for my sis, and there he was, Mr. Karma Chameleon himself, Boy George. Yikes! I certainly wasn't a fan (at least not that I will admit), but man, there had to be 1,000 people there in one of the busiest airports in the world to greet him.

We stayed up in Manchester with my cousin, Peter, for the first week. When we got out to the car garage, he pointed to an Austin Mini. Once he opened what he called the "boot," we got everything in. Then I proceeded to what I thought was the passenger door. Pete looked at me and then threw me the keys. I caught them but was perplexed.

"You're driving, right?" he said.

"No," I replied instantly.

He laughed. "Well, I guess you need to get in the other side then."

Of course, it was jolly ol' England, and unlike our country, the driver's seat is on the right side of the car.

It was a fair hike up to Manchester from Heathrow. I was impressed with how quickly the traffic moved. The vehicles were notably smaller and seemed to move even faster. The architecture was strikingly intricate and ornate. The other thing that caught my eye was how closely together everything was built, which was done to keep the arable land free for agricultural use in the highly populated country. With my motocross racing, we certainly travelled a lot. When doing so, I never felt like a tourist. On that trip I sure did though, and I liked it.

Sports buff that I am, I soon discovered that England was all about soccer and cricket. I knew nothing about cricket, but it was all over the news, because England was in the midst of a battle with the West Indies. I had followed the Vancouver Whitecaps at home, because they had won the Soccer Bowl in 1979.

In the same manner that I went on my own to Canuck games, I did the same with the Whitecaps. It was summer, so the English Premier League had no games scheduled though.

Once settled at Pete's house in Manchester, I asked if he would take me to Old Trafford, the stadium that the Manchester United Soccer Club called home.

Upon arrival, in the same manner that I ogled pretty much every other major professional sports facility, I was spellbound. After touring the grounds and even standing in the fabled "Stretford End," our final stop was the souvenir shop. I love sports memorabilia, and the shop was kind of like the North Pole for Manchester United fans. I had about $500 to spend on that three-week trip, and I easily dropped half of it in there.

While at the shop, we found out that Man United was playing an exhibition game against the Dutch squad Ajax from Amsterdam in two days' time. We quickly grabbed a couple of tickets.

As we were about to leave the souvenir shop with likely the biggest smile on my face in a long time, I opened the door and allowed a gentleman who had just reached for the door handle to enter. He smiled and thanked me with typical British pomp and circumstance. I was out the door and excited to go back to sort through my new collectible treasures when Pete, trying to keep pace, abruptly said, "Stop! We have to go back in the store."

"Why?" I asked.

He looked at me. "Do you know who Bobby Charlton is?"

I had no idea who Bobby Charlton was. Pete quickly told me that he was on England's last World Cup-winning team in 1966 (the year I was born). Are you kidding me? There I was standing face to smiling face with a soccer legend.

Before he could move on, I asked Charlton if he would sign something for me. I reached into one of my bags and pulled out the 1966 World Cup team photo that I had purchased just moments before. I didn't think it was possible, but producing that photo, made Charlton's smile even bigger. He proudly signed it and shook my hand. That man, who survived a plane crash in 1958 in Munich, which claimed twenty-three lives, including eight of his Manchester United teammates, was now certainly on my radar! Sir Bobby Charlton was knighted in 1994.

The game we attended at Old Trafford ended in a 2–2 draw. The game was fun, but meeting England's soccer hero Bobby Charlton and experiencing his genuine value for average people like me left a lasting mark.

After a week in Manchester, we headed back down to the Berkshire Valley—Redding, England, to be exact, which is where my father was born. My grandmother's other nephew, Chris, lived there with his wife and three kids.

That part of my vacation proved to be quite different, because I had a two-week British Rail pass. I could go anywhere I wanted for two weeks. Heck, I could have bombed all the way up to Scotland if I felt like it.

It was fun to get to know Chris, who is my dad's cousin, and his family. Within a few days of touring Redding and other historic sites, including Windsor Castle, I was getting restless. I wanted to do my own thing. On one occasion I took the train into London. Wow, what an incredible experience. The Thames River, Big Ben, Paddington Station, Trafalgar Square, and of course, Wembley Stadium. On that first day, I did a quick reconnaissance trip around Wembley. I found out when the stadium tours were and then took the train back into London the following day. It was about a one-hour trip from Redding.

Touring Wembley was incredible. The most exciting part was running out of the tunnel and onto the pitch at the end of the tour. They had ambient music blasting as well as simulated crowd noise from a hypothetical crowd of 100,000 people. But that wasn't all. The tour ended with a march up the stairs to a hypothetical congratulatory meeting with the queen. They certainly knew how to do pomp and circumstance. I wonder if Evel Knievel had had the gearing right and not hit the last London bus there in 1975, he would have been able to meet the queen. If so, being the gentleman and scholar that he was, he likely would have wished her happy landings.

By now you may have figured out that I'm an "all-in" or "all-out" kind of guy. There are no half measures for this cowboy. On that note, now that soccer was in my blood, I wanted to play. I used to knock around the ball quite a bit, but I never played anything organized. Chris and I went out a few times while I was there. My leg was still not 100 percent (it never was again), and it hurt when I kicked the ball with my right foot. Then I thought I should try goalkeeping. I loved it. I could lunge, dive, scramble, flail, you name it. When I had to kick the ball out, I used my left foot. That wasn't a problem, because I had been pretty much ambidextrous my entire life.

After one knockaround session not far from Chris's house, we went to a pub. It was a typical English establishment that resembled someone's residence more than a pub. After pounding back a few pints of lager, I struck up a conversation with the bartender about soccer. He was knowledgeable and informative. His name was Bill Mowbray, and I believe he owned the pub. I told him that I was from Vancouver and attended Vancouver Whitecaps games regularly.

"I guess you know Bobby Lenarduzzi then," he said.

Of course, I knew who he was. Lenarduzzi was pretty much the most recognizable Whitecaps player. Bill told me that Bobby used to stay with him when he played in Redding. I had no idea.

Bill went back into a room and came out with a handful of T-shirts and things. He put half the pile on one side of my beer and the other pile on the other. "When you get back to Vancouver, give these to Bobby, and tell him Bill says Hi." I was starting to like that country. I no longer felt like a tourist.

The three weeks in England flew by. Before I knew it, I was back home in Chilliwack. What a great experience. I will be eternally grateful to my grandmother for making it happen. Sadly, she became ill a few years later and passed away in 1987.

Now that I had no plans for school, what was next? I had no idea what I wanted to do in life. I loved sports, but I didn't want to even go near a motocross bike, so I knew I needed to find a real job. I continued on at the Pizza Factory, but I was hunting for more. First, however, I had to get to a Vancouver Whitecaps game to introduce myself to Bob Lenarduzzi, and give him the things that Bill had asked me to pass on to him.

I headed into BC Place well before game time. After finding out where the players parked and entered the building, I waited there armed with everything that Bill had given me as well as something else. The year before, the 7-11 stores sold collectors' trading cards of the Whitecaps players. I had collected them all. (I've been a card collector for almost my entire life.) I thought it would be cool if Bobby and the other players could sign them.

When Bobby showed up, I introduced myself and told him how I came to be there to meet him. He had a huge smile on his face, impressed that in a country of millions, I ended up meeting a man who had played a role in his soccer development. He didn't spend a lot of time with me but told me to meet him in that spot half an hour after the game.

As I sat and watched the game sipping a glass of beer, I thought, *I'm going to make my fortune in collecting trading cards and sports memorabilia.* The thought made perfect sense. There I was at a professional sporting event and getting a good glow on. I loved the feeling. It was conviviality at its finest. Nothing hurt, my body was relatively healed, and I just wanted anything but to be broken again. Bobby followed through on his promise, and it felt good to make a connection with him, which started in England.

Back at home in the Clare Avenue neighbourhood, I had a group of good friends with whom I often played ball hockey. They included Jeff Long, Lance Price, Steve Sache, Chris Neufeld, and David Archibald. David was an up-and-coming Western Hockey League prodigy who was heading into his first full season, at age fifteen, with the Portland Winter Hawks. He had aspirations of playing in the NHL, which he eventually did.

Roller blades had not come out yet, but the Winter Hawks had a line on some of the first ones ever made. I got a set through David. I loved them, and I skated on them everywhere. When I say everywhere, I mean miles and miles and miles. I loved to skate; it was one of the greatest endorphin releases I had.

That fall I decided that I was going to give hockey a serious go. I was never a superstar wherever I played, but I was a good skater and had a hard, accurate shot. Every league I played in, I seemed to have a knack for scoring goals. With no Junior A team in Chilliwack—the Colts had folded—I decided to go to the Merritt Centennials/Kamloops Blazers joint training camp as a walk-on. I had no idea what to expect, but I seriously thought I could make the team. I had extended family in Merritt with an open invitation to winter there, if needed.

The first thing that brings a smile to my face when thinking about that ordeal was that I couldn't believe I was on the same sheet of ice with Coach Ken Hitchcock. Not just with him, but also the likes of the high-flying Blazers. Greg Evtushevski, Rob Brown, Gordie Mark, Darryl Reaugh, Greg Hawgood, and Robin Bawa were some of the top Blazers that season. Kevin Mitchell, you will be happy to know that our own hometown Vernon Vipers current and successful coach, Mark Ferner, was also a Blazer that year.

On one occasion, I went over to Brown and ask him a question about his quick release or something. I was an eighteen-year-old at that camp and could see he had some serious talent. As brief as it was, that was a cool moment. He posted 173 and 212 points in his final two seasons in Kamloops. He was also a gold medal winner with Canada's 1988 World Junior team. The year also saw Rob Brown finish fifth in the NHL's scoring race with 115 points as a member of the Pittsburgh Penguins as Mario Lemieux's line mate.

Everything on the ice happened quicker than I had experienced. It was so cool to experience such top-level energy and enthusiasm. In my heart, I knew I had no chance at being a Blazer that year but knew the Cents were interested in me.

I ended up on the Merritt Centennials final trading camp roster along with thirty-nine other players. Over the next few sessions, I gave it everything I had. I was always watching out of the corner of my eye to see if Coach Chuck Tapp and his assistants were taking notice. They were a typical coaching staff—sweat suit, clipboards, and spectacles. I didn't know what they were looking for. Only ten players were returning from the previous year, so I figured I had a good chance of landing a spot. They included the likes of Pat Ryan and Rick Boyd. Also in this camp was my good friend and Chilliwack Minor Hockey Rep team, teammate goalie Todd Rutledge.

With a few days left in camp, we hit the ice for our first full red-and-white scrimmage with coaches on the bench, the whole bit. Midway through the second period, Chuck tapped me on the left shoulder. "Do you see that guy?" he asked, a serious look in his eye.

"Yes," I replied.

"Go out there and find out how tough he is."

I had seen that movie before. I knew he didn't want to know how tough the big, burly defenceman from Hope, BC, was. He wanted to know how tough I was.

I knew how tough the kid from Hope was. We played them often in minor hockey. He was a gorilla who had hit me many times. On one occasion we ended up in a bench-clearing brawl, which ended with parents slugging it out in the stands. Damn, I wish my dad had been at that game. Our team bus ended up needing a police escort out of town.

I got on the ice figuring for sure I'd be dropping my gloves with that guy. The puck was dumped into the corner of their end and straight to the guy who coach Tapp wanted me to take on. I was about half a dozen long, hard strides away from him. I hit the afterburners to get in a good solid hit before he could get rid of the puck. He saw me coming and kept his head up. I knew I wasn't supposed to, but due to his huge size advantage, just before impact, I began to leave my feet and braced myself. Sensing the hit, he pirouetted to his left to avoid it. Too late! I was committed. By the time I made contact, it was with the back of his shoulder, and I unceremoniously drove him headfirst into the boards. That wasn't my intent; I just wanted to hit him fair and square as hard as I could.

When I landed on top of him, I felt like I had just hit a cement truck. I sprang to my feet and awaited what was next. The whistle had already gone, and I was ready, holding my gloves at my fingertips, ready to drop them. Things seemed to take forever. Finally, after seeing my foe reeling from what I believe was the biggest hit up to that point in training camp, (for me anyway), I skated away.

During the next shift, it didn't take long for me to find someone else to mix it up with. I didn't fight very often when I was young and usually only when I was drunk. Hockey was different though; fighting was an accepted part of the game. I never got hurt playing hockey other than a few concussions, but back then, what even were concussions anyway? I did have some dental work done though, as my capped teeth had broken out of my mouth twice on the ice. No, we didn't wear mouth guards, either.

That final tussle ended up being a glorified wrestling match. I grabbed my combatants jersey and yanked him in tight for all I was worth. I always felt safe inside and put up with the blows that he landed. We ended up on the ice, and I was on the bottom.

When I got to my feet, everything was silent. No heavy breathing, just two teenagers, completely breathless. I skated back to the bench and sat down. Coach Tapp came over and asked how I was.

"Not that good," I said. He seemed puzzled, because I had handled myself well. But it wasn't that at all; it was my right leg. When we landed in a pile, it got twisted badly, and I felt a horrible pop. I'm not sure why, but I didn't notice the pain immediately. I was probably too fuelled with adrenaline from trying to fight my way onto that Junior A hockey team. After telling Coach Tapp what the deal was, he gave me the key to the dressing room. I was devastated. This was it, my damn bum leg was going to cost me my Junior hockey dream.

I sat in the dressing room and slowly and methodically took off my gear. When I got to my right skate, the door opened. It was Coach Tapp. He wanted to know what it looked like and how I felt. I explained that I had broken it five times previously and that it was just tender. I also told him that if I iced it that night, I would be good for the final scrimmage the next day.

He left the room and came back with a trainer, who went through some range-of-motion tests as I gave him the history of my leg. He didn't say much and wasn't with me long. The scrimmage was still going on, and he headed back to the bench.

Just as I finished getting dressed, Coach Tapp returned. I figured he was just going to thank me for coming out and wish me luck in the future. What else could he do? What happened next was a miracle of sorts. Coach Tapp looked at me and said, "Head home, rest up, and report back to the Nicola Valley Arena in two weeks' time." I was so happy that I could have leapt to the moon. I had made the Merritt Centennials team and was going to be a Junior A hockey player. *Move over, Happy Gilmore,* I thought. *I'm coming for your records, bro!*

Upon returning home from camp, one of my friends made me an offer on my pickup. The truck was great, and I loved it from day one. It was pretty reliable for a 1967, but I needed something more fuel efficient. I had been driving my dad's Toyota Corolla most days, anyway. I sold the truck and then purchased the Toyota Corolla off my dad. That car could go for a week on $5 of fuel. I had no plans to ride a dirt bike anytime soon, so in my mind, it made perfect sense.

I had been home a week, and my ankle was still sore and huge. I had it X-rayed but was still waiting to hear from my doctor. That Friday I got a call from the Canada Employment office. We had a family friend there, Judy Douglas, who was now married to Sam, my dad's best friend. A Canada Works grant job was available in the bush up in the Chilliwack Lake area building trails and campsites. It wasn't a full-time job, but it was six months guaranteed, and the pay was good. Now I had a huge quandary. I really wanted to go to Merritt and give hockey an honest go. However, the other part of me that was enjoying an unregimented partying lifestyle knew that money was the fuel I needed to keep me in action. The job was starting in a couple of weeks, and if I didn't make an immediate decision, it would go to someone else. I took the job and didn't go back to Merritt. I never bothered to even contact the organization. I'm sure they got over it quicker than I did, but that is one example of how my morals and accountability were deteriorating. Knowing what I know now, I wish I had chosen differently.

I was invited to try out for one the better teams in our men's recreational hockey league (a.k.a. beer league). Called Ponderosa, they were sponsored by a local car lot. Our team was a charismatic mix of characters. Most of them had played top-level hockey at some point. I fit in well and, at age eighteen, brought some youthful energy to the team. Our coach was a goaltender who was out of action, because he had been hurt in a car accident. He did a good job.

I still laugh at one of things that happened at a game at the Vedder Twin Rinks. We had just finished the first period, and my mom was there watching, standing at the north end just outside our dressing room. As we walked to the dressing room, I stopped to talk to her while the rest of the team continued into the room. When I went into the dressing room, the coach came over and said, "What'd that lady want?" I didn't know what the heck he was talking about.

"Nothing," I said. "That's my mom."

Finally, some colour returned to his face. He had recognized her from court or the law firm where she had worked previously. He thought they had sent her to the game to spy on him. We all had a good laugh at his expense.

One of my good friends, Darcy (one of the two Frey twins), also played on that team with me at times. He was a tall, strong skater with whom I had played most of my minor hockey. When we were on the same line, I always knew where the open ice was. Darcy was a great playmaker and, more times than not, put the biscuit where I could bury it. Darcy and I, along with his brother, Dale, had been pretty tight in high school. Now that it was over, and I was no longer chasing racing, we had lots of time to get into trouble. That was never the intention, but unfortunately, it was the reality I would endure for the next few years.

That fall, much like we had done many times before, Darcy and I headed to Vancouver for a BC Lions game. These road trips always required booze. We had a six-pack in the front to drink on the way there, and another dozen in the trunk. The plan was to get to the case in the trunk once we reached the stadium parking lot. Darcy was driving a 1976 Mercury Bobcat, almost identical to the Ford Pinto from that year. Those cars were nicknamed the "Molotov Cocktail," because many of them had exploded when rear-ended. The gas tank was in the rear of the car right below the rear bumper. As many as 180 people died due to that issue.

We had just passed Abbottsford on what was usually a one-hour drive into BC Place. I was in the passenger seat and well into my second beer when I noticed Darcy stretch his neck to get a good long look in his rearview mirror.

"What's that loser doing?" he asked. Before I had a chance to react, there was a huge bang and a crash. My head and neck snapped back against the headrest. I became dizzy but maintained consciousness. We were doing the speed limit of fifty-five miles an hour and had been rear-ended by a pickup truck.

When we got out to survey the damage, we couldn't believe our eyes. The truck that had hit us had a large steel winch on the front. The winch had impaled the trunk of Darcy's car, buckling it in. Worse, the winch had scraped right across the top of the car's gas tank, exposing it. We looked at each other, realizing how lucky we were that that car hadn't exploded. It turns out the driver of the pickup had fallen asleep at the wheel, though he claimed in his statement that we had deliberately slammed on our brakes to try to cause the accident! What were we to do?

We were drinking and had just been hit on the Trans-Canada Highway. Then the driver of the pickup left the scene, but Darcy got his licence plate number while I salvaged our case of beer from the trunk. The case was a little mangled, but none of the bottles were broken. Darcy and I decided to hide the beer in the ditch, head to the police station, report the accident, then go back and get our beer and continue on to the football game. It seemed like a good idea at the time.

Like a well-oiled machine, our plan went off without a hitch. We reported the accident, then went back to retrieve our hidden treasure and proceeded to the game, refreshments in hand. Darcy had to go to court, but the other driver was deemed 100 percent at fault. As for the Lions, they ended up winning the game. I wasn't worried about or wanting to win anything. That was kind of strange at first, but I didn't give it much thought. All I cared about was blocking out the turmoil of my life by getting to know my newest friend, John Barleycorn, a whole lot better.

14

Crossing the Invisible Line

The 1984/1985 hockey season saw the Edmonton Oilers back up their first Stanley Cup championship with another title. Also hitting the ice for the first time was a soon-to-be phenom out of the Quebec Major Junior League, Mario Lemieux. As for me, I was happy to settle for beer-league glory. Even though most game nights included me departing the dressing room with a belly full of beer, it was a lot of fun. Having fun has always been a key variable in my life. However, fun was fleeing faster than I could break bones. Weekends pretty much became a blur with hockey, partying, and trying to hold onto my job delivering pizzas. It was good money, and I got paid daily. It also afforded me the freedom to scope out the Chilliwack party scene. I was doing my best to make up for lost ground in that regard.

Gerry, a friend I had gone to school and played rugby with, worked at another pizza place called Minos right across the street. When out delivering on weekends, we often checked in with each other for a little beer break. It seems insane now for me to be driving around to all hours of the morning delivering pizza while getting a glow on. I never worried about the police though, because my Toyota Corolla always smelled more like the Pizza Factory than a brewery.

Things were starting to get a bit out of control though. One night after our shift, at 3:00 a.m., we decided, in our infinite wisdom, (likely mine) that a road trip to Seattle was in order. I hopped in the passenger seat of Gerry's car, and off we went to the Sumas border crossing. We had decided that when we got to the border, we would tell the officials that we were headed to Mt. Baker to go skiing.

When we pulled up, no one else was in line. Had I not remembered what happened just two years back at the Minnesota crossing? It was another perfect example of how I was developing a flare to defy authority. I don't remember what the questions were, but I knew immediately there was no way we were getting into the US. The final thing the border guard said before he sent us inside to be searched was, "If you're going skiing, where's your ski gear?"

"We're going to rent skis," I said. That seemed to piss him off even more. I should have kept my damn mouth shut.

The next room we got shuffled into felt like a weigh station of sorts. Gerry looked at me and said, "Now what?" When he found out the next phase entailed a full-body search, he started to change colour.

Gerry was a big guy with an easygoing demeanour. However, when he lost it, he freaking lost it. He was like the Incredible Hulk in that manner. I had seen him like that on one occasion. I started to worry that things would get out of hand and we would end up locked up for a long time. The officer told us that if we were going to proceed into the US, we had to consent to a strip search and provide him with someone he could call to come and pick us up. We were in no shape to be driving. In that moment of seeming insanity, I think the customs official knew what our response would be. Would he actually let us turn around and head back to where we came from in the condition we were in?

I had given him Rick Albee's name as a contact. (I had raced bikes and stayed with Rick in Bellingham years earlier.) He wanted Rick's address and phone number. I had nothing and was starting to get wigged out from the bright fluorescent lighting.

The officer looked at Gerry and said, "You obviously haven't had as much to drink as your friend." As messed up and hurting inside as I was, that comment brings a twisted smile to my face. If I had $100 for every time I heard an officer say that about me throughout my drinking career, I'd have enough money to replace my Wayne Gretzky rookie card. The officer told us to head home and not to attempt to cross the border again within the next twenty-four hours. I know by today's post-9/11 standards, that might seem like a bit of a stretch, but that was our experience, foolish eighteen-year-olds that we were. I hope everything is going well, Gerry, and thanks for looking after me when I was too drunk to do so myself.

It amazes me that, considering all that I've put my body and brain through, I can still retain most of what happened. Soon there would come a time though where if I wasn't blacking out, my psyche was starting to block things out in the name of self-preservation.

Toward the end of the hockey season that year, our team had a big dance to raise money at Chilliwack's iconic Evergreen Hall. I sold my share of tickets and was excited about the event. When I say these were big parties at the Evergreen Hall, they were huge. It's also imperative to add that my new best friend's name was Bacardi (white rum). I was jealous as hell; he certainly had a way cooler name than I did.

On that note, soon I began judging myself according to my peers' approval. Why not? I had always gained positive comments and interactions even with people I didn't know from my motocross racing success. Things were quickly changing, so much so that when I showed up at the party, the first thing one of my teammates said was, "There's the liquor pig." I took it as a compliment.

I was pretty blitzed at that dance early in the night. I had not taken a date or anything and was there for one reason only: to get bombed. I remember calling the Pizza Factory and ordering pizza to be delivered. After that my memory fast-forwards to driving much later that night down Yale Road right in front of where O'Connor Chrysler was located. I was headed southbound and doing a poor job of staying between the yellow line and the sidewalk. I knew I had to get home, some five kilometres away.

I woke up the next day in my bed. That was the first time that I remember waking up afraid—afraid of what I had done the night before and how I had gotten home. I couldn't remember that part at all. Finally, I mustered enough strength to convince my badly vibrating body and brain to look out my bedroom window. It put a smile on my face, because the driveway was empty. That meant I had at least had the sense not to drive home. No sooner had I done that than I rolled my head a little bit to the left. I was dumfounded. There it was, parked right in the middle of our front yard beneath our two cherry trees, the Corolla. In that moment I knew I had a big problem.

The spring of 1985 saw Rick Hansen set out on his Man In Motion world tour. Over the next twenty-six months, Rick circumnavigated the globe, wheeling over 40,000 kilometres through 34 countries. His goal was to raise awareness about the potential of people with spinal cord injuries. Rick's goal wasn't just to create awareness but also to make a difference in their quality of life through accessible and inclusive communities. I should also mention that we had a new prime minister in Brian Mulroney. He was elected the eighteenth prime minister of Canada in September 1984 and served as our country's leader until 1993.

Now that hockey season was winding down, I began to wonder what was next, employment-wise. The Canada Works job had come to an end, and I was starting to become somewhat unreliable at the Pizza Factory. John always cut me the slack I asked for, but I knew leaving him shorthanded hurt his bottom line. If I didn't show up, he would send his own family members out on delivery. His son, George, who has been one of my best friends since they came from Greece, was one of those unfortunates. George put in countless hours on my behalf when I didn't show up, and I don't even think his dad paid him for it. Nothing against John; he was just old school in the sense that family helped whether they got paid or not. Little things like that, and my increasing unaccountability, saw me fall out of favour with many of my friends. One night I even had the audacity in a drunken stupor to go in to the place I should have been working at and write John a cheque that I knew full well was bad to get money to drink! I didn't return to the Pizza Factory for some time. Finally, my conscience got the better of me, and I went in and paid John and apologized. I can still see his ear-to-ear smile as he cuffed me on the side of the head. John, you are a good man, and I appreciate how you looked out for me.

My Aunt Betty called and told me there was a great job at a sawmill in the Vedder Crossing area called Uneeda Wood Products. I had never heard of the place, but she said it was solid work for great money.

On my first day, I was given a set of earmuffs and a pair of gloves and put behind a re-saw to stack lumber. I thought I did a great job. I kept up to the feed and stacked many of carts of freshly re-sawed timber. I loved the smell of fresh-cut wood, something I got used to in the bush with my dad. But more than anything, I liked the fact that the starting wage was $13.91 an hour. With that kind of money in 1985, I could have sponsored myself to a motocross comeback if I wanted, but motocross was the furthest thing from my mind.

I made a lot of hard-working blue-collar friends at the mill. I was making good money, and I loved the endorphin release from treating my job like a workout. Being a day job, I took that endeavour a lot more seriously than I did driving around getting half-licked while delivering pizzas. The crew at Uneeda was a good bunch, and I got along well with most of them. I also participated in many social activities with the guys and their families, including golf, baseball, and hockey pools. For the most part early on, things couldn't have gone better. I was a hard worker and never missed a shift during my first year. Before taking the job there, I had been completely lost with no real direction or ambition.

That's the thing with people like me, who from pretty much the time I could walk wanted one thing and one thing only, to be a motocross champion. Take that away or have it removed, and there has to be a legitimate replacement. I realize now that everything I was doing was an effort to recapture what motocross did for me. Sadly, it took me more than twenty-five years to realize that.

Bruce Springsteen's "Born in the USA" was blasting on the radio, and it spoke volumes to my freedom. I had not been into a motorcycle shop for almost two years. One Saturday I was cruising through downtown Chilliwack and was drawn into Champion Cycles (our local Kawasaki dealer) by the shiny, fast, and stealthy look of that year's newest Kawasaki "crotch rocket," the Ninja. I was smitten and had to have one. I picked up my brand-new Ninja that Wednesday. Getting the bank's approval was no problem, because my job and credit were both good. I rode the bike off the lot without even getting a proper licence. I had a driver's licence, and that was good enough for me. I don't even remember my insurance agent bringing it up. Damn, I miss the 1980s.

I was free once again and on two wheels. That thing was fast, and I loved it. I rode it to work every day, and pretty much any free moment I had I was out testing its limits. I had visions of grandeur and saw myself riding it all the way to Florida the following spring for bike week. Some of my friends had street bikes, but the way I rode, I preferred to go solo. I loved putting that thing up on its rear wheel while going through the gears. I knew it was dangerous, but I never felt like I pushed the envelope too hard—until one day on the way home from work.

Still living in my parents' house on Fairfield Island, it was a fair trek out to the mill. Coming home one day, I approached Wolfe Road from the Chilliwack mountain side. Wolfe makes a ninety-degree right turn at the foot of Chilliwack's sewage plant. I had just passed a carload of waving young gals and figured I would show them how fast I could rail the upcoming right hander. I was less than 100 feet from the corner, and the speedometer was still at 160 kilometres per hour. I knew I was going way too fast to make the turn, but I wasn't worried, because the road carried on beyond the turn, although it was gravel. With not much time to think, my front wheel grabbed the gravel and started to skate. Using every bit of my motocross might, muscle, and experience, I grabbed way too much front brake. Down I went, hard. I must have slid on the gravel underneath the fairing shroud with the bike on top of me for thirty feet.

When I finally came to a stop, everything was silent and dark. I sat upright in the eye of the huge dust cloud I had created. Without even looking, I felt blood running from both of my right appendages. The thing I forgot to tell you is that I was wearing a T-shirt and Nike jogging shorts. That's right, shorts. Where was my head at? I'm not even sure if the carload of girls saw me crash. I also knew that had my old man seen me ride that bike with shorts on, he would have kicked my ass.

I collected myself and the parts of the bike that had broken off. The bars were bent, the fairing was toast, and the right signal light and brake lever were broken off. The bike fired up no problem though, and I rode home. I thought maybe I should go straight to the hospital, but I hated that place. Besides, I was worried I would get busted for not having a proper licence. I had broken many bones before and felt I had dodged a bullet with that one. The ride home seemed to take forever. Realizing how bad that crash could have been, to say I was wigged out was an understatement.

Upon arriving home, I knew I had to do one thing and one thing only: sell the crotch rocket before it finished me. The next day at work, one of my colleagues made me an offer, and it was sold. Still wanting a road ride, I purchased a KZ-750 and found it a little more to my liking. Eventually, I hung a "for sale" sign on that bike, too, before I did any more harm to myself.

Home life was pretty much non-existent at that point, and what was left of it was different. I came home one day to find my father sitting in a kitchen chair in front of the oven. Perplexed, I asked him what the heck he was doing.

"Making muffins," he replied. Was that a joke? My dad, who was all bronze and brute, was now baking. Was the world ending, and I had not been notified?

I mentioned that when Roger died, my dad quit drinking. None of us took him seriously on that one, but he did it. I saw a slow transformation as my dad became more and more like an everyday joe who could do whatever he put his mind to. I should have never doubted that he was serious about quitting, because when he made his mind up to do something, he didn't talk about it; he did it.

That was new, and part of me liked it. However, the other part of me that had endured most of the garbage that went with his drinking was stumped. I was wetting my whistle regularly, and my dad was so dry that I feared lighting a match around him. That only seemed to make things more difficult at home between my parents and me. Fortunately for me, or so I thought, if Dad wasn't away in camp, he was in New West staying with my mom and sister at their apartment there.

Nightclub life was also becoming part of my weekly routine. I turned nineteen that June and was finally of age. Let's just say this cool cucumber was well on his way to becoming a pickle. I still loved sports though, and continued to pursue soccer and hockey passionately.

One day while knocking around in the schoolyard with some of my friends, a guy approached me. He had been watching me tend the net. I loved the feeling of stopping seemingly unstoppable shots—long, full lunging airborne dives, you know the kind. I loved challenging the strikers and foiling their attempts. He was a curly-haired guy named Ron, and he was the coach of the Olympic Sports soccer team in the Fraser Valley League. He asked me who I played for, and I told him that I had never played organized ball. Then he told me that his team needed a keeper, and he thought I would be a good fit.

Excited at the prospect, I attended the team's next practice. Before the kick-off of our first game, Ron called us in for a pep talk. At the end of the talk, he said that now they had a goalie who could stop the ball, he felt they could get their first victory of the season. They were zero for four up to that point.

In the first game, I let one in over my head and was mad as hell at myself. I had come a little too far out of the net to charge the forward. About forty feet out, he smiled and chipped the ball over my head into the back of the net. I learned my lesson on that one the hard way. However, that was the only goal they got on me in that game. We ended up in a 1–1 draw. The next game at Cultus Lake on the Soowahlie Reserve was where we got our first victory.

That was the only season I played organized soccer. I lost interest after the original Vancouver Whitecaps folded in 1984, following a ten-year tenure. Professional soccer returned to Vancouver in 1986. That was also the year that Vancouver hosted Expo '86. The mill provided us with three-day passes. Fittingly, the new soccer club was called the 86ers. I attended one game at Swan Guard Stadium, but it was not the same as the original North American Soccer League.

That fall things went well for me at the mill. I loved the work and got along well with my coworkers. In all honesty, though, the thing I liked the most about the job was the money. It allowed me to partake in pretty much anything I chose. I went to games and concerts and spent countless hours and dollars in nightclubs. I wasn't required to pay rent at home, because I was now the house sitter, so to speak.

My dad had a passion for old cars. He bought and sold many over the years. At that time, he had a 1966 Ford Mustang in original mint condition. That car was sweet; it even had an immaculate leather Pony interior. One day he looked at me and said, "I'll sell you that car for forty-five hundred dollars." I bought it in a heartbeat. The car was special to my dad, and I knew it. Today that car would easily fetch $50,000 or more. I loved it and looked after it, just as I had my motorcycles.

Other than the hockey cards, which I was still buying like a madman, knowing they would have huge value one day, I didn't have any other real interests. Sports, sports, and more sports have been and likely always will be the favourite flavour in my life. Even as my morals and health were starting to deteriorate from my somewhat derelict lifestyle, I always found time for sports.

That winter the Frey boys convinced me to come back over to the church hockey league in which they played. The Chilliwack Men's Fellowship League. That proved to be one of the roughest and dirtiest leagues I ever played in as far as cheap shots and stick work went.

Our team was called Martin Stucco, sponsored by our friend, Milne Martin. We had a pretty decent cross-section of players. I was excited to play right wing on the top line with the twins. Thinking back on that season and how out of control our games got at times has me shaking my head. By mid-season we were one of the top teams, and my line mates and I lit the lamp often.

As we geared up for a playoff run, some of the other teams got under our skin. The gloves were off, and suspensions were handed out. I was sitting up in the stands one night (while under suspension for fighting) when I started talking to the guy next to me. He was scouting our team, because we would be playing them in the next round if we won that game. I told him that I played for Martin Stucco. He paused for a minute and then said, "You're dirty number four, aren't you?" I still laugh at that, because in my mind, I was anything but dirty. Unfortunately, my rap sheet and list of suspensions contradicted my self-concept. Our team won that game, so off to the next round we went.

The next game was at Vedder Twin Rinks. Early in the first period, I was parked in front of the net, where I did a lot of my best work, when I got pitch-forked by a stick in the eye. I couldn't see a thing as I skated over to the bench. By that time a full-scale gloves-off brawl was taking place behind me.

Dennis, our trainer, tended to my eye. I could still see somewhat out of my left eye. I was fixated on what was happening on the ice. One of my teammates, Darren, who was a fairly small guy, was getting worked pretty hard. The Freys were also out there holding their own with two of our big defenceman. Seeing our guy get worked like that prompted my teammate, Oly, over the boards. He was a wiry kid with decent height. He could skate like the wind, and had a wicked shot. As soon as he leapt over, I broke away from our trainer to do the same. No sooner had I opened the bench door than our coach tackled me to the floor. They knew it was an imminent suspension if I hit the ice to join the altercation. Through all of this, I was a gentleman with our coach. The boys still laugh recalling me saying, *Let me go out there, Mr. Muth!*

I had no idea how good of a fighter Oly was until he got to the melee and laid a whooping on the biggest guy out there. And let me tell you, that league had some real farm-fed giants. The only saving grace for me out of that game, which we won, was that by not getting on the ice to join the fight, I didn't get suspended for the next round. I did end up needing stitches to close my eyelid gash though. However, with half of our best players suspended for the next game, we wound up losing. I could write an entire chapter on some of the other crazy things that happened that season.

I was dating a girl who I had met through the Frey boys. She had recently split up with her husband. She loved the Mustang, as most people did. In fact, at first I wasn't sure if she was into me or the car. Our relationship was anything but spectacular. Keep in mind that if I wasn't already certifiably insane, it was coming. I was starting to do weird, random, crazy shit. I had no idea why; I just craved chaos and excitement. In fact, the Frey boys used to joke by saying, "Worrall will do it if no one else will. He's crazy." When they said that, it egged me on even more.

One such time was at the Cultus Lake cliffs. The first time I was there, one of the Frey boys said, "Have a look over the edge, and see how far down it is." Without even looking, I leapt. I fell for what seemed like an eternity, so much so that I even had time to wonder why the hell I had just done that. I finally splashed down in the water overeighty feet below, narrowly missing an outcropping of rocks. If you are from the Chilliwack area, you probably know the place

I'm talking about. Was it stupid to jump? Maybe, but not only did I love those guys like brothers, I trusted them. Unfortunately, they trusted me, too, and my craziness almost killed us all more than once!

Before the summer was over, Darcy made me an offer on the Mustang. I didn't want to sell it, but I needed the money. I still had the job at the mill, but my trips to the furnace room at the nightclubs were getting expensive! Part of the deal we made was that I got his Honda Civic. It was pretty hooped, but it ran, and was good on gas. In short course, not only did I regret selling the Mustang to Darcy, but shortly afterwards, he wrote it off when he hit a pole one night on his way home. It was the 1980s, and the best way to sum it up now is that common sense wasn't so common.

Within that same timeframe I had also bought and sold another hot rod to Darcy's brother, Dale. That one was a nice mint Firebird. Once again, I loved the car, but when I needed fuel to feed my habits, I did what I had to do.

Needless to say, my romantic relationship was failing, and living the way I wanted to, being single was an attractive option. The only accountability I wanted in my life was to go to work, so I could continue to afford the "vitamins" that I used to block out the mental and emotional pain. What pain? Trust me, there was a lot. I didn't realize it for many years, but being away from the sport that defined me was killing me.

That fall, we were back on the ice for another hockey season. The church league team (despite my shenanigans) wanted me back. They had added a couple more ringers to our motley crew. We won the first game handily, but the celebration didn't even make it into the dressing room when the referee, Vic Isaac, skated over and gave our coach the news. It read as follows: Worrall, Frey Boys, Olson, Thompson, all suspended from the Men's Fellowship League for the season for what was deemed "dirty play"! What a bummer. We had a great team and knew we could win. What now?

It turns out Vic (who I knew from town) ran a team in the men's recreational league. He told all five of us that we were welcome to play for his team. That's exactly what we did. Little did I realize it would be the last season of organized hockey that I ever play in Chilliwack. One of the lowlights of the season came at a tournament in Hope. We had our own mini-game in our hotel room with a hard puck and lots of liquor, the night before the tournament started. The liquor bottles when finished were stabbed into the walls, along with puck holes in the doors

and walls. Topping it all off, waking in the morning, I shouted "Good Morning
Vietnam, and smashed out the room's window screens. Halfway through our first
morning game, sitting on the bench, I noticed three police officers approaching.
It was literally a scene out of the cult hit, Hockey movie "Slapshot." They called
us by name, and hauled us off to the station in handcuffs. I will never forget the
look on our coach, Vic Isaacs' face as he pleaded to the RCMP, "Where are you
going with half of my team?" Another untimely date with law enforcement.

The nightclub life continued, and it was taking its toll. Seven days a week, I
was always in action somewhere. I was even starting to lose interest in sports, of
all things, not watching, but playing. I was nineteen years old and should have
been feeling strong and confident. Unfortunately, the magical elixir I had found
just a few short years before, alcohol, was starting to turn on me. I know it's a
cliché, but that boomerang effect was serious.

In the early days, alcohol was an escape. Drinking gave me the sense that everything was going to be okay. Under its influence, I could rationalize pretty much
everything, including the many bad choices I was making. I didn't understand
what was happening to my body. It was changing, and I didn't like it.

Oly's brother, Brian, who was also an incredible hockey player in his day,
managed one of the nightclubs that I attended regularly, Earthquake Annie's.
Brian was a great guy, and always treated me well. He knew I had a problem, as I'm
sure most did. Brian looked out for me, and I sure appreciate that. RIP old friend!

One day, he asked me about motocross racing and why I wanted no part of it.
I did my best to explain, but now that I was no longer feeling physically broken
from moto all the time (even though I limped like an SOB, my right leg half an
inch shorter than my left one), it wasn't an easy sell.

Brian asked if I wanted to put together a stunt team and start jumping cars
in the nightclub parking lot. I thought it was a pretty cool idea, and got excited
about it. I still had my 1983 CR 250 parked in the garage, where it had been since
the 1983 Vancouver Supercross. The idea definitely had potential, but I was in
no shape to be risking my life. I was getting to the point where everything I did
outside of work included alcohol. Weekends were beginning to start on Thurs-
days, and they were usually followed up by a call to work on Friday morning,
saying I was sick. Many of those weekends I didn't even sleep. More often than
not, I could be found sitting on the doorstep of the house party I was at in the
wee hours of the morning trying to come down as the sun was coming up. It

was insane. My heart raced uncontrollably. There I was, bad heart valve and all, just looking to stay immersed in the new white lie I had found.

Throughout that winter my condition deteriorated rapidly. I woke up in the morning after trips to the nightclub and found my pockets full of lighters and cigarettes and other strange things. I didn't smoke; I was allergic to cigarettes and hated smoking. What was happening to me? That scared me, because I realized that when I was in that state, I was capable of anything. I had a great upbringing. Why was my good moral fibre failing me in the face of addiction? Was I defective? I was starting to feel that way, but I felt more like a failure than anything.

One night at Annie's, the lights came on just shortly after last call. Jim, one of my friends from school, approached me with two glasses of beer in hand. He had a huge smile on his face, and was happy to see me. I had also just grabbed two pints, knowing it was last call, and had one in each hand. When Jim extended his arms to clink glasses. I looked at his beer glasses compared to my large pint-sized mugs and, in the blink of an eye, smashed the bottoms of my mugs down on his, exploding his beers everywhere. My mugs didn't break, and I turned away, laughing so hard, I thought I would piss myself.

The bouncers quickly grabbed Jim and threw him out. I thought nothing of it and continued interacting with my drunken friends. When it was finally time to get out of the club, Dale told me that Jim was outside waiting and wanted to fight. Thinking nothing of it, I was up for the challenge.

Right outside the front door, we squared off. I swung as hard as I could and missed. I was so drunk that throwing that first punch sent me off balance and to the ground. There I laid, laughing my head off wedged up against the side of a car. I didn't laugh long. Jim jumped on top of me, landing blows to my head and face. My arms were trapped, and all I could do was turn to the side as each blow landed. Finally, the group that had gathered dragged him off me. We stood face to face again. I will never forget the look in his eye. It said, "You crazy SOB! What's wrong with you?" You know what, Jim? Put my name on the list of those who wanted to know the answer to that question. I wasn't the same Brent Worrall who had become one of Chilliwack's best-loved sons through his accomplishments at the motocross track.

My sick days at work were catching up to me. My work ethic, which had been appreciated by so many, was now a shadow of its former self. I often didn't even make it to work on time, sleeping through my alarm.

When the calendar flipped over to 1987, my boss, Bob, took me aside. "I have a feeling 1987 is going to be a lot better year for Brent than 1986 was," he said. I could read between the lines. I never worried too much though, because deep inside, I felt I was destined to fail. I'm not sure why, but the confidence I had as a young, aspiring professional motocrosser was no longer even a memory.

That year Grandma Pearl pass away from cancer. She wasn't even seventy years old. RIP, Grandma. I know we don't talk about you often, but I will never forget how amazing you were. My dad, being sober for seven years by that point, was handling life and its untimely situations much better than I remembered as a kid. He was much more responsible, and his all-around demeanour was almost friendly. If I asked anyone who knew my father to describe him, I don't think "friendly" is a word they would have used. Burly, yes! Friendly? No!

The hockey team that I played hockey for that winter had a year-end party one weekend in Chilliwack. I was without a vehicle at the time, because I had smashed mine into the ditch at the Fraser River. I wanted to go to the party, but I needed a vehicle. One of my friends, who I met on the Canada Works job, had a nice truck. It was an old Ford, like the one I used to have, with a canopy on it. The truck was clean and in what I would call mint condition. I had been over at his house having a few beers and watching a movie with him that afternoon. Later that night, I pleaded with him, saying I needed a truck, because I had a date, which was a lie. Yes, I had been dating, and I even had a girl fly out from Montreal (who I was even briefly engaged to, Marie-France), but I wasn't looking for a relationship at the time. It's not that I didn't want to have a meaningful relationship; I just knew I was incapable. One-night stands weren't my thing either, but I had my share. Donny agreed to let me take his truck out that night. However, he cautioned me to park it safely, because he had his work tools in the back. I told him not to worry, because we were only going out for dinner and then to the river.

How could that same person who, apart from stealing from the co-op in grade three, turn into such a liar, even to his friends? The answer is simple. I was no longer driving my own bus, so to speak. That position was now held on a full-time basis by the thirsty committee of demons in my head.

The first place I ended up that night was a house party on Woodbine Street. I parked the truck on the street and made sure everything was locked. After a few hours of dumping back Bacardi and Coke, I headed to the Fraser with a couple of friends, having heard of a big outdoor party out on Gill Road. Most of the guys from my hockey team were there, including the Frey boys. Sitting on a log as the sun came up, I knew I had to get Don's truck back to him. I stood up and announced to the one hundred or so people who were still standing at 5:30 a.m. that I was going home. Anyone who wanted a ride should jump in.

I can't remember how many of us piled into that pickup truck. I dropped one person off somewhere on the way home. Finally, there were four of us left in the cab: the Frey boys, a guy who I think was their cousin, and me. That truck was a three-on-the-tree stick shift. It had no power steering either, just "Armstrong steering." We only had about four blocks to go before the twins' house. I was headed west on Berkley Avenue doing thirty-five miles an hour, according to my last look at the speedometer. We were rapidly approaching the three-way stop at Corbould Street.

As we approached the corner, I thought, *I'm going to show these guys how fast I can blitz that three-way stop, left-hand corner without even slowing down.* Being as drunk as we all were, under the extreme g-force of the turn, we all fell over onto each other. Holding the wheel for all I was worth, it was impossible to avoid crashing into a car parked on the curb, a brand-new white 1987 Ford Mustang. I had hit it at about thirty miles an hour!

We came to an explosive and sudden stop. Thankfully, the truck's large steering wheel stopped me where it did, but I had to fight to stay conscious. My ribs were a mess, but I was too drunk to care about anything physical. As I looked up from where I sat, I saw a huge mushroom cloud of fibreglass and smoke hanging ominously. The morning sun was just cresting over the neighbourhood's rooflines. Not a soul was in sight.

My passengers were all ejected on impact. The door had blown open, and out they went. As I looked out the passenger door, I saw Darcy barely able to hold himself up from laughing so hard. I couldn't see the others, but I knew it was no laughing matter. I looked at Darcy as I put the truck in reverse. I had the clutch fully engaged and ready to drop it and bolt. The laughter continued; he was hysterical. He couldn't even get a word out.

Finally, Darcy said, "You can't back up. Dale is stuck underneath the truck." I didn't believe him. We had to leave then or get busted. Just as I was about to drop the clutch and back up, something inside stopped me. I believe it was a miracle, some form of divine intervention. I got out of the truck and walked around to the passenger side. Sure enough, my good friend Dale was trapped between the curb and the truck's front wheel. I was instantly sick to my stomach, realizing how close I had come to running over him!

We got Dale up, and the laughter continued. We were a mess. Still not one person had come outside to see the what the hell had just happened. Maybe they looked out and saw what kind of craziness they would have to confront if they did.

I told my mates that we had to get the hell out of there immediately. We all climbed in the truck, and then I drove them home. That was just the beginning of the end. There was no going back now; I had crossed an invisible line.

15

A Geographical Cure

After I dropped the boys off at Dale's house, I went to return Donny's smashed-up truck. I had not noticed until I parked it at the bottom of his driveway, but his canopy door was also open. Sometime during the night, someone had broken into it, and his tools were gone.

He was an early riser and greeted me when I walked through his door. The first thing he asked was how my night went. Wrong question.

I told him straight up what had happened. He glanced out the window and saw his truck at the end of the driveway. He started to laugh, thinking I was just telling him a story. "Brent, you're just pissed," he said, still laughing. "Go lie down on the couch and sleep it off."

At that point I didn't argue, because the couch sounded inviting. I flopped onto it and was out like a light in no time.

Donny was a redhead like me, with similar facial hair. By that time one of the witnesses to the crash had called it in with a full description of the vehicle and its driver. Within half an hour of me falling asleep, the police arrived at Donny's door and arrested him for the hit-and-run on Corbould Street. He tried to explain that he wasn't driving, but they wanted no part of that. He matched the description, and the evidence was parked in his driveway.

About an hour later, they came back from the police station, realizing they had the wrong guy. I was awakened from my drunken slumber and hauled into the Chilliwack RCMP detachment. I was hung over, but the football inside my stomach was more from what I was becoming than what I had just done.

When I look back on my drinking days, I realize I was in trouble with alcohol from day one. Why didn't I have more self-control? Why was I unable to apply myself to the problem and put that seemingly formidable foe in its place? I didn't have the answers, and it troubled me. I felt lost and defective inside. The world was my vampire, and I seemed to be its daily blood donor. I had no idea what would happen next.

The crash happened on a Saturday morning. After finishing up at the police station, I headed back home to Fairfield Island. My parents were in New West and were not scheduled to be back in Chilliwack until later the next week. I didn't know what to do next. I came up with a bullshit line at the police station and told them that I had not had a drink up to the point of the accident. I told them that I had started hammering whiskey when I got to Don's as a result of the trauma. Realizing they didn't have what they needed to convict me of the DUI and hit-and-run, I was charged with a lesser count of leaving the scene of an accident.

As you might have guessed, my parents were not impressed. We had some pretty serious discussions. I could see how heartbroken my mom was. She couldn't understand how someone so young and with so much talent could be such a train wreck. I know my mom loved me, but she didn't understand the way my father did. "Just get your shit together, kid," he said. Right. It wasn't that easy, because there was an underlying problem. I was an alcoholic and had crossed the invisible line from social drinker to full-blown drunk.

My dad had been in the same predicament but sobered up when Roger died. I was dumbfounded that he found a way to put the plug in the jug. My dad had not said much up to that point through my escapades, but he could see I needed an intervention. Much like he was with my racing and pretty much every other thing he taught me, he was tactical. Dad went to a twelve-step program when he first sobered up. He had a friend named Ron Arnett who he had raised hell with in Chilliwack while growing up. Now Ron was living a happy, healthy, and productive sober life. He and Dad had reconnected in the program. After I expressed a willingness to attend my first meeting, Dad asked Ron to take me. That weekend I went out and got hammered. I figured I had nothing to lose, because I would start the program in earnest on Monday.

Ron picked me up on Monday night, and man, was I nervous. I was afraid, though I didn't know of what. I guess I was afraid I would lose my best friend (alcohol). That may sound ridiculous, but that's what alcohol had become to me, a friend that I could rely on to pick me up when I needed it, to take away my physical and emotional pain, and to make me feel like I could overcome anything or anyone. But those were only in the early days. Now the weapon that I had forged had come full circle. Now it was starting to do *to* me the things it used to do *for* me.

Instead of feeling confident and strong, I became weaker and paranoid. If alcohol wasn't on my breath, it was oozing from my pores. The hangovers that I never got early on became the norm. At work I was becoming a hanger-on. While running a trim saw, I just wanted to run my hand into the saw. I was so sick some days that for the first six hours of the eight-hour shift, I vowed to never drink again. But more often than not, all I could think about during the last two hours was how good the booze was going to taste.

My first meeting was out in Vedder Crossing, at the old army base. It was a closed men's meeting, and what an assortment of untrained yard apes they were. When I walked into the room though, something happened immediately. I couldn't put my finger on it, but I felt like I was in a good place. These people were happy to see me. It had been a while since I had experienced that. Hands were extended and shaken, coffee was poured, and I was seated.

An orderly of sorts at the end of the table chaired the meeting. It went by quickly. I didn't understand a lot of the dialogue in reference to powerlessness or a higher power or anything like that. I just figured that if a person was willing to go to those lengths of admission, they were likely to succeed in defeating their demons. It didn't work quite like that, but it was my first start in the right direction in a long time.

When asked to share, I didn't say a lot, but I did share some of the experiences that led me to the meeting. For the first time in my life, I saw a look of understanding in the eyes of my peers. I didn't want to let go of my newfound best friend, Mr. Barleycorn, but I certainly wanted the kind of contentment those individuals had.

I got drunk before the next meeting and even went directly to the nightclub after it. I was failing and shared that when I was asked to speak. Again, more of those damn smiles and nodding heads. It was starting to bother me. How could my pain and suffering precipitate such bobble-head-like approval? They were starting to make me crazier than I already was. Many of those individuals told me, with that same smile, to "Keep coming back." *Easy for you to say*, I thought. I had my entire life of having fun ahead of me.

Ron continued to mentor me as a sponsor. I was starting to realize that if I was going to succeed at anything in life, all I had to do was not have a drink today. I thought that was some kind of a trick at first. However, one day it hit me like a brick, and I got it. The little twenty-four-hour-a-day book one of the attendees gave me had a passage in it that read, "If we do not have a drink today, we will never get drunk as it is always today." They had me there. Not God, the queen, the pope, or even the Easter Bunny could argue that one.

That week at work, I heard on the radio that Rick Hansen and his Man In Motion World Tour would be passing through Chilliwack. The day he came through, I heard it again on the lunchroom radio. I wasn't sure why, but I was intrigued. The radio announcer claimed that at around 2:30 p.m., Rick would pass under the Lickman Road overpass. After the lunch horn sounded, that was all I could think about.

I worked at my station, and watched the clock closely. I didn't know why, but the thought of leaving my post at 2:15, so I could be at the overpass to witness that hero-in-the-making roll by, was strengthening. Anyone paying any attention to what I was doing would have seen nothing out of the ordinary. I always watched the clock, and to my boss's displeasure, I often left early. Finally, I shut off my saw and walked into the office and said I was going home sick. Not even waiting for a response, I bolted.

When I got to the overpass, it was a wet spring day. A few hundred people were there, and I was happy to be one of them. Rick pressed on, and from where I was, I didn't even get to make eye contact. I was impressed to see how calculated and determined he was with each movement of his arms and upper body. That man had almost finished his 40,000-plus-kilometre roll around the world, and I got to witness part of it. Many days I had left work early to get a head start on that day's buzz and felt guilty about it. After seeing Rick, I had not one ounce of guilt about my decision to leave early that day. Beautifully enough, I got to meet Rick face to face many years later in Vancouver and shared that story with him. My compulsion to do that validates why I have and always will follow my heart. There are no such things as accidents or coincidences.

I managed to string together a couple of weeks sober and was starting to feel pretty good. I was still going out to the clubs but not drinking. Ron hated that.

He used to say, "Brent, if you sit in a damn barber's chair, eventually you're going to get a haircut." It took me a while to realize what he meant.

It was 1987, and the Edmonton Oilers were back in the Stanley Cup finals. They had lost the previous year's Smythe Division final on an unassisted goal by Steve Smith in game seven against the Calgary Flames. I think every Oiler and Flames fan knows the goal I'm talking about. That year's final saw the Oilers face off against Ron Hextall and the Philadelphia Flyers. I had seen Gretzky play a few times in Vancouver, but this was the playoffs.

When I got paid that week, I went straight to the travel agency. Games one and two of the series were scheduled for Edmonton's Northlands Coliseum. I bought tickets from a scalper and sat in the first row, right behind the players' bench.

The Oilers' theme song that year was "Still The One" (by Orleans). I had my Oilers home jersey on and tied the orange scarf they gave everyone around my head like a bandana. It was incredible to be ice side watching my hockey idols Wayne Gretzky, Mark Messier, Jari Kurri, Dave Semenko, Glen Anderson, and Grant Fuhr. They were the best that game will ever see!

On the other side of the ice, the Flyers were no slouch. They had rebounded after tragically losing their goaltender, Pelle Lindbergh, on November 11, 1985, in a car crash in Somerdale, New Jersey. Ron Hextall, who was nicknamed "Hackstall," became the team's number-one goalie. The Flyers were a great team with power forward Tim Kerr, who was coming off a fifty-goal season. Coached by Mike Keenan, the Flyers also boasted the likes of Brian Propp, Dave Poulin, Mark Howe, Pelle Eklund, Rick Tocchet, and Ron Sutter. They also had Dave Brown, and a player I grew fond of watching with the New Westminster Bruins, Craig Berube, to try to deal with Dave Semenko, if needed.

Game one was tied 1–1 after two periods. I was having the time of my life, enjoying some great hockey. Two gals seated beside me had season tickets. We chatted throughout the game. As the clock wound down on the second period, they mentioned they were headed up to the bar for a drink. I had made it that far and had not even thought about drinking. I was too enthralled with the game. However, up to the bar I went. On the way up the stairs—and let me tell you, it was pretty much at the top of Northlands—I told myself, *Whatever you do, don't take a drink!*

No sooner had we got there than my new friends asked what I wanted to drink. The old me kicked in before I knew what the hell was happening. Not to be caught short, I reached into my wallet and grabbed one of the few $100 bills I had left.

A few drinks later, we made it back to our seats, just in time to see Glen Anderson, Paul Coffey, and Jari Kurri post third-period markers to help the Oilers clinch a 4–2 victory. As for Gretzky, he didn't disappoint, getting a goal and a helper.

Just before the game ended, my new friends invited me to a place they claimed the players went after the game. They couldn't guarantee that Wayne would be there, but they assured me that many of the other players, including Esa Tikkanen, would be. I had a hotel in downtown Edmonton, and the place they were talking about was a fair ways out. If having those beers with them at the game was a bad idea, the way my luck had been going, I knew better than to accept their offer. Even though it didn't seem like it at that moment, that decision was a blessing in disguise.

When the game ended, I headed downstairs to get as close to the dressing rooms as possible. I had my program and hoped to get close to Gretzky, to meet him and get his autograph. Remember, I had pretty much learned from the best of the best in con artists when it came to getting through secure areas in my dad. I talked to one of the guys working there, and he hooked me up. He placed me just outside the dressing room at the door that the players would exit to get to their cars.

The Flyers came through first to catch their bus. I got almost every player's autograph in my game program. One of the cool moments was talking to Kent Nilsson, who played for the Oilers. I had heard the commentators on Hockey Night in Canada talk about how long his stick was. Kent was carrying a stick with him, and it reminded me of the comment. He looked at me and said, "I don't know where they got that from. I've always used that length" I thought it was cool to get the goods straight from him. The next guy who came through was "Captain Video," a.k.a. Roger Neilson. I loved Roger, and I'm pretty sure I speak for the entire Vancouver Canuck Nation when I say, RIP, Roger, we fans love you.

My program was getting full of signatures but still no Gretzky in sight. I kept asking the guys as they came by if Wayne was still in the room. Most didn't want to answer until I put the question to Coach Glen Sather. He didn't give me much of a look, but said, "He'll be out soon." I had been standing there for well over an hour. I didn't know what to believe, but it was already after midnight.

Before I had a chance to think about my next move, there he was, the "Great One." I didn't think many people were still around until he stopped to sign my program. A crowd gathered instantly. Calmly and politely, I congratulated him on the victory. After he signed my program, I wished him luck and stuck out my right hand. I got to meet my hero, and he certainly didn't disappoint. Had I accepted the invite to the bar, that likely would not have happened. I was excited about that bucket-list encounter. I have lost many of my valued treasures over the years, but I'm so thankful to have that treasured program back in my life.

I wound up getting ten points on my driver's licence and a $500 fine for hitting the parked car. My mom and dad, seeing that I was somewhat serious about getting sober, invited me down to New Westminster. I stayed with them on and off that summer, because work had slowed down at the mill. While there I met some new friends at the New West Alano Club. I attended meetings regularly and enjoyed the big-city vibe. I realized that most of those I gravitated to and hung out with were normal, intelligent people while abstaining from substances. I fit that category too.

I found some work helping a guy from the club who cleaned carpets for a living. Things went fairly well that summer. However, I was devastated when one of the guys who I thought had it all together died of a heroin overdose. I didn't understand how the same guy I had gone to a Vancouver Canadians game with just days earlier could be dead.

In the fall I was back in Chilliwack, where I was placed on the night shift at the mill. Life was lonely once again, but only because I chose it to be that way. After work I would veg out with a six-pack of tall boys and other herbal remedies, only to awake and repeat the cycle. I kept the lights off and never answered the door or the phone. I was sinking further and further into a reclusive shell.

In the spring of 1988, I lost my job at the mill. I don't remember much about the night that led up to it. I was supposed to be on shift but filled in on a hockey team instead. After the game I was dumb enough and drunk enough to go see one of my buddies, who was working at the mill. He and I had played hockey together, and his brother, Randy Maxwell, was in the NHL with the Minnesota North Stars.

The next day my boss caught wind that I had been roaming the floor of the mill in that shape and not on shift like I was supposed to be. He handed me a two-week suspension. I remember thinking, *Good, now I can go get loaded without work getting in the way.*

My parents no longer wanted me in their Chilliwack home. My list of friends who wanted me around was also shrinking. For a short period of time, I lived in Uncle Al's crawl space. I would go in there with a bottle of something and not come out for days. I was even too ashamed to go upstairs to use the bathroom. I conveniently re-filled the bottles I was in the process of emptying with my own urine.

I moved back home again briefly. I don't think my parents even knew I was there. In the Clare Avenue house, I had a small bed hidden under the stairs. I was seriously messed up and paranoid. I was also without a vehicle. I had pretty much liquidated anything I had with wheels, including my CR 250, which I sold to Darcy Frey. I had a few glimpses of hope, and my parents tried to help as best as they could. My dad even took me out and bought me a nice Mazda B-2200 pickup with a canopy on it. But much like before, it was only temporary, and soon I was drunk again. I sold the canopy first and then sold the truck to get my next fix. I was starting to believe I would be dead before long. I was a wanted man and on Chilliwack's most-endangered species list. Finally, I rented a car and took off to the West Edmonton Mall.

I was officially certifiable by that point. I holed up in the Fantasyland Hotel, and nothing made sense. If I told you I had visions of hijacking the mall's submarine and blowing shit up, would you believe me? I figured you might. The trip was just a Band-Aid, an escape from the reality of my current situation of not properly addressing the roots of my problems. I was repeating the same cycles and expecting different results. I couldn't go back. One of the guys at my meetings summed it up when he said "Son, alcoholism is like bad breath. You're the last one to know you have it." I did, however, know that I was and always would be an alcoholic. The saddest part was that I still wanted to drink.

One day I ran into an old motocross buddy from Chilliwack, Rick May. He had stopped racing a couple of years earlier, too. Rick was a bit of wild man in his day, but he was starting to settle down, as most people do when they mature. I stayed at Rick's for a couple of nights, which turned into a month. He knew I was a mess and did his best to help me to make solid choices.

I didn't return to the mill after my suspension. I didn't even bother to get a separation slip to file for unemployment insurance benefits, because I knew I owed so much money that it was a waste of time. Nothing I was doing made sense to anyone, me included.

While staying at Rick's, I ran into another hockey friend. He had a gargantuan bag of magic mushrooms, which he fronted to me. I didn't think it was possible, but my train wreck of a life was about to get a lot worse.

That fall, the day after Kirk Gibson and my Los Angeles Dodgers won the World Series, I left Chilliwack for good. I had been in contact with my old friend, Howard Dedels. He and his brother were living and working in Calgary. I told him my predicament, and he bought me a bus ticket. I climbed on that bus with a plastic garbage bag and the clothes on my back. I had a few items of clothing in the bag, but it was mostly just the magic mushrooms. They were a valuable commodity that I could sell in an effort to stay loaded.

That was Calgary's Olympic year, and it was sure evident when I arrived. The boys picked me up at the bus depot and put up with me for a while. Calgary was a nice change of scenery, and I loved the Albertan vibe. Now all I had to do was find a job. We had some partying to do first, though.

We infiltrated the bars on Electric Avenue, and I was eating more mushrooms than I was selling. One night I ended up behind the wheel of my friend's car. I got pulled over on Deerfoot Trail in the vicinity of where Ikea currently sits. It's a miracle that I didn't get us killed. I had made a wrong turn, and I was driving on the wrong side of the road on a four-lane divided highway.

I answered some questions, and then the officer moved on to quiz my friend, who owned the vehicle. I heard the officer say I was a total liar. I sat and awaited whatever fate lay ahead. He gave me a twenty-four-hour roadside suspension, and placed a "Denver Boot," a device used to lock the car's wheel, on the car. Now what? We were miles from our apartment in southwest Calgary. I was drunker than hell and ripped out of my gourd on mushrooms.

We walked for what seemed like miles. When we got back to our neighbourhood, we made a quick stop at a 7-11 to fill my famished gullet with 3-for-99-cent chili dogs, then went home to sleep it off.

When we got into our elevator, the motion had me hurling. Nothing pretty, just pure, volatile, venomous vomit everywhere. My friends laughed and laughed. I didn't think it was funny until one of them unzipped his fly, and pissed all over it. It was totally disgusting, but it was my life at that time.

Back at the apartment, one of the boys, who was quite big, picked me up and pile-drove me headfirst into the floor. I couldn't move. As ripped as I was, I knew something wasn't right. I went to the hospital the next day to get checked out.

The results were inconclusive, but when I broke my body into multiple pieces at Walton Raceway in 2011, it was thought that I had also broken my neck. My neck was broken, but it didn't happen in 2011. The scar tissue over the fractures in my neck show that they were from years back as a result of that incident.

When we arrived back at the apartment from the hospital, someone had cleaned out the elevator. As soon as the door opened, it reeked of disinfectant. My gag reflex engaged, and once again, I was vomiting in the elevator, and the boys were my supporting cast of laughter. Man, I was messed up.

The laughter continued into our suite. Howard and I headed out to the balcony, and we started pissing off their fourteenth-floor balcony. They say timing is everything, and it was only fitting that just as our golden showers were about to touch down, the landlady walked underneath us. Bingo, we had just pissed on the head of the same lady who would have to clean out the elevator for a second day in a row.

Minutes later there was a knock on our door. As soon as she asked if someone from our suite was peeing off the balcony, we broke into laughter. I can't imagine laughing at such disfunction today, but such things were par for the course when I added alcohol to my body. Needless to say, we were evicted, but not before I stooped to a first-ever, all-time low. Grey Cup Sunday saw my friend and I pool our limited (mostly found in the couch) resources to buy a can of Lysol. And no, it wasn't to help the landlady clean out the elevator.

I was broke, so I called my mom to see if I could get a few bucks out of her. I told her a BS story that I had a job lined up but needed forty bucks to buy a pair of work boots. She knew better, and sent me nothing.

I hit the paper trail, applying for a few jobs in the northeast. I landed a couple of jobs, one at Smed Manufacturing and the other at Con-Force Structures, but I never managed to make two pay periods. At Smed, I ran into a guy who I had worked with at the mill in Chilliwack. He had left town under similar circumstances.

After the eviction, I got my own place in Bowness. It was just a room in a rooming house, but it was mine, and I could be alone. The house was on the hill, on the way up to Market Mall. My friend Howard's cousin, Brent, lived close by. He was attending the University of Calgary, and we became good friends. He was into hockey, so it was a perfect fit. I went to the university and skated for hours on the Olympic speed-skating oval. We also played outdoor shinny at the Bowness Rink almost daily that winter. Brent also got us a smoking deal on Calgary Stampeders season tickets. We attended many Calgary Flames games that season, too.

One night I went to the Flames/Winnipeg Jets game on my own. I was way up in the nosebleed seats. It was 5–0 for the Flames, and I was hammered. At those games when I got drunk, I got vocal. A jersey-wearing Jets fan stood up and told me to shut my mouth. I leaned over and took a drunken swing and missed. Falling headfirst, I tumbled, ass over tea kettle down four or five rows of seats. The police were called, and I was kicked out of the building. I wasn't too worried though, because the Flames were up 5–0 anyway. The next day, I was shocked to read that the Jets had come all the way back, and the game ended in a 5–5 tie.

My dad made a road trip out from BC to bring a few of my belongings. He stayed for a few days, and it was good for both of us. In his heart, he was starting to accept that his son had a serious problem, and might not be around for long.

My parents mailed me a plane ticket, and I spent Christmas 1988 with them in New Westminster. I had put on quite a bit of weight. My regular frame of a buck fifty was now pushing 200 pounds. My face looked gaunt and tired. On top of my alcoholism, I was also allergic to the barley in the beer I was drinking. My hangovers were getting much worse. It was nice to see my family for Christmas. My Grandpa James even came and spent it with us. I had not seen him since our days drinking together back at Chilliwack's old Royal Hotel. From a period of my life where I don't have many positive memories, that Christmas restored my faith in family.

About a month or so earlier, I had applied for unemployment insurance benefits. When I returned to Calgary, three cheques from the government were in the mailbox. I now had $1,300 and was only paying $180 a month in rent. Suddenly, I felt like the Sultan of Brunei. I went to the bank, cashed the cheques, and put the money in my wallet. It was New Year's Eve, and out I went.

One of my buds and I went bar hopping in the neighbourhood of 3rd Avenue. We met a couple of gals, and had just changed venues when I went to grab my wallet. It was gone. It must have fallen out in the car, because I know I had it when we stopped. My friend, who was driving, and had the keys, said, "I'll go grab it and be right back." Thinking nothing of it, I trusted him. Besides, someone had to keep the two nice ladies company.

Five minutes later when he had not returned, I knew something was wrong. I went out to where the car had been parked, but it was gone, and so was my wallet. I knew I had been duped. It was a horrible feeling to tell the girls that I had to leave. I didn't expect to see my friend back, because I knew where he was headed with my money.

By February 1989, I was sick and alone. When I looked in the mirror, I didn't recognize my reflection. That scared me more than anything. Still drinking daily, the self-torture continued. I didn't want to die though. I knew I had some serious issues, but I also knew I could defeat my demons. All I heard going through my head was the preamble of the twelve-step groups I had attended: "If you want what we have, and are willing to go to any length to get it, then you are ready to take certain steps." I was ready and knew exactly what to do. For the first time, I realized that my survival depended on getting sober. I also knew that I had to act fast, because I suspected that narrow window of willingness would close quickly.

I called a hotline, and a fellow took me on a twelve-step call. We had coffee. All he did was share his experiences, strengths, and hopes. That's all one drunk can ever do for another, but you know what? It works. The next day I called Renfrew Detox. I was admitted within twenty-four hours. Uncertain and afraid, I weighed in at 196 pounds of quivering diarrhea. That turned out to be a great move on my behalf, because good things were about to come back my way.

16

Dr. Quincy

The year 1989 marked the beginning of the end of the Cold War. Walls were coming down abroad, and dictatorships were contested. The Soviet Union also ended their nine-year occupation of Afghanistan. Ronald Reagan bid his nation a farewell in a nationally televised event, and George Herbert Walker Bush was sworn in as the forty-first president of the United States.

On a darker note, on January 24 serial killer Ted Bundy finally received his just fate in an electric chair in Florida. I was always aghast hearing news of such individuals. I know that some will argue that two wrongs don't make a right, but I'm good with one less wart on the ass of society.

Being in Calgary, I had picked up Flames fever. That team was loaded with talent for the 1988/1989 season. I felt like they had a chance to win the Stanley Cup. It wasn't all roses in the NHL though. That season Buffalo Sabres goaltender Clint Malarchuk almost lost his life due to a gash from a skate blade. In one of the most horrific on-ice scenes you can imagine, Malarchuk's jugular vein was sliced open. If not for a quick-thinking Buffalo Sabres trainer, who had served in Vietnam as a combat medic, Malarchuk likely would have died. The 6-inch gash took 300 stitches to repair. As for Malarchuk, much like me, he has found a way to put his life-changing adversity in its place. Clint, even though I have never met you, I feel like you're my brother.

It was a brutally cold winter in Calgary. It was minus thirty or colder every day for weeks on end. I had no vehicle, and public transit saw my shadow frequently. On February 21 I took the bus up to the Renfrew Detox. I was alone, which was a good thing. I had finally accepted that I was the problem, and wherever I went, I took me with me. I was the only one responsible to get me well. At that point, looking back on even the last two years of my life was a titanic struggle.

When I arrived, it was so cold that the front doors were frozen shut. They had to let me in around the back. Once inside, I felt safe. The place was clean and quiet. I had some medication with me, because only the week before, I had been diagnosed with scabies. Upon hearing that they almost didn't let me in. I can't say I blame them, but all I cared about was getting well.

At the detox, my blood pressure and vital signs were monitored regularly. I had a few sleepless nights, but fared pretty well overall. We had to attend daily meetings, which proved to be a game-changer for me. They were speaker meetings, meaning that others who had been down a similar road came in and shared their stories. Those meetings were a key factor in my recovery.

The speakers were a couple, and they took turns sharing their stories. When it was Dan's turn, I identified with him immediately. Like me he was a hockey player and an athlete. For the first time in a recovery setting, I looked at an individual as an equal. Prior to that I had always compared myself to others. The old saying, "Without points, it's pointless," applied there. But sitting there at twenty-two years old, I realized that this man was no different. He was a drunk, just like me. But unlike me, who was still suffering from a seemingly hopeless state of body and mind, he had recovered from that. That was all I wanted, to be in charge of my faculties and emotions. In that man, for the first time, I saw real hope.

One of the key points in Dan's therapy was "The House," and he referred to it often. It was a place in southwest Calgary called 1835 House. It was run by the Recovery Acres Society and spearheaded by the late Blair Moody, who had made it his mission to work with those addicted to substances after his own child was murdered by such a person.

After the first meeting at Renfrew, I approached Dan, and we talked for a bit. I wanted to know more about his journey and 1835 House. After connecting some of the dots and getting his contact info, I had new hope.

Later that week, the detox centre scheduled a visit to 1835 House to attend one of their noon meetings. I loved it. There I was, sitting in that facility with more than thirty individuals who, in my opinion, were walking, talking miracles. They had sobriety, and I wanted it more than ever. I put my name on the house's waiting list. I don't remember how many beds they had, but it was around thirty. Within the week, I was released from detox, and admitted into 1835 House.

Life at the house was structured. It was mandatory to attend daily in-house meetings. I was also encouraged to attend at least five meetings per week at other places in Calgary and outlying areas. We also had counsellors and other in-house mentors in whom we could confide. The self-discipline aspect of my life needed a serious overhaul. The survival skills I had learned up to that point had kept me alive, but I knew that what I was doing to stay loaded was killing me.

The food at the house was well-prepared, though it was a bit of a shock to my system at first to be eating three square meals a day. If an individual wasn't putting 100 percent effort into his or her recovery, it was pointed out. If the behaviour or negative attitude continued, the individual was asked to leave. I never had to worry too much about that, because I treated that opportunity as if my life depended on it. By then I had parted ways with any friends who were still drinking. I didn't care if they understood; I just needed to get well.

After two weeks in the day program, I was required to go out and look for a job. That was a something they believed in. I was down with that, because I always enjoyed a hard day's work. I hit the trail in the northeast putting in resumes in the industrial area, and within two days, I landed a job as a shipper/receiver at an oil emulsion plant. I liked the work and fit in well quickly. The company made their own products on site. When the trucks came in to fill our tanks with crude oil, I was in charge of helping off-load, weigh in, and so on. We also filled our own oil drums on site, which was a little sketchy at times.

When I was hired, I was told it was a seasonal job. I was okay with that, because the money was good, and it being March, the layoff date of October seemed too distant to worry about.

The next spring they called and offered the job back. I liked the job, the crew, and the Calgary area, but I turned the offer down. I regretted doing that until I heard about a serious accident at the plant. I was quite taken back when I got the news.

The two other guys who I worked with were responsible for the same job that I did. One day they were sent into the SP-6 container to clean it, but the propane canister they were using began leaking while they were in that somewhat airtight industrial-sized drum. When they ignited their flame, it exploded, and they were killed instantly. That news was hard to take. I couldn't help but wonder how my own celestial alignment had kept me out of harm's way!

While living in that house, through working the twelve-step program, I began to feel better than ever. My confidence was back, and I felt strong mentally and physically. My days started at 5:00 a.m. and finished at around midnight. Now that I had a clear head, there wasn't enough time in the day. I also realized that living life on life's terms rather than my own wasn't such a bad thing either.

The house had a baseball team, which I played on, and many of the guys golfed. We were always somewhere doing something constructive. I bought a gas guzzler off one of the councillors and had wheels again. I got pulled over one day and was worried that my BC warrants might show up. (Yes, I still had some of those. However, in due course, I got a chance to right those wrongs.)

Around that time my miracle started in earnest. I had accepted that I was physically and mentally different from those who can drink socially, and I knew I could never drink alcohol safely again.

The other revelation was that I had accepted a god of my own understanding. I needed some help with that at first, because every time the word "god" was mentioned, all I could think about was sitting in that church at six years old with wet piss pants burning my ass! All I had to do was decide to turn my life and my will over to the care of God, as I understood him. That wasn't easy, because to me it was a god I did not understand. My sponsor was okay with that and encouraged me to start addressing that power greater than myself as the "God I Don't Understand." My willingness to make such efforts opened many new doors. No, I didn't shave my head and head out to the airport and start banging tambourines or anything like that. The journey I was embarking on was spiritual in nature.

After addressing most of my shortcomings, one of the steps included a thorough and fearless moral inventory. It was an arduous process. I was required to look at my part in some of the wrongs that I thought had unjustly come my way. From there I was to find someone to confide in to do the fifth step. I was to admit to God, myself, and another human being the exact nature of my wrongs. Many of my peers had chosen a certain ordained minister. I wasn't sure about going that route. In the end, I decided that if I was going to tell my deepest and most highly safeguarded secrets to anyone, it would be someone who was sworn to secrecy. His name was Father Delisle. The day I headed off to do my fifth step, I joked that I was off to see Father Denial. It was no joking matter though; I was carrying some pretty serious shit.

One of the things I was carrying I hadn't told anyone. Remember back when I told you that Andrea had a new boyfriend? For the longest time I used to look up to the sky and wish he was dead. A couple of years prior, I was talking to my Uncle Larry, and he told me that the guy, Adrian, had died in a skiing accident. He had struck a tree and was killed instantly. I was horrified and sick to my stomach when I received the news. I felt responsible. If I hadn't wished those things, would he still be alive?

I sat with Father Delisle for over two hours. At one point, I thought I would have to poke him with my pen to see if he was still awake. He provided me with some feedback, but it wasn't what I was expecting. I saved some of the best stuff for last. When I told him about Adrian and what I thought was my part in his death, he stopped everything. "In the grand scheme of life and the world," he said, looking at me, "do you think you're important enough to have God act out on your behalf like that?" I had no response. I was happy to have completed that vital step in my recovery.

That June, the Calgary Flames won the Stanley Cup, defeating the Montreal Canadiens in six games. I almost leapt out of my second-floor window when Doug Gilmour scored the winning goal. Gilmour was a key piece, added to an already-great team that had at least ten players who had sixty points. One of them was the man with the signature handlebar moustache, Lanny McDonald. The Flames also got great goaltending in that series from Calgary native Mike Vernon. It was also cool to see young, feisty Theo Fleury as part of that winning formula as a rookie.

As soon as the game was over, the torch on Calgary's iconic tower, which had been extinguished when that year's Olympics concluded, was ablaze once again. We headed downtown and joined the celebration. It was certainly different to wake up the next day remembering what had happened the night before. Toward the end of my drinking days, I had reached the point where I couldn't remember the night before even when I tried.

While working through the recovery program, I started to think about getting into journalism or broadcasting. I had always loved to write, and whenever no one was around, I would turn the television down and do the play by play for whatever game I was watching. Kind of embarrassing, right? I went to Columbia

Academy, and they wanted $6,000 for their program. At that price, it would have to wait. I checked out SAIT, and their program, which started the next fall, was more reasonable.

I also contacted the *Calgary Mirror*, a local newspaper, because a friend had given me the number of the managing editor. I landed an interview, during which he told me that his paper was focused mainly on local events, people, and stories. I hit him with an idea. A fast up-and-coming Calgary kid was racing road bikes at Race City Speedway. I had met him at one of the Calgary bike shops I had meandered into. A big national event was coming up at the speedway in a week's time. The editor approved, and off I went to get the story. I had not been to a motorcycle race since 1983. I had not even thought much about bike racing. The merry-go-round that my alcoholism had me on left no room. More than anything I think my brain was trying to block it out. Now that I was sober, things were different. My brain was starting to function like I remembered it. That was a good feeling. As I mentioned earlier, I seriously thought I was one of those individuals who my peers claimed was "incapable of grasping a manner of living that demanded rigorous honesty."

It was so much fun to be back at a racetrack, even if it wasn't a motocross track. One of the first people I ran into was my old racing friend and nemesis, Robbie Mutch. Are you kidding me? I had not seen Robbie since 1981, but I had heard through the grapevine that he had gotten into road racing and was good. Robbie was a talented kid on a dirt bike, but it turned out he was just the right kind of crazy to be even better on a road bike. Robbie and his mechanic were pretty excited to see me. It was a bit humbling to tell them that I had fallen out of favour in Chilliwack but was now addressing my issues. In true Robbie fashion, that little SOB started a huge food fight in the Race City cafeteria that day! I couldn't help but smile and think about how some of the good things in life never change.

The day went by quickly, and I got what I felt I needed for a solid story on the rider I was focused on. That Wednesday, upon returning home to 1835 House from work, I got a nice surprise. My half-page article had been published in the *Mirror*, and the house director had cut it out and posted it on the wall where we all lined up to get our meals. Before I even had a chance to see it, I received several compliments. That was certainly different, because the shoe was now on the other foot. I had read many newspaper articles about me in the *Chilliwack*

Progress, and now I had a chance to write my own. To me that was key, because I was always able to identify flaws in the writing of a journalist who didn't know the sport like I did. That was a perfect example of the type of thing I was learning in my new life: how to be part of a solution and not the problem. Penning that article from a racer's standpoint, a racer who had spent enough time behind the right kind of bars (handlebars), was a proud moment.

I made it out to Race City a few more times that season and even went back to Vancouver for a weekend race at the old Westwood track, reconnecting once again with many people I had not seen for years. That marked the last time I attended that fabled facility. Sadly, it closed the following year after hosting high-profile racing for over thirty years.

Back at the house, Dennis, one of the guys I respected a lot, was into horse racing. I had never been to a race. I knew of my grandfather's days at the track through some of the stories my dad told me. Not a lot of positive things were said about horse racing in our home. Both my parents' fathers had done their share of gambling. My dad went to the track on occasion, but he usually kept it to himself. He never had a problem, and he enjoyed it when it made sense to do so.

Quite a few at the house were attending Stampede Park's races regularly. Dennis, invited me out one Sunday. I had no idea what to expect. I had $220 in my wallet. I admit that even though I was losing, early on, the excitement was real. That changed over the course of the racing card. I was losing more and getting frustrated. I had worked damn hard for that $220. Heading into the last race, I was down to my last $20. I put all my infinite wisdom aside, and when I got to the window, I said, "Ten dollars to win on the number ten horse in the tenth race."

I headed out the corridor toward the north end of the home stretch. The horses went into the gate for their six-furlong dash. My horse broke dead last and must have been twenty lengths off the lead heading to turn one. As they approached the final turn, he caught the pack but was still last. My heart was in my throat. He was making up much ground on the outside. I didn't think the straightaway was long enough though.

When they hit the wire, it was close, but I thought my horse had come up just short. The photo finish would require a print. When they flashed number ten on the board as the winner, I was electric with excitement. Get this, the horse's name was "Fairly Reasonable." To me that day was when horse racing itself became "fairly reasonable." But wait a minute, where was my regard for all the no-good, cheating, damn loser horses that had plagued me up until that final race? Much like my drinking, in my first day at the racetrack, I went through a similar collection of negative emotions. Was I in a self-deceptive state once again that fooled me regarding my values? No pun intended, but you bet I was!

By October's end, I had been at the house for nine months. Their track record showed that most people who stayed there for a year remained clean and sober afterwards, though there are no such things as guarantees when it comes to alcoholics. I continued to do everything necessary to give myself the best chance. I knew there was no such thing as a cure. What I was given was a daily reprieve from my condition, based on the maintenance of my spiritual condition, nothing more and nothing less. But if I continued to do what I was doing, history proved that my chances were better than average.

My parents had sold their home in Chilliwack and bought a nice new place in Delta's Sunshine Hills. My mom had also opened as a notary public on Vancouver's Granville Street. I was in contact with them fairly regularly. Other than that one-off trip to Westwood though, I didn't see anyone from my family at all. Once again, I believe getting away to Calgary helped me take the steps I needed to get well.

With my job at the oil plant coming to an end for the season, my mom offered me a job as her receptionist. I liked the idea of being in the high-profile setting of Granville Street, but I wasn't sure about sitting behind a desk for eight hours a day. However, that type of position would suit my current lifestyle. I accepted her offer and couldn't wait to get back to BC. I missed my family a lot. Now that I was no longer trying to hide from them—or the world, for that matter—it seemed like a logical choice.

My dad drove out to Calgary to pick me up, along with my belongings. As for my gas guzzler of a car, I sold it to one of my "cell mates."

Back in Vancouver again, I revelled in big-city life. The job was a bit confusing, but my mom put up with me. I did the best I could, but I knew I wasn't cut out for office work. Remember, I'm a Gemini, a double-headed monster who thrives on excitement and activity.

I also did what was emphasized as imperative by my mentors when I left Calgary: I went to as many meetings as I could. A Tuesday nighter took place right up by our house in North Delta. There was also Pike Road, Strawberry Hill, and a good old "Rootin' Tootin' Newton" group close by. I was a regular fixture and soon knew most people by name. I met a guy named Ken who built homes. We got along well. I told him my story, and he gave me the opportunity to work for him in the spring of 1990. That's right, the "Neon Nineties" had arrived.

By that time, Grandpa Jim had sobered up as well. It was crazy; all of us drunken Worrall adults were now sober. I guarantee you someone was losing money on those odds somewhere. But the thing that comes to mind first when I write this is, recovery works! I know it works. I was hopeless, or so I thought. My grandfather was a hopeless alcoholic, too, or so I thought. And my dad, don't even go there. I would have bet my own personal Funny Farm on that never happening. However, there's a power in the universe that provides a way out for us drunks. I didn't believe in miracles until I started to have some faith in the things that I couldn't see, feel, hear, or touch. Think about that for a bit. I have many times, but rather than overthink and complicate what is so simple today, I have just learned to go with it.

While working for Ken, it felt good to have a real job again and money in my jeans. He taught me a few of the framing basics, and other than that, I was pretty much a grunt. I enjoyed working outside though, and my penchant for fitness always saw me challenging myself.

With money in my pocket, I also began to get curious about Vancouver's horse-racing scene. Exhibition Park (now called Hastings Park) wasn't yet open for the summer meet, so I settled for the "Buggies" (standardbreds) out at Cloverdale Raceway. I didn't know the game well, but that didn't stop me. Through the balance of that meet, I don't think I missed one race. Win some, lose some, the money was only fuel. Before long I knew everyone at the track by name. That proved to be my favourite new social environment. I still attended meetings, but if they fell on one of the four nights that horse racing took place, I was at the track. I rationalized it in my head, and it made perfect sense to me. My dad came along every now and again. It was fun to be in a racing environment with him once again. That fun didn't last long though, because he was a little more appalled at losing money than I was.

Something was happening to me that I didn't realize right away. My twelve-step program sponsor was the one who pointed it out. He asked me why I liked playing the ponies the way I did. I gave him my take, and he didn't buy it. When I was there, he told me to take a look around and tell him what I saw. Many answers came out before he stopped me. He pointed out that most people who were there couldn't afford to be, and they had a problem, the same kind of problem I had with drinking. That wasn't something I wanted to hear. I pretended to be listening and assured him that I would never let it get that bad. After all, I had overcome the demon that was killing me, and it was my prerogative to have a little fun, wasn't it? I also pointed out that I was starting to see many people who I recognized from my meetings at the track. His response was, "I rest my case." Now I was confused. He told me not to worry; I would figure things out in due course. I hated to hear him talk like that, because he was rarely wrong.

I combatted that thought by going to the meetings at Cloverdale Raceway's backstretch. People had to be an owner or a horseman to get in, but I had an angle. One of the guys that I had met who trained horses signed me up as part-owner of one of his horses. Now I had my own horse owner's licence and could go anywhere on the grounds. Once again, I felt like a somebody at a racetrack, although the circumstances were a bit different.

One night at Cloverdale Raceway, I was heading out of the men's room when I ran into one of my old motocross friends, John Snow. We were excited to see each other. He was there with his dad, who was a thoroughbred trainer. They were at the track that night, because they had done some work on a horse for someone. Throughout our motocross racing days, I never knew that he and his family trained race horses for a living. Now I couldn't wait for that summer's thoroughbred meet to start in Vancouver.

In 1990 my grandfather, who was now sober, moved from Chilliwack to White Rock. It was nice having him around for family dinners and other social events. We also made a few trips to the track together. Grandpa had a phone-in account, and sometimes I went over to his place, read the racing form, and then we called in our bets. By that time Grandpa was in his seventies. His health wasn't great due to years of abuse, but I was thankful for the opportunity to get to know him a little better. My grandfather may have been many things to many people, but he was always a gentleman, in my opinion.

When the summer meet began at Hastings Park in Vancouver, I was having the time of my life. There I was, in the trenches of that racetrack, rubbing elbows with a who's who of the sport. I would drive straight to the track from work and head into the backstretch. John and his family treated me like gold. I was and always will be grateful for that. Because of them I got to witness and experience many exciting things in the sport of kings. That affliction was my new elixir for life.

Working for Ken that summer building houses, I made some new friends, one of whom was a guy who worked at the lumber yard that we frequented regularly. He was in our twelve-step program, and we got along well. They had me over to family barbecues and became a valuable part of my support system. Their son, Jay, was a BMXer. I told him about my racing days. One thing led to another, and in no time, we were hitting jumps at the Surrey BMX track. It had been years since I had even been on a BMX bike. After doing a couple of laps, I was sure that one set of jumps could all be jumped in a single leap. They spanned about twenty-five feet, but there was a good downhill run, and in my head, it was doable.

The sun was already setting. It was a hot summer day, and I was feeling it. I had already worked the entire day outside in the sun, but the sight of that quad jump gave me a familiar adrenaline rush, and I was going for it. Despite grabbing all the speed I could, it wasn't enough. With no suspension on the rear end of the BMX bike, I was catapulted over the handlebars and driven face first into the hard-packed pavement-like soil. I was knocked unconscious, but not for long. About the safety gear I was wearing…I wasn't wearing any! No helmet, no riding pants, no protective jersey, nothing. I was dressed the same way I used to rip around the neighbourhood on my BMX bike as a kid: shorts, runners, and a T-shirt.

Once I came to and saw the amount of blood running from almost every part of the front of my body, I went into shock. After a call to 911, I was taken to Surrey Memorial Hospital. Luckily, no bones were broken, but I had broken my front teeth again and suffered yet another nasty concussion. I didn't miss a lot of work over that incident. In fact, the crash was on a Wednesday, and I was back at work the following Monday. When I was sober, I didn't believe in missing work.

Around that time, I started to date a girl I had met at one of my meetings. It was a relationship of convenience more than anything. In my heart, I knew she wasn't going to be my permanent main squeeze. I have always believed there is a soul mate on this planet for each of us. I also believed that having such an individual cross my path would be the challenge.

We ended up renting an apartment together in Coquitlam. Things lasted until one night when she failed to return home. The lure of the fix that put her in my path in the first place had claimed her yet again. I was put out by the hassle of having to relocate but thankful that the apartment we shared was the extent of our commitment.

For the first time since the Vancouver Supercross in 1983, I attended a moto-cross race, at the Stetson Bowl. I had noticed signs advertising the race while frequenting the Cloverdale Speedway. I didn't know what to expect or who I would run into. Being keen on motocross was something I had not experienced in a long time. That Stetson Bowl race was a pretty big deal. I had been down a fairly dark path since leaving moto and wasn't sure what to expect.

Upon arrival I re-connected instantly with many old friends. One of the first guys I ran into was Steve Crevier. Even though he had moved on to a high-profile road-racing career, it was fun to share some old stories about our motocross days together. Sitting in that packed grandstand on a hot summer night with the smell of the freshly watered track invigorating my senses, I couldn't help but miss the sport. Many thoughts raced through my head. At twenty-four years of age, I felt like my window of opportunity was pretty much closed.

After the race night was over, I ran into my old friend and mentor, Wally Levy. He was still active in the sport with promotions as well as doing track announcing. At the end of our conversation, he asked how old I now was. After I told him, the next thing that came out of his mouth caught me off guard. "Brent, you're still young enough to make a career out of motocross if you want to." I was pleasantly surprised to hear that.

I left the Stetson Bowl that night feeling a lot better about myself than I had in years. It had been a long time coming, but to finally reconnect with my passion and its people was sheer awesomeness.

By the fall of 1990, Kelly had moved out of our family home and in with her boyfriend, Richard Lemieux. He was a hard-working guy who grew up in a large hockey family. Oddly enough, he first took note of my sister as she was doing a header down the stairs at his Junior A hockey game in the old Queens Park Arena. With Richard now in our family mix, I got back into hockey, playing for the New Westminster Police Department in the Metro Vancouver Police League. Brian Burke also played in that league. It was a fun, tough league. I lit the lamp often, and many praised my on-ice skills. I loved the game so much, and it felt good to be on the ice again.

Richard worked at the BC Hardwood Flooring Company, which was based in Vancouver's East End just off Hastings Street. Hardwood flooring was making a huge comeback. I was offered a job there and accepted it immediately. It was a union shop with solid pay and benefits, and I looked forward to learning the trade. Richard was a "sander man," but I joined the installation department. The job was physically demanding, but I liked it. When I say that job was physical, how long do you think it takes to bang together a complete tongue-and-groove gymnasium floor? In addition to the hard work, it also allowed me to be creative.

Being the only union shop in the province that installed hardwood, we got most of the government jobs. We also did a lot of high-profile jobs. Many of these saw me working in homes for the likes of Jimmy Pattison, Bruce Allen, and even late Vancouver Canucks owner Frank Griffiths. Writing Frank's name brings a smile to my face. The day we were at his house in West Vancouver, I had no idea whose house it was until I went into a room with all kinds of wall-mounted photos of the Canucks, one of which was a photo of the team's airplane, Air Canuck. When I saw that photo, I looked at my colleague, "Ace," and said, "Whose house is this, anyway?"

"Frank Griffiths, owner of the Vancouver Canucks," he said just as Frank's wife, Emily, entered the room. She smiled and nodded. From that moment on, that job had my full attention.

Part of the job involved being flown in and out of remote areas to work. On one occasion we took a Harbour Air flight to a private island owned by the CEO of Hewlett Packard. Three of us were scheduled to be on that tiny, remote island for five days on our own. We ended up staying for a couple of extra nights, because the weather was too severe for our float plane to get us. Making things even worse, on the return trip, our pilot flew us into downtown Vancouver. That was a problem, because our vehicles were at Vancouver International Airport out in Richmond.

I was often paired up for work with Ace, a.k.a. Doug Kessel. He was a hard-working individual. He showed me the ins and outs of the trade, and we got along well. Doug also respected the fact that I no longer drank. I never felt much pressure to do so on that job. It was also rewarding to look back at the end of a long day, and appreciate the new look we had given to our jobs.

Doug also wound up saving my life one day—literally. We were working in a high-rise condo complex being built at 2088 Barclay Street in Vancouver's West End. We were responsible for installing hardwood on every floor. As the job wore on over a series of weeks, we continued our ascent up that tower. At lunchtime we often ate on the balconies, enjoying the views of Stanley Park's Lost Lagoon and surrounding area.

On one of those days, we were on about the fifteenth floor. Before we sat to eat, we headed to the edge of the big balcony and looked down. Just like every other floor, the view was incredible. As I approached the edge of the deck, I had not noticed that a railing had yet to be installed. In a muscle memory-like response, I leaned forward to grab it. With nothing there for my hands to grab, I felt my body become weightless. Just then, my quick-thinking colleague grabbed the back of my sweater with a clenched fist. Just beyond the hinge point of falling to certain death, Doug saved me.

One other significant event happened while I was working for that company. It was on a job up in West Vancouver on a street called Montiverdi Place. The large home, cut out of the sharp, jagged, West Vancouver landscape, was on a hill. The driveway was blocked, and tradesman had to park on the street. I had to park about half a block up the street at the top of the hill. No problem; just a bit of a hike with all my tools and a few trips back and forth were needed.

At day's end, thinking nothing of it, I packed up my toolbox and headed for my car. It was an overcast day and quite peaceful once I exited the work zone. Walking head down with my portable table saw in one hand and my toolbox in the other, I was happy to be heading home. As I slugged up the hill to my car, my thoughts drifted to how the commute home would be over the Lions Gate Bridge. No sooner had that thought crossed my mind than, for reasons I will never be able to explain, a voice inside said, "Look up!"

I did, and just in time! Right in front of me, the car that had been parked first in line at the top of the hill was coming straight at me! It was fifteen feet from me when I dropped my tools and launched myself into the ditch. The driverless car exploded when it hit the cliff at the bottom of the long hill in front of the job site. All the tradesman were out checking the damage before I even collected myself. I was in a state of shock. I had not heard the car coming, and something told me to look up before it wiped me off the face of the earth. Why was I still there and surviving such near-fatal events? Days like those and some of the other near-death experiences I will recount later have only increased my appreciation for pretty much everything. I didn't think of it that way at the time, but I believe something was and has always been looking out for me.

Over the next two years, I continued to increase my involvement in the horse-racing world. My friend, John Snow, got his trainer's licence. I was fortunate enough to become part owner of his first racehorse "Jazz N Time." It reached the point where I was spending more time at the track (even when races weren't on) than I did anywhere else. I would take a clean set of clothes with me to work and shower at the track. Much like motocross, it was the people, environment, and excitement I craved. Remember, Geminis thrive on excitement.

I also dated many beautiful gals in that two-year period. A date with me usually included a trip to the track's backstretch to meet my horse and then on to the owners' boxes.

My sponsor quickly pointed out that everything I craved at the racetrack wasn't much different than when I drank. I was confused. I was sober, and I didn't have to lie, steal, or cheat to enjoy my newest passion. He reminded me, much like in our program, that when I made comments like that to always add *yet*. "You haven't done that *yet*," he would say. He reminded me that compulsive gambling, much like alcoholism, was a disease that was progressive in nature. I ignored him and carried on as I saw fit. However, I discovered the truth of his words in short course, and I learned it the hard way.

On a side note, growing up I regularly watched a TV show called *Quincy*. It starred Jack Klugman as a forensic pathologist who worked for the Los Angeles County Coroner's Office. Jack was in Vancouver working on a sequel to his other hit, *The Odd Couple*. He was also into horse racing. He was at our track one night, because he was friends with my trainer's bloodstock agent. He sat in our box, and I must admit, I was a little starstruck. Then things got even better. My friend's horse, "Counting On You," won her race. Off to the winner's circle we went for our photo. I have seen that photo time and time again in the last few years. However, when I looked for it to put it in this book, I couldn't find the damn thing anywhere. Great memories, nonetheless. Jack Klugman passed away in 2012. RIP, Quincy.

17

Chaos, Disguises, and a Miracle

Full steam ahead into the Neon Nineties, there was no stopping this stubborn, independent redhead. I'm not even sure if I had any kind of long-term plan. I lived for the moment and never worried too much about the future. Up to that point, I had managed to survive what I was starting to think was a chronic case of bad luck. Or was it? Today the dots are much easier to connect, knowing what I do about addiction.

I had a brand-new Nissan pickup that was wired for sound. My flavour in that regard was also changing with the times. I still appreciated Van Halen, AC/DC, and other metal tunes, but the nineties mellowed that a little for me. My speakers now chimed to the likes of Barney Bentall, Jim Croce, Nirvana, Tom Cochrane, and U2. I even went on a date with a gal to a Gloria Estevan and the Miami Sound Machine concert. I didn't know what to expect and went with an open mind. That concert was Gloria's first tour since her 1990 tour bus crash in Scranton, Pennsylvania, which almost killed her. The crash broke her back, and she needed titanium rods to be installed and her vertebrae fused. I couldn't help but be impressed with the incredible full-circle comeback performance she put on for us at the Pacific Coliseum. Seeing someone so talented and determined to overcome her adversity stayed with me.

The year 1992 marked for the first time in history that the World Series championship flag flew in a ball park outside the United States. Our own Toronto Blue Jays defeated the previous year's winner, the Atlanta Braves, in six games. The Jays made some key off-season moves to solidify their veteran winning lineup. I remember exactly where I was when Dave Winfield hammered his game-winning two-run double down the left field line at Atlanta's Fulton County Stadium in game six. The Blue Jays, on the power of Joe Carter's ninth-inning three-run homer, won the series again in 1993. Baseball fever was contagious, and it seemed like our entire country was infected.

I had started to leave my job early to get to the racetrack earlier. Looking back now, that makes no sense, because most of the racing cards didn't start until 6:00 p.m. on weeknights. I just felt I needed to be there schmoozing with the who's who (jockeys included) to get any information that might help me make my millions. Sometimes it worked, and sometimes it didn't. I learned many things quickly, and knew who I could trust.

I had another friend who had a horse that had speed. The problem was, he was a bad actor in the starting gate. By the time his race started, the horse would be spent from the ruckus it had created.

One night he drew the ten post. That was good news, because he would likely go into the gate last. It didn't always work that way, so I talked to a friend on the gate crew. I pleaded with him that if that horse went in the gate calm and the last one to load, he had a great shot to win. The guy who trained that horse thanked me and told me that he had bet twenty to win on the horse for my efforts. When the gate dropped in the six-furlong dash, it was the number-ten horse straight to the front and winning the race in gate-to-wire fashion. I headed to the test barn with my date to congratulate my friend and his horse. He had an ear-to-ear smile on his face as he pulled out the ticket he had purchased on my behalf out of his shirt pocket. His horse had gone off at 25–1 odds. When I gave the ticket to the teller, I received just under a week's pay, over $500. That horse racing game was much like trying to capture a bolt of lightning inside a bottle, in coal mine, but I always had a plan. Sometimes they even worked.

I was falling out of favour at BC Hardwood, for obvious reasons. It didn't bother me though, because I had teamed up with another co-worker who had started his own company. It was a short-sighted decision, but I liked the idea of being paid more regularly, and most times, it was untraceable cash, though it meant saying goodbye to my union job with full benefits.

I started to attend off-track betting sites on non-racing days. Simulcast wagering wasn't legal in our province, so some of the places I went were a little shady. I knew some of the people there from their involvement at the races. The places I'm talking about were unmarked and usually just a locked room at the back of a coffee shop on Commercial Drive or in the surrounding area. I even got to sit and play with some high-profile athletes. No names mentioned, but having an NHL all-star and captain of his team buy me a cappuccino certainly floated my boat.

I was starting to wear out my welcome at home once again. I didn't see my parents much, because my new lifestyle allowed no time. I didn't pay rent and always dodged the subject if it came up. I knew I was pushing my luck, but in my mind, I needed the fuel to gamble. I moved into a nice home in south Vancouver at 41st and Trafalgar. A guy who I hung out with regularly at the track rented me a room. He only charged me a few hundred dollars, and that was about the only financial responsibility I could handle. On many occasions after a win or a big hit, we headed south for some serious gambling. Eventually, I screwed that up too. Dave, my old friend, like the many others in this story who helped me along my journey, please know that you were appreciated.

Dave wasn't the only person for whom my financial responsibilities were falling short. Many of my bills were delinquent, and I was starting to owe money to friends and horseman around the racetrack. The right thing to do would have been to pay them off, but I went another direction. On race days I avoided my regular hangouts, like the backstretch restaurant, the barns, and the paddock. I would sit way down on the end on the grass or way up in some obscure spot in the grandstands. Sometimes I even wore a fedora and large eyeglasses to change my appearance. What the hell was I becoming? I was completely irresponsible and only fooling myself about what I was really after. My dad even called me on it one day. "Brent, there's a whole lot more to lose gambling than just money," he said. That pissed me off, but I discovered the truth of his words soon enough.

When my parents took me back in for the final time, I headed straight for my hockey cards—my highly treasured and safeguarded Wayne Gretzky rookie card, which was in mint condition, to be exact. No, I didn't want to look at it; I was curious about what I could get for it. It was a few days from payday, and the shoes I was wearing were trashed. I also needed money to play the Wednesday night card at the Cloverdale Raceway.

There was a sports card shop on 72nd Avenue close to my parents' home in North Delta. I sat in the parking lot for a good five minutes staring at the card. I had three of them at one point, but that perfectly centred, razor-sharp cornered card was a mint gem. I was torn. I had met Wayne and, like most in the hockey world, was a huge fan of the greatest to ever play the game. Something deep inside told me that I may never see another Gretzky rookie card in that condition again. One side of my Gemini brain said, "No," but the other half went to work rationalizing my decision to go into the store. The card was worth around $1,000. I hoped to get at least $500 for it.

When I got in the store, the guy I showed the card to told me that it was the nicest one he had ever seen. He had a few in his shop though, and unless the price was right, he didn't want it. Most people in their right mind, which I obviously wasn't, would have walked out. I pleaded with him for $300. I walked out the door minus my highly treasured and dearly loved Gretzky rookie card and with $200 in my wallet. It was getting close to 5:00 p.m., and racing started at 7:00. My pride would no longer allow me to show up at my happy place with beat-up shoes. Part of the horse-racing game was that it was also my social scene. I didn't want to look like a down-and-outer. I was better than that, right? Thankfully, there's no space for your answer in this book.

When I arrived at the track that evening, I headed to where I usually met my friends before the race, a place in the grandstand basement called—get this—the Stand Up Bar. I laugh when I write that now, because had I been in a wheelchair back then, maybe they wouldn't have let me in. In all seriousness, once again, it was me and the usual suspects in their usual places. Everyone was studying their race programs. I had bought a new pair of kicks, and had just over $100 in my wallet. The guys were going off about the big pick six carryover that night, which was nearing $60,000. I went over the racing form and put together a ticket. It came out to $64. I asked two of my friends if they wanted to go in on it with me. Excited at the prospect, they asked who I had selected and then looked at my picks. The pick six involved picking the winners of races two through seven. We could have more than one horse in each race, but we had to multiply each line by each other. It got costly quickly.

In the fifth race, I had picked a horse named Balthazar. He was a New Zealand-bred horse that had won a lot of money up to that point. But there was a problem. He had been in Canada a while now, and his current form was terrible. My rhyme and reason for selecting him was that, amidst my schmoozing, I had met a trainer who had wanted me to claim (buy) a horse with him. We met at the track many times and spoke often. He loved the New Zealand-bred horses and could get them turned around and back on point like none other. He even went as far as to say, "Brent, if you ever see me claim a New Zealand-bred horse, grab a piece of the action if the odds are to your liking." I had two others in that race on my ticket just in case. That fifth race was a real mixed bag of low-end claiming horses. The reality is that in races like these, anything could happen. My friends wanted no part of my ticket and played their own. I was left with the quandary of spending $64 of my last $100 on that ticket—or removing some of my selected horses to lighten up the cost. I ended up spending a practical, to my mind, $16 on the ticket.

In my head, I told myself that if Balthazar came through for me, I would be in a good position to be one of few with a live ticket. The horse didn't disappoint. He won the fifth race by open lengths and paid, get this, $64 for a $2 win ticket. I had no money on him to win, but I did have a live pick-six ticket with two horses in each of the remaining two races.

Before race five, I headed to the men's room. Upon exiting I ran into a guy I had met in Calgary, "Off the Wall" Paul. He was a player, and a big one at that. He flew out for that race because of the huge pick six carryover. Like most others, he had been put out in the fifth race by Balthazar. I told him I was still alive, and he asked to see my ticket. He looked at me and then pulled out a nickel. You know the kind, five $100 bills. For that he wanted half of my live ticket. Seeing that money was tempting, but I said no. He smiled and then told me if I changed my mind, he would be in the bar.

I headed back to my friends and shared what had transpired. Saying it out loud had me rethinking the situation. The damn thinker I was born with is always in overdrive. Before the gate dropped on the next race, I went searching for Paul. Before I even reached his table, his arm extended with the five brown bills poking out of his hand. I was elated to have them in my wallet. To me that was a win. I had gone to the track with just over $100 and now had $500. I didn't go back to my friends. Instead, I went and sat by myself in the grandstand.

I knew that pick six was going to pay huge if I hit it, even with giving up half for a nickel. One of the owners, Don, who I had befriended, saw me sitting on my own and joined me. I talked with Don superficially for a bit, and then we got to the brass tacks of the pick six. I told him I was still alive and showed him who I had. He liked my ticket and my chances. I was getting nervous and even caught myself starting to hyperventilate.

I made it through race six and was still alive. The seventh race had a scratch and would be a six-horse race. I had the one and the two horses. At that half-mile oval, the inside posts were more favourable. I know one of the horses was Columbia Nipper, but the other escapes me. All I knew was "One, two, come on, one, two, come on...."

The race was almost anticlimactic, because it started and finished the same way, 1–2. I had the two best horses in the race, but more importantly, I had a winning pick-six ticket. My friends found out where I was sitting, and when I turned around to acknowledge them, a huge crowd had gathered. Everyone knew I had what was likely one of the only winning tickets. When the tote board lit up, I thought my heart had stopped. There were three winning tickets, each paying the rightful owners $17,840. I was one of them! Paul came with me to the window to collect the loot. The teller told me it would be a while before they could issue a cheque. I didn't like that idea. The way I saw it, they never let me bet with a cheque, so why should I be paid with one?

The teller had no argument for that. My friends encouraged me the whole way, promising to act like the six-foot-plus thugs they were when I headed to my truck. For the record, even though I was only five feet eight inches, I was considered a thug at that time, too. Once I paid Paul, I couldn't get home fast enough with my share of the jackpot, $8,770. Seven of these bills were $1,000 bills. I had never even seen one before.

I mentioned how I had fallen out of favour at home as a result of my new affliction. To me this was the perfect opportunity to show my parents that I was a winner. It still haunts me today what I put my mother through that night and as a result of that win in general.

When I got to the house, I told her that I needed to talk to her about a problem I had. She sat and waited. I think she was expecting me to admit I had a problem with gambling and needed help, the same way I needed help with my drinking. My first sentence was just that, "Mom, I have a gambling problem. The problem is, I've gambled, and now I have too much damn money." She almost stopped breathing when I threw the money into her lap.

She pleaded with me to do something constructive with the money rather than give it back to the track. I think she already knew what the math would be on that one though. Her response hurt me a lot. I knew in my heart that she was right. Having no argument in response, I went to bed, because I had to work in the morning.

The next day I told Dave, for whom I was working, about the win. He was impressed that I even came in the next day following such success. The truth was that even though my fuel tank was now temporarily full, it wouldn't be for long.

Life was pretty good for a while, or so I thought. I had a decent supply of fuel and a set routine. I had been back to my normal body size for quite some time since weighing in to the Renfrew Detox at almost 200 pounds. Being an alcoholic and allergic to the beer I was drinking was literally killing me. On top of that, my liver was pretty much on life support. I wasn't drinking, but I only seemed to eat regularly during the workday. Once I departed for the track, food was the farthest thing from my mind. I had an appetite for one thing only: excitement and adrenaline. I couldn't have weighed more than 130 pounds during that stretch. My friends at the track even encouraged me to become an exercise rider for the horses. It never happened, because I have never trusted horses. That may seem strange, because I considered myself fearless on a steel horse at one point.

That winter while playing a game of pickup hockey at the Queens Park Arena, I suffered another serious concussion. One of the guys I worked and played with, named "Gronk," was a giant. He was six and half feet tall. He wasn't the best on skates, but when his stick was planted, he was an unmovable tripod. I had just skated out over my own blue line with the puck. Being a right winger, I was on the opposite side of the ice. When I looked up, the centre man and left winger were just ahead of me on the left side of the ice. I still had decent wheels and hit the afterburners as I headed to the right. Just as I crossed centre ice, I took another quick look left. Before I even knew what the hell happened, I ran headfirst at full steam into the unmovable Gronk. Making matters worse, after hitting him headfirst, my helmet-less head bounced off the ice. Everything was bright, but I couldn't see anything. The guys helped me to my feet. Once at the bench, I needed help to get to the dressing room. I was in trouble, and I knew it. The last thing I wanted to do was go see another damn doctor.

I went back out to the bench for a bit. I tried a couple of shifts and started throwing up. It was back to the dressing room and out of my gear.

Not long before I had suffered a bad concussion at the BMX track. Added to that I had fallen through the opening of the stairway at my uncle's new home and landed headfirst on the concrete basement floor. My noodle might as well have been inside a spaghetti strainer rather than the helmets I was or wasn't wearing.

For a few months after that header, I had a hard time focusing. I also got dizzy and delirious at times. One night coming home from New Westminster after dark, the headlights on the other cars had me struggling to stay on the road. I pulled over and walked around Moody Park until I felt better. That bout lasted about an hour. Eventually, I was able to get back in my truck and navigate the Queensborough and Alex Fraser bridges. Bouts like that and the general sense of being dizzy and loopy lasted for months. Not even thinking it might be related to my head injury, I thought I was getting too much wheat. That is also a symptom I get when my system becomes wheat or candida toxic. My brain is not nearly as sharp, as if I'm in an altered state. Even so, I still include wheat in my diet, but it has to be monitored.

I thought that all I needed was to buy some vitamins. Being the all-or-nothing guy that I am, I was all in. When it came to taking them, my rationale was, if one was good then more would be better. That proved to be mistake when it came to taking garlic and chili pills to improve circulation. It felt like I was on fire and going to combust. Eventually, the concussion symptoms subsided though.

There was no more hockey for me that winter. At the top level, the Stanley Cup final was contested between Wayne Gretzky's Los Angeles Kings and the Patrick Roy-led Montreal Canadians. Gretzky had been traded to Tinseltown in the summer of 1988. Hockey was now a Hollywood hit thanks to team owner Bruce McNall. McNall, who was also a thoroughbred race horse owner, was the NHL's newest visionary owner. Sadly, the Bruce McNall era in Los Angeles did not have a Hollywood ending. In 1994 the courts ordered the sale of the Kings, because McNall had defaulted on his $90 million Bank of America loan. He was also charged with defrauding several banks of more than $236 million. McNall pled guilty and did his time. He was released from prison in 2001.

The Kings lost the final to Montreal in five games. I watched that series like a hawk. My mom, who had been a lifetime Leafs fan, was also cheering for the Kings. I have great memories of watching a couple of games in that series with her. LA won the first game, but in the second, while up 1–0, Marty McSorley was called for an illegal stick. Montreal scored on the ensuing power play, and won that pivotal game in overtime. The series went back to Montreal tied, but the Kings didn't win another game. Patrick Roy was voted series MVP. As for Gretzky, he was traded the following season to St. Louis as result of the McNall debacle. I'm not sure we will ever see Bruce McNall in the Hockey Hall of Fame, but when gauging his impact on hockey, I think we only need look as far as this. When the Kings wanted to retire Gretzky's sweater, he would only allow that to happen if his friend Bruce McNall was in the building. That is a powerful statement coming from the greatest ever to play the game.

By the summer of 1993, I still had no real plans other than working and playing the ponies. It was a struggle to keep up physically, financially, and mentally. I was growing increasingly more unreliable in the employment department. My work schedule was now three or four days a week rather than five or six. I wasn't worried though, because I figured I was just another big win away from certain happiness. What I didn't understand was that my fascination with the ponies, even though it cost a lot, wasn't about money. My underlying problems were the real culprit. Gambling, drinking, a compulsive desire to eat mashed turnips, whatever it was, it was just a symptom. I had heard that, but I didn't understand it yet.

I was in need of shoes again, so I figured a trip up to my lucky shoe store in the Scottsdale Mall was in order. That was a bit odd, because I was never really that superstitious about anything, but I was desperate.

When I got to the shoe store, I stood along the west wall trying to decide on a new pair of sneakers. The clerk acknowledged me and then let me do my thing. Not more than a minute or two later, a beautiful Fijian girl approached. She stood beside me and didn't say anything at first. Then she told me that she was being followed around the mall by someone who was making her uncomfortable. I thought nothing of it and acknowledged that it was okay for her to stand with me. After some time passed, we left the store together. I didn't know what to make of that experience and just decided to go with it. We ended up back at the place she had rented and played some basketball. One thing led to another, and we got busy getting to know each other and having some fun.

I was anxious to introduce her to my family and friends. It was the first time in years that I had met someone who I could see myself having a future with. Everyone in my circle seemed to approve. I believe most people were just happy to see me happy somewhere other than at the racetrack, although most of our early dates and outings were to the track. I also found out that my new partner, Seema, had a daughter, who was born in 1991. Her name was Sonu. She was in Portland, Oregon, and being kept there by the mother of Sonu's father, at least that's the story I was told.

My mom, being the legal beagle that she was, jumped into action. I don't know how it shook down, but after some legal work was done, my mom and Seema went to the border and picked up Sonu. She was a gem and still is today. She has been a daughter to me ever since that day. Just two years ago, for the first time since then, Sonu made a trek south to visit her biological father. At the time I met Seema, he had been deported.

Our first Christmas together came with the news that we would be expecting our first child in August 1994. Many raised their eyebrows when that news dropped, but I thought it was what I needed. It was a chance to get my life on track and live like a responsible adult. After all, wasn't that what most people did at age twenty-seven? I will admit I was and always will be a kid at heart. But I dug in harder at work and prepared the best I could for the new addition.

I still went to the racetrack almost every night, justifying it to myself that I could win again. I also maintained my connection with a few of my twelve-step friends. On February 21 I celebrated five years of sobriety. I was sober, and drinking was no longer an option. If I picked up a single drink, I knew it would set up the phenomena of craving, and I would likely die quickly. I didn't want to die. I had a child on the way, which I saw as a new lease on life.

We needed to find a home, and I was getting stressed about that. The size of place we needed cost well over $1,000 a month. I started to bet bigger, hoping my returns would be bigger. One night I blew an entire paycheck. I was sick to my stomach and realized I needed help. I had heard it many times before at my meetings, "God doesn't go into bingo halls." I didn't even know what the hell that meant at first. Maybe that's a good thing, because I didn't buy it. I had a new plan. I headed to the casino in Surrey to play the roulette wheel. I had played a little bit before, but to me, casinos were for losers. No one ever won there, did they? Maybe I'm one of those losers; I'll let you decide.

I'm not sure how it happened, but my numbers of double zero and thirty-six red never let me down. Before long I had a stack of $100 chips. I even had a pit boss come up to me at one point and ask me how much I was up. In those places they only do that when the house is losing their shirt. I had gone into that casino that night with $200 and was smart enough to walk out when I tipped the scale at $4,000.

As short-sighted as they were, my prayers had been answered. As far as God not going into bingo halls, I will never know, because that was a casino. I maintain that a power greater than me, who I choose to call God, has always looked out for me. It's part of my routine to thank him daily.

We rented the top floor of a massive home on 64th Avenue in North Delta. It was $1,150/month plus utilities. It was a spacious home that would give us the room we needed. My family did their best to help us, and I busied myself with home projects while not at work. I even started to do little pedalling again on my unicycle and mountain bike in the Panorama Ridge area of Sunshine Hills. Living as a young growing family, we fared pretty well at first.

Early in 1994 my dad's father became quite ill. He had lung cancer and passed away that spring in White Rock. I'm sad that my grandfather didn't get to see my firstborn child, but I'm grateful that my father got to make peace with him. I also feel blessed that our family was able to spend a few quality years with him. That would not have happened had he not sobered up. Until we meet again, Grandpa, thanks for all you did for us.

As I noted earlier, my grandfather loved his money. He was a stingy bugger too, which was one reason why he had so much dough. He lent me money often at the track or the casinos when we went. I was always cautious when I asked him though, because I knew he would want to know exactly when he would get it back. He knew where I worked and when I got paid. If I was a late repaying him, I knew a phone call was coming.

I don't know how much money my grandfather had when he passed away. That was none of my business. However, shortly after his service in White Rock, my dad took me aside and told me that Grandpa had wanted to help me out. I'm sure my dad had some misgivings about that, but he wanted to honour his dad's wishes. I received $10,000 as a partial inheritance as well as my grandpa's prized Cadillac. Here again was hope that I would put the money to good use. I still had a few thousand owing on my truck. I could have paid that off instantly and gotten rid of the $200/month payment. That would have put a smile on my grandpa's face. However, my brain didn't work that way. I rationalized the decisions I made with my own committee.

Off to the bank I went. It was just a deposit to start, because I wanted to see that $10,000 in print in my bank book. I should have taken a picture, because it didn't stay there long.

I went to the track that Wednesday night and spent a modest $200. I had a bit of a code that I stuck to sometimes. The code was $200 in my wallet, and if I needed more, I got the rest through a bank machine. My rationale was, more times than not, if I couldn't win on $200, I wasn't going to win on $400. One of my dad's old sayings rings true here: "Don't go looking for luck, son. Let luck find you."

That night at the track, I tried to recruit some friends to go to Vegas. Most were down on their luck, and I had no takers. I wasn't paying anyone else's way other than my own. I drove straight to the Seattle Airport after the last race that night at Hastings Park. By 6:00 a.m., I was on a one-way Alaska Air flight to Sin City. I had convinced myself that my alchemy would continue down there.

It didn't. It was horrible, I lost time and time again on the roulette wheel. I was determined to prevail and kept withdrawing more money. At one point when I returned to the wheel after grabbing some more cash, the dealer was pulling the ball out of my number, thirty-six red. I can't tell you how sour I felt seeing that. After three nights of self-torture, I departed for the airport and flew back home.

I didn't put any of my grandfather's money toward my truck. We didn't go without at home for a while, though. With the baby expected in August, we still had some time to prepare. Sonu settled into our new place nicely. Right from day one, that girl always had a ton of affectionate energy for life and people. I used to take her to the track with me every now and again. She was pretty small, and I carried her around on my shoulder.

One night, I approached a friend of mind named Dooley. He was an older fella, and I greeted him by name. Riding on my shoulders, Sonu took note and welcomed him with a great big, "Hi Doofy!" We all had a good laugh. It may not have been Chuck E. Cheese, but I was never too proud not to take my kids to the track.

That spring also gave us something to cheer for that we had not had for a while. For only the second time in their history, our Vancouver Canucks were in the Stanley Cup finals. They were up against a powerful New York Rangers team that had not won a cup in fifty-four years. Glen Sather was the general manager in New York and had brought many ex-Oilers with him, the most notable being the "Moose," Mark Messier. What an incredible series that turned out to be. Game one was on May 31, the day before my twenty-eighth birthday. I had been to the conference finals-clinching game at the Pacific Coliseum against the Toronto Maple Leafs. That Canuck team was good and versatile. Led by "Russian Rocket" Pavel Bure and backstopped by goalkeeper Kirk McLean, the team had also added some key ingredients from St. Louis in the form of hometown boy Cliff Ronning (who I had cheered for as a New Westminster Bruin), Vancouver Island's Geoff Courtnall, and the guy I called "Momentum," big Mo, Sergio Momesso. The Canucks had their hands full with that powerful Ranger team.

The Canucks won the opener in New York in overtime after tying the game late in the third. I still get goosebumps thinking about what was on the front page of the *Province* newspaper the following day. It was a full-page photo of the Canucks celebrating the winning goal with an image of their late owner, Frank Griffiths, looking down at the team in approval. That was extra special, because I had been in the Griffiths' home recently.

I didn't get to any of the home games in that series, but game seven was memorable for many reasons. It was held on Tuesday, June 14, at New York's Madison Square Garden. Headed back home to North Delta that day after work, I felt the excitement and anticipation building. Game seven was a big deal. Mom and Dad even came over to watch. The Canucks fell behind 2–0 early but fought back late in the game. Team captain Trevor Linden cut the deficit to 2–1. The Rangers got another, and then so did Linden. With time winding down, a player who had recently been called up from the farm team, Nathan Lafayette, rang one off the post. That near miss with around five minutes left in the game certainly didn't help my heart condition.

As the clock ticked down in the final minutes, the Canucks' unwavering assault on the Rangers' Mike Richter continued. It was to no avail, because when the buzzer blew, the Rangers were 3–2 victors! As a fan of that team from day one, I would be lying if I said I wasn't disappointed. I was happy to see the effort they put in though, and unlike their 1982 Stanley Cup final, I believe they were just one good bounce away from winning. Recognizing that and not hating on my team for losing was a sign that I was maturing. Please don't let your hopes get too high though, because I still had a long way to go.

By midsummer work was slow. I was struggling to keep up with my current employer's demands. I had started out as his main installer, but due to my unreliable nature, he found others. He did his best to keep me afloat on the jobs he trusted me on. Nevertheless, a few months into our new life together as a young family, finances were tight. The truth is, had I just buckled down and gone to work and performed the job I was capable of doing every day, things would have been fine.

One night at the track, one of my friends, a used-car salesman, made me a solid offer on my Nissan pickup. With my best short-sighted thinking at work, thinking I still had Grandpa's Caddy, I accepted it. Somewhere in the back of my mind I felt that letting that truck go was also releasing my last connection to dirt bikes. Even though it wasn't a regular thought, I always visualized myself riding again one day. After all, my friend and mentor just a short while before had encouraged me that it wasn't too late. In my heart I was slowly making peace with that never happening though. I was torn. Some days I would go out and rip through the trees and mulched pathways of Sunshine Hills' forests as if I was winning a national title. I knew what it felt like to be a winner, but that feeling was already becoming a long-distance call at best.

On the night of Wednesday, August 24, I headed out the races in Vancouver. I had not worn out my welcome there yet. You see what I just did there? Like my sponsor had suggested, I added "yet." Later I learned that the affliction of compulsive gambling that I was suffering from was also a progressive disease. I know some people get a little funny when they hear the word "disease" mentioned in relationship to these disorders. I balked at first, too. But then I had a mentor put things into perspective. He said, "Dis-ease, you get that? You are at dis-ease." I certainly couldn't argue with that. I was usually restless, irritable, and discontented until the sense of ease that came from a first drink or a bet. That was a huge wakeup call, because I was starting to realize that gambling was also beginning to cut me up. I wasn't drinking, but the character defects that I had recognized and removed when I sobered up were once again controlling my life. To many on the outside looking in, that was perplexing. With booze it was obvious what my problem was. With gambling one of the things I heard around my loop fits well: "You can't smell a deck of cards, can you?" No, you can't, nor could anyone smell the hundreds of dollars of pari-mutuel tickets in my pocket on any given night.

That Wednesday night card at the track got cut short due to a fire. Just below the track at the foot of the Second Narrows, or Ironworkers Memorial Bridge, an industrial supply building caught fire. The smoke was so intense that it blanketed the track and the barn facility.

I headed back home to North Delta, which was a godsend, because when I got there, Seema was in full-on labour. We gathered up Sonu and a few things and drove her to my parents' house a few blocks away. Then we headed for Royal Columbian Hospital in New Westminster, because our family doctor was there. He was also one of the Vancouver Canucks' physicians. He was a great doctor and a great human being. Whether it was me or any one of us, I always felt like he genuinely cared.

So far, I wasn't nervous at all, but as I accelerated over the Alex Fraser Bridge toward New Westminster, that began to change. I'm not even sure if my headlights were on.

When I pulled into the emergency parking lot at Royal Columbian Hospital, it was quite dark, but I spotted an open space. As I began a U-turn at a pretty good clip for a parking lot, I slammed headlong into a concrete lamp standard. It made a helluva bang! Parts of my Grandpa's poor Caddy were everywhere. I had other concerns, so it didn't bother me too much. I just did a quick survey of the damage and then parked the car.

We went into the hospital and got signed up to have a baby. I was nervous but excited. I felt we were going to have a beautiful child. That's exactly what happened. At 1:29 p.m., August 25th my beautiful baby girl, Sara Lynn Worrall, was born, weighing a healthy eight pounds seven ounces. Sara had beautiful brown eyes and a full head of hair, and there were no real complications. We were excited. Even though I had no idea what fatherhood would be like, I was determined to be a great dad.

My mom and sister in New Westminster, Christmas 1989

Christmas 1997 in North Delta, with Grandma Jean (my mom's mom)
at the head of the table

Seema, Sonu, Sara, and me in 1997

Grandma Jean and her seriously overweight grandson

In Richmond with Lori, Sonu, and Sara, 1999

Nolan and me unicycling in the rain on top of Richmond's Kwantlen College

Big sister Sonu with her little brother, Nolan, and sister, Sara

Mom and Dad and the kids in Richmond, 2000

Overtime call with the City of Vancouver after a windstorm

Our winning Vernon Winter Carnival entry in the name of my late mother,
"Grandma's Fairyland Clowns"

Gisela and I in 2008

Outside our second Vernon home.
The Adventure Bay condo across the lake in the background, 2005.

Dad, Gisela, the girls, and me at Dad's Armstrong farmhouse, 2008

First year back racing in twenty-six years. Nanaimo, BC, championship, first moto holeshot.

Two wheels for all at the Merritt ranch the year after Mom passed away

A full-time racer once again at the tender age of forty-three

2009 Walton TransCan on the 250 cc two-stroke Yamaha

Heading to the line of the Kamloops Pro National 2011
with Travis Acheson as my mechanic

Airborne at the Kamloops National in 2011 on the Valley Moto Sport KTM

Shaun Greenaway and me on the line together at the 2009 Walton TransCan

Sonu sending it on the TTR-125 at the Westering's house in Chilliwack in 2009

Riding the unicycle on Highway 17 on our way to Walton in 2011,
not far from the Terry Fox Memorial

My amazing sister, Kelly, her husband, Richard Lemieux,
and sons, Justin and Joshua

First race indoors in my old hometown of Chilliwack. Wearing my Blair Morgan, MX-Forum T. (James Lissimore photo)

Gisela and me stretching our legs on the way to Walton Raceway in 2011

At the West Edmonton Mall in 2008, highlighted by a Blair Morgan sighting

Just before heading to the line at the 2011 Walton TransCan

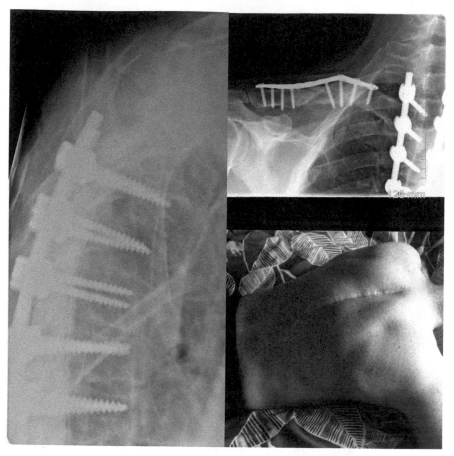

This is what the "Smart Car" that's holding me together looks like today.

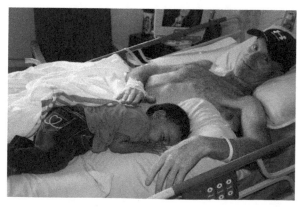

Granddaughter Ava's love was and is always appreciated.

My first flight after returning home from GF Strong was to Victoria to celebrate Gisela's parents' fiftieth anniversary.

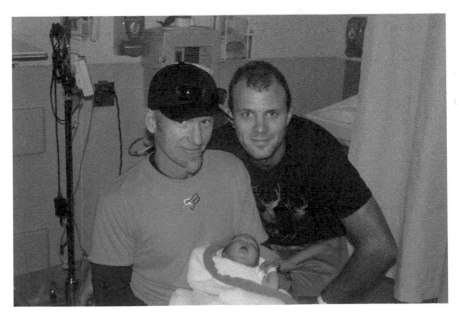

My son-in-law, Colin Jones (married to Sonu),
and I welcoming their newborn son, Mason

It put a huge smile on Rick's face when I told him about the day that I was compelled to come see him on his "Man in Motion" Tour.

Curling with Okanagan Para Peers Scotty James, Mike Foote,
and Paralympic gold medalist Sonja Gaudet

2012 Seattle Supercross, cheering on Kyle Beaton. Jess Pettis and Pat O' Conner,
gunning in the background.

The Canadian Moto Show is born.

Gisela and me on the job at the Kelowna Dirt Bike Club

Danielle Alessi, Mike Alessi, Mike Mamula,
and me at the 2015 San Diego Supercross

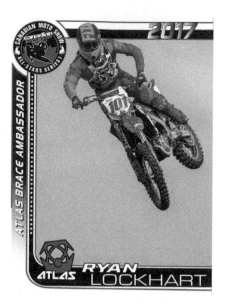

Atlas Brace rider Ryan Lockhart on one of our signature trading cards

Tyler Medaglia and I will always have special Walton connections.

On the Thompson Train at the 2016 Calgary National

2016 Christmas gift to our grandkids, Ava and Mason

Carol Henderson ran like crazy and saved my life.
You are my angel without wings, Carol.

Interviewing "The Man" Roger DeCoster at Angel Stadium at
Anaheim-3 Supercross in 2014

Supporting Canadian racer Dylan Wright at Glen Helen in 2015

The first live broadcast at Walton in 2015 with Lee family patriarch Chris Lee

I suggested to the Champ, Mike Tyson, that we have a go!

My friend, Reed LePine, at the Dawson Creek race, boosts me up into the tower

Calgary National 2015 with Chris and Ayrton Pomeroy,
along with pro woman's national #7 racer Dominique Daffe

My dad and his wife, Doreen, along with Gisela and me in Chilliwack 2017

Gisela and me catching the action trackside at Walton in 2016

Cheering on Cycle North Honda racer Summer Knowles trackside
at Walton in 2015

It was an incredible honour to be nominated for a Coast Mental Health
"Courage to Come Back" award in 2016.

Future West Arenacross live broadcast with the always-smiling Kevin Tyler and the fast and talented Shelby Turner

A surprise visit by the Enticknapp brothers, Adam and Tyler, to *Canadian Moto Show* headquarters

Hanging out at the Kelowna track on a practice day with my good friend, "Hammertime" Rick Hamer-Jackson

A play day with Ava in our neighbourhood

Handcycling today is a freedom that I absolutely love!

Jim Holley and Doug Hoover at the Toronto Supercross

Wearing my last racing jersey in support of the Humboldt Broncos

The Adventure Bay Peninsula, where I believe my higher power orchestrated one of my many miracles

One of our favourite spots away from the races is the Okanagan Rail Trail.

My birthday brother Tony Alessi and family,
two days before the 2017 Kamloops National

Day's end at Gopher Dunes in 2014 with Hayden Halstead
and Dunes patriarch Frank Schuster

Under the Legends tent at Walton in 2014 with Canadian pro women's east organizer Leah Clarke. The 81 bike belongs to two-wheeled legend Carl Bastedo.

Arizona Supercross 2015 with Ron Lechien, Steve Matthes, and Jason Weigandt

2016 Western Canadian National in Raymond, Alberta,
with our good friend, Trevor Unger

Gisela, Ava and Mason at Halloween.

Our sport has been made better by this man's involvement. His name is Brent Carlson, and I'm thankful he is our friend.

When I set out to write this book, I went to Evel Knievel's Snake River Canyon jump site to get a feel for where my two-wheeled story began.

Sitting on the spot where Evel launched from was one of the most powerful connections I have ever made to where I now sit.

Gisela and I at the Snake River Canyon in 2017

#LifeIsGold, friends, live it.

The Dreamer's Disease

Now that I was a dad with a family of my own to look out for, the world certainly seemed a more daunting place. That year was when our new North American Free Trade Agreement went into effect. We no longer had Brian Mulroney and his Conservative party leading our country. That job now belonged to Jean Chretien and the Liberals. South of the border, Bill Clinton was the forty-second president of the United States. Overseas, Serbia continued its onslaught in Bosnia. In South Africa Nelson Mandela was elected president in that country's first fully democratic election. Mandela headed the African National Congress with almost sixty-three percent of the vote.

In the sporting world, most of us had witnessed O.J. Simpson's "slow-speed" chase to infamy on the Los Angeles Interstate 75. On the pitch, the United States hosted soccer's World Cup. Powerhouse Brazil prevailed as the champs, defeating Italy in the final. As for the four-wheeled racing the world, 1994 saw the tragic passing of Formula One Superstar Ayrton Senna. On another sad note of the moral fibre kind, let's not forget the Tonya Harding/Nancy Kerrigan saga. It was a terrible incident that played out time and time again on our five o'clock news broadcasts.

I got to know Seema's family quite well. I took a liking to them. They had immigrated from Fiji a few years prior. We were regulars at their house in Port Coquitlam. Being the pasty-white, redheaded Englishman that I am, I never ate or craved spicy food. That was about to change in a big way. My palate soon took to the delicacy of that newfound culturally-diverse relationship perk. They always treated me like a king, and I can't thank them enough for that. They were good to us and helped us out in any way they could.

With money vaporizing quicker than I could earn, borrow, or steal it, I came up with a new plan: I would start my own hardwood flooring company. I had made some decent connections with contractors through my previous jobs. More than anything, I was tired of doing someone else's dirty work for little pay. At least that was how I rationalized my decision. In all seriousness, had I stayed with the BC Hardwood Flooring Company, things would have been okay financially. My problems at that point were no different than they had always been—entirely of my own making. Until then I had survived most scrapes I had gotten myself into financially. The biggest reason I put so much value on the people in my life today is that many of my personal relationships didn't survive those tumultuous times.

I would like to be able to say that things went well for a short while with my business, but that never happened. I did a few jobs on my own. I had a couple more quotes to give, and after the first one, the homeowner reached into his pocket and pulled out a cheque. I thought nothing of it until he asked me how much of a deposit I wanted for the materials. I'm surprised my head didn't combust when the lightbulbs went on in every single one of the many demons in my head. That was it, deposit cheques. Now I had a licence to go out and solicit work and collect deposit cheques for the materials I would be required to order. This was great. It would buy me time with money between jobs if I needed it. I don't know what the hell I was thinking, but things were definitely getting out of control.

My inner circle of friends at the track knew I did hardwood floors. I did a couple of jobs for some of the horseman, which went so well that the good word got around quickly. One of those jobs was for a friend of my horse trainer's aunt. I also had a good reputation with two of Vancouver's main hardwood suppliers. They had no reason to doubt me. They shouldn't have either, because my intentions were 100 percent pure when I took those deposits. I had every intention of doing those jobs well and on time. I prided myself on that. However, the reality of what I was dealing with in terms of my out-of-control progressively deteriorating gambling problem would pen a completely different plot.

Seema and the girls had gone to spend a few days with her family. I was knee-deep in work, which was a good thing. I had managed to keep the bills in check up to that point. In my mind our future as a family couldn't have been any brighter.

With my new responsibilities, I wasn't able to attend the races as regularly as I had before. That wasn't by choice but more out of a growing necessity to become a more responsible adult. You may have figured it out by now, but I'm still not sure I know what that means. I had seen enough dysfunction in my life. I also believed it would give me some kind of insurance from repeating such mistakes. Sadly, it didn't, because I was about to go into what I call "blackout mode."

Blackout mode was a big part of my drinking days toward the end. When it comes to alcohol and drinking, it's a no-brainer. I don't care who you are. If you dump enough of that stuff into anyone, eventually, they will black out. Alcohol wasn't the only thing that caused blackouts in my life. I also suffered periodic blackouts from some serious traumas that lay ahead. I have seen a lot and experienced a lot. Now I believe those blackouts protected me from doing some serious damage to myself or others.

I took advantage of having some time to myself. It had been a whirlwind of change up to that point with the many new responsibilities, but I loved my family and believed that was my destiny.

On Wednesday night that week, I headed to the track and I sat in my usual spot in the owners' box. I had met a guy over the years who was a bit of a bad seed, if you will. I'm not going to go to deep into it, but even he called himself a degenerate gambler. Every time he said it, it made me laugh. In essence, whether I realized it or not, I had become the same thing. I began to hang out with him more and more. For whatever reason, I became infatuated with some of the crazy and creative (mostly illegal) things he was doing to fund his gambling. He had been in and out of jail for most of his life and done some hard time. He was a clean-cut older gentleman, and for argument's sake, I will call him Sam. When it came to wagering, he was a heavy hitter. It was common for him to place $200–$1,000 win, place, or show bets. I was just a punter in comparison to how he was laying down the green.

That night he came back from the window with a wad of cash. When I saw that, I had another lightbulb moment. That's what I needed to do, bet a whole lot more!

I had nothing to lose, because I was in thick with the in-crowd at the track. Besides, if I lost I could just double up and get it back, right? Lady Luck had always taken care of me up to that point, so I had no reason to believe otherwise. If I did I'm sure my committee extinguished any resistance instantly.

I left the track that night down $1,000. I was sick to my stomach. I knew that kind of money would not be easy to recover quickly. The only option in my mind was to keep trying. I had nothing left to liquify. Looking back on that now, a song races through my head: "The Devil Went Down to Georgia" by the Charlie Daniels Band. We pretty much wore that tape out in our motorhome during our racing days. I loved the band and that song. Now I know why, because that's exactly what I was doing—selling everything I valued, including my soul, to fund my gambling addiction.

Within a few days of that latest quandary, I managed to burn through $5,000. Now I had my back up against the wall and was desperate for resolve. I had jobs to do, but I had already spent the deposit money. It was impossible to ask anyone for a loan, because most who knew me knew my current lifestyle. I didn't want to die, but for the first time ever, I contemplated taking my own life. What I did next many may never understand, but I believe it prevented me from following through with my exit plan.

I reached out to Sam and asked him if he could help me. He had a huge smile on his face when I told him how much money I had burned through in short course. He agreed that I was now stuck but told me that I could stay at his place until I had a plan. He also told me that no one would know I was there. Remember, he was cut from a similar cloth, and had burned through many a dollar himself. In the real world, most people wouldn't understand, but there's a saying that my old sponsor used to say, "Misery likes company, son. We often seek the lower companion to make ourselves feel better." I was finally starting to understand it. He also told me that it was progressive and would always get worse and never better. He even went as far as to say that if I progressed far enough, "The lower companion will start to look for you."

That one was a bit deep for me, but I knew many were now looking for me. I was a wreck. I was terminating everything in my life that I had ever valued, including my family. After about a week in Sam's basement contemplating how I was going to die, he showed me the door. I ended up at his son's house, who I had met through Sam. He lived in a part of Surrey that I usually saw on the 6:00 news. I didn't care; I just needed a place to hang until I could figure out what to do next. I'm not sure what kind of a bullshit story I gave him, but he and his roommates put up with me for a while.

It was a party atmosphere pretty much 24/7 at that place. Many people came and went regularly. Many things were passed my way, but I never picked up. That is, until an orange cooler with alcohol inside was offered to me. I had not had a drink in over five years. Was I going to do the unthinkable and take my drinking problem back into my own hands? Sadly, my will failed me. I had reached the moment that they spoke of in my meetings: "There will come a time when we have no mental defence against a first drink. That defence must come from a power greater than ourselves." I asked for no help from God or anyone else in that moment. I took the drink and was officially back on the garbage truck. We all know where the garbage truck ends up, don't we? At the dump!

I don't remember much about the next month, but some of what I do remember still haunts me. I know for a fact that there are still a few unsettled accounts out there. I liked to think I grew up in a tough home. I also know that as rough, tumble, and unorthodox as my father was, he had a code. The only codes I was experiencing at that time were on the butt ends of bullets. I know it's impossible to change any of that, but I still hate myself for abandoning my beautiful newborn daughter and family. How could anyone do such a thing? At least that's what I used to say when my mom told us stories about her dad. No, the fact that the apple does not fall too far from the tree doesn't make living with myself any easier. My supreme moral fibre, which I had prided myself on, was gone. I wanted desperately to be well and back with my family. That seemed impossible though, because I felt like a loser and a chronic fuck-up. What I didn't realize was that I wasn't a bad person who needed to be good, but a sick person who needed to get well.

In my absence, my mom and dad helped my family re-locate. I don't know how long I was missing in action, but it had to be at least two months. I made the call I feared the most and was reunited with Seema and the girls. They had moved into a place right beside the Sundowner Pub in North Delta. I didn't make any promises. I just wanted to be with my girls and help raise them. Things were not great, but we did our best to survive everything I had put my family through.

Sara's first Christmas was a memorable time. My mom always went over and above for Christmas, and her grandkids were the benefactors of that. I didn't work much at all when I returned home. My name was mud now at the track and also in the hardwood flooring business. I had not made any financial amends or righted some of the accounts I still had outstanding. My dad was working close to home on a contract falling trees on Abbotsford Mountain. He needed someone on the job with him, so he put me to work.

During that period, even though I was back home and living somewhat responsibly, I was still drinking—not regularly but wherever and whenever I could. It was a form of self-medication that was helping me cope with what I had become. I'm pretty sure my old man could smell the booze coming out of my pores on the morning commutes. I think back to many nights staring out my kitchen window at the neon "Open" sign at the Sundowner Pub. Some nights I would even make it to three minutes to eleven (closing time) before I bolted out the door for a six-pack of Colt 45 or XXX beer. The stuff was horrible, but it was around 8 percent alcohol. Multiply that by six, and it usually equalled a solid buzz. That's what drinking was for me, a buzz and an escape from reality. Drinking was never about flavour, wetting my whistle, or socializing. It was a necessity.

I stayed away from the track, because I owed a lot of money there, too, but I hit the casino every now and again, and continued to frequent the underworld of East Van's betting dens.

When the gate dropped on 1995, I arranged to do the last floor I had outstanding. The owner was good about it, and I did a decent job. He paid for the material, but had it delivered on his dime. I arranged to pay him back over a period of time. I still haven't completed that and still owe him $3,000. He and his family are on my amends list. I don't believe in leaving this earthly journey without having these accounts balanced. I'm not sure where I picked up on that, but it's something I stand by, no pun intended. Okay, maybe just a little.

Once again, for the time being life was pretty decent. I had my immediate family at home, and my parents and sister close by. Dad and I went to a few hockey games together that year. It had been ages since we had done that. It felt good, because going to hockey games together was a big part of my upbringing.

Someone else in my family was having huge success on the ice. My cousin, Doug Ast, who had led the Chilliwack Chiefs in scoring, was now a big leaguer. He didn't go the Major Junior route, because he had attended UBC in hopes of getting his teaching degree. After his Junior career was over, he tried out for the Vancouver Voodoo of the Roller Hockey International League. Much like his entire career, Doug went into camp well under everyone's radar. Not only did he make the team, he soon led the team in scoring. The games were played on the floor at the Pacific Coliseum in front of huge crowds. Doug became a fan favourite and was nicknamed "The Paperboy," because he always delivered. Over the course of that team's tenure in Vancouver, he was the leading scorer with 84 goals and 68 assists for 152 points in just 51 games. I might add that he was coached by the one and only Dave "Tiger" Williams. Doug was fortunate enough to play alongside heavyweights like Sasha "The Pitbull" Lakovic and former Canuck Craig Coxe.

Doug's roller hockey success wasn't overlooked by the Vancouver Canucks, who invited him to that year's training camp in Whistler. Even though he didn't make the team, he landed a spot on their Syracuse Crunch farm team. That marked the beginning of a stellar professional career, which saw Doug play for the Long Beach Ice Dogs and the Manitoba Moose before finishing up with eight years in Germany. Way to go, Doug. Your cousin is proud of you.

In non-sporting news, 1995 saw homegrown terror on US soil. On April 19, 1995, just after 9:00 a.m., 168 unsuspecting souls lost their lives in the Oklahoma City bombing, an act of domestic terrorism. I remember looking at the TV, despairing at the damage and wondering, why? That year also saw O.J. Simpson acquitted of the two first-degree murder charges of his ex-wife, Nicole Brown Simpson, and her friend, Ronald Goldman. The Simpson trial was high profile and lasted for nine months. In the end, the infamous glove didn't fit, and O.J. Simpson was a free man.

Right around that time, I got news that my old friend, Robbie Mutch, had died of a drug overdose. That hit me pretty hard, because Robbie was a big part of my upbringing and my first true two-wheeled colleague. I'm not sure what happened, but the bottom line was that his journey had been cut way too short.

The first person to greet me at his funeral was his dad, Bob. He took me into the room where Robbie lay at rest. Seeing that formerly vibrant young man lying completely devoid of life couldn't have hurt more. At the service, which was held in Surrey, it was cool to catch up with old moto friends who I had not seen in years. When my father and I left that day, my head was filled with silence the entire way home. Robbie's death was a huge wakeup call, which I took seriously. Drugs were no joke, and now I hated them even more! Making things even worse was the fact that Bob took his own life only a couple of years later. Receiving that news gutted me and my father. We were close to the Mutch family. RIP, fellas, and thank you both so much for your special place in my journey. Robbie, you better have that track dialled in when I get there, brother. We have a score to settle.

By that time, I was back up to 200 pounds again from my wheat intolerance while on a steady beer diet. Keep in mind that my normal healthy body weight is about 155 pounds. We still lived on 64th Avenue right across from the shopping centre and next door to the pub. I was drinking pretty much daily, but still managed to find the odd flooring job. The sad part was that if I didn't have work, instead of looking for it, I sat in the underworld bookie shops until my last dollar was gone. I was starting to feel hopeless and defective again. I did my best to be a good dad. I loved and still love my children more than anything. Sonu was attending Pinewood Elementary, and to most on the outside looking in, we were a pretty normal family. Then again, "normal" is just a setting on the dryer, right?

During the summer of 1997, Seema took the kids into Vancouver to visit her brother's family on Argyle Street, as she often did. While there, they needed to go out and get something. Luckily, the kids didn't go on the outing. Shortly after leaving his house, the car was broadsided by a car that had failed to stop. Our car was totalled, and Seema was in rough shape. I had known they were going to be out overnight, and had passed out on the couch, drunk, while watching a CFL game. I didn't hear the phone ring and didn't find out about the accident until later that evening.

Nothing was broken, but Seema's head and the side of her body had significant trauma. The car was written off, and Seema eventually recovered. If it seems like I'm being brief and maybe even a bit cold, remember, this is my story and what I was experiencing at the time.

Our relationship was deteriorating for many reasons. I fought it for the longest time, believing it was my calling and that I needed to be there for my kids. I blamed myself for everything. We had many arguments, and things that didn't make sense to me were happening. Again, this is my story, and I can only speak to my parts and what I felt. It's not that I was starting to dislike Seema; I just didn't understand where many of her seemingly irrational accusations were coming from. I did the only thing I knew how to do, and that was to keep trying harder. My upbringing had taught me that if I put in the appropriate effort, good things would happen eventually. I was putting in the effort, or so I thought, but I was fooling myself about certain values.

My dad took on another job as an urban faller and worked out of Stanley Park with the City of Vancouver's Park Board. With his body pretty broken down from years of packing those godawful heavy chainsaws through the bush, the new gig was a nice change of pace for my incredibly hardworking father. He told me there was a longstanding joke in the bush about tree falling. If the strip they were cutting was flat, they joked it was "just like falling In Stanley Park." Now that was where Dad would apply his skills, knowledge, and abilities.

I knew the city's head arborist, Paul Montpellier, appreciated my father, because he told me so one day. I get that, Paul. My dad has always been and always will be my hero. I hope it's not a spoiler alert, but I don't think any of my three children will ever say that about me. Yes, I'm responsible for that, and I have to live with it for the rest of my life. Why? Because I still had a shovel in my hand, and much like the hole I had dug and hidden in when I was a kid, I was not finished digging.

Through my dad's new job and connections at the Park Board, you will never guess who they hired next. That's right, yours truly. I was hired out of Sunset Nursery in the ethnically diverse neighbourhood of 51st and Main Street. I was hired as a water truck driver in the Arboriculture Street Tree Department. The pay was great, and I was guaranteed six months' work. I caught on quickly, and I can't thank Mac Stairs, Dieter Jablonowski, and Paul Montpellier enough for the opportunity.

After learning the ropes, I was put on night shift. I liked that, because I could come home and polish off a six-pack of strong ones while everyone else was asleep. Looking back now, it seems demented that pounding back beers was a highlight. Where was the resolve I had to be a champion? Sadly, I had blocked out everything I had learned about alcoholism. It's a progressive disease, meaning it only gets worse for people who are afflicted. That's not the case for everyone, but for me, my family's history was repeating itself. Making things worse, I no longer cared, and felt that was how I would die.

Now that I was working regularly again, I bought us a nice newer Nissan sports car. One of my new friends at the Park Board bought my grandpa's Caddy. I wanted to keep it for sentimental reasons, but fuel was getting way too costly. I was in no position to be collecting vehicles.

I had gotten to know the guy pretty well when he helped show me the ropes while working for the City. Amidst our conversations, he had told me that he planned to take the Utility Arborist Climbing Course in hopes of landing a full-time position with the Park Board. The idea of climbing trees in hazardous situations was appealing to my type-A personality. Not long after hearing that, I began to pick the brain of my supervisor, Mac Stairs. He told me that if I had that course, the city could justify hiring an individual full time. The course was held over a few weeks at the EITI (Electrical Industry Training Institute) in Surrey.

There must have been over twenty students at that course. I knew a good mark would go a long way to ensuring a solid position with the City. Incredibly, through most of my life, even with the addition of many bad vitamins and head injuries (the biggest ones still to come), I had maintained some smarts. We had a week in the classroom and then went out in the field to put the knowledge into practice.

I loved climbing trees wearing a belt and spurs. I was fearless but always heeded the dangers of the uncontrollable variables while spurred in with a chainsaw in my hand. Making that course even better was that it couldn't have been taught by a better individual than John Monk, a man who had done tree work in direct proximity to highly energized power lines for BC Hydro for most of his life. The city had over one million trees that needed attention. If you know anything about hydro lines and trees, working around them requires the utmost caution.

I'm not sure if it was the highest mark in the class, but when the grades were handed out, I was told that I was one of three people in the class who got 97 percent. I was ecstatic. For the first time in as long as I could remember, I applied myself to something as if my life and well-being depended on it, which they did.

Following the course, I was called in again as a temporary employee. On my last day of work, all the temps were saying their goodbyes. I started to do the same thing but was cut off by my boss, who said, "You're not going anywhere." He added that they were keeping me on to plant trees over the winter. I was over the moon with excitement, because I knew that meant I was becoming a full-time employee. I was officially hired in the Arboriculture Department as a Pruner 1.

January 1998 saw the untimely passing of my Grandma Jean (mom's mom) at age sixty-nine. She had a rare bone and blood cancer that spread rapidly. That hit our family hard. My dear grandma, who had raised eight children under such adversity and hardship, was gone. She had become our family's rock. If you ever met that beautiful, sweet lady, you would never know what she had seen and lived through. My grandma believed in unconditional love. As far as I know or anyone can remember, she never bore any grudges against anyone. That takes a special person. RIP, Grandma, you deserve the happiness that I believe you now have.

My new full-time job was great. I had a full benefit package, and my family would be taken care of. I loved being in the trees and felt like a monkey at times. Still based out of Sunset Nursery, I was on street tree duty. It was never the same job twice, which helped keep my interest, for the time being anyway. I was also PSSP (Power Systems Safety Protection) certified in order to work around power lines. Some days I was paired up with a colleague and put on an elevated boom truck. The boom trucks were a ton of fun, because they extended fifty-five feet in the air.

I got along with almost everyone, although I was certain a few people had it in for me. I wore my heart on my sleeve, but I was a hard worker. In fact, one day in the office, one of the long-term employees asked a supervisor who had done the most on a certain job. I was shocked to hear my name come out of his mouth. The colleague in question approached and told me to slow down a little, because I was making everyone else look bad. I was perplexed, and the first thing that came to my mind to say was, "You don't need my help for that. You're doing a pretty good job of that on your own."

Not smart. I gave it some thought, remembering that my father had warned me that at the City, it was best to go with the flow. I understood that, and it was never my intention to make anyone look bad. Simply put, when it comes to work, I have only had one gear. For me the endorphin release is part of the complex equation. Hard work was also my way of correcting for past mistakes and proving my worth. I know my colleagues didn't understand that, but my supervisors didn't seem to mind.

That job helped me in many ways. One of the best things about it was that it got me back on a regular work schedule. I drank much less during the week, because I knew I would be putting myself and others at risk if I did. As far as the gambling went, I still hadn't made financial amends at the track, so I stayed away for the time being.

That winter the Olympics took place in Nagano Japan, and the Goo Goo Dolls and the New Radicals were breaking out new hits over the airwaves. I was captivated by the New Radicals' tune "You Get What You Give." I had always believed strongly in karma. The lyrics made so much sense to me at that point in my life.

> Don't let go, you've got the music in you
> One dance left, that world is gonna pull through
> Don't give up, you've got a reason to live
> Can't forget, we only get what we give
> We only get what we give

I certainly understood those words, because I had been a fighter and a survivor up to that point. I also had the "dreamer's disease" that the band was singing about. I'm a bit torn on that one, but part of me hopes I die with the same affliction. After all, without hopes and dreams, what's left?

I was still miles away from my eventual rock bottom, but there was big trouble ahead that year for my immediate family and me. Home life wasn't great, but I continued to do my best to be a good father. We maintained our connections with our extended families, and our kids had much love from all. Sonu was as smart as a whip.

One time I walked to the video store with the kids. I had my bank card and $20 in my pocket. Upon entering the store, we only made it as far as the claw machine, those godawful things that never pick up exactly what you want. A gimmick, right? Not to me. If anyone could decipher that Jurassic claw and break the Toy Bank, it was me.

I put my twenty-dollar bill in the machine. Twenty unsuccessful attempts later, seven-year-old Sonu looked at me and said, "Okay, now what are we going to rent a movie with?"

Damn, she had a point there, didn't she?

That incident sums up how I was, and still am, at times. I'm either all in or all out. In my program they talked about how "half measures availing me nothing." I understand that fully and completely.

We did many cool, unique, and fun things as a family. I had some issues with Seema at times, which was frustrating. More than anything I didn't understand some of the rationale she constantly threw in my direction. We kept moving forward with the hope that things would get better.

I continued to blame myself for everything. Looking back now, I realize that I made some terrible mistakes. However, I also know that the relationship that I was trying to hang onto had no chance whatsoever.

Later that year, Seema made a trip back to Fiji. We had planned for the trip and saved for it. I had no problem with it, and knew it was impossible for us to go as a family. I stayed home with the girls and got some help with places for them to stay while I was at work. On one occasion I even drove them to a friend's house in North Vancouver from North Delta before I started my 7:00 a.m. shift. I sure don't miss those commutes.

The girls missed their mom when she was away, but we managed pretty well on our own. When Seema returned home, I assumed everything would be fine, but something was off. I didn't know what it was, and just assumed it was something I had done, or something she thought I had done. It was none of the above. It took a while to get it out of her, but I found out that while in Fiji, she had gotten married.

What the hell?

I'm still not sure about all the details, but the marriage was supposed to help someone gain access to our country or something like that. Either way, I was devastated. I knew I had some problems, but I loved her. I also wanted my kids to be raised by both their parents under the same roof. That was no longer going to happen.

I went deep inside, and did some heavy soul searching. I felt that the only person responsible for that was me. That didn't last long, because I quickly began to realize Seema had some serious issues of her own. I could no longer stay under the same roof feeling like that. I reached out to my mom and dad for a place to stay while I figured out my next move. They wanted no part of that, and told me to figure it out on my own. That only made things worse. I was heartbroken at home, and now I was confronted with sleeping in my car.

Then I came up with a brilliant idea. That weekend I drove into the nursery I worked out of and slept in the change rooms. I had keys and an alarm code, so there were no security breaches or anything like that. For the first time in an eternity, I had a chance to think about my life and what it meant to me. I had to figure something out soon. I could no longer continue to hurt like that or keep hurting others. I had heard about another twelve-step program in regard to gambling. I had no idea where that thought came from, but I thank my Higher Power for it. All the conditioning that I had absorbed through my five years of sobriety was starting to come back. For the first time in a long time, I wanted to be sober and free of my obsession to gamble.

I called a hotline and found a Tuesday-night meeting that week at the Vancouver Recovery Centre. Though I was a bit nervous when I walked through the doors, I felt at home right away. I had heard it around the hood in my previous tour of twelve-step duty and it fit there too: "You can't con a con." The folks in that room, even though they were of different ages, sexes, races, and sizes, all had something in common with me. Not only a common problem but, more importantly, a common solution. The solution was don't gamble, read the damn book, and go to meetings. It was that simple, as long as I didn't get in the way and try to complicate it.

I met many new friends at those meetings, and attended regularly. I also put the plug back in the jug and started on the other program as well.

I met a gal at one of the groups. She was of Asian descent and had a nice condo on Vancouver's Beach Avenue. She took me in, and I lived with her for a while. I had the girls come and stay a couple of times on the weekends, but it was awkward for them. I understood that completely. I never imagined them seeing their mom and dad living separate lives. They were deeply hurt, and I felt it every day. But there was no other way, because the relationship that had failed was toxic long before that.

One night upon returning home from a meeting, we were dumbfounded by what greeted us when the elevator door opened. Sitting on the floor was Seema, a friend of hers, and Sonu. That was insane! What was she doing there? Was she stalking me? It turns out Sonu had been on a field trip the Vancouver Aquatic Centre with school, and had told her mom that I lived in the building across the street. Seema took it upon herself to come and confront me that night face to face. It was just plain weird and definitely something that none of us needed to experience. That was early in December 1998. I tried not to let it bother me too much, but it did.

Through it all, my mother did everything she could to help out with the kids. She even had them for a couple of nights on one occasion. The next day she went to take them home at the time she had agreed to have them back to their mom. She called me and told me that there was no answer at the door. I sensed immediately that something was wrong. Seema had never led my mom astray before. I told my mom that I felt like something was wrong, and she needed to get into the house.

As it turns out, Seema had made a suicide attempt and was found unresponsive. She was rushed to hospital where, after a lengthy stay, she made a full recovery. A note and a disturbing picture were found beside her. I will not elaborate on that, though. I think I have painted enough of a visual of how trying those times were for all of us.

On December 23 I was somewhere that no one ever wants to be, especially at Christmas. No, I'm not talking about the shopping mall; I was in family court, and based on the evidence I provided, I was awarded custody of our two daughters. I had been to court many of times before. However, that was the worst and most emotional experience in a courtroom for me ever!

19
Dear Nolan

As we approached the new millennium, it seemed like, globally, there were way more questions than answers. The world was preparing for a worst-case-scenario Y2K computer bug crash. That may have been a legitimate concern for most, but I still didn't even own a computer. In the political world, Bill Clinton was about to be impeached. How can one not recall seeing Clinton say under oath, "I didn't have sexual relations with that women, Miss Lewinsky"? The impeachment trial, which ended in February 1999, saw Clinton charged with perjury and obstruction of justice. After what I had just been through, I'm sure you know how I felt about that one!

The spring of 1999 marked sadness and a celebration of sorts for the man known as the Great One. Wayne Gretzky announced his retirement, and his iconic number ninety-nine was retired throughout the NHL. Gretzky, who finished his twenty-season NHL career in New York, amassed point totals and records that will probably never be broken. I know records are made to be broken, but let's face it, there will never be another Wayne Gretzky. I'm so thankful I got to see him play in a Stanley Cup final and meet him in his prime. Thanks for some incredible memories, Wayne!

Early that year, I rented a place in Vancouver's high-rent Shaughnessy district. The house was only a few blocks from my mother's notary public practice at Granville Street and 64th Avenue. She sold her business that year to facilitate her and Dad's retirement dreams (more on that later).

The new pad was a perfect fit. Making things even better was the fact that I had been clean and sober for over a year and a half. I also no longer had the constant urge to gamble, although I did miss the racetrack and my friends there. When I say the Snow family took me under their hospitable thoroughbred horse wings, I mean it. They treated me like gold. Thank you all for sharing your passion with me. I'm not only thankful for that, I'm thankful that I realize how lucky I was.

I was determined once again to show the world and myself that I could succeed at whatever I put my mind to. I went to work, putting my own personal flare on my new place. Whether I knew it or not, I was feathering a new nest.

Though far from gothic, during that period almost everything I owned and wore, was black. Ribbed black tight-fitting cotton-poly blends were the norm. Why not? I was starting to get pretty ripped from all the tree work and the long unicycle rides. I shopped at places like IKEA, and got my Go Juice from Starbucks. My tall cans of Budweiser and shot glasses of tequila were now grande dark roasts or my old favourite, Americano, always straight up, no cream or sugar. When I'm in a good groove in life, abstaining from my demons, I eat like an athlete. It's probably some of the leftover positive life conditioning from the great sport of motocross.

In fact, I was starting to see how many things in my character and life skills were acquired in those racing years. In addition, not only was I missing motocross, I felt like I would never ride again. If there is one thing that I have learned, and believe wholeheartedly, it's to never say never. I have seen way too many improbable miracles unfold right in front of my uncomprehending eyes. I joke with friends and say, "Thank God I'm an atheist." Some laugh, and some ignore the comment, but I get a kick out of it for that reason. An atheist is someone who believes in nothing. We all believe in something, don't we? Once I started to believe in me or anything else, for that matter, good things happened.

Having rekindled my unicycle fetish, I rode it back and forth to work. That was a healthy escape and workout. The unicycle requires the utmost focus and concentration. It also is the best way I have found to tone abdominal muscles. I was proud of what I called my "mid-life six-pack." Even after a long day as a "tree monkey," I often went bombing into downtown Vancouver or even out to UBC. There were no limits, and my freewheeling Gemini soul loved it. I don't ride a unicycle anymore. In fact, after my spinal cord injury, I gave my last one to Kyle Beaton. I had not shed a tear over my injury up to that point. That changed the day I parted with my favourite unicycle. I was hopeful that it would help

Kyle win a national title. After all, he was the son of a man I spent most of my formative years with at the motocross races. I know you don't get a chance to read too many books from cover to cover, Brian, so I'm going to thank you in advance for reading mine. Also, while I'm at it, I want to thank your son Kyle, for coming into the GF Strong spinal cord rehab centre with the jersey he wore while winning the San Diego Supercross LCQ.

Between my job and the girls, my responsibilities in life had increased exponentially. If the kids weren't in school, they were with me, my mom, or on a supervised visit with Seema. Even though Sonu and Sara had love all around them, I know that was a difficult period for them. Their home structure of a mom and dad under one roof was gone, and they were too young to understand why. It still hurts me to know what they endured.

Sometimes at work I was put in charge of potentially dangerous equipment. I was so thankful to be sober. It's not the best recipe to be fifty to sixty feet above a sidewalk (and likely power lines, cars, and people) running a chainsaw while trying to shake off the booze demons of the night before. I loved the challenges that the job presented. We had regular pruning jobs and storm damage jobs. I was on a twenty-four-hour call-out list for storm emergencies.

On one of those emergency calls, I was out for over twenty-four hours. On more than one occasion while at the City, we had some catastrophic windstorms. My dad's crew in Stanley Park had their hands full during those times. We were also called in when needed. I still have a great love and respect for trees. No, I'm not a "tree hugger," if that's what you're thinking. I grew up with a tree killer for a father, remember? Speaking of which, here is how I know my Higher Power has a sense of humour. My dad spent the first part of his career killing trees, and now he was hired to save them. Who knew?

Dad always taught me where to look for hazards in a tree and its surroundings. I'm not sure where it ranks in terms of dangerous professions, but I have known a few guys personally who lost their lives on the job. In fact, just a little while back, one of the guys I took the climbing course with and worked alongside at the Park Board was killed on a job in a Vancouver park. RIP, Jody. Godspeed, old friend.

I knew every tree species by name, including the Latin names. Most of it was part of the curriculum with the City, because they were always sending us on a course somewhere. Fortunately, I still had a solid memory. I still love driving down the street with my wife and listing off the names of the different tree species.

I was based out the City's south department, called Sunset Nursery. The secure, fenced-in grounds housed the Arboriculture and Horticulture departments. They had many large greenhouses to propagate all the city's annual plants and flowers. (The trees were grown at a tree farm in Langley, at which I spent a tour of duty as well.) An added bonus was the Sunset Arena, which was a City of Vancouver rink, right next door. We were on the ice often, and I'm thankful for all my friends at the Park Board who made that happen.

One Saturday, I went in to work looking for an extra set of keys I had for the new house. Our change room was on the other side of the yard in a portable. When we got our work duty for the day, we had to go into the horticulture side, because that's where the keys were kept. That's where I ran into Lori. All I knew about her was that she was outgoing, blond, blue-eyed, and beautiful. We had exchanged hellos on a couple of occasions. However, on that Saturday morning, with the sun high above, beaming fresh rays of relationship hope through the glass of greenhouse one, we met again. Lori had to work on Saturdays, because someone had to keep all those plants alive. I assured her that she was perfect for the job. No one else was around, and we chatted as she worked. Multi-tasking away, I didn't want to bog her down. I have always had pretty good perception when it comes to reading people. I could see that she didn't want to jeopardize her position with the Park Board, and I took the hint. I felt a mutual connection though, and that kept my hopes up. I don't even remember if I got my keys.

We went on a couple of dates, if you want to call it that. Everything in life was happening so quickly. I don't know how my heart didn't explode from all the energy I was using. Maybe it was just the age I was at, but my life was just the way I liked it, wide open and busy with good stuff, no more bullshit. I was done with all that, or so I thought.

I told Lori my entire history pretty much right off the bat. Why not? If you're serious and you care about the future of your relationships, there's only one way to roll. She didn't seem to mind any of the baggage or collective karma that I brought to the table. She had seen her share of dysfunction and was a survivor herself. Her dad was a horse logger. That's right, he used horses to skid the trees out of the bush. Her brothers were cool, and into downhill mountain biking and hockey. I'm not going to tell you Lori's story, but I can tell you that I quickly fell in love with her. We had a lot in common. Like me, she was outgoing and had a great sense of humour. She was also intelligent, and I loved how we connected on many subjects.

Our first movie date was to see Austin Powers in "The Spy Who Shagged Me." I will never forget when I burst into uncontrollable laughter in the theatre after something Fat Bastard said to Mini Me, "I've got corn in my shit bigger than you!" When I realized no one else was laughing, I looked at Lori, and asked why I was the only one laughing so hysterically. She was laughing, too, and agreed that the crowd was just being reserved. What was that? Come on, people, pay your money and have some damn fun. Mike Myers was definitely one of the more brilliant funny men of that era. I always loved *Wayne's World*, and the incorporation of Stan Makita's donuts was a brilliant play on our love of hockey. Sadly, Stan Makita passed away in 2018. RIP, Mr. Makita, and thanks for the laughs, Mike.

Within a matter of weeks, I helped Lori move all of her belongings into the Shaughnessy house. She had been living in New Westminster and now was way closer to work. We kept our relationship down low at first, because working at the Park Board was a lot like high school. Sad but true. My dad warned me that the gossip there spread faster than Federal Express. In fact, we had a saying there, that if you hadn't heard a rumour or story by high noon, it was time to start one. I didn't like that aspect of the job at all. I didn't grow up in an environment like that, but I did my best to go with the flow.

One of the things that I was conditioned to believe with that tour of civic duty was that it wasn't always how things were that mattered most, it was more about how they looked in the public eye. Knowing that we would all be seen swimming in the Park Board's public fish bowl, our backyard was an out-of-sight playground of sorts. Maybe it was the times, or maybe we were just a bunch of reprobates. I know many of the things we did on a regular basis would not fly today without a grievance or even a lawsuit filed.

The down low only lasted until Lori came in to pick me up on her day off. We were standing outside the office waiting for the 3:30 buzzer, so we could bolt out of the gate. Before the buzzer blew, she walked through the gate all gussied up and planted a great big kiss on my lips right in front of everyone. I thought nothing of it until a large roar of childish oohs and ahhhs came from my peanut gallery of colleagues. Yes, the Park Board was just like high school.

By summer's end my mom and dad were living full time in Merritt, BC, building their dream home. They had bought an acreage that overlooked the pristine Nicola Valley. Kelly and Rich had also relocated to Kamloops on Overlander Drive along the North Thompson River (close to the Kamloops motocross track). Richard had left the BC Hardwood Flooring Company and bought his own company in Kamloops.

Lori and I also needed a bigger place, because my girls would be living with us. That was awkward at first for the girls, but we all did the best we could. Lori treated them well. She was patient and always keen to teach them new things. She had a unique and off-the-grid type of creative flair.

It took some searching, but I managed to find us a home to rent in Richmond on Blundell Road. It was an older home on a four-acre blueberry farm. It needed a coat of paint, among other things, but the landlord offered to buy the supplies as long as we did the work. The house had a garage-type shop, which I liked. Considering the time of year when we moved in, I never gave much thought to what the place would look like in the rainy season. Let's just say there's a reason that blueberries grow so well in Richmond.

With the exception of the driveway, which was elevated, and a portion of the front yard, our property resembled swampland during the winter months. Richmond was also crawling with rats, and they were all keen to come and greet us. Poison worked to get rid of them, but they stank when they crawled into a crevasse to die. It was horrible. In bed at night, it often sounded like we had cats dancing on our linoleum and hardwood. We even found rat shit in our oven! We were troopers though. That place wasn't great, but at just under $1,000 a month, it was affordable for our family of four. But hold the phone, we had more good news. Lori was pregnant, and we were expecting our first child together.

Apart from the chronic issues with our old house, Richmond was a good fit. It was just a short jaunt for me to work across the Knight Street Bridge. It only took me about fifteen minutes each way. The kids were active in school and the community with friends.

I picked up several side jobs while employed at the Park Board to make ends meet. I wouldn't go out of my way to solicit side jobs while working on shift. I didn't want to jeopardize the job, which took care of our needs. Getting one of those jobs was like winning the lottery in the sense that I had to be pretty lucky to land one. I usually did the side jobs after my shift ended. When I landed a job that was too big to handle on my own, I employed colleagues. Most of these jobs were removals. The work itself was climbing, de-limbing, and then bucking up the trees into firewood sized chunks. One of my buddies used to joke that any idiot could dump a tree, but it took a real man to clean it up. Most of the time on those jobs, being a real man meant many trips back and forth to the city dump in my Mazda pickup. We had also purchased a newer minivan for our growing family. These jobs were a difference maker, so much so that without them, I don't believe we would have had anything left over after the bills were paid. My position paid well, and the benefits were great, but big-city life has always come at a hefty price.

During that year at work, I connected with a fellow who was a few years younger than me, and into motocross. His name was Phil Golding, and his mother was dating a guy named John Persic, who I used to race with in the 1980s. Sadly, John has since passed on. Godspeed, old friend. Phil had a pretty trick Noleen 125 cc Yamaha. He and I talked about bikes and my racing days. He shared a few of the stories John had told him about our heyday. There I was, for the first time since leaving racing, wanting to ride again. My cousin Darryl hooked me up with some gear, and off to the Tsawwassen motocross track we went.

Since the Vancouver Supercross, I had been to a race at the Stetson Bowl in 1990 as a spectator, and ridden an Enduro bike at a family campout, but that was it. No seat time whatsoever, but boy, was I aching to ride.

When we pulled into the track, there must have been twenty vehicles there. I hadn't been nervous before that, but I was then. Phil got ready first, did a couple of laps, and then pulled in, and asked if I was ready.

The Tsawwassen track was parched, rock hard, and blue-groove dry. It had many jumps and some of the deepest rhythm section whoops I had ever seen. I rode a couple of laps to get a feel for the bike and track layout. On the backside of that track was a big triple jump that was about 110 feet in length, if cleared completely. Coming out of the left hander that led up to it, after only two laps in sixteen years, I went for it. I'm not sure how or why, because I just did what I had always done on a dirt bike, and that was to go for it. Not with a "checkers or wreckers" attitude either. I knew I could still do it. That jump fit my eye, and I felt confident and comfortable. I overjumped a little, but what an incredible feeling to be in the air again, flying freely without a worry in the world. I hit it again the next lap no problem. Then I swung by the starting line area where Phil was and told him to grab the video camera. While he went back to the truck for it, I started to blaze another lap. Man, it felt good.

On that lap, as I crested the face of the big triple, I noted my body weight was positioned a little too far back. By the time I tried to adjust, I was airborne. In the air, the bike was instantly front-end light. I lost my footing on the pegs, and there was no way I could tap the rear brake to bring the front end down. All I saw was the sky. I felt like I would hit the moon before the ground. I had enough time to think that landing off the back end of the motorcycle like that was a bad idea, so I hit the eject button and did my best to land on my own without the 220-pound steel horse. One hundred and thirty feet later, I landed right knee first on the ground, which resembled pavement, well beyond the downslope of that jump.

I felt my knee explode inside my pants and knee cup. It was one of those injuries that I often had in my racing days. The pain was unmistakable. Knowing I was messed up, I focused my thoughts on the rest of my body. Fortunately, nothing else hurt—yet. After about a minute or two, a few guys headed over to see if I was okay. I got to my feet and remounted the bike before they could get there. As I passed them on my way back to the pits, I gave them a thumbs-up. I didn't want anyone worrying on my account. I knew in my heart that my knee was destroyed though.

Phil hadn't seen the crash, because he was at the truck grabbing the camera. I told him what had happened, and he asked what he could do for me. After he loaded up the bike, he wanted to know if I needed the hospital or a medical clinic. My response was neither. I told him to take me straight to London Drugs. I needed to medicate, quickly!

During my tenure at the Park Board prior to that, I had a couple of injuries. At 5:00 a.m. one morning while loading trees the winter before for planting season, the loader operator lost sight of me and dropped the bucket on my shoulder. That injury healed up pretty quickly, but it introduced me to pain pills. Only a couple of months after recovering from that one, I messed up my ankle when my boot rolled after jumping off our boom truck. Once again Tylenol 3s were my friend. Strangely, I don't remember ever taking pain meds when I hurt myself racing in my younger years. Things had changed. Not only did the meds work for the pain, they also gave me a sense of euphoria. I liked the feeling, which was an escape from everything that ailed me. Another bonus in my messed-up head was that, unlike booze, no one could smell the pills. There was a huge problem though that would only get catastrophically worse for me: each Tylenol 3 contains 30 mg of codeine, 15 mg of caffeine, and 300 milligrams of acetaminophen.

I didn't have any T-3s, but I knew I could buy some T-1s at London Drugs. I had experimented with them before, but they only had 8mg of codeine phosphate per tablet, so I just took more. That posed another huge problem, because the T-1s have 300 milligrams of Acetaminophen per tablet, which is hard on the liver. My liver was already messed up; it didn't need any more help. A person can safely take up to nine or ten of those pills a day for a short period of time. Even at that dose they are detrimental to one's health.

Despite my damaged knee, I could still walk through the front door of my own home, but barely. Thankfully, our benefit package included full long-term and short-term disability insurance. They were also good at getting us back to work in a light-duty capacity when injured. Without that my family would have been sunk.

At the doctor, it was the usual song and dance of MRIs and eventually a rehab protocol. I hated it. Once again, I was busted up from a dirt bike and feeling like a failure. I hit the pill bottle hard. I was taking T-1s and grinding my doctor for the good ones. Some of the excuses I gave him were almost childish, such as "I went to Kamloops on the weekend and left them at my sister's house." What I was failing to see, or at least choosing not to recognize, was that I was addicted to a substance yet again. If I told you I was taking thirty to fifty T-1s a day, would you believe me? To give you an idea of what things are like when my addict is in overdrive, try that one on for size.

Within a day or two of being back at work, where my job was driving around the city with a clipboard assessing trees, one of the guys gave me what he called a "rookie cookie." I didn't know what it was, but he promised it would make my day go by a lot better. It was huge and grainy and as green as a cow pie. I gobbled it down like it was my last meal.

I left the yard and felt pretty decent for the first couple of hours. At around 10:00 a.m. I was out in the UBC vicinity when I started to get a massive buzz! I got uncomfortable and paranoid. I didn't feel like I could continue to drive safely, so I pulled the truck into an underground parking lot at the UBC campus. I must have gone out like a light instantly. I didn't wake until 5:00 p.m.

I panicked, because I was supposed to have the truck back to the yard two hours earlier. When I got back there, the gate was locked. I had a key, but I was worried that someone was wondering where I got to. I hung up the keys and went into the washroom to wash my face, still feeling groggy. When I looked into the mirror, my eyes looked like a road map of New York City. They were beet red and looked as if the veins had been embossed on the whites of my eyes. Seeing that I thought what a loser I was. When I got home from work that night, I told Lori I wasn't feeling well and went straight to bed.

The fall of 1999 brought more heartache to the sporting world. I was only a few blocks from home on October 25 when news came over the radio of Payne Stewart's tragic passing at the age of forty-two. Stewart, who was a professional golfer, had won three majors, including that year's US Open. A crowd and media favourite, he also had a couple of distinct wardrobe signatures. He could usually be found in a colourful pair of knickers topped off with one of his stylish flat caps. Payne always appreciated the fanfare surrounding his swing and his attire.

The airplane that Stewart was flying in lost cabin pressure just after takeoff from a Florida airport. With traffic control getting no response, it became a lethal ghost plane scenario. The White House was briefed and ordered the Lear Jet to be followed and visually inspected by the Air Force. There was a worry that the inevitable crash would put many in harm's way. The plane eventually ran out of gas and spiralled to the ground in South Dakota. Stewart, two of his agents, and three others on board perished in the crash. Stewart was posthumously inducted into the World Golf Hall of Fame in 2001. Rest in peace, Payne.

Halloween was nearing, and that was always a fun time for the kids and me. That first year in the Richmond house, however, more sadness hit when one of our local heroes, Maple Ridge, BC's Gregg Moore, lost his life in southern California at the final Indy race of the season. At just twenty-four years of age, Moore lost control of his car and slammed into the infield wall at 200 mph. I was home watching the race on television. Even though it was almost twenty years ago, I still get the same sick feeling thinking about that tragedy as I got when it happened. RIP, Greg Moore.

Ringing in the new millennium at home with Lori and the kids was fun. I'm not sure what the world was expecting to happen with the Y2K deal, but thankfully, not much came of it. Our life at that time was pretty simple. Lori and I continued to do our best to provide a healthy, stable environment for the kids. For the longest time, looking back on that period depressed me. I guess it should have, given how things were about to play out, but now I know I did the best I was capable of at the time. I had a lot of unresolved issues that needed to be dealt with. Over and above that I was also chipping away at a few different things over which I was powerless.

Somewhere in that space of time, I had picked up a drink again. I never advertised it or told a soul, but my addict went back into overdrive. It was almost childish how I would sneak off here and there. If I had a couple of drinks at work or after, I would eat whole cloves of garlic to cover the smell. I tried not to think about it too much, because it only made things worse when I started to internalize. I had lost touch with my twelve-step groups and could easily come up with an excuse for why I was no longer going. I figured if I continued to work hard and was a good dad and partner, everything would be okay. You guessed it, the master of self-deceit was at it again, fooling himself about certain values.

Between my job, my side jobs, my kids' activities, and the sports that I was involved in or a fan of, it seemed I was always doing something. My legs were restless, and for whatever reason, I was always more comfortable when I buried myself in people. Whether it was at a Canuck's game or pedalling my unicycle around downtown Vancouver and False Creek, the freedom gave me the ability to be whomever or whatever I wanted. I didn't realize it, but at thirty-three years old, I was starting to have a mid-life crisis. I wanted to be successful, but I wanted more than success. I wanted to do something beyond the mainstream and even a little extreme. Why not? It was the new millennium, and everyone was pushing the envelope.

One day as I approached False Creek from Terminal Avenue, I was captivated by Vancouver's signature geodesic dome, known as Science World. Sara was in Brownies, and they had a sleepover there one night. I had dropped her off there and then taken a moment to size up that unique structure. I thought for sure that the 110-foot dome needed to be jumped on a motorcycle by yours truly. Once planted, that bad seed of an idea never left me.

One day at work as a colleague and I drove up Terminal Avenue toward Science World, I hit him with my idea. He burst out laughing as we approached the Quebec Street stoplight. I thought silently about how potentially cool that stunt could be. My colleague's name was Al. Once he realized I was serious, he stopped laughing. Then I went into detail about how I thought the stunt was doable. I'm not sure Al was picking up what I was dropping, but I was certainly excited about the prospect.

From that day forward, the thought of that jump and how to make it happen consumed me. I researched the building's dimensions and the part of False Creek in which I anticipated landing. The landing would be parachute assisted. I believed I needed to achieve at least 150 feet of air to have my base jump-style parachute deploy safely. That chute would help to absorb the impact, because water is denser than concrete. I should add that upon conducting that research, I learned that False Creek at Science World has a notorious history of highly polluted water. Swimming is not advised; critics have long suspected the City of Vancouver's sewage natural outflow as the main culprit.

That idea captivated me for many reasons. I believe the biggest one was that I thought it was the perfect gig to define who I was as a human being. I had grown up idolizing the likes of Evel Knievel, Doug Danger, Gary Wells, Seth Enslow, and Johnny "Airtime" Roger Wells, the most successful ramp-to-ramp jumper who ever lived, in my opinion. I even contacted him in regard to the jump as I began to research, what it would take to make it happen.

With thoughts of Science World on my mind, regular life was a struggle. But with our newborn on the way, I did my best to balance my inner struggles with my adult responsibilities. Looking back now I feel horrible, because I was always off doing something. One of the most valuable lessons I have learned is the value of time. At that stage I took it for granted.

We had everything in place, and come June 5, we headed into BC Women's hospital. I was nervous but excited. I don't remember it being a difficult birth, but to keep things in perspective, let's remember it was Lori, not me, having our baby. He came into the world as beautifully as we could have hoped. Born with red hair, blue eyes, and happiness in his heart was our son, Nolan Jaylee Worrall. I believed Nolan's birth was the only insurance I needed to keep my shit together. Sadly, much heartache was just around the corner for my family and me.

20

No Moral Compass

With our newborn son at home, Lori and I set out to raise our children. It took a bit of extra effort to get Nolan feeding properly, but within no time, he was a solid eater. Lori embraced motherhood and was determined to make our home a happy one.

I mentioned earlier that she had seen a certain level of dysfunction, because she had been in a relationship with someone who had issues similar to mine. I knew she was watching me closely and that I couldn't screw up anymore if I wanted our relationship to last. I started to exercise more and work even harder at work to get the endorphin releases that I craved. That proved problematic, because during that period, I was physically extended. I began to get hurt at work every other week. They weren't always big injuries, but my name was always on a disability form for something. I enjoyed the time off to be with my family, but the City wasn't fond of it at all. I knew they were watching me closely. It didn't bother me too much though, because deep inside I knew I wouldn't be there for long.

Back on the pain meds once again, I was taking them by the handful. Within a couple of months of Nolan being born, I pulled another disappearing act. I have not had much difficulty yet while writing this book in regard to piecing together a timeline—until now. I realize I was so stoned that I was pretty numb for most of that period. When I returned home, Lori gave me an ultimatum: clean up my act for good or be locked out. I knew she was serious, and I cleaned up my act for the time being. My God, I will never forget how awful it feels when the body's natural pain receptors are not kicking in, because they have grown dependant on the codeine. That coupled with chronic diarrhea for a solid week. Detox from that poison is horrible. I wouldn't recommend it to anyone. Sadly, I went through that same process a few times during that stage of my life.

It wasn't all doom and gloom during that stretch. I loved my kids with all my heart, and nothing made me happier than laughing and playing with them. We played many ball sports at home and loved going on bike rides together. I also donned a clown costume for the first time at the City of Vancouver's truck rodeo that year at Manitoba Yard. It was a good fit for me, because I could ride my unicycle while entertaining the masses with my tricks and wit. With the exception of the few who had it in for me at work, I got along well with most people. I also knew I had to work pretty hard to get fired from the City, so I didn't sweat it too much.

I also landed a spot on the City hockey team. That was great for me, because I had missed playing organized hockey. One of the problems with hockey for me though was booze. By my adult years, after not going back to Merritt to embark on a Junior A career, hockey meant getting drunk. Whether it was going in to watch a game or playing a game, the best part for me was getting drunk afterward or even during. Sadly, I did the latter way too often.

When I joined that team, it was commonplace for me to pound back three or four Mike's Hard Lemonades in the parking lot before going into the dressing room. No one ever said a word, until one game when, just after the first period ended, I had an explosively volatile vomit session, spewing a massive red concoction all over the ice.

My rationale in my alcoholic brain was that if I drank before the game, the smell of the booze would be gone by the time I got home. I figured you might not understand. That's okay; you're not alone, because my bad heart and liver could never figure out what the hell I was doing, either. Once again, I was only fooling myself. My alcohol demon was back with a vengeance.

There I was, a full-blown alcoholic Gemini with the Jekyll-and-Hyde traits that my groups had warned about. In regard to alcohol, I had lost the ability to choose; I was powerless. My only hope was to get back to my meetings and start over. I couldn't do that, could I? I had no time. Besides, how could I tell everyone that I had screwed up again? So, I hung onto those vices as a coping mechanism. What I should have realized was that each life problem that I had wasn't being made any better by drinking or drugs.

As a family we were dealing with several stressful things. The biggest strain on our lives was dealing with the legal issues surrounding the girls. Seema was doing everything that she could to prove she was a fit mother. She lived all the way over in Maple Ridge, and we were in Richmond. Given the distance, it meant long commutes back and forth to accommodate visits. Many times, when we arranged to meet at certain locations, she was over an hour late. Going through that constantly had a profoundly negative affect on our lives. How could it not? My kids didn't need that; no one did.

That winter I attended quite a few Vancouver Canucks games. Once again it was the big-city action and vibe that my Gemini sign craved. As alone as I felt inside, being around large groups of people was a distraction that made me feel okay.

I took Sara to a game one night, and the seats I had bought for us were up in the family section. I thought nothing of it when I purchased the ticket. Once inside I grabbed a couple of Mike's Hard Lemonades, and then we headed up to the seats. When we got there, I found out that alcohol wasn't allowed in the family section. I should have taken the hint that life was trying to give me. Mike's Hard Lemonade plus kids does not equal quality family time.

That night on the way home, I came close to hitting a car parked in the curb lane on Cambie Street. My dear unsuspecting Sara was sound asleep. I'm getting wet eyes writing this, Sara. I'm so sorry, my baby girl. Please know that your father loves you.

By the time Christmas rolled around, I had started to put on a bit of weight, not back up to my "full Monty" weight of over 200 pounds, but I had put on a few. My liver was in huge distress from all the acetaminophen in the Tylenol that I was using to try to eradicate my emotional pain. Looking at photos from that period, my colour was beginning to change to a greyer, gaunter look.

Christmas has always been a time for reflection on the past, as well as a look ahead to what the future might hold. As messed up as things were, I believed there would be happiness in my future. I didn't know what that looked like, but I believed I was a good person, and eventually, karma would take care of me.

Seeing Nolan experience his first Christmas at just six months old with Lori and the girls was precious. My reflection that year focused on what I was grateful for and what I needed to do to keep it.

By the spring of 2001, my body and spirit were sick. "Toxic" is the word that comes to mind. I began to miss many days of work to do side jobs or to go and case out Science World. I even got a hold of my old friend and graphic artist from Chilliwack, Gord Siemens, to help me put together a logo and some other promotional graphics. Lori supported my efforts to a certain extent, but I wasn't one hundred percent certain how much. Who could blame her? It seemed the only person that idea made sense to was me. That isn't totally true, because I had confided in about half a dozen people who believed in me. In my heart I had resolved that if I could pull off the jump, it would be my own personal alchemy.

In late May 2001, we received some tragic news. Our lifelong friend and the best man at my mom and dad's wedding, Sam Douglas, was missing and presumed drowned. Sam, who had fished the Fraser River his entire life, had fallen out of his flat-bottomed boat just below the Agassiz-Rosedale Bridge. Sam, who I only ever knew as a kind and gentle soul, was gone at sixty years of age. That gutted our family and our close friends at the Cheam First Nation Band. Sam was a grand chief and chief of the

Stó:lō Nation from 1969–1992. He was a great man who always advocated for his people and their rights. Over and above all that, Sam was a man of his word, and whom I was always happy and comfortable around.

My dad and I attended the memorial service together on the Cheam Reserve just across the river from where Sam drowned, right beneath the Agassiz-Rosedale Bridge. As we left there that day, I realized one of the key pieces in my upbringing and a true salt-of-the-earth human being was gone. RIP, Hielamacha (Warrior of the Water). We will meet again, old friend.

After the service I rekindled my friendship with Sam's son, Charles. He, along with the other two Douglas siblings, Sammy and Lisa, also played a big role in my upbringing. Charles was into motocross as well, and had a couple of nice bikes. He invited me out to the reserve for a ride a short time after the service.

I can't tell you how good it felt to be again riding around on the Douglas property, where I had burnt so much fuel as a kid. At one point, Sam had even built us a track with his bulldozer right behind their home. I had a few close calls that day with Charles. They put a smile on Charles's face, but left a stain in my shorts. Like everything else in life, timing is everything, and my angels had my back that day. I think the ones who were still around were starting to get tired of it, though. Damn, they had to be!

I continued through that year with no real sense of direction, other than trying to keep my job and my family together. By that time, I knew deep in my heart, that our relationship would fail. Maybe that's what I had programmed based on everything I had experienced up to that point. I'm not sure how Lori was feeling, but she seemed concerned often. Her concerns were legitimate, because I was starting to do increasingly irrational things. Pushing the envelope, being a rebel, an idiot, an a-hole, insert pretty much any negative word you want, and it would have fit. I certainly didn't regard myself that way, but the world was judging me by my actions. I was also sensing that as young as they were, my kids knew their dad had some serious issues. That revelation didn't help how I felt about myself one bit. My confidence and physical well-being barely had a pulse, let alone the will to keep fighting. But I had been raised to never give up. Where had all that good moral fibre gone?

I think back to a time when one of my sponsors in the program pointed out that, "Day by day, I was getting worse and worse." He also noted that, at times, I was even starting to "look like tomorrow." I may have been perplexed at the time, but I certainly get it now, Cecil. Even though it took a few years, your efforts with me have helped immensely. Today you are now genuinely appreciated, old friend.

On one of my disappearing-act weekends, I ended up in Kamloops at the horse-racing track. No live races were scheduled, but they had a licensed off-track betting facility. I played there for a couple of days and then decided I should go farther east. I wanted to be anywhere but home. The booze, drugs, and constant desire to gamble were in control of my thought process. Trust me when I say that diseases like drug addiction, compulsive gambling, and alcoholism are insidious. I was starting to give up, and for the first time in a long while, I had thoughts of ending my life.

I left Kamloops with a tank of gas, but other than that I was broke. On my way out of town, I had an idea that would help me with some creative financing. I would pay the money back one day, or so I thought. In front of God, I now sit judged and have somewhat forgiven myself. I am and always will be my own toughest critic. It's a curse I guess, but if you don't have a plan for success, how can you succeed?

I left Valley View and headed to Vernon. I hadn't been to Vernon for years. The only thing that I knew about it was that it was the hometown of Steve Fonyo. Fonyo, who later fell on hard times, gained fame for his cross-Canada run, called the "Journey for Lives." Much like his predecessor, Terry Fox, Fonyo had lost a leg to cancer when he was a kid. Fonyo completed his coast-to-coast marathon in 425 days, on May 29, 1985. He also became the youngest person ever given the Order of Canada that same year, at just nineteen years old. The order was later revoked due to some of the things Fonyo was charged with. I recently watched a documentary on his life and current situation. It left me with a newfound respect for Fonyo and some of the things that he has overcome. I love seeing stories like that. They remind me that I'm not alone and that winners never give up. That's right, folks. In my mind Steve Fonyo is a winner and always will be. We are human beings, and no one is perfect. I can only hope that my story resonates with someone else one day as much as Fonyo's did with me. Strength in numbers, friends. We are not alone and don't have to be. Unfortunately, it took me years to figure that out.

On that random and seemingly senseless debacle of an escape, my Higher Power was about to give me a sneak peek into my future. Keep in mind that I don't believe in accidents. Based on experience, I'm convinced that everything happens for a reason. As senseless and reckless as I was living, and as painful as it was for everyone in my family, that was our journey. That is not easy to write, because Lori and my children deserved better. I can't change a thing I did yesterday, and I'm thankful I no longer own a shovel. My main coping mechanism today in regard to dealing with the wreckage of my past is knowing that, be it good or bad, we all change over time. Not all cons do their time and become hardened lifelong criminals. It may come as surprise to most, but some change if they discover what I have: a capacity to be honest with themselves.

On the road to Vernon, I called Lori. She was mortified. Where was I? What had I done? And of course, the inevitable, why? I had no logical explanation other than the obvious symptoms of booze, drugs, and gambling. It's important that I classify these three disorders as symptoms of deeper underlying issues. I'm not sure why Lori was willing to take me back, but she agreed. That wasn't the first time I had taken off like that. I had told her where I was, and said I would be home later that night. I never said a word about heading to Vernon first. I had no idea why it was so important to get to Vernon, but I knew there was an off-track horse-betting parlour at Vernon's downtown Kalamalka Hotel. I knew where every one of those places was located, even if hadn't been to them.

I found the betting parlour easily at the corner of 30th Street and 30th Avenue. It was an older bar that had a small-town "everybody knows everybody" feel. I sat at a corner booth and in no time was talking horses with the locals. I had learned quite a bit over the course of my tenure at the thoroughbred tracks in regard to pedigree, among other things. In my polluted head, I figured that I had time to play the afternoon races, before making the six-hour drive back to Richmond. I didn't win big, but I also didn't lose any money that day. Really though, it didn't matter to me either way. By that point gambling was no longer about winning or losing. It was merely about the action. Money was the only fuel needed to stay in action, and nothing seemed to hurt while in action. I could yell and scream at the monitors and beat the shit out of my leg with my program pretending I was helping my horse along to victory!

As I looked out the window to the southwest, I saw that the sun was starting to go down. If I hoped to salvage anything at home, I had to get going. Outside the hotel I ducked into Gerry O's Beer and Wine store and grabbed a six-pack of tall boys for the drive home. Once again, my not-so-sensible alcoholic rationale told me that it may be a while before I got a chance to drink again.

From downtown Vernon I headed out toward Okanagan Lake. I wasn't sure about the lay of the land, but I figured once I got to the lake, the road would take me to Kelowna. That didn't happen. However, what did happen I truly believe was God showing me something that I would in short course see a lot more of, and it would even become my home!

As I got past Kinsman Beach, I headed west on a long, winding, picturesque lakeside road called Tronson. The Okanagan Lake views were incredible from up there. Massive mountainside and lakeshore homes were nestled together in the heart of the north Okanagan. About ten kilometres out of town, I still had not yet seen a sign indicating how far it was to Kelowna. Sensing I had taken a wrong turn, I pulled over at a gravel pullout. I had no cell phone, and if GPS was even a thing yet, I didn't have one. Maybe it was from all of those years chasing motocross racing, but I had developed a great sense of direction. In that instance though I knew I had made a wrong turn somewhere.

A couple that was out for an after-dinner stroll walked by my car. I hid my beer and called them over to the window. They informed me that I had made a wrong turn and would have to go all the way back into Vernon to get to the highway. After they continued on their way, I just sat and stared at the reflection on Okanagan Lake. I had not done it often during that period, because in my mind, I was mad at God, but I said a quick prayer asking him to help me be a better person. I was confused though, because even though my actions were contradicting it, I didn't feel like a bad person in my heart.

After asking for guidance and direction, I made a U-turn and resolved that I would go home and repair what was still salvageable of my badly broken life. I knew it wouldn't be easy, but I was ready to fight for all I was worth.

When I got back to Richmond, I was hungry; I hadn't eaten all day. That was commonplace for me when in action. The first thing that hit my mouth most days during that period were a handful of T-3s, followed by booze. As sick as it was, I only felt hungry when I knew I would not be ingesting any more substances. My liver, like me, was on the endangered species list.

I ducked into the McDonalds drive-thru on Richmond's Number 3 Road. A car was ahead of me, so I waited. Then the car in front of me began to back up. Before I could react and hit the horn, the car had backed right into me! Shit. I was pretty intoxicated, and now the SOB had driven into me. He got out and began to apologize profusely. I got out and saw there was some damage. Fearing I would get pinched for a DUI, I told the guy not to worry about it and to carry on. He gave me a funny look and said, "Are you sure?" When I said yes, I think he realized I was inebriated. We went our separate ways, and I finally ended up back at home.

I don't remember what I said to Lori other than the usual, "I'm a shit. I'm sorry. I won't do it again." But as hard as I tried, I knew I was failing, and so was our relationship.

I managed to get everything out of my system for a while, but it didn't last long. I never even went back to any meetings. I may have told people that I was going, but I didn't go. As sad is it may sound, I knew I was not done. In my program they talked about hitting a bottom before one can sober up and make it last. The problem was, everybody's personal bottom is different. It's impossible to paint an image of what a bottom looks like. It doesn't always have to be a geographical place like "skid row" either. A bottom is a state of mind, not a place. Therein lies the narrowest vortexes of opportunity for people like me.

Coming off those pain meds is horrible. I know I deserved it, but man, when your body's pain receptors have been masked by a pain med dependency, everything aches for weeks!

Lori and I continued to do the best we could raising the three kids. They were troopers! I know they were old enough to realize their mom and dad had some pretty serious issues.

Around that time one of the guys at work was retiring. His nickname was "Snack Bar," but his real name was Dave. I didn't know him well, because he was a grass cutter at the Park Board, but I was keen on going to the party at the Legion. Within a few short hours, I was bombed out of my head. There I was, drunk as shit and making an ass out of myself with my co-workers and bosses. It wasn't even dark as I staggered out to the van, knowing I was about to pass out. I drove a few blocks to get away from the Legion, because I figured if I passed out there, someone would find me or see me. I parked along the curb at Vancouver Memorial Park and passed out.

When I awoke it was daylight. It was a horrendous feeling. I had done what I had promised Lori and my innocent, unsuspecting kids that I would never do again. My heart was pounding, and my thoughts raced. What to do now? How could I ever explain it?

I also had another problem. Being the Park's clown, literally, I was expected to be at Evert Crowley Park that day giving kids boom truck lift rides in my clown costume. I called Lori and told her where I was and what I had done. She encouraged me to follow through with the day and do the job that I had promised to do. I went straight to London Drugs and bought some Tylenol to help take the edge off. Then I went in to work. Keep in mind that it was a Saturday, and the Arbor Days festivities was a volunteer thing.

I got into my clown attire and headed to the event. Man, was I ever hung over! I can't even remember what I was drinking, but I can almost guarantee that if I was given a sobriety test before I hopped in to drive that boom truck over to the Fraser View site, I would have failed. None of my colleagues said a word about my condition, but I sensed some knew. There's not a lot of room in those buckets, and on one occasion when I took a lady and her child up, I knew she could smell the booze coming out of me. What had I become? The one-time keen to be world motocross champion was now nothing more than a real-life "Krusty the Clown."

After that latest slip, crash, drunk, or whatever the hell you want to call it, I pressed on into the fall of 2001. Even though I had seemingly everything to live for, I was bent on destruction. These were not always conscious thoughts or attempts. My dilemma seemed a lot like the movie *Groundhog Day*. The best way to make sense of it now is knowing that I was experiencing the addictive insanity that my sponsor had warned me about. I was repeating the same actions and expecting different results. Either that or I knew in my heart what the end result would likely be, and I felt that's what I deserved. I was told long ago in the program that for people like me, there are only two options: sober up or die! No one candy-coated it. I could also see the progressive nature of what I was suffering from. When I looked into my children eyes, I feared how my choices were hurting them. I know that every single person in my life hoped I would get my act together. Unfortunately, it never happened, because my demons never slept. They never let me rest unmedicated either. I don't know what I was addicted to; I was just tired of hurting. So, you could say, I was addicted to feeling good. It was a whole lot better than having to sit through another repeat performance of the B movie that was now my life!

The second week of September that year, my mom came down to stay with us for a couple of days. She loved her grandkids more than anything. Now that she and Dad lived in Merritt, she didn't get to see the kids nearly as often. She was always a rock for my girls and loved little Nolan dearly. Seeing how my parents had changed over the course of their lives gave me hope. Even though I was raised in a totally different era, I believed my parents did the best job they could with me. It was different now. My mom and dad were settling down to be grandparents.

On the morning of Tuesday, September 11, I departed for work at the same time I always did, 6:40 a.m. As I approached Westminster Highway, news came over the radio that an airplane had hit the World Trade Centre in New York City. I was taken aback upon hearing that, but I thought it was an accident. That feeling soon changed to a sense that something tragic was unfolding when I heard that a second plane had hit. As I crossed the Knight Street Bridge, I looked around at the many different people on their daily journeys. I couldn't help but wonder what on God's green earth was becoming of us all.

When I got to Sunset Nursery, I went straight into the lunchroom, where everyone was watching the news live on television. Within minutes of tuning in, the South Tower collapsed. It was surreal to be sitting in that room with about twenty people knowing that our lives were forever being changed. The 7:00 a.m. buzzer blew, signalling us all to go to work. Few of us did. I had not even been to the office to see what vehicle or job description I had for the day.

On my way to the office, I passed a colleague who I had a lot of respect for and got along well with. His name was Vern, and he was a sports enthusiast and a history buff. He was also about six and a half feet tall and looked like Kramer from Seinfeld. I liked working with Vern, because I fancied him a hard worker as well. When I told him the South Tower had just collapsed he looked at me and said, "Do you know how tall that building is?" I had no clue. Vern told me it was 110 stories tall. He knew that and much more.

Vern and I went back into the lunchroom, where some thirty minutes after the first tower came down, the other did as well. I was sick to my stomach. We all were. I thought of my family and my kids. Would they all be okay? I'm sure I wasn't the only one who was having such thoughts. I have a pretty solid gag reflex, but I went into the bathroom and started to heave. With my eyes glassed over and snot spewing out of my nose, my boss walked in. I told him I was feeling sick and would be going home for the day. His response was simple. "Okay, maybe we'll see you tomorrow." We were allowed up to three consecutive sick days before we had to file for short-term disability with a doctor's note.

By the time I got to my truck, I didn't want to go home. I wanted to go and sit somewhere and medicate. I grabbed a handful of Tylenol 1s out of my glove box. I had cut back considerably, but I was still pretty jacked, taking about fifteen to twenty a day. I had another quandary to deal with to. I had promised a side job to some clients in the highfalutin Shaughnessy neighbourhood at 4:00 p.m.

After my Tylenol kicked in and I had a solid buzz going, I went and sat on Jericho Beach with a strong cup of coffee. I just sat and reflected about all those times as a kid watching the news. I don't know how old, maybe eight or nine. I had a TV in my room and would sneak it on late when the 11:00 news started. I saw the horrors in the Middle East and beyond. It always bothered me. It was senseless, and most of the innocent victims never stood a chance. I was brought up in the midst of the seemingly ever-escalating Cold War. In my formative years, it seemed that the superpowers were always looking to scratch an insatiable trigger-happy itch. I was thankful that our soldiers and my ancestors fought for our country the way they did. I never wanted anyone in my family to experience anything close to that, but it seemed like we were on the verge of something that no one wanted to talk about.

When I showed up at my side job that afternoon, I expected the homeowners to be away, as planned, but the terrorist attacks had put the brakes on that. It wasn't a delicate job either. I wasn't too keen to start bouncing things off their home and beautiful yard with them present. I was thankful to have employed one of my co-workers for that job, who was also a great spur-less climber.

That night I pulled into our driveway just as the sun was heading down. Before I even got in the house, my mother came out and met me in the driveway. Up to that point, I hadn't talked to a single member of my family about the tragedy that had unfolded. The first thing that came out of her mouth was, "There's going to be a war, you know." That memory brings a smile to my face now. Why? My dear mother, of course! That's just the way she was, up front with most things! When I got into the house, it felt good to be able to put my arm around my kids. As messed up as I was, I was thankful for everything that I still had.

My boss was somewhat empathetic for my situation, because he had overcome alcoholism. I feel like he looked out for me as best as he could. If he reads this, he will know what I'm talking about. I know many others at the City wanted to see me gone. On a couple of occasions, I felt like I was being set up. It certainly made things uncomfortable, because I had to keep my head on a swivel working around certain individuals. I have always believed that as long as I know who the enemy is, I have a chance. At that stage of the game though, I was my own worst enemy. My attendance was the biggest issue. I was often absent on sick leave, stress leave, or injured from workplace neglect. Where I used to exhibit the utmost respect, care, and caution for my craft, now I was a loose cannon. I was starting to take chances that I never would have taken before. My father had raised me to respect the work I did, because it was always so unpredictable, but I had put that out of my mind.

On one occasion I was fifty feet above a sidewalk when I dropped my brand-new chainsaw on the sidewalk below. Needless to say, it ended up much like I felt at that time, junk. Most of the accidents that I was responsible for were due to a lack of focus. My plate was full at home, and the job I had been so proud of didn't seem to matter anymore. The truth was that my preoccupation with my demons was my real full-time job.

That winter our City of Vancouver hockey team was invited to a tournament in Kamloops. If you have ever been to Kamloops, you may have noticed the sign that welcomed you to the "tournament capital" of our fine nation. I was raring to go. I was also excited to get out of town, because I knew it would be a good opportunity to chip away at some of the things for which I had been jonesing. Kelly and Rich lived in Kamloops, so I would have a place to stay. Rich, who is a great hockey player, was also penned in to play for our team.

Our first game was against Chilliwack. How fitting. I would be pitted against some of the guys who I played minor hockey with. It was cold, and the ice was rock hard. Chilliwack got a couple of quick goals and were up 2–0. We got one back, and then I buried one in the top corner. Shortly after that, Grant Metcalfe, one of the guys I knew well from Chilliwack—he was the captain of our Pee Wee rep team—scored. Seeing Grant skate toward our bench with his fists in the air incensed me. He had his big traditional post-goal, rub-it-in-your-face, ear-to-ear smile blazing loud and proud. I didn't want to hit him, but I decided to do something that turned out to be even stupider. I kicked at his leg in an effort to knock him down. When my knee hit his knee, my knee exploded. I knew almost instantly that the same knee I had landed on just a year earlier was toast once again. I felt like an idiot.

I pretended my knee wasn't hurt that bad and continued to play through the excruciating pain. Before the period was over, I headed to the locker room to start the medication process. One thing led to another, and soon I was into the team's beer. Man, I was a wreck. I was sure of that, but I had no idea how long I could survive. If I hadn't lost all hope already, it was just around the corner.

The injury warranted more time off work, that and more manipulation of my doctors for the elixirs I craved. Those meds were helping to keep me numb, to keep me from feeling anything that most normal people experience on a daily basis. Codeine creates a numbness of the body and its senses. My body may have been going through the motions, but my mind was in neutral.

As Christmas neared we all planned for the time of year that we loved. With the house nicely decorated and the tree up, we were ready. To me Christmas was always a good time to put aside life's struggles and enjoy special moments with family. That was the way it was when I was young, and that is what I wanted for my own family. However, I had an overpowering sense that it would be the last Christmas we would spend together. I won't go too deep into it now, because writing that last line has brought on a flood of sorts. All I can see right now is the image of my dear mother proudly holding the gift basket Lori put together for her. Nolan loved the Grinch movie, and the girls loved everything Christmas always brought to our household. We were blessed and had so much to be thankful for.

Kelly and her family also came down that Christmas. Her two growing boys, Josh and Justin, were always part of my girls' upbringing. With all of us boys into hockey, we went to a Vancouver Giants game at the Pacific Coliseum. That was the Giants' inaugural season in the Western Hockey League. It was so fun to experience something new with my dad, brother-in-law, and nephews. Hockey was always a huge part of our lives and family dynamics.

One of the highlights of the night came just before the game started. We had just gotten settled into our seats, and Richard told me to look beside me. Thinking nothing of it, I looked to see that the person two seats from me was none other than Kurt Russell. Kurt and his wife, Goldie Hawn, had a place in Vancouver. They were also in the midst of raising their son, Wyatt, who was a hockey player. Wyatt Russell played for a couple of teams in the BC Junior Hockey League as well as the Ontario Major Junior League. He also followed in his family's footsteps as an actor. Russell is most noted for his role as Paul in *The Walking Dead*. He has had many other high-profile roles in other movies. It was cool to see how the offspring of two major Hollywood headliners was now into hockey. I believe a man named Gretzky had something to do with that. Kurt also starred in the re-make of the movie *Miracle*, playing the late Herb Brooks, the coach of the 1980 United States gold medal-winning hockey team. The movie was filmed on location in BC in many of the venues where I skated. Great job, Kurt Russell. RIP, Herb Brooks!

When 2002 hit, I had no real resolve or resolutions. I never believed in that kind of thing. I also deemed them pretty much useless in terms of the demons that were controlling me. The one solution—getting back in the program—that would have worked was the last thing that I wanted to do. My rationale was that it didn't work for me anymore ,or I didn't have time now that I was raising a family. However, if I didn't get help soon, something bad would happen.

When I wasn't working, loaded, or busted up, I rode my unicycle for escape. On one occasion I had Lori help me load Nolan into the backpack carrier she had for hiking with him. That afternoon with him over my back, I set out on my unicycle for what turned out to be a more than two-hour ride. We ended up at Richmond's Kwantlen College. As I was navigating a tricky section at the top of the stairs, one of the *Richmond News* photographers grabbed a cool shot. I told him a little bit about my history with motocross. It turns out he had also spent some time at the tracks I had raced at. Without telling him exactly what my plan was, I told him that I was working to put together a high-profile stunt in downtown Vancouver. He had me come back to the newspaper office, where I gave a reporter enough details to run a story. Even though it was cool, it left many around me with more questions than answers.

I was all over the map and never seemed to be home with my family. It seemed I always had a reason to be either working or at an appointment. Just a short time before that, I had taken my frustration out on one of our solid doors at home with my fist. It may have released some pent-up frustration, but it left me with three broken bones in my hand. That pretty much sums up how I was dealing with what was burning out of control inside me. I knew it was just a matter of time before I did something that I would regret forever.

I didn't miss a lot of work due to my hand injury. I was also back on the ice with my hockey team shortly thereafter. I'm not sure how the bones healed, because I was so heavily medicated that I couldn't tell if it was sore or not. In early May, as our season wound down, I headed off to play what would be my final game of organized hockey, on Tilbury Island.

After my usual few drinks on the way to the game, we were up 3–2 in the second period, and I had already scored two goals. As the other team skated out of their end, the guy carrying the puck started to get away from me. I sensed that if he got by me, he would be on a breakaway and could likely score. I managed to get back alongside him and, without thinking about the consequences, pulled him backwards over my extended left leg. Just as he began to fall backwards and his feet were airborne, I saw he was going to land hard on his back and maybe even his head. Realizing I had to break his fall, I hit the ice. The guy landed with all his body weight right on my left arm and shoulder. I felt it snap. The pain was instant.

When I got to my feet, I didn't say a word, just skated off the ice and headed straight to the dressing room. I was gutted. Why had I tried to trip that guy like that? It was dirty, against my own code, and I knew it. My attention quickly turned to not being able to lift my arm. Not again, another injury! I had so many injuries to overcome, some work related but most just a result of the reckless and heavily medicated person I had become. I felt like that one could even cost me my job. I knew the City would love to get my reckless and insubordinate ass off their payroll.

The next morning, I called in to work, as I had often done, to explain my injury. I'm not sure what was said on the other end, because the addict in me didn't care. I knew I needed a doctor's appointment, so I could get assessed and get some more pain meds.

My doctor's office was in New Westminster, so the next day I headed in. On the way there, as I drove eastbound up Marine Drive, my head started to get some crazy ideas. I reasoned that seeing as I was about to lose my job, my family, and everything else that I loved, I might just as well leave the big city and go somewhere and end my life. I never even stopped at the doctor's office. I hit the Trans-Canada Highway and headed east. I figured the world would be a better place without the grief I was causing. I couldn't take the emotional pain any longer. I just wanted to die!

21

Adventure Boy

As I crossed the Port Mann Bridge, I couldn't get out of Vancouver soon enough. I had not packed any clothes, because my decision to leave was like most at that time, random and spontaneous. I had filled up my Mazda pickup. The fuel gauge no longer worked, but I knew I was good for at least 400 kilometres. I didn't give a shit about any of that, though. All that mattered was getting out of town, medicating, and then putting an end to my misery for good. I wasn't sure how that would play out, but I was confident that I would find a way. Maybe I would just drive off one of the massive drop-offs on Highway 97. Maybe I would drive headlong into an oncoming semi-truck. Either that or just dump another 100 T-1s on top of a belly full of vodka. Something had to happen, and quickly. For the first time in my life, I was considering doing harm to others as a way of lashing out for what I was feeling inside. I cursed my Higher Power in every moment that was unbearable to me. Was there even such a thing? I was so angry inside that I couldn't even make sense out of life's simplest problems. It felt as if my calling was to suffer until I ended the pain. If I ever needed a miracle, this was the time.

When I reached my old hometown of Chilliwack, I needed some supplies— pain meds, booze, a cooler, and a T-shirt, so I would have a clean one to throw on if needed. After pulling out of the Chilliwack Walmart, I went over to the local off-track betting facility. It was already around dinner time, and I noticed that the race program from Hong Kong was on that night at 10:00 p.m. I grabbed the racing form and decided to get a hotel room, get hammered, and then go play the Sha-Tin ponies.

I don't remember a lot about that night. By the time I left my motel room, I had already consumed close to a dozen beer. The next thing I remember is coming to on my motel room bed. All I could see was the bright sun shining in on my pounding head. It took me a minute or two to get my bearings. I was back in full blackout mode. It's a horrible, helpless feeling.

I looked out to the parking lot to see if my truck was there. It was, but depending on how you look at it, that may or may not be a good thing. Whatever your choice, it was a good thing for me, because it meant I didn't have to go looking for it. Sadly, there were many days where the latter was the case.

When I left Chilliwack, I figured I would head through the Rocky Mountains to Alberta. As I got on Highway 1, I thought back to something I had told a gal a year or two before when she asked, "Brent, with your gambling, where do you see yourself in the future?" My smartass remark was that I would likely be hiding out somewhere on the east coast at one of the "leaky roof tracks" (B-circuit tracks) like an ostrich burying its head in the sand.

As I drove the Coquihalla Highway eastbound, I worked on killing my hangover with Mike's Hard Lemonade and Tylenol 3s. In my current state, it seemed impossible to face even one breath without medicating. I'm not sure how much money I had on me. I wasn't too worried about that though, because I had solid line of credit and a credit card. I figured that was more than enough fuel for where I was going and what I was planning.

When I got to Merritt, I decided to bypass Kamloops and head to Vernon. I figured there would be less chance of anyone recognizing me there. After all, I had been pretty much a regular on other road trips to the Kamloops betting establishment. I didn't want to explain myself or make any empty promises. I was determined that wherever I ended up would be my end-all trip.

As I neared Vernon, I ran out of booze. I was thankful to see the place I had been to just the year before, the Kalamalka Hotel. I had no plans yet as to where I was going to sleep or anything like that. All I knew was that I needed some more medication and some action.

I thought I fit in pretty well with the regulars. I bet lots, and I bet often. That was my kind of place, where I could be the person I was pretending to be, and no one was the wiser. I wasn't totally out of touch with reality, in the sense that I knew I would not be able to stay there long.

I got a room at the Paulson Park Motel right at the bottom of Hospital Hill. I spent my first few nights in Vernon there. I booked the room on my credit card even though I knew it would be traceable. That didn't stop me though, because all I cared about was numbing my life to the point of extinction.

After three or four days of repeating the same cycle of wake, drink, and gamble until it was time to pass out, I moved on, taking Highway 6 toward Lumby. Soon I realized that the route I was taking was a bit of a goat trail and would eventually land me up in the Kootenays. I did a U-turn and headed back toward Vernon.

I spotted a logging road that went up into the mountains. Later I discovered it led to Aberdeen Lake. I was tired and lethargic. It was starting to get dark, and I could hardly see where I was going. I figured if I drove far enough up that logging road, I would find somewhere to drive off the mountainside and crash the truck.

Once I realized I was miles off the beaten path, I got out of my vehicle and hiked up a narrow hillside trail into the trees. After a bit I reached an opening in the pine trees. I wasn't sure what it was, but it looked like the Boy Scouts or Cubs or some similar group had recently camped there. My thoughts went immediately to my kids. I buckled to my knees, and for the first time in a long time began to cry uncontrollably. In that moment all I could think about was how I had sewn Sara's Brownie patches on her outfit for her, so she could proudly wear them on her Richmond Brownie night. It was completely dark. After seeing that campsite and being moved to tears thinking about my children, I decided to head back to Vernon and get a room, then make a phone call.

On the way into town, I swung by Paulson Park to get a line on some meds. In no time I was hooked up with what I needed. Then I headed out of Vernon toward Salmon Arm. As I drove down Highway 97, I did an about-face and ducked into the Midway Motel. Getting another room in Vernon and doing some interior skunk wrestling made a lot more sense than driving east in the dark. I was afraid of driving in the dark, because I had only one taillight. It wasn't just a bulb either; it was a short in the wiring, and I had no desire to spend any of my highly safeguarded money to get it fixed.

Another few days went by, and I still had not notified anyone of my whereabouts. I was not planning to, either. I figured they would find out what happened to me soon enough.

On Sunday afternoon, just over a week after I left my home in Richmond headed for a doctor's appointment, I went to the Kal Hotel. By then the patrons and waitresses knew me by name, as well as my drink of choice. I was just going to go with it until something or someone stopped me.

The sun shines often in Vernon, because the climate of that British Columbia town of about 40,000 people is desert-like. That spring was no exception. It was a warm one. I'm not sure why, but I sat in a different seat than I usually chose on that fateful day. I was soon thankful that I did.

My luck had been moderate that day. Sitting back and taking it all in, doing my people-watching thing, I noticed a pretty lady helping an older gentleman who reminded me a lot of my late grandfather. She seemed preoccupied as she came in and helped him get comfortable. After they settled in, I took note of what they were drinking and had my waitress send them a round. When that beautiful, tall, confident gem of a girl looked in my direction to thank me, I was spellbound. I couldn't believe what I was seeing. I almost turned around to look behind me to see if it was actually me she was looking at with her piercingly radiant and beautiful blue eyes. I could write an entire chapter on what I saw in those eyes in that moment. It was something I had never experienced before. Then she introduced herself and told me her name, Gisela.

I went one up to do my best to impress. After noting the older gentleman was playing the races too, I had an idea. I was pretty sure I knew who the winner of the next race would be, so I went to the mutual window and bought a win, place, and show ticket and gave it to the older gentleman, whose name was John. The ticket was a winner, and there were smiles all around.

After the races were over, Gisela had to move on. A caregiver by profession, she was actually working that day, and John was one of her clients. Before she left she asked if I wanted to go to a barbecue that night. Are you kidding me? What was going on here? Was I already dead? Another lady in my life was the last thing I thought I needed, but I figured I had nothing to lose, so I accepted. I reached into my wallet to find something to scribble down the address of where I was staying.

At 5:00 p.m. on the dot, there was a knock on my hotel door. When I opened it, I was blown away by Gisela's genuine beauty. What was I doing, and where were we off to? Was this an alien who had taken the form of a beautiful woman and come to take me away to exorcise my demons? I had no idea. All I knew was that we were off to Lumby, about thirty minutes east of Vernon on Highway 6.

The drive was long enough for me to let her know who I was, and what I was up to. It felt good to finally tell someone what I had been doing for the past two weeks. Again, I had nothing to lose, because I had no intention of jumping into another relationship. How could I? I didn't even have a relationship with myself.

The barbecue was fun. It felt good to be around people who had no preconceived notions about me. Yes, I had certainly earned my reputation, for the most part, but it didn't make life any easier knowing that people were just waiting for me to screw up. But from that day forward, May 26, 2002, there has not been a next time—not that I didn't have a whole lot of heartache waiting for me just around the corner. Speaking of May 26, remember the new T-shirt that I bought on the road the week before? It was an orange American Eagle Outfitters shirt with a large number twenty-six on the front. Coincidence? I already told you; I don't believe in those anymore.

I'm not sure that either of us was in any condition to drive back to Vernon that night. I took the initiative and got us back in one piece. As we approached town, Gisela invited me out to her place right on Okanagan Lake, which she had just leased. She said it was at the tip of the Adventure Bay Peninsula facing southwest toward Kelowna.

As we drove toward Gisela's place, even though it was dark, the road seemed eerily familiar. I thought nothing of it and just tried to keep the car on the road. It seemed to take forever to get there. After about a twenty-minute drive from downtown Vernon, we reached her lakeside home. The incredible view, coupled with the sound of the waves serenading the shoreline, was awe inspiring. Was I even still alive? Maybe I had finally driven over the edge of something. I almost pinched myself but soon found out that I didn't have to.

In no time flat, our clothes were off, and we were in the lake skinny dipping. It was pitch black out. I was confident that no one was any wiser to what we were up to. I fell on the rocks on the shoreline a few times on my way back up to the deck. The next morning, I woke up in the loft bed beside Gisela. She was quick to rise and told me that she had to be at work shortly. Then she gave me the option of a ride back to town to get my truck or to just hang out there until her day was done.

Not even sure what was happening, I fully expected an escort from some kind of celestial weigh station of sorts to intervene, much like in one of my favourite movies, *Heaven Can Wait*, with Warren Beatty. In that epic movie, Beatty played Los Angeles Rams Quarterback Joe Pendleton, who was summoned to heaven ahead of schedule by an overzealous escort. In my case I was still alive and had no clue what to do next. For the first time in last two years or more though, I no longer desire to die. I still had a mountain of misery just ahead in my personal life, but I certainly wasn't going to look that gift horse in the mouth.

Gisela went to work and left me with her spare keys, so I could meander around the property, docks, and inviting lakeshore. After a couple of cups of Joe and a few Tylenols, I decided to go for a walk to think. With the sun out in full force, the view back toward Vernon and the Monashee Mountains was postcard perfect. All I could see on the way out there the night before was the moonlight casting its reflection off the lake.

When I got to the top of where Adventure Bay Road began, I noticed the sign for the road that we turned off said Tronson Road. That was the same road that I was on when I was lost there, the only other time I had ever been to Vernon. Seeing the sign, I knew that the pullout where I had made the U-turn on that trip was nearby. I walked a little farther until I found it. When I got there, I stopped and said a prayer. No, it wasn't one of those "Dear son of a bitch" or "What the hell now?" prayers. It was deep and heartfelt. All I wanted was some answers. Answers to questions like, why do I always end up on the run? Through all that insanity, I knew that God was looking after me. You may have heard of the poem "Footprints." I definitely felt that was true for me. God was carrying me. I had no other explanation. A guiding force was at work. There are no such things as mistakes or accidents. Everything happens for a reason. Knowing that and believing it in my heart is huge. However, it hasn't made dealing with the aftermath of my quandaries any easier.

When Gisela returned from work, she drove me into town to get my truck. Then I returned to her place, where we continued to talk through some of the events that led me to Vernon. She was a good listener. It's not that I didn't have any of those in my life if I had looked hard enough. I was just convinced that everybody was tired of hearing about my problems. My name was on that list, too. With no idea what my future held, I realized the only thing that could save me was a quality that had long since left me: honesty. I had become a train wreck in that department. I used lies to cover up lies, and I hated it. I didn't even know who I was anymore. I just knew I was badly broken and considered myself to be permanently damaged goods.

Within a few days, Gisela asked if I planned on returning to the coast. I knew I had to face the music sooner or later, so I planned to go that weekend. She went to work, and I told her I would contact her soon. I thanked her for everything and promised I would see her again.

That morning, a Friday, I cleaned out the inside of the truck in the parking lot for the trip home. I must have thrown out a half a dozen empty 200-count bottles of Tylenol. Then I headed into town to fill up with gas. After that I went straight to the beer-and-wine store to grab a half snap of Mike's Hard Lemonade. To give you an idea of how powerless I was, my next move was to go into the Kal Hotel. I was greeted "Cheers style" by the usual suspects. Many of them were a little surprised to see me still in town. I told them that I was heading home that day. It never happened.

Before Gisela's workday was over, I headed back to her Adventure Bay home. When she got there, she was surprised to see me. We went into the house, and without a lot of pomp and circumstance, I told her that if I headed out on the highway on my own, I would likely end up anywhere but home.

Due to my alcoholism, drug addiction, gambling disorder, and collective brain injuries, I was physically and mentally unable to do anything constructive. The only thing that could or would help me was some form of divine intervention. I didn't know how or what that would look like, other than my own funeral. However, I did believe through my program and meetings that God works through people. I still believe that, and my track record validates it.

I worried that Gisela would see me as weak and irresponsible for leaving my family. Why wouldn't she? If the roles had have been reversed, my red flags certainly would have been waving. But I had been so honest with her, and we had covered so much ground, she felt safe with me. She did encourage me to at least make a call though.

That weekend Gisela's parents were scheduled to come to town for a visit.

Meeting them went much better than I anticipated. When they arrived, I helped her dad unload the canoe they had brought with them. It was a nice housewarming gift for their daughter's new lakeside home. We took it down around to the side of the condo property, where the boathouse storage unit was.

Then Gisela led us, including her mother, Lennor, into the house. They had many questions for both of us. I don't remember it being too uncomfortable, though. I believe God orchestrated everything just the way it was meant to be. Whenever I attempt to connect certain dots to different events in my life, that answer is often the only one that suffices.

It wasn't long before I was in love with Gisela. I knew I had a mountain to climb to have a chance at a successful relationship though. The feeling on Gisela's end was mutual. The day that I told her I loved her, I had no idea what to expect. What happened next still blows my mind. "Brent, I have been waiting for you my whole life," she said. It's important that I convey that these were her words and feelings. She wasn't the messed-up one; I was. Gisela has always had an A-plus reputation with anyone who has ever met her. Over and above that, she is the sweetest, dearest, and hardest-working person I have ever met. Apologies will never be enough for my dear children, my parents, Lori and other family members, but I believe that had things gone any other way, I would be dead.

As our first summer together moved along, I stopped going to the Kal Hotel or into Vernon, for that matter. I stayed out at Adventure Bay while Gisela was at work. I did my thing in my time and was accountable to no one but my newfound love. I got to know most of her clients, and they were all happy for her. It was never easy to answer their many questions about my life. For the most part, I was honest and didn't pretend to be something I wasn't. That was certainly an improvement over the mid-life crisis of wanting to be the guy who jumped Science World on a motorcycle. (Easy now, I still might do it once this book is written.) Instead of the Kal Hotel, I went off to places like Kelowna, Penticton, Salmon Arm, and even Calgary on a few occasions to play the races. On one trip to Calgary, I ended up posting a letter to my family. I desperately wanted them to know I was okay, but I also wanted my whereabouts to be a secret. I feared facing the music would finish me.

By that time vodka was my drink of choice, coupled with more liver punishment in the form of handfuls of Tylenol 3s. My trips to the racetrack were also getting costly. My credit card was maxed out, and so was my line of credit. Gisela encouraged me to contact my bank. I wanted no part of it. As long as I was in action, money was fuel, and its only purpose was to be burnt.

Once my money was gone, Gisela took care of most of my financial responsibilities. She paid for everything, but it bothered me. By the fall I was deteriorating physically. When I met her, my waist size was thirty. Now it was thirty-eight. My liver was in huge distress. I was up to a full forty-ounce bottle of vodka daily. In the morning as she was having her first coffee, I would pour myself a triple vodka and cranberry juice. My sustenance came from the half dozen Tylenols that I washed down with my blood-red elixir of life. I was back up to taking a 200-count bottle of Tylenol every three to four days.

When winter came the reality of facing life without my family was tough. Christmas was always a time when family was together; that's how I was raised. I decided that we should go and dig a tree out of the ground and have our own "live" tree for our first Christmas together. Then one day I went out and collected a bunch of pine cones and needles and painted them with gold spray paint. That was it, just a small, simple tree that paid homage to our families' strong Christmas values.

Just before New Year's, we took a road trip to Vancouver Island for Gisela's parents' fortieth anniversary. To say it was awkward with all the baggage that I was carrying is a huge understatement, but it was good to be with such a kind and loving family unit again. Gisela's dad, her brother, Roland, and her sister, Renee, and their families also attended. I'm not sure they or anyone else understood how sick I was during that period. Gisela did though, and she was starting to worry that I may die sooner rather than later.

On the way back to Vernon from Vancouver Island, I pulled over on the Coquihalla Highway just outside Merritt. There in full view across the valley on the hillside, about a kilometre away, was my mom and dad's brand-new dream mansion. I saw the Christmas lights illuminated in the distance. Seeing the smoke billow out the chimney brought a tear to my eye. I had helped my brother-in-law, Rich, put the hardwood floor in that house the previous March. Now my mom and dad were living there full time. I can only imagine how difficult it was for everyone not knowing what I was up to that Christmas.

Feeling as if my death was imminent, in January I went to a Vernon walk-in clinic. I was a bit worried that my whereabouts could be tracked through my medical card, so I prolonged it as long as I could, but I felt my time was running out. The first doctor I saw in Vernon is kind of famous now, because he's the father of one of Vernon's most famous sons, Daniel Powter, the musician who sings, "So You Had a Bad Day." That makes me smile, because I was certainly having a few bad days around that time. I was in and out of hospital later that winter, and my blood pressure was through the roof. How does 215 over 152 sound? Yes, it was bad, I was dying, and I knew that unless I made some serious changes, my life would soon be over.

Before the snow melted completely that winter, Gisela informed me that she would no longer bring alcohol home for me. I didn't contest it, because I knew why she said it. I improvised and either used her vehicle or walked. I had driven the truck, which was registered to my father, back to Merritt and left it parked on the side of the road close to his turn-off once the insurance expired. I can only imagine what he or anyone else who still cared about me thought. I was convinced they didn't care. How could they? Look what I had done to everything they had taught me to value.

It was a sixteen-kilometre round trip (about ten miles) from our Adventure Bay home to the liquor store. I walked it many times. I also had a bicycle that I rode back and forth to town as well. With the amount of weight I had gained, I believe that regular activity kept my troubled heart ticking.

One Sunday morning I woke up still completely blitzed realizing that I needed to get into town to grab my sports tickets before the Sunday NFL games started. I hopped into Gisela's little red car in the sub-zero morning sun and burned off to the lotto retailer. On my way back up the winding lakeside road, I was doing about eighty kilometres an hour (fifty miles an hour), cutting tight up the inside. The speed limit on that blind uphill corner was thirty kilometres per hour. I wasn't fully coherent, and my focus drifted to the lake. As I looked back at the road, I had just enough time to swerve and miss an early morning pedestrian walking his dog. It was so close that you have no idea what I saw in that man's face when he realized I was about to mow him down. It was similar to when I looked up in the nick of time on Montiverdi Place in West Vancouver, just before the ghost car almost ran me over. Lucky, yes, but I believe my Higher Power was doing what he had done often, which was looking after me—me or the poor unsuspecting soul who I had almost killed. When I returned home with my tickets, I kept the incident to myself.

There were many similar events. One night on that same road coming home from town completely gunned, I lost control on a left-hander and was sliding toward the edge of the cliff. I tried to turn the wheel as the car skated across the ice. Fortunately, before I hit the edge, the car did a 360, stopping right at the edge of the drop-off to the lake. It was easily 500 feet to the water. I didn't beat my chest in celebration or anything, though I knew I had cheated death. I was certain the Grim Reaper would get even eventually.

On February 1, 2003, I awoke in the loft. Gisela had already gone to work. She had left the television on. I had plans that day to help out a friend, Garth, who I had met at the bar. He was fixing up a place to sell in Enderby (about half an hour north of Vernon). Even though I was sick, I wanted to follow through with what I had promised someone who had been good to me.

Before trying to climb out of bed, I heard news on the TV of the space shuttle *Columbia* disintegrating upon re-entering Earth's atmosphere. As I laid in bed, I said a quick prayer for each of the seven deceased crew members. Then my thoughts returned to how sick I was.

I made it into the bathroom, and my morning vomit ritual began. The ritual was followed by bowel movements that were starting to scare me. My body and organs had almost completely shut down. My food wasn't digesting at all, and my movements were always blood soaked. My heart would race in the morning for hours. I'm not talking 100–120 beats per minute either. Try 180–200. The stress on my body from the poison I was putting into it had every one of my system's meters red-lined. I had blood-pressure medication to take daily, and Gisela had bought me a monitor. It helped a bit, but unless I made a drastic change soon, I was on my way out.

Garth called to let me know he was on his way to pick me up. I told him I was hungover and would start walking toward town. I walked for a few kilometres, and my heart rate, which was already high, continued to accelerate. I was so sick that I just wanted to jump in front of the next oncoming car and end the terminal pain that was my life.

Within a second or two of that thought, Garth pulled up. The drive to Enderby was horrendous. I must have had him pull over three times, so I could hurl. When we got there, it continued. I was completely useless. I hated it. I wanted to work. Work always made me feel better. Garth came outside to where I was fertilizing his garden with puke and asked if I was going to be okay. I looked him in the eye and said, "I think I'm going to die." I could see how concerned he was. Seeing that look on his face gave me a deeper understanding of what dying would look like. I didn't want that at all. In that moment I didn't know how, but I knew I couldn't take even one more Tylenol 3—ever!

That night when I got home, I told Gisela how sick I had been that day and that I wanted to get some help for my condition. I knew I needed to get into a detox centre to help get the process started. With any type of substance abuse, especially the amounts I was taking, a detox centre was a must.

I called the Crossroads Treatment Centre in Kelowna and was admitted the following week. Not knowing what to expect, I was afraid.

The morning that Gisela drove me to Kelowna, I thought my heart was going to explode. We barely made it out of Vernon on Highway 97, and I had her pull over at the garbage dump turnoff. She never questioned it, because she could see that I was reeling in discomfort. When I got out of the car, I'm sure I was vomiting before my feet even hit the gravel.

After I was finished, I climbed back in and told Gisela we needed to get there before I changed my mind. In the throes of addiction, it is so easy to give in to the demon burning within. The only answer is total and complete abstinence. It was never the third or fourth drink or pill that got me going. It was always the first one. The first one set up the craving for the next one. Today, I no longer need a second or third or fourth, for that matter. Simply put, I make a commitment each day when I wake up not to drink or do drugs that day. It's such a simple formula, which I remember as long as I'm honest with myself. Self-honesty was a quality I lacked for years. The only person I was ever fooling was me.

I gave Gisela a big kiss and a hug and then checked myself in. That was a Monday, and I would likely be there for at least a week. I told her I would call once I was settled in.

I had been to the Renfrew Detox in Calgary in 1989, but I was some fifteen years removed from that. Making things worse, my addictive personality was no longer an infant but a full-grown monster. Adding to that was how gravely ill I was physically. Upon admitting me, they took my blood pressure. It was around 250/150. It was so bad that the nurse called for a doctor. They shipped me off to the Kelowna hospital in an ambulance. I was happy I had made the move to try and get well, but now I felt like my death was imminent. Making things worse was I thought the next person who came into my hospital room would be a member of my immediate family. I missed them dearly, but I didn't want anyone to see what I had done to myself. If I was going to die, I wanted to be alone.

After they stabilized my vitals and put me on some new heart medication, they shipped me back to the detox centre. I feared the worst and wasn't looking forward to shaking out the booze and codeine demons. But Crossroads was a quiet place, and my time there went better than expected, although I did get banned from the supper table, and I was fortunate I didn't get kicked out altogether.

One night when dinner was served, a younger guy loaded his plate with most of the chicken that was to be served to about a dozen of us. I called him out on it and told him that he wasn't the only one at the table. He flipped me the bird, and before he knew what happened, I stood up and confronted him physically. Every person in that detox centre applauded me—not the staff though. That act personifies how I was during that period of my life. If someone did something that bothered me, and it affected others too, it was on. I had a short fuse.

After a lengthy meeting in the counselor's office and a lecture on anger, I was exiled to my room. They reluctantly decided to let me stay, and I'm so glad they did. Back in my room, I was able to spend the next four days detoxing in peace. I gathered some of their books, including my twelve-step program's big book. Between reading, eating, sleeping, and watching a bit of television, I continued to talk to my Higher Power. He was and always has been a great listener.

Eight days later I was released from detox. The medications they had put me on to control my blood pressure and the seizures that I was prone to were working well. My blood pressure was still high on the top number, but the bottom number had come down considerably. I told them that I would definitely follow up with some twelve-step help. In my heart though, I knew I still had some drinking to do. In all honesty, I only went into detox to kick the codeine addiction. That is where the denial part of my alcoholism comes into play.

I remember the drive back to Vernon through Lake Country vividly—the cool, crisp look of teal-green Kalamalka Lake framed by the flowing, wind-wisped hills of the Swan Lake Valley. Inside though my alcoholic palate craved only one thing: Budweiser!

The first stop that my beautiful chauffeur, Gisela, made (at my request) was Alexander's Beer and Wine Store. That's right, it was only going to be beer. That was my rational in trying to appease the half of my Gemini brain that knew how dangerous any kind of alcohol was for me. Alcohol is alcohol, and no matter what kind or percentage, it's a poison to me. My health, my lifestyle, and my life in general had some serious questions, and they needed some answers soon.

As 2003 moved along, I continued to drink daily, though I was fortunate to have kicked the pill habit. I still had a ton of things to resolve in my personal life, but I had no idea where to start. I realize that much of the heartache could have been avoided with a simple phone call, but at the time, living the way I wanted to on my own terms seemed more appealing than telling the whole world what a screw-up I was.

Gisela picked up a couple of new clients who lived out our way on the lake. Once they found out I had an arborist background, they were keen to put me to work. Two of my first Vernon clients were Ken Steinley, the owner of Kenkraft Sales (an RV shop), and Art and Kay Schmidt, the owners of a longstanding Vernon optical business. Their homes were just down the lake from ours, and they were both pretty stunning. There was no shortage of work, and I worked whenever I could. They paid in cash, no questions asked. It had been well over a year since I had used a bank of any kind—at least legally, anyway (more on that later).

Even though I was working three to four days a week, my body was continuing to swell inside. When I wasn't working, I was either hiking, biking, or walking the Adventure Bay mountainside. All the exercise in the world couldn't bring my weight down or reduce the amount of water my body was holding, because my liver was so stressed. I could say it didn't bother me, but that would be a lie. I hated trying to squeeze into clothes that had fit me the year before—that and looking at myself in the mirror. It grew increasingly difficult to tolerate with each mounting day of unresolved family issues. How could it not? I don't consider myself a bad person. I have heard it said that when it comes to mental health, people are sick not weak. Now I know just how sick I was!

I needed to know how my three children were doing. Were they okay? Would Nolan even remember me when I eventually saw him? My thoughts raced daily. Were my girls still living with Lori? Did the court system decide they could go live with their mom?

I started to enjoy the daily hikes up the mountain behind our home. That soon became my number-one daily ritual. It was about an hour and half to the top of the mountain, about two thirds of the way back to Vernon from our home. Downhill and homeward bound, it took about an hour. I never thought in a million years that I would enjoy hiking or walking, but my type-A personality loved it. Yes, my ankles, knees, legs, and everything else I broke racing dirt bikes hated it, but I loved it. During those hikes or bike rides, I was at one with my Higher Power. I talked and prayed often. I prayed that my kids were okay, and that he would help me resolve the defective parts of my being, which were preventing me from amending my life.

That year for my birthday, Gisela bought me a downhill unicycle. I took it with me everywhere. It was cool to pass the odd person on the mountainside in the middle of nowhere while riding it.

In August 2003 the Okanagan Mountain Park Fire started near Rattlesnake Island on Lake Okanagan. It was a horrendous fire, and many homes were lost. The tinder-dry desert-like vegetation was no match for one of Mother Nature's most powerful forces. The fire was started by a lightning strike and displaced some 30,000 residents and burnt nearly 250 homes on its path to infamy. As for my path of destruction, I had accepted in my heart that what I used to call home, would no longer be.

That year I began to work at the RV shop that Ken owned, Kenkraft. Ken was a bit of curmudgeon, but he treated me well, because I was a hard worker. He had been in business in the valley since 1968, and everyone knew where Kenkraft was. He hired me as a grunt, and I had his yard in tip-top shape in no time. Over the next eight years, I was given much more responsibility and got to know the RV business well. Ken, my friend, I wish I had been well enough to attend your funeral. RIP, Ken Steinley, your legacy will last forever.

In the fall of 2003, I had cycled into town to the Village Green Mall. I had my eye on an engagement ring for Gisela. By that time there was no doubt in my mind that meeting her was fate. I realize that may not make sense to some, but that is my story, and it makes sense to me. Gisela had jetted off to Mexico with a friend, and when she returned that weekend in October, I presented the ring to her. When I asked if she would marry me once I had my shit together, she told me the same thing she always has: "Brent, I have waited my whole life for you." I was happy she wanted to wear the ring I had given her.

As the long cold Vernon winter settled in, I got laid off at the RV shop. Once again, I was back home and hiking to top of the mountain daily. Each time at my favourite lookout, I prayed to the God of My Misunderstanding. That's the way it was for me. I knew and believed in my heart that God had a plan, but I didn't understand what it was. That's why I called him the God of My Misunderstanding. Nothing revolutionary came out of my prayers, or so I thought.

Gisela and I continued to live at Adventure Bay throughout the winter of 2003 and into 2004. By then I had accepted that my family would likely never want to have anything to do with me. Why would they? I was AWOL and now a deadbeat dad.

In early August 2004, I was cycling into town for booze. It was hot, like only Vernon can get on a midsummer afternoon. About halfway there I passed an individual who my Spidey senses told me was a bit unsavoury and out of place. Keep in mind that out on the Adventure Bay Peninsula, the building lots along on the water start selling at $1 million. It's off the beaten track and too far out for the riff raff. So, it was not hard to detect when someone was out of place. I sensed he was up to no good, but hey, what did I know? I was the one who was messed up. I went into town, grabbed my beer, and then rode home with a twelve-pack of Budweiser in my backpack.

A few weeks after that encounter, I headed up the mountain for my usual hike. It's a beauty, straight uphill for the first five kilometres. As I exited our driveway onto Adventure Bay Road, I noticed something didn't smell good at all. As I followed my nose to the far-right side of the road, where it drops some 300 feet to the lake, I recognized the smell.

Years back, one of the hardwood flooring jobs I had was to replace the floor in a room where a woman had died. Not only had she died there, she wasn't found until a few weeks later. Her decaying torso had soaked through her bed and into the wood flooring below. That job was so damn gross! As soon as I detected what the smell was, I stopped in my tracks. I knew there was a body about fifteen feet below me, but I wanted no part of being the guy who discovered it. I crossed the road and continued uphill on the other side. Throughout the hike, I was torn about what to do. I had been brought up to do the right thing. But without taking a single thing away from my mother's part in my upbringing, I was also a student of my father's codes. What was my code? I was now a full-grown man who had been living like a child for the last two years!

Back at home I paid close attention to the news, often wondering if I would ever show up on Crime Stoppers. I have not mentioned it yet, but let's just say there was a warrant out for my arrest. One of them was for a count of robbing my own bank with the deadliest weapon known to humankind—a piece of paper! I agree, no matter how you slice it, that will never look good on my resume. That's fine though, because I don't need one. I'm a writer, right?

On the news, I learned that a local man had been murdered. He had something advertised for sale, and the guy who showed up under the pretense of buying it beat him to death with a crowbar! RIP, seventy-five-year-old retired carpenter Bill Abramenko

It turns out the guy who I saw on the road that day who had my red flags a-blazing, was convicted killer Eric Fish. He had been unlawfully at large from the Howard House in Vernon for six weeks prior to Abramenko's death. The National Parole Board was under extreme media fire after Fish was arrested. They admitted he was at high risk to violently re-offend. Incidentally, Corrections Canada eventually closed the facility.

About a week to ten days after I first noticed the festering smell on the hillside, Gisela and I headed off to play golf. We were in the Salmon Arm area playing a beautiful course called Hyde Mountain, which has an incredible view of the valley and Mara Lake. I loved that course and am thankful I got to experience it.

After our day of golf, a sport we played together often, we headed home. I usually did the driving, but likely had more than my fill at the "nineteenth hole." Heck, our car was the nineteenth hole every day all day, at least for me anyway. When we turned down our quiet little lakeside road, I was mortified by what I saw. Police were everywhere! I'm not sure why, but I felt my heart stop as if I had just slayed a unicorn.

"There's Randy!" Gisela said. He was Vernon's chief of police and one of Gisela's clients. As we rolled up to the crime scene, it was a given that my hiking boot prints were all over and around it. That didn't bother me though, because I was innocent—of that crime anyway. What I was guilty of was the sorrow that I had caused everyone who cared about me. I had discarded them all as if they meant nothing to me. That is the life sentence that I still live with. Even though I understand more of why I lived the way I did, it doesn't make it any easier.

The police asked if we lived in the area and told us what had happened. I sat in the passenger seat and didn't say a word. That night we watched the story on the 11:00 news. I was a little wigged out when they showed Fish and the van he had stolen in the murder of seventy-five-year-old Bill Abramenko. I had seen that van parked on our road and walked right by it. I had even spoke briefly to Fish. Fish was eventually charged with the murder of Jeffery Drake, whose body was dumped on our road.

I didn't sleep a wink that night. The entire thing seemed weird. It was being driven by something that wanted me to reach out. Reach out for what? And why? Heck, I didn't know. I just knew that I couldn't live on the lam forever. On the outside, I projected the image of a normal person, but on the inside, I was a zombie.

The next day I had a job on the other side of the lake. It was directly across, and I could see the yard from our front window. Twenty kilometres round trip, off I went to cut grass and rake leaves. As I neared my client's driveway, I noticed the Global Okanagan News crew setting up. I'm not sure why, but I stopped.

"What are you guys doing over here?" I asked. "The bodies are turning up over there."

He looked at me, kind of perplexed. "Yes, we know," he said. "We're just getting set up here, to do the story from this side of the lake." I pointed to where I lived and told him what I knew. I felt that if he knew that, he would put me in the piece, which would air on the news. It was a chance to be seen. I felt that doing that would expose my whereabouts to anyone who even searched my name.

It worked. For the next two or three days, the story ran with me telling my piece. It was well done as they highlighted me as Adventure Bay resident Brent Worrall.

The day after the story first aired, Gisela and I had just returned home. One of our neighbours had rented out his condo, and the renter was looking for the boathouse. He was more than happy to have me show him the way down there.

When we got to that place, which is not part of our complex, I saw someone sitting on the grass. I said hi, kept walking, and then stopped in my tracks when I realized it was my cousin, Mike Sowpal. He had seen me on the news, and he had headed straight out to Adventure Bay to find me. I had been found. Now I knew I could start to amend my life. But with his first words, my world began to darken yet again. "Brent, you have to come home. Your mom is dying."

I went and got Gisela, and we brought Mike into our house. He told me that my mom had been diagnosed earlier that year with a massive tumour in her lungs. She had just returned from taking my children on an outing and had a pain in her chest. She was rushed to hospital, where she was told that she needed to get her affairs in order, because she would not live two months. No matter how many times I try, I can't write that without crying my eyes out and blaming myself for what I put my mother through.

Mikey, I know it wasn't easy for you to do what you did. You came out to Adventure Bay and waited there all day for me, and I can't thank you enough.

I managed to get over to my parents' place with Gisela within a day of Mike coming over. When we pulled up to their Merritt mansion in the sticks, Mom was out front lying in the porch swing with my dad. As I got out of the car, I could see she had been through the wringer. By that point she was exhausted.

They had tried every possible treatment, but she was dying, and she knew it. That feeling of helplessness, seeing my mother, who I loved so much and always wanted to make proud, now dying, changed me forever.

We talked and talked about our lives together. We talked about forgiveness and forgiving ourselves. She assured me that she loved me and understood why I was the way I was. She told me to look after my dad when she was gone. When she said that, I could no longer hold back the tears. As our conversation continued, she told me that one of the hardest things for her to deal with was that many who came to visit her, looked at her as if she was already dead.

We continued the visits in Kelowna and Penticton as Mom had a couple more treatments there. Her wish was to be in the beautiful home that her and my dad had just built when she passed. My dearest mother, Donna Lynn Worrall, was called to a higher purpose on September 11, 2004 at 58 years young. Rest easy, Mom. You are and always will be my biggest angel.

22

Together We Can

My mother's funeral was held in Merritt. The service was the first time in almost three years that I saw most members of my family. It was awkward, but none of that mattered to me. I was just happy to see my girls. They were understandably guarded though. I know my mother's death was hard for them. They loved their grandma dearly. She had always been there for them, their rock when things went sideways. Later I learned that my mom had been granted a temporary custody order in my absence. The courts eventually ruled that the girls be returned to live with Seema on the coast. Lori had also come up with her brother, Kory, but she had left Nolan home. There were many in attendance, both family and friends, who I had some serious history with. But none of that mattered. Every person in attendance was there to honour my dear mother's life and legacy.

As I sat in silence, my thoughts raced. How could this be happening? Part of me wanted to believe it was my fault. I was fortunate enough to have been able to talk to my mom a few days before she passed. During that conversation, she pleaded with me that she understood why I did the things that I had. She also told me that she didn't want me to feel responsible in any way shape or form when she was gone. Even though it has taken some time, I have forgiven myself somewhat, but I will have to work on it for the rest of my life.

Back at the house after the service, it seemed like the entire world was in a holding pattern. The many who had come to pay their respects were departing. By night's end the reality of what that day had signified was suffocating. I didn't have a lot of conversations with anyone that I can remember, at least not until later in the evening, when it was just my father, sister, and immediate family. I'm thankful Uncle Al took me aside. I will never forget the words he spoke to me. They were a lightbulb moment. He told me that he understood that I had done some things that I wasn't proud of, but what he said next was something that I had never given much thought to. "Brent," he said, "we are family, and blood is thick." He also insisted that everything would heal in time. How could I argue with him? After all, remember what his father had put him and my mother's family through.

As for my dear father, I couldn't even imagine what he was going through. My parents had a long list of people who cared about them and their well-being. It was comforting to see most of them doing what they could to support us all.

My dad was never one for family pep talks or anything like that. In the past he had shown his affection in roundabout ways, every one of which was brilliant and unique. Mom's passing changed that too. He took me aside and told me to hang in there, that things would get better. He also told me that, now Mom was gone, we were going to be strong and be together, just the way Mom wanted it. I wasn't completely sold, but coming from my dad, it was powerful. We were all raw with emotion. I had no idea what would happen next or what to do, but I made a pledge with myself that no matter the outcome of my situation, I would never do anything voluntarily to harm my family again. It was a tall order, but I was serious.

Within a couple of weeks of Mom passing, my girls came up to Vernon for a visit. Again, it was awkward at first, because they had many feelings to sort through. We made the best of our time together though. I was keen to show them around Adventure Bay Peninsula. I had spent many days hiking aimlessly while wondering how or if such a reunion would ever even happen. I'm so thankful that it worked out that way. I know the kids (Nolan included) will likely have questions forever, but it sure felt good to have the girls back in my life.

That Christmas I went to spend some time with my dad to help get ready for the big day. Mom loved Christmas. She always had her own way of putting a special touch on everything related to it. We were spoiled rotten when it came to Christmas. Now it was important to us all to rally together and have the kind of Christmas that Mom would have wanted us to have.

Dad and I drove up the mountain in search of a tree. As I climbed into the passenger seat of his beautifully smelly 4x4 work truck, it reminded me of times that Dad and I went out for firewood or the many days that I got to go into the bush with him as a kid and watch him fall trees.

One time I went along with him on a strip that he was falling on a mountainside in the Fraser Valley. He had a smaller chainsaw that he used for under-brushing. I usually carried that one for him. Dad always showed me where to look in the tree, on the tree, and around it to assess any potential hazards. Tree-falling is an incredibly dangerous profession. At that tree Dad pointed out its potential to "barber chair," which meant the tree could split from the butt upwards and outwards before the tree's holding wood was cut through. It could happen quicker than lightning, so it was important to have an escape route pre-cleared and pre-planned. Sensing that potential hazard, Dad pointed to a spot in the distance where he wanted me to stand. Then he told me to take the chainsaw I was carrying and place it adjacent to the trunk of another tree that we had just felled. Everything went according to plan—until the tree split, spun, and landed to the right of the intended target area. I was mortified as the top portion of that tree demolished the chainsaw that I had been carrying. Dad didn't notice it. I said nothing and started to walk away. Then he said, "Hey, where's the saw you were carrying?"

"Right there where you told me to put it," I said as I pointed to its apparent burial ground. It turns out as Dad was falling the tree, he made some improvisations and forgot where the saw was. Better the saw than me, I guess.

We got a beauty of a tree that would have made the Griswolds proud. It towered up to their great room's vaulted ceiling. More importantly, I knew my mother was smiling down on us, because it had been ages since my dad and I had done anything like that together. My mother's dying wish was for me to look after my dad. Mom, I have done my best since your passing. I have not been nearly as strong or as helpful as Kelly, but I'm pretty sure Kelly got your gene in that regard, and I have Dad's.

Between Gisela and me, my dad, and my sister's family, we managed to survive our first Christmas without our family's matriarch. It was anything but easy. Seeing the kids play, laugh, and smile with each other was soothing though. It was the music that our souls badly needed. Mom was there with us in spirit every step of the way, and I certainly felt it. When the sun set that Christmas Day, I asked God for something I knew I was going to need in the year ahead: strength.

On Boxing Day as we sat in the living room, my father turned on the television. On every channel news was breaking about a huge earthquake in the Indian

Ocean. The epicentre was off the west coast of northern Sumatra. The earthquake was massive, 9.1–9.3 on the Richter scale. The ensuing tsunamis hit no less than fourteen countries, including the hardest-hit countries of Indonesia, Sri Lanka, Thailand, and India. That Boxing Day tragedy killed over 250,000 people.

When the news broke, Rich picked up his phone and began dialling. His nephew was in Indonesia and in harm's way. Thankfully, he was found in short order and was okay.

It's important for me to write about some of these events that shaped our world for a couple of reasons. First, as I've said, I am and always will be a history buff. Second, such events are a good reminder that life happens, and we are never alone. Everyone on this great planet has to deal with something unpleasant at one time or another. I have long since learned that we are all in this deal together, and not one of us is getting out alive.

When 2005 arrived, I sensed that change would be a popular flavour for me—or should I say, us. Most of my life I have considered myself a lone wolf. However, I'm a Gemini, which means I'm a social creature. The double life I had been leading up to that point was a by-product of my demons. In no way was ingesting any of those ingredients a recipe for success. I knew that, but I didn't seem to care too much, or at least that's what my actions indicated. But I did care about my family and friends, and I wanted everyone to know it. Now that my mom was gone, I wanted to show her and the world that she had raised a winner, not a loser. That would be no easy task, but I was ready to roll up my sleeves and put on whatever gloves were needed, work or boxing!

The lease on our condo was up that summer. One of Gisela's clients, who lived directly across the lake from us, was planning on retiring and travelling during the winter. The Carters, Mike and Donna, had a beautiful home and put a brand-new entry-level suite on the main floor. That home had a stunning lake view. It seemed like a perfect fit for us, and it was considerably cheaper than locking into an inflated lease. Best of all, we would still be on the water. Go figure, our address at Adventure Bay was 8800 Adventure Bay Road, and our new address was 8888 Okanagan Landing Road. I was excited for the move, because in certain cultures, the number eight is good luck. We were good in that department. Our address now had four snowmen in it.

I was certainly going to miss Adventure Bay mountain, and hiking and unicycling up and down it, though. I will always have a soft spot in my heart for that damn road, onto which I made a wrong turn long before I ever saw the reasons why. I believe it was perfectly tailored for where I needed to be during those troubled times. Today I'm thankful I got to spend as much time hiking and cycling as I did. The old saying, "You never know what you have until it's gone," comes to mind. I have thanked my Higher Power many times for looking out for me. I have no other explanation for how I survived my many experiences, and that is okay by me.

The day we moved, my dad came and helped. I will never forget leaving the house with the final load in the pickup. After locking the door one last time, Gisela climbed into our canoe and paddled it across the lake to our new home. We beat her there, but just barely.

The Carters were super-nice people. I believe that move was another "God shot." We had water (the lake, which we loved) and a mountain behind us that led right up to Predator Ridge Golf Course. With more coniferous trees and a much rockier surface, that mountain proved to be a happy place for me.

I was still drinking beer quite heavily, about eight to twelve a day. That was pretty gross, and my body hated it. My liver was swollen, and my heart went sideways again.

One weekend I went over to spend a few days with my dad in Merritt. Something always needed to be done over there. Shortly after getting to work in the backyard, my heart went haywire. I had been getting quite a few symptoms associated with my irregular heartbeat and mitral valve issue. The doctors in Vernon had me wear a halter monitor more than once. That time my chest pain was intense. It felt like I had just been shanked in a prison yard. My heart was racing uncontrollably, but the last thing I wanted to do was tell my old man that I needed to go to the hospital. Damn, he had spent enough time there with my mom. But that was as bad as it had ever been, and I feared I might drop dead right in front of him.

The Merritt hospital brought in a cardiologist, and he ordered an angiogram. They didn't have the means to do it in Merritt, so I was sent to Kelowna the next morning by ambulance. I laid there on the gurney wondering if my lifestyle was finally going to get the best of me.

When the nurse came in, her first words were, "You're a little young for this, aren't you?" As she said that, my life flashed before my eyes.

Luckily, the angiogram showed no blockages. The doctors changed my blood-pressure meds and warned me that if I didn't stop drinking, I would likely not see another birthday. I took the medication, and was happy to be back home. As far as the drinking goes, I wasn't ready to let that go just yet. If you are wondering how I could even entertain such thoughts, let's just say addiction is insidiously stubborn and painful.

I continued at the RV shop that spring. I also did many landscaping side jobs for Gisela's clients. My girls were back in my life, and things were slowly getting better on that front. They came for weekend visits often. The Carters, who had raised children of their own, embraced the girls. There was no drama in our home, but our neighbours got the benefit of seeing me dropped off in a police car more than once. At the time I didn't care about drinking and driving one bit. In fact, I would drink four beer from the time I left work in Lavington until I got home out on the lake. The two dots that I couldn't connect were summed up in a saying from my twelve-step program, "I was an alcoholic, and out of my alcoholic malady, my life had become unmanageable." It was that simple, and I knew my life depended on me figuring that out again quickly.

That year also proved to be a powerful year for my mom's side of the family. Earlier on I mentioned James Champ, the son that social services had taken away from my grandmother. It was in 2005 that he reached out to my Uncle Larry, and let him know who he was and what had happened. I can only imagine how tough that was for my grandmother to be sworn to secrecy. I recently stopped by Merritt to visit my Aunt Cheryl, my mom's oldest sister and the oldest of the nine kids. She was old enough at the time to know what had happened, but she, like my grandmother, feared repercussions, and did as the ministry requested.

That summer was the first time we all got to meet the man who was born James Champ, though he was raised as Randall Barr. He grew up in a loving home and taught high school until he retired in Quesnel, BC. The thing that is most compelling to me about that story is that when the only mother he had ever known became ill, she told him that he was "different" from the other adopted kids, in that he had been taken from a family that would have loved him and care for him. That didn't sit well with him, and he reached out to find his birth siblings.

That summer, like every other summer, our family gathered on the Merritt property high above the Nicola Valley. It was an annual campout event that we called "Camp Champ." It was always a good time to get together with my extended family on the 150-acre parcel of property. It was my first time back at Camp Champ in four years. I missed my family a lot, and it was important for me to be there that year.

When I met Uncle James (Randall Barr) for the first time, I couldn't believe how much he looked like my other uncles. There was no doubt in my mind that he was my mother's brother. Mom and Grandma Jean, we all felt your presence at that incredibly powerful reunion. There were many wet eyes around our campfire. I will go to my grave believing that you both had something to do with that.

With the reunion of family, it was only fitting that I be reunited with something else that weekend. The campout with all my cousins and their kids and friends usually included two and four-wheeled mayhem. Almost every one of my cousins, mostly as a result of my racing involvement, were moto heads. Uncle Al's son, Jeff, had brought along a 1997 YZ-250 two-stroke. When he asked if I wanted to take it out for a ride, I was a little hesitant. He had a slick-looking kit to wear, and it had been years since I had cast a shadow in motocross gear. It was crazy, but when I put it on, something changed. Wearing that colourful out-of-date 1990s MSR kit gave me a power I had not experienced in ages. I had forgotten how good it felt. I had thought about dirt bikes often, but the part of the equation that I always settled on was that was then, and this is now! I thought I would never ride a dirt bike again.

I rode the bike a lot that weekend. It gave me a sense of freedom that I had not felt in ages. I can't tell you how good it felt to have my family and a dirt bike back in my life. I realized I had many mountains to climb in terms of dealing with the wreckage of my past, but I was prepared for it no matter the cost.

That September Uncle Al called me in Vernon to tell me that he was now the owner of that YZ-250, and he wanted to know if I wanted it. Are you kidding me? That was too damn good to be true, or so I thought. I didn't expect to get it for nothing, but with Uncle Al, I never knew. He is a kind soul who always had nice surprises for everyone in our family. I paid him $1,900 for the bike and then met him at my dad's place in Merritt to pick it up. I got in a few good rides at our Noble Canyon area before the snow fell.

Winter 2005 was tough for me mentally and emotionally. After having had the year to process what I had put my family through and losing my mother at fifty-eight years young, that came as no real surprise. I reached daily for my favourite cure-all, alcohol. Like every winter before, I was laid off at the RV shop, but I did a lot of snow removal to keep my pockets insulated. I also hiked often, even in the snow, up to Predator Ridge and where the Sparkling Hill Resort now sits. I had to. It was an escape that I had fallen in love with since arriving in the Okanagan Valley. I also figured that if I was going to continue to poison myself with alcohol, the exercise would help offset the damage. This is a good illustration of how unwilling I was to let go of that vice. It had a death grip on me that seemed incurable. I needed something, but what? Divine intervention? I had already had a couple of pretty strong God moments. No one could argue that. What I needed more than that was to find a weakness in my formidable foe's seemingly impenetrable armour. My willingness to be well had to coincide with a vortex of my desire not to die.

That winter I was hospitalized at least half a dozen times. Heart meds and depression pills were on my script. The anti-depressants had me wanting to jump off the cliff at the top of Sparkling Hill or run headlong out my living room window. I had tolerated the mental torment I had put myself and others through, but now my mental health was starting to fail, and that scared me.

Two days after we rang in 2006, I sat at our kitchen table with a beer in my hand. I looked over at the television and when I saw that the hockey team I had bet on was not doing me any favours, I had seen about enough. No, I wasn't going to snap or anything like that; that wasn't my style. I did have my moments though. I threw our phone halfway across Okanagan Lake the day I got the call that my mom passed away. This feeling was different though, and somewhat strange to me. Something inside changed, as if a switch had been turned off.

"That's it, I've had enough," I told Gisela, though I didn't explain what I was talking about. Like everything else that I had decided to do, I was all in. I was going to take that narrow opening of willingness and run with it. Something or someone was listening to my prayers, and I knew they wanted me one way only, and that was sober. It had taken a few years, but I had finally figured out that if I was going to achieve any of my remaining life goals, I had to get sober. In truth though, I was just tired of being sick and tired. Was it too late for me? I didn't know.

My mind was filled with memories of how genuinely happy my sober friends were to see me when I attended meetings regularly. It had been almost five years since I had attended any kind of twelve-step program. I dug out the "booze clinics" directory and called their twenty-four-hour hotline. I'm so glad that I made that call immediately. With any kind of addiction, the willingness to change can be fleeting. I was no longer afraid to fail, and was determined to succeed.

My first meeting was a Tuesday night free speech and open meeting at the Kindale Centre in Vernon. When I arrived, it didn't surprise me to see all the smiling people. They had what I wanted: happiness. I knew that if I could somehow lock up the demon inside of me that had an insatiable appetite for alcohol, it would create room for more happiness in my life. It wasn't going to be easy. Alcohol was a good friend who I feared I would miss dearly. I went to the meetings almost daily, and I got a new sponsor. I became involved with that program as if my life depended on it, which it did.

By the time Vernon's winter carnival rolled around that February, we put in a comical entry with Gisela, my girls, Kelly, and her two boys, Josh and Justin. We called ourselves "Grandma's Fairyland Clowns" in honour of my late mother. The theme of the carnival that year was "The Orient." I sewed over thirty miniature stuffed pandas onto my clown costume and wore it while riding my unicycle and playing an accordion. It was so fun to get out and participate in that great community. It was also cool to recognize a few people from some of the meetings. That was a tangible proof of how much my life had already improved, physically and mentally, in just under two months. Our entry didn't win top prize—we were defeated by the Shriners and the Kalamalka Caring Clowns—but we got our revenge the following winter, when we were voted top comical act for the parade. It was such an honour to have the huge trophy with our names engraved on it in our home for a year. We love you, Mom, and I know how proud you are of us.

I rode my dirt bike moderately over the following year. I was more focused on working through the steps of my twelve-step program and my job at the RV shop. Along the way, Sonu and Sara had expressed some interest in riding dirt bikes. In the summer of 2006, we bought them a new Yamaha TTR-125. It was a lot of fun to share a family tradition and one of my true first loves with my girls and Gisela. Our yard was huge, and it was a great place to get them started. They loved it. I was a little worried about Sara, because she had taken a header on an MR-50 at Camp Champ on one of the years that I was away. Once they were accustomed to the bike though, and I was confident they could ride well enough, we hit the Noble Canyon riding area often. Another spot that we liked to ride was the Barnhartvale area just outside of Kamloops. It was a lot of fun, but I shake my head now. Some days we were miles from anywhere on our bikes. If things had gone sideways, I can't imagine how we would have dealt with it. I don't consider myself to be a bad father (at least not anymore), but having a life-changing injury has certainly changed the way I look at things. Older, safer, smarter, I'm not sure. One thing I'm sure about is that wheelchairs are highly overrated.

With my girls living on the coast with their mom, things were not great for them. I'm not sure what the issues were, but they both expressed an interest to live with us. I know their mother also had some demons that needed addressing. She also had two other children from a different father. My girls were young and innocent and deserved the best possible chance at life. I believed Vernon was a lot better for them than the Greater Vancouver area.

They took to our town, its people, and its activities well. They attended Fulton Secondary School, where they made good friends before they graduated. It was anything but easy, but I'm so proud of them both. How could anyone not be? They had been put through the wringer. Girls, I'm so sorry that you had to experience such dysfunction.

During the summer of 2008, I reconnected with an old high school friend from Chilliwack, Wayne Oberst, on Facebook. We had hung out a lot when I was younger. He was a great guy and came to a lot of my races. Believe it or not, that was also the first year that Gisela and I got a computer and cell phones. I never had any use for those things until then. We didn't have an abundance of technology in our home growing up. With the expenses lavished on our two-wheeled hobbies, there was never a lot of room for such luxuries. I can't take one iota of credit for the two cell phones we had or our Macintosh laptop. One of Gisela's clients, who was an emergency room doctor in Vernon, took a job in Dubai. One of the stipulations was that he could only take a few select things with him, at least that's how it was explained to me. The price of "free" fit our budget nicely, so we were very thankful. Thanks, Shim family! We miss you here in Vernon.

I was excited to drive up to Chilliwack and see Wayne. It had been years. He got me up to speed on how some of the people we had graduated with had faired. That reunion was healing in the sense that I had not been back in Chilliwack for years. The fact that I had also been sober for a couple of years was surreal. When I left there in 1987, I was a mess and had a substantial number of outstanding debts from my "step one" days, step one being that I was powerless over alcohol and that my life had become unmanageable. In fact, for many years I didn't dare pull off the highway into that town. Today things are quite different in that now one of my twelve-step promises has been fulfilled, that being, "I no longer regret my past, nor wish to shut the door on it." Pretty powerful stuff, isn't it?

Wayne convinced me that I needed to buy a new or newer YZ-250. He had done quite a bit of riding and racing in his day. He was more into BMX racing, but he was also hardcore moto enthusiast. We rode a lot together. He found a 2006 YZ 250 two-stroke in the Harrison area, and we got it for a great price. Up to that point I had not been back on a track, but I fancied hitting the big jumps. Being airborne again on a dirt bike at almost forty years old was an incredible feeling. I had no fear, and it felt as if I was a kid again. The big Barnhartvale freestyle jump, the jumps at Peg Leg on the Fraser River, the jumps way up in Noble Canyon, I was all in to air it out. Even when I was a kid, my dad would scream at me to keep my wheels on the ground and stop "showboating," as he called it. "And none of those damn cross-ups either." Those are now called "scrubs," Dad, and if done right, they help to get the power back to the ground as quickly as possible.

The bike that I had just bought had only ever been ridden up and down logging roads around Harrison Lake. Its power and suspension system was a considerable upgrade from the 1997 model that I had been riding.

When I returned to riding, I did everything pretty much like I did when I climbed off my bike that final time at the Vancouver Supercross in 1983. Sadly, apart from one-off rides with my friends Phil Golding and Charles Douglas, I had not ridden at all. In my mind, all I needed was a good helmet, a pair of boots, gloves, and goggles—and, of course, a pair of sweet riding pants with a matching jersey. The bikes were much faster, and I soon found out why the safety equipment had evolved to match.

On one ride at a track in Chilliwack, I had just gotten my girls outfitted and ready for their day of riding. Then I climbed onto my bike and took off, but I ran out of gas mid-air on a jump on the first lap. It sent me over the handlebars, and I ended up with a broken collarbone. That turned out to be a good thing, because my friend George, who watched the end-over-end crash, saw my helmet impact my collarbone and break it. That prompted me to buy the piece of equipment that I believe saved my life in 2011. I will get to those details shortly, but for now, all you need to know is neck braces save lives. From everything I have experienced, I believe they should be mandatory if you are racing a dirt bike. I also think they should be worn when riding for recreation. I have no financial connections with neck brace companies whatsoever. I also no longer have any voluntary connection to anything below my arms.

In the summer of 2008, after having ridden a lot, I started to think more and more about motocross racing. Up to that point my rides had mostly been for fun. I loved jumping though. To me it was the best freedom one could have. It felt good to be the old guy who was still doing all the big jumps—that is, until I rekindled my habit of not landing as one with the motorcycle. But what the heck, right? I had put myself and my family through the wringer. Was it because I had lost track of who I was and what mattered most? I'm sure many answers could be inserted by any number of people. What mattered most to me was the moment. I had spent most of my life trying to live up to everyone else's expectations. As my brain slowly became unglued from years of alcohol abuse, my ability to visualize success grew stronger quickly.

That summer we took a road trip to Edmonton with the girls to visit the West Edmonton Mall. We also went to the Edmonton round of the Canadian motocross pro national series at Castrol Raceway. It was a fun trip. For the first time that I could remember, I was doing something with my family while completely sober.

When we pulled into the track, I was shocked at how many people I recognized. I had been to a race at the Stetson Bowl in 1990, but that was my first outdoor motocross race in twenty-five years. Wow, had it been that long? No wonder I was so messed up.

One of the first people I talked to was the Kawasaki team's truck driver and my old friend, Jim Small. I grew up racing with Jimmy, who was a big, burly redhead with the number forty-two on his bike. Jim, who achieved much top-level success in the late 1970s and early 1980s, was also later the team manager of the Yamaha team I had ridden for. After the surprise reunion at that event, I got to see Jim and his son, Greg, quite a bit more at the races. In keeping with a "small world" theme, Kelly (my sister), who is a nurse at the Kamloops General Hospital, works with Jim's wife.

I'm not sure if Jim smiled when I showed up at the track because he was happy to see me or because I was there with a two-stroke. I'm sure you older moto heads will see the humour in that one. When I got back into moto, the four-stroke thing confused the heck out of me until my friend, Brock Hoyer, confronted me at the Williams Lake track and said, "Dude you need a four-stroke." Maybe I did, but I was having fun, and that's all that mattered for the time being.

Another individual I ran into that day in Edmonton was my old friend Brian Beaton. I had raced with him back in the late 1970s and early 1980s, and he was a big part of my family's racing circle. His son, Kyle, was on the track that day racing the 250 pro class on his GA Checkpoint Yamaha. I was impressed with how fast Kyle was and with how far our sport had come, both on and off the track. When I hung up my boots prematurely in 1983, a full factory ride meant you rolled in a cube van. Nowadays the factory rigs were all semi-trailer trucks with all the bells and whistles. I was impressed.

That day I was privileged to witness one of Colton Facciotti's best rides. I hadn't seen him race before that day, but what I saw in Edmonton was exactly why he's a sixtime national champ. The other rider who impressed me was none other than our Canadian "Superman," Mr. Blair Morgan. Blair didn't have the best first moto that day. However, the second moto for Facciotti's Blackfoot Yamaha teammate was a good one. He charged hard all the way to the finish, and I believe he finished second. I was impressed with Blair's race savvy and determination to keep on pressing in the late stages of a long tiring moto.

We had promised the girls another day at the West Edmonton Mall on the Monday after the big race. They had to get ready for school, which was starting in a few weeks' time. We headed over to the mall early. It was good to be there on a Monday, because it wasn't nearly as busy as it had been on Saturday. Some of the rides the kids had wanted to go on had huge lineups, but now there were none. We figured it best to get the rides done before they were packed with people.

While the girls lined up to go on the roller coaster, I saw someone I thought I recognized. I did a double take and then looked at Gisela and said, "That's Blair Morgan over there with his kids." I was a little starstruck and kept my distance. The entire time though I watched and admired him as he spent some quality time with his kids. I'm not sure how old they were but likely a few years younger than my girls. I told Gisela how cool I thought it was, because I know how demanding the sport can be on families. When one gets to the top level in any sport, the immeasurable sacrifices required are not often talked about. So, seeing that world-class motocrosser and snowcross racer spending quality time with his kids made a lasting impression. Later that year, in October, when word came in that Blair was paralyzed at the Montreal Supercross, I cried my eyes out. It was weird. I didn't even know Blair, but from that experience in Edmonton, I felt a solid connection. I bought three MX-Forum Pink Palace Blair Morgan fundraiser T-shirts and I'll treasure them forever!

On the way home from Edmonton, all I could think about was motocross racing. It had been ages since I had felt that kind of fire burn inside me. When I got that bike a couple of years earlier, I didn't think I would ever race again. I figured that ship had sailed, and it was time to just have some fun. Riding was fun, but "once a racer, always a racer."

Back at home I started poking around on racing websites to check out schedules, results, and those kinds of things. A race was scheduled at the Whispering Pines track in Kamloops that September. I told Gisela and the kids that even though I wasn't sure how it would go, I wanted to give it a try.

First, I had to get over to the Kamloops track and get in some practice. One hot August afternoon—it had to be close to 100 degrees—I unloaded my bike at the track. A friend from my twelve-step program came with me. I was excited to be at the track and even more thrilled to have someone there who was a talented photographer. Making things even cooler, I got a call from Wayne, who happened to be in Kamloops. When I told him, I was at the track about to throw down some laps, he said he would come out to watch.

Everything was ready. It was hot, windy, and dusty. Thankfully, I was the only one silly enough to try and ride in that searing heat. That's how I've always rolled. No half measures for this cowboy. If I'm in, it's all in. After a little motivational music, AC/DC's "Thunderstruck," which bellowed so loudly from my stereo that it could likely be heard in Raleigh (across the river) I threw a leg over my bike and fired it up.

It's impossible to put into words how good it felt to be back on an official motocross track, one that I would hopefully be lined up on again in a few weeks' time. The clock was ticking, and I needed to make sure I didn't waste a single second. That signalled a big change in my attitude toward many things. I had been the proverbial procrastinator for years, and now I was taking initiatives that were scaring some people. The difference was having the biggest missing piece of my identity back in place.

After I navigated the first laps to get a feel for the track, I told my photographer friend, Jeff, that I was ready. He looked a little surprised and wasn't sure what

I meant. I told him that I was ready to start going much faster and doing all the big jumps. I showed him where to position himself to catch the best shots.

As I headed back onto the track, my mind was clear. I was confident and ready. As I approached the tower turn finish-line jump, I got a little more airtime than I bargained for. Cresting the peak of the jump, I moved my body weight to the left, the direction the track went after the landing. I was also preparing to turn my wheels in that direction with my best scrub efforts. No more than twenty feet into what promised to be a good-sized leap, I got hit by an insanely powerful gust of wind. It was a huge shock; I wasn't expecting it at all. Talking with the locals after the fact, I learned that surprise gusts are a known issue in that valley. That gust came directly from the north. With the way my body weight was positioned to scrub to the left, I had no chance to stay airborne with the motorcycle. For the first time in years, I was confronted with hitting the invisible eject button. I have always considered myself to be a graceful crasher. If I had done nothing else at all in my racing days, I managed, at least in my mind, to make crashing as graceful as possible. After hitting the eject button and getting as far away from the motorcycle as possible, I saw the ground coming up fast. Reacting on instinct, I extended my left arm to break my fall.

When I hit the ground, I felt a jolt of electricity shoot through my body. It started in my left arm and went all the way down my left side. When my body finally came to a stop, I was sitting upright. Then I did what I had always done when I crashed: I performed a rapid self-assessment to see if I had broken anything. My left arm hurt so much that I was afraid to look at it. It felt like it had just been ripped off my body. I don't think any one of my broken legs ever hurt that much. When I finally turned my head to the left, I nearly fainted. My arm wasn't there; it was gone. As I rolled my head over to the right, completely aghast from thinking I had just torn off my arm, there it was. My left arm had broken off at the radius, right inside the shoulder socket, and was twisted completely around my back. I have a pretty strong gag reflex when it comes to seeing boo boos, but that one was a mess.

By that time Wayne had shown up, and so had Kelly. That was good news, because the next series of events was pretty ugly. Jeff had called 911, but they told him it would be about an hour before they could get an ambulance to the track. I will give them a break on that one, because I know it's at least a forty-five minute drive to the Kamloops hospital from the motocross track. Of all people, I should know.

Kelly, who is a nurse, helped stabilize my rapidly deteriorating condition, so much so that I was even able to pose for a few photos with my seriously messed-up wing. Sadly, enough "Airmail," yours truly, was once again sentenced to some more time in life's "No Fly Zone." I felt everything was going to be all right though. It was nothing compared to what I had put myself through for the last twenty-five years without motocross. I had gotten hurt doing something that I loved doing. I had hurt enough mentally and emotionally without motocross in my life, so whatever the outcome, I was okay with it. I still believe that and will take it to my grave.

When the ambulance finally showed up, it ended up breaking down. In fact, it didn't just break down with me stuck in it, the damn thing broke down on the McLure Ferry, which they decided to use to cross the river. I hit the laughing gas or whatever they were giving me as hard as I could; the pain was severe. The next thing I remember is coming to at the hospital. To give you an idea of how long it took them to get me there, Gisela arrived at the hospital from Vernon before I did.

I was assessed via X-ray, and it was confirmed that my humerus was badly broken and dislocated. The doctor determined that the only way I would have a chance at an arm that would rotate in the shoulder socket again was through a delicate operation that required six long screws to be inserted from the top down into my humerus. Making that more complex and riskier was the fact that I had severed my deltoid muscles from the arm. They would have to cut my rotator cuff completely in order to put in the screws. With not guarantee of success, I reluctantly opted for the surgery. I was certainly disappointed that I wasn't going to get an opportunity to line up on a motocross track that fall, but I was determined to maintain the path I was on, heal up, and be ready for the 2009 outdoor motocross racing season. I had to, because I believed God had given me a second chance at living rather than just existing.

23

The Road to Walton

I had a one-week wait at home in Vernon before returning to Kamloops for surgery. My arm and shoulder were massively swollen. The bruises were some of the largest I have ever seen. I knew it was going to be a long road back to health. During that week I did some more soul searching. I remained committed to my plan to line up at a motocross race on a dirt bike.

When the orthopaedic surgeon met me before we went into the OR, he reminded me of the complications. I heard him, but I only visualized one thing: that I was going to heal up 100 percent. Those memories of being sick and tired of being so busted up many years earlier were gone. I needed to get better now. It was imperative for me to make peace with the sport that had defined me as a youth.

Being sober and fit due to my compulsive itch to exercise helped a lot. Even on workdays (up to the time of that most recent physical setback) I exercised at great length. Mountain biking, unicycling, elliptical training, weights, stretching, I had my eyes on the prize, though I didn't know what that prize would be. I just wanted a chance to go out and give it my best shot and be able to say I did it. That was a whole lot better than going to the "other side" not having tried.

After the surgery, I slept on my sister's couch for the night. There's not much that I have experienced in life that hurts as much (physically) as when the surgical sedatives wear off after hardware is installed. Before I left the hospital, the doctor offered me a prescription for Tylenol 3s, but I rejected it. I didn't want to jeopardize my path of being clean and sober.

I woke up at 3:00 a.m. reeling in agony. I rolled off the edge of the couch and onto my knees. I needed something and called out to my sister. Kelly hooked me up with a few pain meds, which allowed me to get back to sleep. Things like that are a no-brainer for most people, but someone like me can't be too careful.

That injury proved to be a good test of many things. It also gave me a chance to think long and hard about the pros and cons of what I was hoping to get back into.

The rehab protocol that fall and into the winter was brutal. My surgeon instructed me to keep my arm in a sling for six weeks, because it was the only way the deltoids would have a chance to re-attach. I forget the exact formula he quoted me on how slowly they heal. My rotator cuff also had to be snipped and re-attached to facilitate the screws, and everything was likely going to atrophy after six weeks of immobilization. I wasn't one to argue, and I did everything that was asked of me to get well. Time was on my side, because the gate on the 2009 outdoor racing season didn't drop until April. Besides, it had already been over twenty-five years since I had sat behind a gate, so a few more months wasn't anything, right?

By January 2009 I was still pretty messed up. I had been to rehabilitation with a few different therapists. They determined that I would likely never be able to raise my arm above my head to a twelve o'clock position. I worked on that daily with a hockey stick. I would lie on my back with the stick in both hands and then try to stretch it back over above my head. Progress was painstakingly slow. I began to make peace with the fact that my arm would likely never extend fully upright.

Around that time, I got a call from Uncle Al, who informed me that he was full steam ahead on a new home he was building on one of his spec lots in Chilliwack. He asked if I wanted to come down and paint it when it was ready. It turned out to be a big job. After making a couple of calls to some of my high school buddies to ensure I would have a place to stay, I accepted. Again, I have to thank Wayne and his wife, Lory, for putting me up. The same goes for George Velonis from the old Hilton Drive neighbourhood.

For the next three months, I spent lengthy stretches in Chilliwack working. I also continued to work on making my arm stronger and getting more mobility. Wayne even came up with the brilliant idea that if I laid on the floor in the manner I did with the stick in my hand, he would grab it and lift me up in an arm curl. We did okay, Wayne. I think you might have pried another half a degree of rotation out of me. You probably could have made a few bucks arm wrestling, my friend.

By February I was getting itchy to get reacclimated with my motorcycle. The racing season was starting in two months. I had only about four laps on a moto-cross track on the 2006 YZ-250. Fittingly, Chilliwack is home to one of the best west coast winter riding areas: the Fraser River. To me that opportunity was gold, because I was able to ride in the place where my two-wheeled passion was born. I never imagined such a beautiful fate. I was able to include the girls on a couple of the trips down as well. Sara rode mostly for fun and wasn't interested in racing. Sonu, however, was determined to be the next Jolene Van Vugt. When we went to the motocross nationals the year before in Edmonton, we got to witness our country's top women race. I'm pretty sure the yellow Suzuki that Jolene was riding that day had a big number four on it. That also had my attention, because it was my hockey hero Bobby Orr's number as well as the number of the Greatest Of All Time (GOAT) in our sport, Ricky Carmichael.

It was also nice to be able to share the riding and racing experience again with other members of my family. My cousin Lisa Westeringh (who is married to Harvey) also had bikes, and so did her kids, Kyle and Jessica. They had a sweet little track in their backyard. We hit it up one day, which I will remember it for the rest of my life. Once again, it was so nice to be creating such memories, and for the right reasons. Everyone ended up out on the small, but fun track spinning laps on that sunny winter Fraser Valley afternoon. I got to be trackside with my daughter and teach her the basics of two-wheeled flight. Wayne and his daughter, Isabella, also came out. I think the Boiler Makers Union had my friend George tied up somewhere on that occasion. I believe my Higher Power was behind every bit of that long-overdue reunion.

The painting job went slowly. I told my uncle that it was because it was winter. I argued that the paint rolled on slower when it was cold, so he turned up the heat. In all honesty, the job went well. I set up a pulley system in the basement with paint cans attached to improve my mobility and strength, the latter being my main issue of focus. I had worked my backside off to be fit and healthy and ready to race. I was back down to my racing weight of 150 pounds. Where I had once been obsessed with self-destruction, I had undergone a 180-degree reversal of lifestyle and attitude. It had been years since I had felt that good, if ever.

Back at home Gisela worked her tail off. The girls went to school and worked part time. I'm not sure if they missed me when I was away, but I certainly missed them. As the saying goes, "You don't know what you have until it is gone." They may not have been gone, but I was at one time. I'm so thankful for my girls' forgiveness. I think about it and feel it every day of my life.

The Chilliwack job concluded at the end of March. Back at home I had my eyes set on racing the first CMRC race of the year in Quesnel. The race wasn't until April 25. Before that I would line up at the Alberta old-timers season opening event in Kamloops at the track on the North Thompson River, the same place where I almost severed my arm the previous August. I was excited but didn't know what to expect.

Sonu and I loaded up our bikes, and off we went for the two-day event. I was nervous, but I was confident that I was doing the right thing. My arm had not healed as I had hoped, but I accepted that. My range of motion was brutal, and my shoulder hurt constantly. But by some stroke of luck that most motocrossers will understand, the pain went away when I climbed on the motorcycle. You know what else went away when I threw a leg over my dirt bike at the racetrack for the first time in twenty-six years? Almost every single ounce of the emotional pain that I had bottled up during that time.

Saturday was a practice day, and Sunday we would race for bragging rights. I felt good during practice and quickly got used to the track layout. I can't tell you how good it felt to be out on the track with one of my childhood idols, 1979 Canadian National 500 cc champion, Stan Currington.

On Sunday they split us up into an A and a B class to separate the skill levels. When I got to staging, I was asked if I was an A or a B rider. I was a top-level racer when I packed it in, but that was years earlier. I immediately thought of the conversation I had a few weeks before with the CMRC head office when applying for my racing licence. I explained my scenario and was told that I could apply for an intermediate licence instead of the pro ticket if I wanted. However, if I beat someone, and they protested, the results could be overturned. Not too worried about it, I told them to just send me the pro licence.

I selected my gate just to the inside of the doghouse (where the starter operates the starting gate). Sitting there on my bike looking down the straightaway to the first turn, I was overwhelmed. Just over my left shoulder was a man I idolized, and I was about to race against him and many others. My eyes started to well up. The thirty-second board wasn't even up yet. I put my goggles on to disguise my emotions. Once they were on, covering my face, I have to tell you, I cried my eyes out with joy! For the first time in twenty-six years, my soul was complete.

At day's end, I couldn't get back to my truck quick enough to phone Gisela and tell her how it went. Sonu and I had survived our first races of the year in one piece. We were both excited about the Quesnel race in three weeks' time.

Our racing licences showed up the week of the first race. I was excited to finally have mine in my hand. Seeing my name and new racing number (114) on it made it all the more real. Sonu, who was born in 1991, was fittingly ticketed to run number 91 in the ladies' class. After everything I have experienced in the moto world, it's so cool how it has become a true family sport. If you get a chance, get out to a motocross race. Kids can start racing as early as four years of age. The sport does not discriminate against age, sex, race, colour, or creed. I have seen many take up motocross, fall in love with it, and excel at it like nothing else they have ever accomplished.

I contacted my long-lost uncle, James Champ (Randall Barr), who lived in Quesnel. I couldn't believe it when he told me the track was just down the road from his home. He and his wife, Jean (go figure, that was my grandma's name), were happy to host Sonu and me at his house.

We awoke to a light dusting of snow on the Saturday morning of the two-day event. Pulling into the track on race day is a feeling like no other, a feeling that I had long since forgotten, but was happy to be experiencing again. We signed in, and then I walked the track with Sonu and a fellow I had just met, Jim Watchell. If you have been to the Quesnel track, you know there are a few good-sized jumps on it. Sadly, a rider was killed on one of them. Having only been back on the bike for a short time, my timing on some of those jumps was likely to be off. Fortunately, I got things dialled in pretty quickly. After our practice session, I made sure our bikes were ready to head to the starting gate.

On my first official first race day in twenty-six years, I signed up for only one class. Sonu did the same, signing up for the ladies' class. Guess what? They put us on the track together for our race.

Having had the benefit of the Kamloops fun race helped tons on that day. It was different, but we were both ready. I wasn't at all nervous. The wet eyes I had in Kamloops were dry. The thirty-second board went up, and shortly after it went sideways, the gate dropped. As I screamed wide open toward the rapidly approaching first corner, I was third. I made a quick move on the guy in front of me out of the left-hander and then had the leader in my sights.

As we approached the biggest jump on the track (a step-down double with a big but forgiving sixty-five-foot downhill gap), I committed to it. I stayed a little bit to the right, because I wasn't sure if the leader would move over into my leaping path. It was a wise decision, because he backed out halfway up the jump face. I was in the lead and marched on to what I would call a fairly easy win. I managed to get around my daughter a few times, because she didn't quite make as many laps as the rest of us. I can't say enough about how good it felt to feel like a winner at the motocross track again. Making it even more special was how proud I felt of Sonu. It was a repeat performance in the second moto, the only difference being getting the holeshot and not having to risk anyone's life (my own included) jumping over them.

Awards, trophies, and payouts were handed out at a ceremony at the conclusion of each racing day. I finished first overall in the plus-forty class. I have a huge smile on my face right now just thinking about it. I never imagined such a divine fate for this drunken bum. When they called my name, I felt so proud, especially considering I was always my own worst critic. I can't thank my Higher Power enough for allowing me to recognize that. I received an envelope with some money in it but no trophy. I was tempted to reach into the envelope and ask one of the kids who had just received a trophy if I could buy his. I won over 300 trophies way back. Who would have thought I would ever want another? After all, didn't money make the world go around? Not on that day, my friends. I still have the envelope, but the money seems to have disappeared (wink, wink). I should add that I compared totals with pro-class winner Brock Hoyer. My gratitude doubled when I found out that my overall payout was more than his. Remember that, Brock?

Day two got started, and the great weekend continued. No snow on the ground, and the sand-based track was ready. When we headed over to the staging area, Sonu and I were both a little more relaxed than the previous day, having both finished day one with better results than expected. When I decided to go back and race, I had no idea where I would stack up. It didn't matter though. Just the fact that I was back in the motocross world compared to where I had been mentally and physically was a miracle in itself. That is, until I won Saturday's race in convincing fashion by winning both motos. Remember, I'm all in or all out. And for the last time before you slam this book closed, "once a racer always a racer."

When the gate dropped on day two, I was out front and leading. On the second lap, as I approached the whoop section (rollers), I noticed Sonu's bike lying on the side of the track. She had fallen and was being attended to by medics. I slowed almost to a stop and then carried on for another lap. The next lap around, when I landed the jump that led to the whoop-de-doo section, I saw the yellow-and-red cross flags waving feverishly to signify a problem ahead. My old friend Rob Crawford, who I had raced with some twenty-six years prior, waved me over. Sonu was still down and unconscious.

When I got to her side, the medics were careful not to move her. Worried, I kept talking to her. In between my words, I pleaded with the powers that be to help. One of the guys who had seen the crash told me that she had fallen off the side of the bike, and her neck had twisted badly. Thankfully, she was wearing a neck brace. We both were! After what I had experienced breaking my collarbone, that was a no-brainer. She was rushed off to the Quesnel hospital in an ambulance. I headed back to the truck and quickly packed up everything.

At the hospital it was unclear how much damage had been done. Sonu was alert and remembered everything except the crash. I was thankful she was in no immediate danger. After a call home to Gisela to tell her what had happened, we were on our way back to Vernon. However, we were required to go to Kelowna to see a neurologist for some more tests that week. Thankfully, everything checked out okay. After all was said and done (with the exception of Sonu's misfortune), it was a memorable first weekend back at the races.

I felt recharged and reborn. After trudging through years of despair, I was empowered to succeed. Having completed the next round of racing in Kamloops, I had my sights set on the first provincial championship race of the year. It was scheduled for Nanaimo, on Vancouver Island. I had not planned on going, because it was a bit of a trek. However, now that I had some seat time in a racing scenario, I figured I could challenge for the title. Sonu, who was working while going to school, had to work that weekend. She would not be able to come with me, and neither would Gisela. Sara stepped up and volunteered to be my co-pilot, mechanic, and partner for the trip. Adding to the family flare was the attendance at that race by Gisela's sister, Renee, and her husband, Warren. They were able to get some great photos, including one of me with a giant power slide out of turn one, with the holeshot. I have included that photo in this book. I can't thank you guys enough for coming out to spend the day at the races with us. Also, Sara, that trip would not have been possible without your support and help. I thank you for that.

As we neared June, I noticed on social media that there was a "legends" race of sorts planned for the Kamloops round of the pro motocross national series. With the CMRC being the main sanctioning body at the time, one of their foot soldiers and former pro racer Ryan Gauld was in charge. I reached out to "Gauldy," as we all know him, and told him my story. I also told him that I wanted to be in that race. Why not? Aren't most of us old, broken motocrossers legends? His response was a thumbs-up. I was excited for that big race on the grandest stage our sport has in Canada. I was determined to get back over to the Kamloops track again and get in some more practice before the big event.

The Sunday before the event, we headed over for a day of practice. Kelly's son, Justin, was also riding, and the day started out as real family event. We were all there at the track together.

After changing the clutch plates in my bike, I hopped onto the busy track. With the nationals just over a week away, everyone was looking to be ready when the gate dropped. I headed onto the track and was a bit perplexed by how many bikes were out there. There must have been thirty bikes on the track, which was a little under-watered. Small bikes, big bikes, fast riders, slower riders, there was no rhyme or reason. It was chaos.

On the second lap, I got "roosted" (a powerful blast of dirt off the rear wheel of the bike in front of me). It incensed me. Even though I was wearing goggles and a helmet, it was like I had been punched in the face. I twisted the throttle and passed the rider who had roosted me but was going way too fast to slow down for the finish-line jump, the same jump I broke my arm on the year before. I knew my landing was going to be flat and a hard impact. I didn't panic though. Once I was airborne, I mentally prepared for the worst.

My suspension bottomed out in the breaking bumps for the tower turn, but I stayed upright and didn't fall off. However, upon impact, I felt my foot and ankle shatter inside my boot. The pain was unmistakable. I pulled off the track and rode slowly back to our pit area. Gisela and the rest of the family were still trackside, wondering why I had headed in. When they came back, I told them what had happened. We loaded everything up, and I decided it was best to go to emergency back in Vernon, over two hours away.

By the time the X-rays were taken, my left foot and ankle were three times their regular size. After the usual wait, the doctor came in and told me that nothing was broken, that it was just a bad sprain. I have had over sixty fractures in my life, and I know what broken bones feel like, but I was thankful to be wrong on that one!

By Wednesday of the week of the Kamloops race, I still could not put any weight on my right ankle. Seeing as it was only a sprain, I figured I could still race. I told myself to suck it up and went to the shower to see if I could stand without pain. After adding the slightest bit of pressure, the pain was through the roof. It was horrible. I was in sheer agony, but I wanted so desperately to race that weekend.

As soon as I got out of the shower, the phone rang. It was my doctor's office. They told me that my doctor needed to see me as soon as I could get in. I hung up and said to myself, "I knew it." Like I said, any time a doctor has ever called to see me, it has never been a good thing. Before I landed at his office, I had pretty much concluded that I had broken my ankle again.

The news from the doctor was worse than I figured. My heel bone (calcaneus) was shattered. According to my doctor, such heel fractures are not always detected immediately by X-ray. He explained that it was like stepping on an orange, and there was no quick fix. It would take at least three months for it to heal properly. Here I was again, broken bones keeping me off a dirt bike. Damn, that one gutted me. I was just getting back into the groove of something that I loved, something that I thought was gone forever!

We attended the race as spectators. I was also able to meet up with a few of my friends, who I had not seen for years. Even though I was long gone from the barbecue before the "Scottish Meathooks" started flying, it was a fun event. While there I was able to meet for the first time a good man that I'm now proud to call my friend. His name is Brett Lee, and he was one of the CMRC's hardest-working individuals. He was also behind an event that he now runs, the Walton Raceway Grand National Championship, which is held annually in Huron County. It's the biggest annual celebration of motocross in Canada.

After chewing the fat for a while with Brett, he asked if I wanted to come out to Walton. He added that if I was able to make it, I would not regret it. I told him my situation with my foot and that I needed three months before I was even saddle worthy, let alone race ready. "Well, maybe next year then," he said.

When we left Kamloops that weekend, I looked at Gisela and said, "I'll be ready for Walton." My head and body were saying something else, but my heart cast the only ballot that mattered.

Getting to Walton was going to be a challenge. I was confident though, because my body weight was back to a buck forty-five, and I was ripped. I was in the best shape of my entire life. All those hours on our elliptical and up and down the mountainside to Predator Ridge with my unicycle had paid off. When I showed up at meetings, some of those who saw me when I first arrived were astounded by my physical transformation. I wasn't. I fully accepted that I had an allergy to alcohol and could no longer drink with the impunity of normal people. I was okay with that, because I had all the pieces to the puzzle of my life right back where they belonged.

As crazy at it may sound, lying on the lake in my sun chair soaking up Vitamin D for the next six weeks never felt so good. For the first time in my life, I didn't second-guess anything. Not only did I recognize the reflection looking back at me when I looked in the mirror, I was starting to like who I saw. I had hated myself for years, though I'm not sure why. I suspect it was partly because I wasn't faithful to my passion and who I was as a person.

My plan was to do everything the doctor said for six weeks. After that, even though he told me I would have to keep weight off my foot for twelve weeks, I would start testing it slowly. I kept it elevated, ate good food, and basked in the sun for the extra Vitamin D. I even quit drinking coffee for a bit, because I heard it hindered the kind of blood circulation that promotes healing.

At the six-week mark, I knew I had to start bearing weight and doing some road cycling at least. If I was going to drive 9,000 kilometres to and from the race, I didn't want to do it for nothing. My goal was to line up with forty of the best riders in North America and finish in the top ten. A lofty expectation? Maybe, but without expectations like that in this sport, you may go a lot of places, but the podium will not be one of them.

The big race was scheduled for the third week of August 2009. I had hoped to take Sonu and Sara with me. Gisela would stay home and hold down the fort. Sonu, who was still riding and racing, was keen on the idea. Sara, on the other hand, wasn't that interested in motocross. Nevertheless, I thought that would be a perfect opportunity for them to see our beautiful country firsthand.

Before we could go anywhere though, I needed to heal up first. To put that in perspective, I had been back for a total of four races. In that period I sustained a badly broken arm, a broken collarbone, four broken ribs, and a shattered heel bone. But I was happier than I had been in twenty-six years, because I was making peace with something that used to make my heart beat loud and proud. I didn't just want that back in my life, I needed it.

On June 25, while I was lying in the sun in a lawn chair, Sara and I heard over the radio that Michael Jackson had passed away. That was sad news for many, me included, who grew up in the era that most of Michael's popular music was from. Death is always tough to hear about, no matter who it is. I'm not sure when, but a while back, I started adding a hashtag to all my social media posts: #LifeIsGold. I have been quite humbled and overwhelmed by its beauty and value since I started writing this book. My life is the most valuable thing that I will ever have. This is no dress rehearsal; it's the real deal. It took a lot of pain for me to finally realize that, but I'm grateful I finally did.

When I threw a leg over my road bike to start my cycling regimen, my foot, heel, and ankle hurt like hell. I pushed through it though; I had to. I kept telling myself, "If it stays on the pedal, you'll be okay." It did, and I rode the bike twice daily for the first week, employing elevation, ice, and Advil in between. I didn't know if I was healing or doing more damage. I decided to stay the course despite how it looked and felt.

After a week on the bike, I dragged my unicycle out of the shop. I felt like it was a better workout for my core, balance, and cardio, and it was! The only problem was, if my foot came off or I had to stop suddenly, I would likely have to stab my foot to the asphalt, setting me back to square one.

I was cautious as I rode the unicycle every day. Riding a unicycle is such a fun, incredibly freeing feeling. It felt good to be doing something that gave my heart the kind of flutter it craved. But let's get back to reality. It was just two weeks until the biggest race of the season, and I had yet to test my leg on a dirt bike. I didn't even think I would be able to kick-start the bike with my right leg.

Gisela and I packed up the bike and headed over to the Kamloops track for the acid test. When I got there, I ran into my friends, Zach Ruff and Sam Nicholls. It was a typical hot, dry, and dusty August afternoon in the Whispering Pines Desert. I didn't even try to start my bike with my right leg, because it still hurt a ton. I felt awkward on the bike at first. I rode a couple of laps and then pulled off. I knew it was going to hurt, but this was insane. I went back out onto the track a few more times and managed to burn a tank of gas. That was my goal. I figured if I could do that without setting myself back any further, I had a chance to be ready in two weeks' time for Walton. Win, lose, or draw, I didn't care. I just wanted to be a part of the big show on the grandest stage in our country and give it my best shot. I had lost a lot in my day, but hope was beginning to return. And where there's hope, there's always a chance. The life I have lived is all the proof I need of that.

Ten days before the 2009 Walton TransCan kicked off, Sonu and I headed east. No toy hauler, no motorhome, and no minivan for us. We had everything we needed to spend the next two and half weeks on the road in my Chevy pickup. I also brought along my unicycle, thinking it would be a good way to exercise before race days.

Sonu had turned eighteen that year and had a learner's permit, so I was thankful she would be able to do some of the driving. I was torn that Gisela and Sara were not able to come, but I was nervously excited and proud of myself for following through with my intentions. It was important for me to obey that small, quiet voice from within, the same one that I thought I had drowned with alcohol.

It was a good drive east, one I had done a few times before. To be sharing it with my daughter made it even better. They may have paved paradise and put up a few more parking lots, but our country's beauty is still enamouring. As we drove, I was flooded with memories of our family trips east as a much younger racer. It was surreal to be doing it again after so much time.

When we got to Thunder Bay and headed out east on Highway 17, I showed Sonu where I saw Terry Fox in 1980. Then we went and checked out the memorial on the north side of the highway near where the Marathon of Hope ended. I was a little reluctant to pull in, because I wasn't sure any monument or statue could express how I felt about Terry and his legacy. But I was pleasantly surprised. The monument and statue are built on a hill overlooking the highway with a breathtaking view of Lake Superior's Thunder Bay. After spending some time there soaking it all in, and reliving my personal connection with Terry, we moved on.

A little farther up the highway, I pulled over and rode my unicycle on the exact same ground Terry ran. It was an amazing feeling of freedom. RIP, Terry, you will forever be my hero.

After two nights in tents, we landed up in Ottawa at Gisela's brother's house.

It was a bit out of the way, seeing as Walton is in Southwestern Ontario, about an hour from London. We had planned on going that route though, because it allowed us to visit Roland and his family, sleep in nice warm beds for a couple of days, and play tourist in our nation's capital. I can't express how cool it was to circumnavigate our country's grand Parliament buildings with my daughter.

After refreshing ourselves, we drove south to Walton Raceway. It had been years since I passed through Toronto, another cool experience to be sharing with Sonu.

After passing everything on our way, from famous monuments to amazing scenery, and even a few horses and buggies, we finally arrived at "the holy grail" of Canadian motocross, Walton Raceway. (The town of Walton is located at the intersection of Huron County Road 12 and Road 25, forty-five kilometres east of Goderich.) When we drove in to Walton Raceway for the first time, it was everything I had hoped it would be and more. I had heard many stories of how well manicured the vast facility was, and all my expectations were met.

By the time we arrived, the pits were already quite full, but they found room for us right by the starting-line staging area. It was around 3:00 p.m. Before we even unloaded and got our campsite set up, I signed up and walked the track. The Walton racetrack, on the vast acreage of the Lee family farm, has rich, vibrant soil. Being a west coast guy, it is always good to see an eastern racetrack that is not sand-based. Some of you west coast guys may appreciate that. In all fairness, a few easterners from my era killed it on the hard stuff. My old friend, Dave Beatty, who was ranked as high as fifth nationally, comes to mind. As a kid, I always had my eye on those top-ten guys. They had what I wanted, success!

The soil at Walton was a bit deceptive in regard to how easy it was to negotiate. When racing starts, ruts start to surface, and it gets technical. My moto friends know the drill all too well. Before we headed onto that racetrack for practice, it was tilled with discs about eight to ten inches deep. Barry "Weeman" Hetherington and the rest of Chris and Brett Lee's incredible foot soldiers at the time had a great racetrack for us in 2009. If you're one of my moto friends, it was the year you were all drinking out of a prosthetic leg in the awards tent. Sonu and I were camped just across the track and sat and watched all the antics from afar. It was fun for me to witness, because it brought back memories of the 1981 CMA awards ceremony after the Aldergrove Pro National, where I sat in the middle of a food fight with our 1981 national champion, Ross "Rollerball" Pederson. I can't remember who threw what first, but I remember my old friend, the well-respected Lawrence St. Pierre, and his wife leaving when that happened. Hey, we're not perfect; shit happens. I'm sure Lawrence was just tired. I know many of my old friends were in the hall that night. That was one of many Canadian moto celebratory moments.

I had looked at images of the Walton track on Facebook, but nothing beats being there to see it and feel it. My dad taught me to visualize and feel the track. He never pushed me. He only told me what he thought I could do, if I asked. I think that's huge for upcoming riders in terms of developing confidence. I have seen too many kids pack it in when their confidence is shattered. It doesn't usually break in one crash. However, a collection of injuries will undoubtedly break your confidence on a dirt bike. It certainly did in my case. It also shattered my dreams of being a champion. Confidence at pretty much anything is built through gradual, repetitive success. There are no instant winners in motocross. All champions, at all levels, have paid a price for their success.

The biggest jump at Walton, which had me a bit worried, was the "natural double." But when I got out onto the track for the first time, I felt pretty good. My foot was so swollen that I could barely get it into my boot. It hurt a lot, but I blocked out the pain as best as I could. That was the biggest show in our country, and it was the most important thing in the world for me to be there. I was there to get the best results possible, given my situation.

On my first lap, I stopped at the top of the corner that led to the natural double. As I rolled down the descent toward it, I told myself it was going to be no problem. I wouldn't do it on the first lap, but the next time around, I would pull the trigger. I had to do it that way, or else I would end up overthinking it and psyche myself out. That can happen quite easily. I learned long ago that if I knew I could do something on a dirt bike, I just did it.

As I headed toward the face of that jump, the landing was totally blind, but I had calculated my speed perfectly. When I landed the large gap on the downslope, it was a great feeling, not only because I had made it with relative ease, as anticipated, but because I figured doing that jump would put me in a better position to finish in the top ten.

In my first moto, I was just off my mark and finished eleventh out of forty bikes. At that event each class races three motos, and the overall positions are awarded based on total points scored.

In my first Vet Class moto (which is any rider thirty years or older who has ever held an intermediate or pro racing licence), I got a mid-pack jump when the starting gate dropped. Halfway down the starting straightaway, my goggles got blasted with mud, and I couldn't see. I managed to stay upright, and had just hit the rear brakes as the bikes I was with were approaching the first corner. Out of nowhere I got tagged from behind by a rider who also had his goggles covered with mud. I went down hard, with bikes lying on top of me. I couldn't see a thing. My visor had broken off and had pushed into my face. I could hear my YZ-250 two-stroke screaming wide open. The throttle was stuck from the impact of the other bikes and the ground.

Several people rushed to our aid. One of them was the guy who ran into me and knocked me down. A tough way to make a new friend, but mission accomplished. The rider who hit me, (who is now a colleague of mine and senior writer at *MXP* magazine) was Mike McGill (a.k.a. "Magoo"). Later I found out from Sonu, who was right there when it happened, that Mike was the first one to pull the bikes off me. When I stood upright, he reached out toward me as if he was going to punch me, or so she thought. In fact, he was trying to pull my crushed visor out of my face, so I could see. When I did eventually make eye contact with Mike, he apologized profusely. He had lost sight of everything as well. When he was reaching to tear off his goggles, he ran right into the back of me and others.

The rider who shut my bike off before it blew up was Michigan native Josh Woods. The throttle cable was completely stretched, and my dreams of a top-ten Vet Class finish were out the window. I only had a short break before I had to head to staging for the plus-forty class. I needed a throttle cable, and I needed it fast. I had brought some spare brake cables but not a throttle cable. You would think it would not be an issue to find a spare throttle cable for a YZ-250, but that was 2009, and almost every motorcycle over 150 cc at that event was a newer four-stroke model. This old soldier was old school, riding a 2006 YZ-250 two-smoker.

With no luck finding a throttle cable from anyone on the grounds of over 800 entries, I made one last stop in a pit called Two-Wheeled Motorsport. I was greeted by a man named Graeme Nelson. He didn't have a throttle cable, but he told me to bring my bike to him to see if he could repair it. I had relearned most of the mechanical stuff with the newer bikes since rekindling my passion, but that one was over my head. Miraculously, with some tinkering, Graeme was able to recoil my stretched throttle cable's spring. It was just in time, because two plus-forty motos were scheduled for that day. Graeme, I can't thank you enough, my friend. You saved my life with that one.

I got to the line and had my best moto of the event, finishing ninth. That result had me excited, because I figured with a top-ten finish in the third and final moto, I would be in the top ten, overall. That would be a monumental accomplishment given everything I was dealing with and had overcome.

On the final day of racing, knowing I was in contention for a top-ten finish in the plus-forty class, I elected not to race the remaining Vet Class moto's. After suffering the DNF (did not finish) result in the opening moto, I didn't think it was worth taking a chance. That decision turned out to be a good one.

When the final gate fell on my plus-forty race, I got a great start. I exited turn one in the top ten and rode a smart and successful race. When I got back to our pit, Sonu ran over to greet me. It was just her and me, and it was beautiful. Sonu, you are a grown lady now with a family of your own, and I'm so thankful for you. None of that would have been possible if you had not agreed to give up two and a half weeks of your summer.

I asked her where I finished, and she figured, as I had, that I placed tenth. It seemed to take forever for the official results to be posted. When they were, we were elated to see my name tenth overall out of the forty racers. When it was official, I was excited to share the news with Gisela and Sara back at home in Vernon. All we had to do now was attend the closing awards ceremony that Saturday night.

We gathered on the grass in front of the grand Monster Energy stage and awaited the gala proceedings. They went through the racing classes from small to large and from young to old. I mentioned earlier that motocross does not discriminate in any way, shape, or form. Walton Raceway has something for every member of the family. If you've been there, I'm preaching to the choir. If you haven't, that place should be on your bucket list. I'm happy it was on mine that year, so much so that all I could think about during the 4,400-kilometre home was coming back to challenge for a top-three podium finish. I was motivated to do so, and when that happens, there is usually no stopping me.

24

Survive, Survive, Survive

The long drive home was painful. I kept my leg up as much as I could, but there wasn't a lot of room in my small Chevy truck. I pulled over in Parry Sound, and when I got out of the truck, I fell over. I'm pretty sure that whatever healing the calcaneus had done had been set back. But all that mattered was getting home safely and giving the other loves of my life, Gisela and Sara, a big hug.

We had a few sketchy moments heading into Thunder Bay that first night. I had done that stretch a few times by then. Highway 17 from Sault St. Marie to Thunder Bay in a Lake Superior storm is no fun in the dark. Nevertheless, the entire way home, all I could think about was racing, racing, racing. It had been so long since racing a dirt bike had made my heart tick. Now that it was back in my life, I didn't want to let it go again. I wanted to get back to Walton and hit the podium. I knew I had it in me, if I took all the necessary steps. I was approaching the sport with a much more mature attitude than when I was younger. For the first time in my life, I felt wise, like Yoda. I was finally going to be able to put my own worst critic, to rest, the one who dwelled deep inside me. I was convinced it was going to be a storybook ending for the ages.

When we got back from Walton, it was nearly time for the kids to return to school. I went back to the RV shop but was starting to feel like it was a dead end for me. I pressed on though, because finding a job that paid well in the Okanagan wasn't easy.

In the racing world, I was excited for the final provincial championship race, which would be held in Kamloops. It was a two-weekend series that had started in May in Nanaimo. I had attended that one and had some solid points to go toward a possible title. Then in practice, my bike's engine blew up. It took me by surprise, because I had rebuilt the top end before Walton. I was bummed at first but was grateful it hadn't blown up in Walton. A good guy from the Kamloops area, Martin Sturm (who was on the Kamloops track crew at the time) lent me his bike to race. That was cool, and I was thankful, but there was a bit of a problem. His 250 was a four-stroker, and I wasn't accustomed to such bikes. It was fun to ride, but everything in the bike's power delivery and the way it handled was different. I finished up third in the provincial championship behind my friends Dino Gatt and Ray Eastman. It wasn't a top-step performance, but I was satisfied. The third-place finish was all the fuel I needed to set out to try to win the 2010 title. If I could do that it would be an incredible feat, because my last provincial championship was exactly thirty years prior. It would be cool to tell the grandkids that. We didn't have grandkids yet, but that would change soon.

When 2010 arrived, I had to make some hard choices in regard to the upcoming racing year. I had decided to hang onto my Yamaha two-stroke bike, rebuild it, and race it for one more year. I had been buying pretty much everything through Barry Wellings at Valley Moto Sport in West Kelowna. I can't thank Barry enough for his support to keep me riding. Barry didn't even sell Yamahas, but he kept me happy as long as I owned mine. I promised that the next new bike I bought would be from him, another fine example of how the sport of motocross creates a sense of brotherhood like no other.

Part of my plan to stay on the Yamaha was to follow the BC provincial championship series. The first race was that spring in Prince George, at the Blackwater track, which now hosts a Canadian national event. I was looking forward to that series. Before it kicked off, I won the Plus 40 spring series, and was third in the Vet class.

Over the course of my reintegration to the racing world, I met many great racing people, the kind of people who I could relate to, whether my day was good, bad, or otherwise. The conversations were invigorating. They made my heart sing with thoughts that maybe it wasn't too late to be successful in my chosen discipline. It also took away some of the pain deep inside of me from chasing John Barleycorn's tail for all those wasted years. Two such great people who helped and mentored me a lot were Travis and Jeanine Acheson along with their son, Daniel. It made a world of difference to go to a race and be able to have my pit area with them. I have not seen Travis and Jeanine for a few years, but I will always be thankful for their kindness.

As we inched toward the first provincial championship race of the year, things seemed to keep getting better. I was riding well and felt confident every time I hit the track. My nephew, Justin, was also riding, and 2010 was his first year of racing. Justin rode shotgun in my pickup, and Kelly, Rich, and my dad followed in their motorhome. It was a two-day event on Saturday and Sunday. I was over the moon to be going racing with most of my family again. We had not done that for more than twenty-five years. I missed being able to share it with Gisela and the girls, but somebody had to be the responsible one and see to it that our family's home obligations were taken care of.

The Blackwater track was pure gold. Its rich clay-like soil packed nice and hard, just the way I liked it. Even though it wasn't near as daunting as Saddleback Park's legendary Banzai Hill or Magoo Double, it had great elevation changes. The other thing that made me smile was the concrete starting gate grid. I always got great starts on them.

In the first moto, I got a great start and led the race through its switchback roller section. After that it was on to the elevated front straightaway, which contained a sequence of technical tabletop-style jumps, meaning riders took off on an upslope, and then the jump flattened across to the opposite side, with riders landing on the downslope.

As I landed the last jump and accelerated away from the pack, I was a bit overwhelmed with what I saw. My father was out on the track giving me hand signals, just like he used to from the pit area when I was a kid. I would like to say that the signal was his index finger pointed at his head to encourage me to use mine, just like he had done over thirty years prior. Dad never encouraged me to do anything stupid; he didn't have to. I never needed an invitation to take such an initiative. In all seriousness, that moment was one of the best I have ever felt in my life. How was that even possible? At one point my life was seemingly locked inside a garbage truck on its way to the dump. Now all that pain and anguish seemed like a bad memory, though I hoped it would never go away. You might think that a bit odd, but experience has shown me time and time again that the day I forget how bad it was is the day that I'm in danger of going back.

I won both plus-forty class motos that day and finished third overall in the Vet class. As the day wound down, one of the last races of the day was Justin's super mini race. It was so much fun to be at a race weekend with Kelly, Rich, my dad and my other nephew, Josh.

As the fast, smaller bikes made their way around the circuit, I noticed Justin approaching the finish-line tabletop with a lot of speed. As he exited the corner and accelerated up the face, I kept waiting for him to stand up to prepare for liftoff. He didn't. Before he even broke free and was airborne, I could see he was in trouble. Justin, who had some incredible skills on a BMX and mountain bikes, was about to learn why I had warned him about "seat bounce" jumping (sitting on the seat of the motorcycle while jumping). As he crested the jump and became airborne, I jumped the fence and ran like hell. Justin must have launched twenty feet straight up and then came crashing down hard headfirst. I saw his neck twist badly on impact. I couldn't run fast enough, because I didn't want anyone to try to move him. Thankfully, no one did. He was in agony but thankfully could feel and move everything. By that time my dad and the rest of the family were at his side, too.

Fortunately, X-rays showed only a badly broken collarbone. Unfortunately, that crash meant my awesome weekend at the races with family was cut short. Eight-Mile (Justin) I'm so proud of you for everything you accomplished in such a short time in your racing career. I'm also proud of you as a human being, because you have always worked your tail off to succeed. I will remember that race for all the right reasons for the rest of my life, thanks to my family.

I stayed behind and raced the final day. It was a weird feeling to go from having all that family support to being a lone wolf at the track. Whenever I rode or raced, I liked having someone there. There are many reasons for that. First and foremost is safety. Second, (and I know most of my moto friends get this), there's a ton of work to do on a race day. More hands make it easier. Finally, what in life is of any real value if you can't share it with the ones you love?

On Sunday, I won the first moto. However, in my fourth and final moto of the day (my eighth that weekend), I was tired and got passed by a local rider named Dean Johnson. By that time the track was rough and getting quite dusty. I had a strong urge to try to get by him, but felt that if I pushed out of my comfort zone, I would crash. In my head, I was already calculating provincial championship points. I had won the first three motos, and already had seventy-five points in my back pocket. To finish second in the final moto would be giving up no points, because I would be heading to the next round with a nine-point lead.

When we crossed the finish line, Dean turned around and gave me a big high-five. Within moments of that, his father was at his side congratulating him. That put a huge smile on my face, because I had shared similar emotions with my father the day before. Yes, I wished it was me celebrating with my dad, because that Sunday was Father's Day! That was a great weekend, Dean. Thanks for the memories, old friend.

The final leg of the BC provincial championship was held on Labour Day weekend in Kamloops. Being the end of the season, my motorcycle, which I had been racing on for almost three years, was pretty worn out—not quite as worn out as me, but close. My goal for that season was to win the provincial title. If I could put thirty-year bookends on that, it would sure put a smile on my face.

It was a cool grey fall weekend at the Kamloops track. That said, some of the best racing conditions in these parts are early spring and late fall. With the point totals the way they were heading into the weekend, I knew I didn't necessarily have to win. I would have to manage my progress with a couple of others who were close, though. When the weekend was complete, I was crowned the 2010 Plus Forty BC Champion. With my family at my side, Gisela included, the feeling of achievement was powerful. You racers who have won titles or accomplished other goals likely get it. In my case, the only thing that could have made it any better would have been to have my mom there.

In the winter of 2010, I headed back down to Chilliwack to race in the Future West Arenacross Series. At the time, it was still owned and operated by John and Jamie Hellam of Chilliwack. I wasn't sure what to expect, because it had been twenty-seven years since I had raced indoors, at the 1983 Vancouver Supercross. As you'll recall, in that event I won the last chance qualifier to get into that night's main event. I finished fourteenth overall in front of 25,000 ravenous spectators. When the race ended, I had no idea it would be the last one for so many years. In keeping with that theme, every one of you racers out there who love the sport the same way I do, make the best of it always. Take the good home and learn from or leave the bad at the track. There are no guarantees in life. When the final flag waves on your racing days, if you're anything like me, you'll miss them. I believe motocross is the best sport on Earth. Without having what motocross instilled in me at such a young age, I don't believe I would have had the fight I would soon need to save my life—again.

That fall things started to get a bit weird for me. I started to have a horrible recurring dream! Back in 2009 at the Walton TransCan, I met a guy from Whistler, BC, named Shaun Greenaway. I had raced against Shaun a couple of times before heading to Walton. Shaun was an Ontario native who had migrated west years earlier. We chatted at Walton and hung out a bit. Being a former top-level pro racer, Shaun was one of many in my class with some serious speed. Shaun was also stoked to see that I had made the trek to Walton, because our western contingent was strong in 2009. That is another great thing about the Walton TransCan; it's a true "who's who" of racers in north America.

Shaun made a pass on me on the far outside of a descent into a valley. That section was after the Dunlop Tire corner that year. It was also a high-speed part of the track. When Shaun's front wheel came up on my left side, his speed was too much for mine. I was already riding on the edge of my comfort level. As I headed down into the valley, all I saw was the number 343 on the back of his TransCan bib. He got by me, and I believe he finished third in that moto. The pass stayed with me. It bothered me that he had passed me there with such ease! I could ride that section like he did; I knew I could. I just needed to get some more seat time.

In my dream, I saw the same moment over and over again, but with a nasty twist. As he went by at the top of the descent into the valley, I swapped out and went head over handlebars. I landed on my head and woke up in the hospital, paralyzed. The dream horrified me. In fact, the same horrifying feeling comes back just thinking about it. I hated it, but I didn't tell anyone about it. A motocrosser has no room inside his helmet for any sort of negative energy. I was able to put the dream into its place eventually. However, seeing as I had never been superstitious, not once did I see it as an omen.

The first night back at Arenacross was awesome. I had no idea what to do with my suspension, so I just stiffened everything up a bit. Arenacross or Supercross races usually have many jumps and obstacles that send the bikes high into the air. That's what warrants the stiffer suspension settings. Fortunately, the Yamaha I was racing had pretty decent stock suspension. On most new bikes these days, the riders customize their setup to conform to their riding style and ability.

The first night at the Heritage Park Facility was a great race for me. I managed to get the holeshot and win. It was an incredible feeling to be back in my hometown doing what had defined me as a lad, the same town that nominated me for athlete of the year in 1981. But let's not forget it was the same town that I left in

1988 with my tail between my legs. To me it was a comeback victory on many levels. It felt amazing. I can't thank my Chilliwack friends George Velonis and Wayne Oberst enough for all they did to help me. For example, George gutted his work utility trailer and outfitted it for me and all my gear and tools for two racing weekends. Damn, it's good to have good people around me, though it took me a while to figure that out. Today I know I'm only as good as the company I keep. For years I was a product of my environment, and when that changed for the better, so did my life.

After the weekend of racing, I came out of the Future West Moto office with my weekend's trophies (plaques). James Lissimore, who is one of our sport's best photographers, captured the moment with my trophy and ear-to-ear smile. Thank you for that, James. That photo is one of the best trophies I have.

Late in 2010, I got some more bad news in regard to some skin cancer spots that had returned. I was first diagnosed in 2003. I have had to have regular radiation treatments for the past two years. I mentioned that I loved the Okanagan sunshine, but it doesn't seem to like me much. Nothing personal; I'm a redhead with fair skin. I have seen a few different dermatologists, and the one thing that they all agreed was that the damage was done long ago. My parents didn't know any better. Instead of sunscreen, they had us slop on coconut oil, and who knows what else. It causes me a great deal of difficulty now, but it can be prevented. As Baz Luhrmann stated in his song to the class of 1999, "If I could offer you only one tip for the future, sunscreen would be it." I have taken that seriously, because skin cancer was the first cancer my mother was diagnosed with, and she left us way too soon.

Our year ended on a positive and happy note. Sonu gave birth to our first grandchild, Ava Lynn, on December 3 in Vernon. She is beautiful, and I feel so blessed to be a grandfather. Sonu has since had another child, Mason, born on October 19, 2014. I'm also thankful they still reside in Vernon. Sonu was married in 2016 to Colin Jones.

When 2011 arrived, I was excited. Gisela and I planned to go to the Western Canadian National, held in Raymond, Alberta, on July 1. After that, if I was still in one piece, we would drive all the way back to the Grand National Championship in Walton. It was exciting times, knowing I would be sharing these incredible events with the love of my life. In fact, parked at the foot of our bed was a brand-new KTM 350. That's right, it was in our bedroom, which I thought was the safest place for it.

I had followed through on my promise to Barry Wellings at West Kelowna's Valley Moto Sport. He is such a great person, and when I deal with him, that's part of the package. He also sold my YZ 250 two-stroke on his showroom floor for the asking price. You outdid yourself on that one, my friend. I was sad to see the Yamaha go, because it was a sweet bike. I always loved my Yamahas, all of them. It also had one of the best graphic kits I had ever seen, thanks to Brendan at Lime Nine, Wayne Oberst (who worked for Pioneer Electronics), and my soon-to-be employer, *MXP* magazine. I should add that Charles Stancer from *MXP* showcased my motorcycle under their display at the Walton race in 2009. The KTM was my first four-stroke, and I could hardly wait to see what all the fuss was about. The KTM was also bright orange, like a pumpkin.

I obsessed over my fitness until the snow melted. I also drove down to Chilliwack and got some seat time on the banks of the Fraser River. That was also a good way to get used the new and improved four-stroke power delivery. What else can I say? It was different. All motorcycles are, and I had ridden a few in my day. All that mattered was that it was even happening at all. I stuck like glue to those who were happy to see me when I came back.

I believe in loyalty, 1,000 percent. The "What have you done for me lately?" attitude doesn't cut it in motocross, or anywhere else in my life. Almost everyone involved in that sport, dealers included, has to work their rear ends off to make a living. We should never forget that. I also noticed almost immediately when I returned to racing that the "free bikes" (sponsored by manufacturers through their dealers) were pretty much only pictured on milk cartons, meaning the heyday of dirt bike sales as a result of winning on Sunday and selling on Monday were no more. But motocross is not the biggest sport in the world either. That said, there are up to 60,000 spectators at a Supercross race. Also, an event like the Motocross of Nations (which is pretty much the Olympics of motocross) can easily draw 100,000 spectators. To put it into perspective, the top riders make millions.

Back at home, with each passing weekend I was desperate for spring to arrive. One February weekend, I noticed the temperature was going to be warm in Merritt. When I say warm in February the term is hopeful at best. I contacted my friend Marc Denis, who raced in my classes, and we headed over for the day. Sara also made the trek with us that day.

There was still a bit of snow on the ground, but other than that, the hills were negotiable. Just to be on the bike outdoors with it running and the wheels moving was good enough for me. I was getting more confident with each twist of the throttle, not just with the motorcycle but also with the conditions, because some patches of ice were hidden in the rich, dark soil. Marc and I were having fun. I pointed out a spot to him that was slick exiting one of the corners on the track we had laid out. Sure enough, my next time around, I went sideways coming out of that corner and hit the ice. Twisting the throttle for all it was worth in an effort to save it, I was ejected from the motorcycle and landed headfirst. I regained consciousness fairly quickly, but my head and face were a mess. I knew I had another concussion and that my riding day was over.

Two weeks later Marc and I headed south to ride in the Oliver area. Even though winters can be tough in the Okanagan, sometimes the southern parts are rideable. That area was known as Stinky Lake. There we met up with our friends and Vet Series colleagues Ray Eastman and Dino Gatt. It was cold, but we were still riding. We pounded out motos, one after another. I was feeling confident and loved gauging my progress with my friends. It felt great to be with like-minded people. Late in the day I accelerated out of a corner and saw Dino. I thought about choosing a line for the upcoming whoop section. The rollers were huge. It was a sand-based track, and I don't think it had ever been groomed.

After that I don't remember how I got there, but I was sitting on top of the adjacent mountainside. There I sat looking at my convulsing body on the ground. How was that possible? I was still alive, wasn't I? The next thing I felt was a warm, powerful aura of energy and light behind me. It was a cold wintery day. Whatever was trying to persuade me in its direction was the most unfathomable, incomprehensible, and powerful energy of freedom I had ever experienced. I had a vision of Gisela and my girls sitting down at a dinner table without me. In my vision they were forlorn and sullen. Were they mourning my death? They couldn't be; I was still here, wasn't I? I had no idea, and I started to get angry. I refused to turn around and acknowledge that powerful, persuasive energy. "I have to get home to my wife and kids!" I screamed. "I told them I'd be home for dinner!"

Then my eyes opened. I was cold, and it was silent. Dino and Marc were there. They hadn't seen the crash, but Dino said that when he got to me, I was still doing the "funky chicken." I was sick to my stomach, and everything was way too bright.

I don't even remember riding my bike back to the truck, which was some distance away. The guys asked me if I needed to go to the hospital to get checked out. I refused and crawled into Marc's truck. That was a bad one, and I knew it. I had just had a concussion not two weeks before. If I had to put a number on it, I have easily had twelve to fifteen wicked hits to the head, and that is a conservative estimate. I didn't want to go to a hospital; I hated those places, and still do.

As we drove through Kelowna, Marc insisted on taking me to the hospital, but I refused. I told him that if I was still symptomatic when I got home, I would go in Vernon. Marc and his wife, Kelly, were also an integral part of my return to the races. Marc, thanks for your help and genuine concern for a wounded brother.

When I got home, life was instantly awful. My head hurt like a son of a bitch, and with every step I felt like I was falling. I was light sensitive and nauseous daily. My comprehension of even the simplest things was non-existent. I didn't get off our couch for a week. When Saturday night rolled around, and the Supercross racing was on television, I couldn't even keep up with the action. That scared me! I finally booked a doctor's appointment. I had put that off, because I feared the worst, the worst being that he was going to shut down my plans to race the WCAN or even Walton in August.

He wanted to order a CT scan, but I refused. All I wanted to know was how long I could expect the symptoms to last. He told me there was no blueprint for that. That wasn't what I wanted to hear. He also told me that I should stay off my bike for at least three months. I knew that was likely the right choice, but I had come so far and was so close to realizing an improbable dream. My doctor ended the visit by telling me that if I sustained another blow to the head in the next few months, it could be fatal. He advised me to avoid exerting myself in any way physically until my symptoms disappeared.

My doctor's advice didn't keep me grounded. It was more a matter of my dexterity and motor skills being so bad that kept me parked. Racing season started, and I missed the first two races. I went out and flagged at the Kelowna race to be at the track and make a few bucks. I wasn't even racing that day, and I fell off the mound I was standing on to flag. That was horrible, and my symptoms were not going away. I felt my hopes and dreams of getting back to Walton that year were slipping away. I couldn't let that happen. I had to fight through it and get well enough to get back on my motorcycle.

After not riding for a month, I couldn't take it any longer. I entered a race at the Kamloops track, my first on the KTM 350. I had two goals for that weekend. The first was not to crash and hit my head. The second was just to finish the damn race weekend.

In practice, I felt pretty good. A friend from Vernon who owns Rider's Edge Suspension, Ian McKill made a nice comment about how I looked in practice. That made me feel good. It also took away any negativity I was feeling about being behind the eight-ball with the year's racing plans.

In the first moto, my motorcycle's engine blew up. Later I discovered it was a problem with the manufacturing, and a recall was eventually issued for it. That was a costly repair. I have the utmost respect for KTM Canada as well as the shop that fixed the bike, Valley Moto Sport in Kelowna. It never occurred to me until writing this book that maybe that setback was a blessing in disguise. It's always possible that I could have landed square on my head the next weekend.

I was so focused on motocross and achieving the best results possible in Walton, that the Vancouver Canucks being on the verge of winning their first Stanley Cup took a backseat. Like most ravenous hockey fans who had cheered for the Canucks long and hard and seemingly forever, I wound up disappointed once again. After winning the first two games of the series, the turning point and momentum switch came in Boston's 8–1 game-three victory. The Canucks managed to claw their way back and regain the series lead in game five, but they lost the final two games to the Boston Bruins, prompting an Armageddon-like riot in Vancouver. It was their third trip to the big dance, and without taking anything away from the Bruins, it was tough for many fans to swallow. Yes, my name is on that list. I'm hopeful that given the Canucks current and talented core of up-and-comers, I will live to see them win a Stanley Cup.

By the time June came, I had a few solid race weekends under my belt on my better-than-new KTM 350. We were still a month away from the western national in Raymond, Alberta. The pro national was scheduled for Kamloops's Whispering Pines track on the second weekend in June. It had been twenty-six years since I last rode a pro national, and I thought I would give that one a shot, to qualify and be on the line among forty-two of the best racers in the country. I will admit, I wasn't a hundred percent, but I was committed to trying. I didn't want to hold anything back that year. I was worried I might not get another chance. The sense of closure and being able to make peace with that great sport motivated me all the more.

Forty-eight bikes signed up in the 450 class, and only 40 would make the gate, with two alternates. On the track in my qualifiers, I felt good, but not great. Even though I knew I had better in me, I was happy to have qualified forty-fourth out of forty-eight riders. Being on the line when the gate dropped with the best of the best wasn't meant to be. I can't thank my friend Travis Acheson enough for pitting for me and helping me with everything. It was also a great feeling to be able to share that with Gisela and my family. I'm proud to say that I raced professional Canadian motocross nationals twenty-six years apart.

The Western Canadian national that year in Raymond went well. My goal heading into the big event was to be on the podium among the top three. The Lethbridge Motorcycle Club did a great job at that event. At the trophy presentation, I felt like a blessed man considering the company I was in. Canadian motocross legends Pete DeGraaf and Mark Boot were two fast local guys who finished ahead of me. I was okay with that, because I felt my stock was on the rise and that I would be ready for Walton. Like I said earlier, success in motocross starts with consistency. For me that meant consistency in not crashing. But almost everyone in that sport knows it's an unattainable expectation. In motocross, it's not a matter of *if* you will crash but *when*. I knew that better than most, but I pressed on. I had to. The life I left behind was no longer an option.

My father was pretty much done with living on the Merritt property in that massive home by himself. Mom had been gone for seven years. Dad had gotten back on two wheels and bought himself another Harley. It was a helpless feeling to see him hurting. He would never admit it, but I know those years after mom passed were tough on him. I didn't know what to do. I felt responsible in certain ways, and in others I just didn't understand. Maybe we're not supposed to understand. Maybe if I could see the plan, I would have given up long ago. I didn't want to give up ever again. I wanted those who cared about me to be proud of me. Maybe that would take away some of the pain in our hearts. The only thing I knew was that riding and racing my dirt bike was my allegiance to the real me.

Dad sold the home in Merritt and bought a place closer to us in Armstrong, BC. He also generously helped Gisela and me buy our first home. We moved out of the Carters' place on the lake, and into Vernon's Okanagan Landing area, close to the north end of the lake. I'm a bit of a procrastinator when it comes to certain things. We didn't have a lot of time before we headed to Walton. I felt compelled to get the house deal done before we hit the road that August. I have always had a pretty good Spidey sense, and that voice came through loud and clear.

It was a huge relief to have all the paperwork done before we hit the road for Walton. We would take possession and officially own our own first home together while we were at the event. With my best friend Gisela at my side in the passenger seat, our almost 9,000-kilometre round trip to Walton was now a reality. Nothing fancy, just our modest black Chevy pickup packed up with everything we needed to conquer the holy grail of Canadian motocross.

When I bought the KTM from Barry, he gave me a little KTM gnome. Seeing as there had been news stories of different famous travelling gnomes, I figured we should bring him along and get some stellar shots of him at some of the iconic landmarks in our great country and the United States. We had planned to cross into Michigan at Sault St. Marie. Walton is located about three hours northeast of Detroit. I was excited at the prospect of driving through Michigan again. The border would be a challenge though, because I still have a record that shows up from that regrettable night at the cemetery.

The journey across Western Canada was pretty uneventful. The weather was great, and our country's sprawling landscape never disappoints. That trip provided Gisela and me a chance to share our fondest family travel memories with each other while creating some of our own, which I will treasure forever. Gisela's parents, who were both teachers, used the summers to travel the country as a family in their Volkswagen van. I don't know about you, but I get a huge smile on my face visualizing that fab five, the German "Griswolds." Okay, that might be a bit over the top, but if I had known it was you folks at the local tourist trap, I would have winked at your daughter.

When we arrived in Thunder Bay, I wanted to stop and show her the Terry Fox monument. We also had to make a pit stop for supplies there. Daylight was already fading when we arrived. I had hoped to make it to White River that night, then drive all the way through Michigan the following day and then up into London. Some bad weather was coming in on Highway 17 through Nipigon Bay. If you have ever driven that stretch at night in a storm, you will likely vow never to do it again. There are many long-haul trucks, and the lighting is terrible. Noting all that, and expecting a rough go for a bit, we continued past the monument, vowing to stop on the way home, when we had more time. I wanted to be in London the next day, because I had promised my friend Steve

Emery (where we would stay on our first night in London) that we would go ride together at "The 15," a well-known practice area in Southwestern Ontario.

As we left Thunder Bay, the sun was setting, and we saw a bright double rainbow in the distance. We agreed it was a good sign. The drive to White River took forever, but we made it in one piece. Ironically, that was the same stretch of highway where I drove through another horrific storm on the way back in 2009.

The next morning the sun was out. I was thankful for that, because everything in the back of my truck was soaked. I had tarps and tie downs, but you know how that can go. It was as if nothing had been awry in the sky the night before. It was a new day, and it felt like a fresh start. I was a little concerned about the upcoming border crossing, but I had learned many years earlier from my father to only answer the questions they asked. Sometimes they asked about the asterisk that came up regarding my name, and I always told them the truth.

When we pulled up to the crossing, they had many questions for us. Most were in regard to what we were carrying and why we were crossing into the US to race in Canada. It took so long. I'm often patient, but that was different. I wanted to get across and get on I-75 now! At what I thought was almost the end of their laundry list of questions, he asked what I had been charged for. I told him everything. Then he handed me our passports and said, "Sounds like good times. Good luck at your race."

Our KTM gnome was super impressed with the Mackinaw Bridge as we drove in to Michigan. We got out and stretched at the rest stop at the foot of that incredible five-mile-long bridge. To put it in perspective, It's over 8,000 meters long. The Golden Gate Bridge in San Francisco is only 2,700 meters.

It wasn't going to be easy to make London by nightfall. After a long drive up I-75 through many under-construction areas that didn't make sense, we ended up at a KOA campground. It was already close to 10:00 p.m., and we were lucky to get a site.

The next day we crossed into Canada at Sarnia, hometown of 2018 Canadian triple-crown motocross champion Cole Thompson. Two hours later we were at Steve and Jennifer Emery's house. Steve is a Vet Series racer and a solid human being. Steve and Jen are also the parents of Kim Emery, who was a top-level Canadian women's pro motocross racer. Kim was actually out west on the track in Edmonton in 2008, the year we went to the national race with our kids.

Instead of riding that day, we sat around and drank coffee and talked about it.

That is a veteran rider's prerogative. Besides, Gisela and I needed the rest, and it was good to catch up with our eastern friends.

The next day when we arrived at the practice facility, several riders were already there. One of them was another friend of ours from Southwestern Ontario, Mark Hosie. After that day's ride, our plan was to head one step closer to Walton, where we would stay with Mark and his wife. When I got the bike off the truck and onto the track, I had to remind myself it was just practice. We had come that far, and I wanted to at least make it out onto the Walton racetrack in one piece.

After I got the feel for the track, Mark, Steve, and I pounded out a few good laps. My bike felt decent, and I could tell I was getting faster on it each time I threw a leg over. Physically, I was in the best shape of my life. I wanted to do one more moto on that day to give the boots a little extra break-in time. A few laps in, just before the biggest jump on the track, I blew a shift at the bottom of the jump. It was that full-on fourth to fifth gear neutral that I had been hitting. Luckily, I wasn't far enough up the jump face, and I was able to back off. Had it happened another twenty feet up the track, I likely would have crashed hard and not made it to Walton.

When the bike did that, I was concerned. There was no rhyme or reason, and it wasn't happening regularly. I kept it to myself though, because I didn't want to feed that potential problem any negative energy. After the ride day, we packed up and headed to Mark's house, where we spent the night. The next day on his front lawn in the sunshine, Mark and I completely went over my motorcycle. Damn, it looked good. Thanks again to Brendan from Lime Nine for the stellar graphics.

Walton was only an hour away, and I couldn't wait to get there. When we finally arrived at the track, the first person I ran into was a friend from BC, Marcell Ruff. He pointed us toward that year's BC contingent of racers, and we joined them. Pitted alongside the Ruffs, the Carlsons, and the Pettises, we were officially ready for what I hoped would be the race of a lifetime.

After getting signed in, I headed out to the track for a look. I had been there in 2009 but had missed 2010. On MX-Forum (a place where racers chat moto online, started by my friend Rick Hamer-Jackson), I read that they had built a brand-new, large triple step-down jump. Ironically, the racer who started the topic was London-based racer Jamie Ruddock, a.k.a. "Ruddy 116." We had been for dinner with Jamie and Steve and their wives just two days before. Big jumps at races like that can be a game-changer. And let's not forget that jumps are the favourite part of any track for me.

When I walked out of the Dunlop corner, in the distance I saw a mound that dropped down into a valley. As I walked toward the jump, I realized it was the new one they had been talking about. When I approached the slope of the jump, my heart started to pound. I realized the jump had been constructed in the same place that my reoccurring dream took place. That was insane. Here was an obstacle that I knew would be a lot of fun, though it looked a bit daunting to jump the complete distance of well over one hundred feet. However, I knew it was well within my riding wheelhouse. I told myself the dream was just that, a dream. I had had many bad dreams; we all have. It didn't mean I had to stop living.

Practice went well, and my bike and body felt great. The new jump wasn't a problem. I took full advantage of the practice sessions to get used to that year's layout. After a couple of laps, I was sending it all the way to the bottom of that new triple jump. It felt great to be airborne at Walton once again. I figured that would be helpful, because I was certain that most racers in my class weren't jumping as far as I was. Cocky maybe, but I see it more as confidence than anything. Without that in motocross, your days are numbered.

On Thursday, August 18, we were awoken at 6:00 a.m. by the traditional cawing of Walton Raceway's iconic rooster, followed quickly by legendary race announcer Dave Bell's "Goooood Mooooorning, Waltonnnnn!" This was it; the big day was finally here. I was ready. There was no practice on that day, and my first moto was at 10:30 a.m.

After eating breakfast and getting everything ready in my pit area, I decided to go for a unicycle ride. It was a good way to loosen up and get my heart rate up. But there was another reason that still weirds me out a bit. I felt compelled to hop on my unicycle and head through Walton into Blythe. The entire time, I took in every bit of beauty that amazing region has. I smiled and waved as I passed complete strangers. I'm sure they thought the circus must have left me behind when it left town. I didn't care. The realization that I was finally free and in control of my destiny moved me deeply.

An hour and a half after departing our camp, I hustled back to the track. When Gisela greeted me, she had a concerned look on her face. I knew I had been gone a while, but I had no idea it had been that long. I told her that everything was okay. I also told her that day was special, and something different was in the air. I could feel it.

Twenty minutes before my race, we headed to the staging area, where we sat under the tent with the rest of the racers I would be lined up against. It was a great feeling seeing all my two-wheeled colleagues. Some I had seen in 2009, like Saskatchewan's Roland Giroux. Some others I had not raced against for over twenty-five years. The likes of Bill Wallin, Curtis Lawrence, and Frank Watts come to mind. When the starter called my name and number first, I was surprised. I didn't know it at the time, but I was the top-seeded qualifier for that event. Although I thought it was cool, I felt a bit of added pressure as the other thirty-nine racers watched me select my gate.

I opted for the left side of the starting straight. It suited my eye perfectly as the shortest distance to the first corner. One thing that I was a little bit worried about was the height of the concrete below my front wheel. On that side of the gate, some of the concrete seemed to be higher than in other places. That is an issue, because at five feet eight inches, my outriggers (feet) don't always reach the ground with the front wheel upwards.

They gave us a sighting lap before all the big races to check out any track condition or layout changes. I like the sighting lap idea, and I think it should be used more, where it's feasible. When the parade of forty bikes returned, I was one of the last ones. I had stretched my neck in every possible direction to get a good look at where the smoothest, fastest racing lines were.

As I approached my gate, I thought about how lucky I was to be there with the love of my life. As the other bikes cued up, I felt the ground rumbling beneath my feet with excitement. The fans had gathered all around the track. It would take just over two minutes to navigate each lap. We would race for twenty minutes plus two laps. A good start at that event in the first moto was imperative.

As Gisela handed me my goggles, she said, "I love you." I'm not sure why, but when she said that, as she always does before I took off, I almost didn't reciprocate. I was overcome with a strange feeling. I thought that maybe I should wait until after the moto to tell her. Why did I think that? Where was that dilemma coming from? That wasn't me. Of course, I loved my wife! After the committee of demons in my head did thirty wind sprints back and forth across my brain, I responded with, "I love you, too."

The thirty-second board went up, signifying that things were about to get real. It went to five seconds, and then the gate dropped.

My initial jump was a good one. As my front wheel crested the concrete that the steel gate was attached to, my front wheel became airborne. My holeshot device, which is used to keep the front wheel down to prevent that, had disengaged. My great jump was now all for naught. I remained focused and headed for the first corner for all I was worth. When I rounded the apex of the 180-degree left-hander, I was about mid-pack. That incensed me. If I wanted a shot at a podium finish, I had to move quickly. In such races, the frontrunners can get as much as twenty to thirty seconds ahead of the pack quickly.

Through the first quarter of a lap, I made quite a few passes. Some of them were not that friendly either. The adrenaline running through me felt like I had just been punched in the face. It was exactly how I felt in 1980 when I fell while leading the national. I knew what I had to do, and nothing was going to stop me. I wanted the Walton podium more than I wanted anything in the world.

As I approached the Dunlop turn, I was gauging the progress of two riders ahead of me. I had to, because when I exited that corner, I wanted to be in the best-possible position to hit the large triple step-down jump. I needed to be sure I wasn't going to land on anyone or have anyone cross my line after I committed.

I moved over to the right side of the straight. Powering toward that jump in fourth gear, I looked over my shoulder at the rider I was going by just as I lifted off. I had committed to that obstacle with enough speed to land at the bottom. As I prepared myself for that incredible feeling of flying through the air on my dirt bike, the unthinkable happened. My bike jumped out of fourth gear!

I was already airborne and had more than enough speed to fly the one hundred feet, but with the lack of any rotating gyro forces in the rear wheel, my world instantly became one of desperation. I had to decide instantly if I wanted to stay with the bike or try and eject. Being in a perpetual nose-dive position, I hung onto the handlebars, hoping the front end would break the impact. I had enough time to repeat the word "survive" three times before my moment with fate.

When I hit the ground, everything flashed like a nuclear explosion inside my body. As I lay there, all I could see was an overpoweringly bright, warm light. The only thing I could focus on was the taste of my imploded insides.

As fate would have it, my friend Mark Hosie was the head flagger that day. Flaggers play an intricate role in keeping riders as safe as possible. Mark, who was standing at the base of that jump, saw and heard my panic rev. When a motorcycle hits neutral or jumps out of its gear while airborne, the sound is unmistakable. Today, "panic revs" horrify me. Every time I'm at a race and hear one, I quickly survey the track to make sure everyone is okay. I was a long way up in the air, and he knew it was going to be a bad one. He instantly started to wave the red-cross flag for all he was worth. When the red cross flag is waved, it lets the medics know that a rider is in medical distress.

Gisela was adjacent to that jump watching the entire thing unfold right in front of her disbelieving eyes. She had also witnessed my motorcycle fly in the air another fifteen feet upon impact and then come down right on top of me. Talk about adding insult to injury.

I didn't see the medics run, I didn't see anything. My 150-pound frame of physical fitness, which had outwrestled every personal demon imaginable to succeed, was now in for the fight of its life. My lungs had collapsed as a result of multiple fractures to my spinal column and torso, thirty-six, to be exact. The one-time self-proclaimed "Rocket Man" had plummeted to Walton's grass with all the grace of a Scud missile. I lost consciousness and for the second time that year had an out-of-body experience. Much like the day at Stinky Lake, I was hovering high above my body. In that instance the bright warm light wasn't behind me; it was all around me. I felt the bright, warm, enticing energy pulling me into the centre of its circle. I fought its powerful pull with every ounce of energy I had.

The next thing I remember is regaining consciousness on the ground. Medic Carol Henderson began asking me questions. I couldn't feel anything below my neck. Then I looked up into the faces of concerned onlookers. The first face I saw was that of my friend Billy Rainford from Direct Motocross. When I saw the expression on his face, I knew I was in big trouble. Most of the faces I made eye contact with were gaunt with disbelief. As I rolled my head upwards away from the crowd, I noticed a dark cloaked being lurking. He was waiting for me, and I knew it. It was the Grim Reaper, and he wanted my soul, but his efforts were of no avail against the power, love, and caring energy of all those surrounding me. To me, all that was surreal and almost impossible to comprehend. I have always believed, deep in my heart, that God works through people. If you were there at Walton Raceway that day, gathered around me, I can't thank you enough. It was your strength and energy that kept the darkness at bay. Soon I fell unconscious once again.

You Want to Live, Don't You?

The rush to save my life was on. First, they took me to Seaforth Medical Centre, where I was placed in an orange air ambulance helicopter and flown to the London Health Sciences Centre. When that happened, Steve's wife, Jennifer, came and picked up Gisela.

When they arrived at the hospital in London, Gisela was brought into my room and told the grave nature of my condition. The doctors said they would operate to stabilize my spinal column fractures, if and when my vital signs stabilized. She was also informed that if I survived the surgery, I would have no voluntary movement of anything below my neck and be a quadriplegic. She was devastated. A priest was called in and had some words for her. Then he came and talked to me, though I can't remember a thing he said. Gisela was also given her own room, which the hospital reserved for relatives of patients who are not expected to survive.

Things didn't get any easier. I flat-lined four times in the next twenty-four hours. The surgery was put on hold, and it was starting to look more and more like this was the end. There I lay, completely broken and oblivious to everything except the love pouring out of my dear Gisela's heart.

When I came to, I was in a panicked state. I had no idea where I was. I knew I had crashed, but I thought I was still at the track hidden on the grounds in the far back in a MASH-style medical tent.

"Why are they keeping my crash a secret?" I asked Gisela. She told me where I was and what had happened. Then she asked me a question that I wasn't expecting. "You want to live, don't you?"

"Of course I do," I replied. "My kids need me, don't they?"

Her putting that question to me in black and white painted the best illustration of how grave my condition was. By then we also had a full assessment of everything that I had broken. I had over 30 breaks and fractures, including T-3, T-4, T-5, and T-6; a broken L-1 and L-2 vertebrae; every one of my ribs (some in multiple places); a broken sternum; two collapsed lungs; a broken collarbone; and two suspected broken wrists. The wrists turned out to be okay, but they were so swollen that my hands looked like boxing gloves. As far as head trauma went, I rocked my melon pretty good too.

Placed in a medically induced coma, I went into the operating room and was under the knife for eight hours. It turned out that there were more breaks in my vertebrae than they originally saw on the X-rays. They also discovered that my neck had been broken years before—remember when I was pile-driven in Calgary in 1989? I certainly knew something was off. I couldn't rotate my head right or left for months. I smile now writing that, because most of what made sense at the time doesn't make sense now.

In the early hours of Sunday morning, I began to come out of the induced coma. I was in a recovery room, and my entire body hurt more than it had in my entire life. It felt as if piping-hot acid was flowing through every ounce of bone marrow. No wonder; I now had the metal equivalent of a Smart Car parked permanently inside me. I also had to be given a blood transfusion. I found out later from my surgeon that every ounce of flesh had to be peeled away from my spine for that delicate procedure. Today I have a full-length "zipper" from my neck right down to my rear end.

I was sure the pain was going to stop my heart from beating. I fought it for everything I was worth. It wasn't even possible to clench my teeth, because I had broken my front two teeth off in the crash. My entire life, I seem to have had a love/hate relationship with pain. I hate it, but it seems to love me. I knew my life was going to be different from then on, but first I just had to bear down and survive.

As Sunday, August 21, 2011, shifted into the afternoon, I was somewhat more alert. I knew the weather outside was bad, because I could hear the wind howling. A bad storm was coming in off Lake Huron. I heard hospital staff and visitors talking about its potential seriousness. Word was also coming in that the race at Walton had been hugely affected by the bad weather. The final pro moto of that day was cancelled, the track deemed unsafe to ride. Heidi Cooke, the wife of that day's freshly crowned 250 cc Canadian National Champion, Tyler Medaglia, was rushed into the hospital. She was pregnant and about to give birth somewhat prematurely to their firstborn son, Tallon. As more news started to come in, it was evident that that storm was going to take prisoners.

As nightfall came, whatever resurgence I had earlier in the day physically was gone. I was put in an area for the night where my vital signs could be watched constantly. That night, due to the storm, the hospital was under lockdown. The observation area was dark, and it reminded me of a scene from an old war movie. I was in and out of constructive and medicated self-talk. I should have been used to that, right? This was different though. The ring of angels who had protected me at Walton from the Grim Reaper was still with me; I could feel it. The other side, the dark side, the Grim Reaper, he was there too, lurking about. I wasn't sure what was happening with all that energy. It was as if my aura was caught in the middle of a giant tug-of-war between good and evil. I was confused but maintained my faith in the God of my Mis-Understanding. Just as the hospital was under lockdown, the positive spirits that had protected me that far in life had temporarily locked the evil out of my space.

With no one allowed to leave or enter the hospital, that Sunday night proved to be the longest of my life. I was in a dark, cold space. All I could do was close my eyes and try and block out the pain. It was noisy outside. I heard things bouncing off the hospital's exterior. It sounded like garbage dumpsters were being catapulted at the hospital.

I must have finally fallen asleep or passed out, because in the wee hours of Monday morning, I woke up startled and began to panic. Pipes and hoses were all over me. I was hooked up to enough damn technology to medically industrialize a third-world country. In my bewildered state, I began to rip the breathing tubes out of my chest and mouth. Thankfully, I was in an area where I was being monitored, and I didn't get far before I was stopped. They brought Gisela back in, and she stayed at my side to keep me calm. I told her that I was going to get better. "I will heal. I know it. That's what us motocrossers do." In that moment, and for the next few months anyway, I honestly believed I would walk again despite what the doctors were telling me.

On Monday, August 22, we were greeted by a bright, beautiful sunny day. It was almost impossible to believe the weather chaos that had unleashed its fury just the day before. News was beginning to come in of how bad that storm was. At 4:00 p.m. on Sunday afternoon, in the town of Goderich, an F-3 tornado touched down. Goderich is only about forty kilometres from Walton Raceway. The tornado, which tore a strip a kilometre and a half wide, left one man dead and thirty-seven others badly injured. Winds from that tornado reached upwards of 330 kilometres per hour. It was also the most powerful tornado Southwestern Ontario had seen since 1996. Upon hearing all that, all I could think about was all our stuff and my friends back at the track. Gisela and Steve Emery had loaded everything up, and all our stuff was fine. That was certainly not the way anyone of us saw the last national of 2011 going.

Monday was the first day I can remember having any kind of appetite after the crash. That was a good sign, but there was a problem. They wanted me to have a post-surgery bowel movement before I started on any solid food. I wanted pizza. I knew what the answer would be if I had asked the nurse, so I had Gisela order it anyway. If my body weight was 145 pounds before that race, it was likely down to about 125 pounds by that time.

Later that afternoon one of my visitors was a man that I have known for many years, Brent Carlson. Brent had made the trek from BC with his boys, who were also racing. Brent has been around motorcycles his entire life. Back in the late 1970s and early 1980s while I was racing at Little Rock Raceway in Aldergrove, Brent's dad owned the gravel pit next door. His dad never allowed him to race. He always wanted to, and now he had an entire family of racers. Brent, who has a heart of gold, offered to drive our truck back to BC. I'm not sure why, but I had some misgiving at first. I think I just didn't want to put anyone out. I thought about it for a while and then realized it would be a good move for us. There was no point in Gisela driving our truck all the way back home some 4,400 kilometres on her own. Mr. C., I'm forever grateful, my friend. Thank you for helping us in our time of need.

With the Walton race over, many others came to see me. Back at home, Gisela's sister started a website that shared the details of my accident. She also posted daily updates on my condition. There was a place where people could comment as well as a link to a fundraiser. We had no idea what we were going to need and what would be covered and what would not. We didn't know a lot, but we knew we were officially homeowners. Even though we already lived in the home we now owned, we officially took possession the day of my surgery. I'm so thankful that I felt so compelled to get it all done before we left on that trip.

That Monday we got a call at the hospital that we were not expecting. Lori, my son Nolan's mom, called to say she was stuck in customs with Nolan. She had planned to be in England with him for a lengthy period of time. (They still live there now.) It turned out even though I had left years before and Lori had full custody, she still needed my consent to take him overseas. Once I found out what was expected of me, I signed the documentation, which was sent to the hospital.

This next piece was posted by Steve Emery on the website on Tuesday, August 23.

Tonight we rounded up some motocross friends and went to see Brent. I have been there every day, but five of us coming up brought such a smile to Brent's face. I was surprised they let in five at once, plus Gisela. Jamie Ruddock, Bigwave Billy Rainford, James Lissimore, my wife Jen and me. It turns out his arm is not broken, they saw an old break on the x-ray. I know it has been said, but it is funny how concerned he is about his two front teeth being broken. We brought him the results up from the week at Walton and shared some of the funnier stories with him. He was so happy to hear about the racing and talk with a group of friends. It was easy to see the passion he has for motocross and friends. We brought money up to him that was raised by riders at Walton. Many riders donated their winnings from the week. One little boy, (Hunter Scott) that won the 50 cc class and does not even know Brent, put $100 in the box for him. The crowd was speechless, and then cheered and clapped loudly for the boy. It was a moving moment.

Brent Carlson from Mainland Sand and Gravel, who is a big supporter of everything moto, talked Brent into letting him and the boys drive his truck home. That will allow Gisela to stay a few days longer and then fly home. That is a big weight off of Gisela's shoulders. A big thank you to Brent Carlson. After Thursday when Gisela is home, I will continue to visit Brent everyday as long as he is in Ontario. Overall, Brent has looked and sounded a bit better each day. He wants so badly to get on the computer so he can read and respond to everyone's messages and well wishes himself. He is grateful for everyone's messages and good thoughts.

Mark Hosie, who we had stayed with the night before Walton began, was also a frequent visitor. Many others came by to show their concern and support. To each and every one of you who visited or played a role in these difficult times, Gisela and I are so thankful and will be eternally grateful. With a heart full of love from Gisela and my moto colleagues, for the first time since my crash, my outlook was pretty good. But let me qualify that. I may have been happy to see my friends and chat some moto, but inside I was afraid. Terrified. I didn't know what living like that would mean or what it would look like. That was awful. I had spent twenty-five years without motocross, and I finally had it back. I was sober, and I loved life again! Why was this happening? I had suffered enough, or so I thought. Was I even going to be able to use my hands properly again? The swelling in my hands was coming down, but my fingers were numb. As crazy as that may sound, I was lost and afraid, but it wasn't half as bad as when I was terminally intoxicated.

The big boy in me knew it wasn't going to be easy, but I harnessed my twelve-step tools and told myself (no pun intended), "One step at a time. Live in the now. Just for today," and every other cliché I had picked up. These simple tools that I had spent a lifetime complicating were now going to help me recreate my life. I had no idea how or what living the rest of my life severely disabled and in a wheelchair would look like, but I made up my mind that whatever time I had left, I was going to do my best and make it count. It was no problem to start "living like I was dying." I had already been to the other side twice now.

I was on oxygen and had drainage tubes in my lungs. They also had me on an intermittent intravenous drip of morphine and fentanyl. Earlier on they had given me some oral meds, which I had thrown up intentionally when I found out they were Tylenol 3s. I didn't want to be addicted to them again. My experience through the next two years saw me manage pain with varying strengths of transdermal fentanyl patches. My doctor told me that I would know when my body could tolerate life without it. The doctors who operated on me warned that, due to the nature of the intense trauma to my body and the number of fractures that I had suffered, I would need pain management my entire life.

My collarbone was broken, and from what I could see it needed to be plated, or it would not heal. I argued with the doctors that to let it heal on its own, as they hoped it would do over the next six to eight weeks, wasn't good enough. I was on the losing end of that argument and am still not happy with it. If they would have plated my shoulder on the spot like it needed to be, I would have been able to get into spinal cord rehab in Vancouver four months earlier. Four months is a long bloody time when you want to start recreating your life at forty-five years old. That was just the beginning. I spent the next seven and a half months medically incarcerated.

On Tuesday a social worker from the hospital came in to talk to us. She wanted to know if I had any insurance other than my BC medical coverage. My answer was no. I only ever purchased insurance when I went into the United States to race. I had never thought to get insurance while racing in my own country. I had good health care coverage, which I assumed was universal right across the country.

To put it simply, it is, but it isn't. We found that out soon enough—the hard way. The social worker told us that the hospital was making arrangements to fly me home. We were perplexed. My doctors had originally told us that it would be at least a few weeks before I was well enough to fly. Yes, I wanted to be home; who wouldn't? My major red flag was who was going to pay for that special low-flying 4,000-kilometre medical flight. We voiced that question and were told, "Not to worry; it's covered." Talk about a whirlwind change of events. I didn't know what to think, but I sure wanted to be back home in Vernon. I missed the girls, and Thursday was Sara's birthday. We didn't know when the flight was scheduled, but we were notified that there would be little warning.

Gisela's sister, Renee, cashed in her air miles and bought Gisela's flight home. On Thursday, August 25, exactly one week after my crash, I left the London Health Sciences Centre Hospital in an ambulance. It was a warm, humid day as we headed to the London airport. The ambulance attendant's name Kevin. He also worked periodically as a medic at Walton Raceway. He knew who I was, and knew of my crash. We struck up a conversation that continued over social media throughout my recovery.

When the ambulance reached the airport, it drove right out onto the tarmac. I had no idea what to expect, but I was down with anything that would get me home. When my stretcher was unloaded from the ambulance, it was wheeled over to a Lear jet. It certainly wasn't as big as I expected. There was a pilot and a co-pilot along with two nurses. When the attendants got me to the plane, I was introduced to those who would be responsible for getting me home alive.

Before my stretcher was lifted into the plane, they briefed me on how things would play out. My stretcher was strapped to the top of the airplane's seats on one side, my face within two feet of the plane's ceiling. The windows were below me, and I could only see out the top few inches. I was told the plane would be stopping in Winnipeg for fuel. I was claustrophobic before the plane took off, but once it did, I was able to breathe normally. The nurses, who were there in case I went into full cardiac arrest again, didn't have to do a lot, which was a good thing considering all the pipes and hoses still hooked up to me. I just wanted to be in our new home. That's all I could think about.

When we stopped in Winnipeg for fuel, they didn't go up to a terminal or anything like that. A fuel truck came out to the end of the runway and filled us right there. When that happened, all four crew members disappeared for what seemed like forever. There I was sitting on the tarmac in a plane with no one else on it. I was pretty sure no one had forgotten about me. How could they? Our plane was parked right on the damn runway. I don't know what I was worried about. It's not like anyone was going to see the door open and the keys in the ignition and fly away with me. But after what I had been through, I wasn't sure.

Landing in Kelowna some seven hours after leaving London was an incredible feeling. It was around 8:00 p.m. As my stretcher was unloaded from the plane, I was embraced by a warm Okanagan summer breeze. When the air filled my lungs, I was so thankful to be alive and to be home.

As a footnote, in hindsight I believe the London hospital wanted me out of there and off Ontario Health Care's dime as soon as possible. I have a little more information and evidence to back that up, but I will keep it to myself for now.

On the forty-five-minute drive from Kelowna to the Vernon hospital, all I could think about was my girls. Yes, Nolan too, but I had not seen him since 2002. He was in England, and I was starting to wonder if he would ever forgive me or want to see me again. (I still haven't seen him, though I hope to one day.)

My arrival at the Vernon hospital was chaotic. Even though I believe some staff members had my best interests at heart, the hospital was a huge downer for me. I was in there for four months before I could even go to rehab. Had my shoulder been operated on in Ontario, I would have already been off to spinal cord rehab in Vancouver. Instead I laid there and finally had the surgery two months after arriving. The doctor's protocol was to let it try and heal on its own. I'm not a doctor, but when I look at an X-ray and see a full two inches between the bones, not even God's grandmother could knit that together.

The best part about the first couple of weeks in the Vernon hospital was being in quarantine. I don't know what they were afraid of; was I contagious? It's called

MRSA, I think. It's something that can be transmitted from patient to patient, and because I had been in other hospitals for surgery, that was protocol.

My plane beat Gisela's back to Kelowna, and I didn't see her until the following day. I had no idea what was next in my life. I had decided back in Ontario to live, and I meant it deep in my heart. The road that I was on now, much like my sobriety, would be under perpetual construction. Nothing is a given in life; I fully understood that now. There was no rite of passage for being a good guy or at least having good intentions. My prognosis was pretty much in my own hands. I didn't know how, but I wanted to succeed and not leave a legacy as a failure or a quitter. I wanted to show the world that I was just what motocross had made me to be, a winner.

The outpouring of support from friends and family inside and outside of the motocross community was phenomenal. I don't even know where to start. I would like to thank each and every person who showed their care and concern in many forms, including the well wishes on the website and social media. Gisela's sister set up a GoFundMe account to help offset costs associated with spinal cord injury, to name a few. I was able to get on my own laptop and thank as many people as I could. The visits and outpouring of love were heavy. I wasn't used to that at all. If anything, it was the opposite through most of my active addictive life. During that time, no one wanted to see me, because I had burnt most bridges before they ever appeared in my rear view-mirror.

One of the places that I enjoyed going regularly to chat motocross was MX-Forum. Also known as the "Pink Palace," it was started up by a long-time friend of mine, Kelowna realtor Rick Hamer-Jackson, a.k.a. "Hammertime." The Palace was always a good place for me to get the dirt on the sport we all loved. It was there that I read that Blair had been injured. It was also on that forum that I read about the new jump at Walton Raceway, on which I crashed. Reading some of the posts made on my behalf was overwhelmingly cool. Hammertime also started a fundraiser, and many top-level riders donated items to be auctioned off. Chad Reed, Steve Matthes, Kyle Beaton, my old friend Rick Sheren, (whose son, Brady, was launching Atlas Brace Technology at the time). I could increase that list tenfold. The feeling of unconditional love and caring was foreign. I felt compelled to pay it back somehow. I had no idea how, but that would come soon enough. In the meantime, I had a ton of work to do to get healthy and strong enough to get into spinal cord rehabilitation.

When my dad came up for the first time, I saw the hurt in his body language when he walked into the room. It was similar with my girls, but I know they were more afraid than anything. No one knew what to expect, including Gisela and me. Not two weeks earlier, the doctors had called a priest into my room in Ontario, fearing the worst. Now we were on a mission to re-create.

Part of the re-creation process that still puts a smile on my face is due to Hammertime. I'm sure he won't mind me saying it, and if he does, too damn bad. Hammertime loves to cook, and he's pretty damn good at it. On numerous occasions he brought me homemade pastas and many other good eats. We had plenty of time to catch up on some of the things that we did together as kids. He may have been an "Internet Assassin" (sharp tongued and opinionated) of sorts at one time, but he is one of my best friends. We scripted a lot of history together, but drifted apart when my vagabond lifestyle took me out of the motocross loop. Rick also suffered a spinal cord injury, years back. Fortunately, he was able to walk out of where I would soon be headed, the GF Strong rehabilitation centre.

That said, he understands what it's like to deal with the many side effects of a spinal cord injury. Having had his successful experience at GF Strong, Rick prepared me and advocated loudly to get me in there as soon as possible. Over and above all that, on one visit, he went to Future Shop and grabbed me an iPad. I had a laptop, but other than social media and motocross chat forums, I was pretty much computer illiterate. That was to change immensely in the near future. On one visit, somehow Rick convinced my dad (who has a grade-six education) that he needed an iPad, too, and to get on social media. We're talking my dad, a Harley-riding, tree-falling, never-voted-in-his-life, redneck, hillbilly, Neanderthal. (Trust me, they all fit, or at least did at one time.) I don't know if people or things were changing in those fragile, delicate, and emotional times, or if it was just my perception. At any rate, Dad loved the iPad, and he was onto it in no time. I'm sure that more than a few people were shocked when he surfaced on social media.

Life in the Vernon hospital was tough. I was moved around a lot and had inconsistent care. The rehab department of Dana and Ray were amazing though. Within two days of my being there, they were able to get me sitting up on my own. That was a huge step, because I was now a T-3-and-below paraplegic. I had multiple fractures of my clavicle, thoracic, and lower-lumbar vertebrae. In the crushing manner that my body impacted the ground after soaring 130 feet through the air, my spinal cord buckled like a garden hose. My complete injury level starts where my arms are, and downward. I can't feel or move anything below them. I'm so thankful that the original diagnosis of possibly being a quadriplegic with no arm function was wrong. Once I reached a point of balance, I started to pretend I was riding my unicycle. Even though it took a ton of balance, I never thought about it, and just rode and had fun. I immediately began to program that mindset for sitting upright.

It also seemed like every day of hospital life meant more tests and more machines to sit in or lie in. I had no clue what was happening. I was just so thankful to be alive with so many friends who cared. I remember the looks on their faces. I saw the genuine hurt care and concern, but I also saw something else. They were all thinking about safety and how real the possibility of something like that happening was. The Nicholls family, the Acheson family, Ian Mckill (Riders Edge Suspension), the Gatt family, Barry Wellings of Valley Moto Sport, Mark and Kelly Denis, George, Dooner, Wayne, and everyone else who came my way, you all helped me a ton. Thank you!

I would like to thank one more dear soul. Many years before in Chilliwack, going back to my elementary days, I had a friend named Linda. Like many I went to school with, I had not seen Linda for over thirty years. One day while in hospital, I got a message from her saying she was going to be coming through Vernon and wanted to know if it was okay to stop in. I had no problems with that, as the daily visitors helped keep me sane while Gisela was at work. Linda and her husband, Gord Yelich, became regular visitors. On a couple of occasions, they came in the evenings and brought some incredible Greek food. It was enjoyable for Gisela and me to have their company. One day Linda messaged me asking if she could bring someone up to see me. She would not tell me who it was but said that she had to pick him up at the Kelowna airport. My committee upstairs yearned to know who it was. A motivational speaker like Tony Robbins? Not quite but close, and in my opinion, even better.

His name was Bob Molle, and he was a giant of a man, around 6 foot 4, and weighing about 250 pounds. I didn't put two and two together at first, but Bob was a two-time Grey Cup Champion and former captain of the Winnipeg Blue Bombers. He was drafted in 1985, and won the Grey Cup in 1988 and 1990.

When Bob and Linda came into my room, the visit was electric. Bob introduced himself, and told me he had heard about my crash from Linda. He was in Kelowna to speak to a group that night as part of his job as a motivational speaker. He handed me a book that he written called *How to Get Comfortable Being Uncomfortable*. Then he told me about his wrestling career. I know nothing about the sport, but I would not want to face him in a ring. Bob told me about how he broke his back just a few months before the 1984 Los Angeles Olympics. He was devastated. He loved wrestling and had spent many years preparing for a shot at an Olympic gold medal. He would not take no for an answer and baffled his doctors and the sporting world by winning that year's silver medal.

Bob also told me about the only motocrosser he met when he was going to Simon Fraser University. "Do you know a guy by the name of Ross Pederson?" he asked. Are you kidding me? My old friend, Ross "Rollerball" Pederson is arguably the best Canadian motocrosser ever. I'm torn on that one though, because I wasn't that fond of Ross when I had to line up against him. I don't think anyone was, the lion's share of most purses usually went into his bank account. I'm sure that was just the way he liked it.

Bob told me that Ross was an animal when it came to fitness. He said he has never seen anyone as serious about training as Ross. Bob recalled Ross literally running up and down Burnaby Mountain on the SFU campus to train for motocross.

At the end of our visit, Bob looked at me and told me something that I was starting to feel and believe. He said I would write my own story, that I would harness everything that had made me a winner in my sport and do great things.

On September 25, 2016, Bob was inducted into the Winnipeg Blue Bombers Hall of Fame. Thanks for the awe-inspiring and inspirational visit, my friend.

Around that time an Arenacross race was scheduled for Penticton's South Okanagan Centre. I had been on a few outings in the Handy Dart to different appointments, like getting my front teeth put back in. It had all been pretty much medical business and no recreation. I desperately wanted to go to that race. The hospital staff begrudgingly okayed it. I'm thankful they did, because had they not, I was going anyway. However, the day before the race, I woke up and couldn't believe my eyes. My right leg was twice the size of the left one from my groin all the way down to my ankle.

The doctors had me in for an ultrasound instantly. It turns out their decision to prematurely take the pulsating leg boots off had precipitated a blood clot. It was a huge mistake. In London we were told that they would have to stay on for months. That never happened, and I now had another big problem. The blood clot was huge, and it was in my groin area. My right leg must have weighed more than the rest of my entire body, and it looked horrible. Gisela was pissed with my doctor. I was too, but all I cared about was going to the race the following night.

I was advised not to go, but I heard none of it, and our Volkswagen Jetta couldn't get to Penticton fast enough that Friday afternoon. I can't even remember who won the race, but I remember the love I felt in my heart to be back at the track. Yes, I was cold, the wheelchair I was in was as sketchy as can be, but that is who I was. I'm so thankful that I know who I am now. I felt so lost for so many years. I was seriously injured, and I knew the days I had remaining would be difficult, but that didn't bother me. I only focused on what I loved.

Barry Wellings of Valley Moto Sport kindly put us up in his suite. Barry had Jeremy Medaglia in town that weekend to race one of his KTMs. That night as we were leaving in our car, Jeremy chased us halfway across the parking lot. When he finally caught up to us, I rolled down the window and thought he was going to freeze to death. Jeremy had a care package for me from the good people at KTM Canada. My old friend, Andy White, was running the team there. I have been involved in many clubs and different sports for most of my life, and none of them stack up to the genuine love I have always felt from my friends in motocross.

I had surgery to repair my collarbone in October. My mission then was to get it strong enough, so I could go to Vancouver for rehabilitation. Ray, in the Vernon hospital's physiology department, hooked me up with a wheelchair that was propelled by wheeling on the left side, my good side. I got to know that hospital and its staff pretty darn well—too damn well. I was starting to get restless. I just wanted to get down to GF Strong, put my time in, and get back home, where I belonged. When I left the London hospital, I thought that all of that rehabilitation and hospital stuff would be over by Christmas. I was home for a short stint for Christmas, but much more trouble was about to come our way.

26

The Canadian Moto Show and Life Today

The blood clot in my groin was a huge problem—literally. My medical team was concerned about its size and the potential for a lethal embolism. I was started on Warfarin (rat poison) and was on it for over a year. The other unpleasant part of that big nasty was having to have my blood's INR (international normalized ratio) taken every second day. They had to keep an eye on how thick my blood was, so the clot could eventually dissolve. The other issue was physical; I had to be careful not to aggravate that area. So many things were going on with me medically. It was such a blur in the hospital, I knew I needed to be there, but I hated every minute of it. My incredible Gisela brought me home-cooked food every single day. Most days she was there by 7:00 a.m. before she went to work. She finally told me that while I was in hospital, she lived on red wine and Kentucky Fried Chicken back at our new home.

On days when the weather was nice enough, she and I would go into town and meander. On one occasion we even rolled all the way to our condo. When we got there, Gisela asked if I wanted her to bump me up the sixteen stairs to get in. We had two flights of stairs on the exterior with no in-house elevator. I refused her offer, stating that once I got inside, I would not go back to the hospital. I meant it, and she understood my logic. If you have ever seen where the Vernon hospital is at the top of the hill above Polson Park, you can appreciate what she had to push me up to get me back.

I wasn't supposed to bear any weight through my arms, so my collarbone, broken ribs, and sternum could heal. I was diligent and didn't do anything intentionally to aggravate those injuries. I needed to get to GF Strong, and they would not have me until I was completely healed. I believed that down there, my recovery would start in earnest. I got a contact number of one the individuals who worked there from Hammertime. I didn't know what to believe or to be hopeful for. Every doctor I had spoken to so far told me that, short of a medical miracle, I would never walk again. All I knew was that GF Strong had a great reputation. I believed that whatever chance I had in the way of any kind of recovery would happen in Vancouver.

The next bomb that dropped was absolutely gutting. One morning Gisela walked into my hospital room, and I could tell by the look on her face that something was wrong. We had received a bill from Ontario for $30,000 to cover my medical flight home and a charge of over $2,000 that was incurred to jump-start my heart the four times I had flat-lined. How could any of this be real? We were promised by the social worker in London that it would all be covered by BC medical.

We had the social worker from the Vernon hospital come in to see if there was any way she could advocate on our behalf. A week later there was still no resolution, and things were not looking good. I was starting to visualize us losing our first home, which we had only owned for two and a half months. We finally managed to get an email contact for the social worker from London. When the response came in, it wasn't anything concrete. However, she stated that she had believed the costs would be covered. That wasn't the case. That situation dragged on for the next four months, eating away at my moral code. Having lived a life coming full circle, I make every effort possible to follow through with any promises that I make. Now rather than focusing on my recovery, and things that I needed to be learning to survive and live in a wheelchair, I was one hundred percent preoccupied with the bill. We went to our local MLA and pretty much anywhere else we could think of, to no avail. Ontario wasn't prepared to budge one bit.

Ten days before Christmas, I had had enough and told the hospital staff that I was leaving. After having spent a full four months hospitalized, I felt that a few weeks in my own home would help me prepare for GF Strong both mentally and physically. The hospital staff was livid. They told me that my INR needed to be taken every second day, and if I went home, that would be impossible. Once in the condo, there was no way I was going up and down sixteen stairs every second day. I was prepared for that and had looked up a community health nurse who did mobile bloodwork. Now we were set, and it was sure nice to be going home. I had been hospitalized for over three months by that point. The plan was that I would fly to GF Strong the first week of the new year.

Being home was a challenge, but did it ever feel good. Keep in mind that most of the things that I would need to know how to do, like self-catheterizing, transferring in and out of my wheelchair, and things like that, I had not yet learned. These were all things that I would learn in the rehab centre, where I was soon headed. At that stage, because I was healing from so many broken bones, I had no way to begin testing on my own. I would stay in my chair throughout the day while Gisela was at work. If the house had burned down, she would have had to find an urn big enough for my ashes and my hardware. Fortunately, it didn't, and I was able to enjoy the holidays at home with family and friends. I feel like my Higher Power was looking out for me, because I badly needed that break.

A day or two after Christmas, I got a bladder infection, my third one in three months. As horrible as they are, I have now had over forty of them. Bladder infections are, no pun intended, crippling. Add to that the lack of physical dexterity or ability in a new paraplegic, and you get a pretty good visual of my 2011 holiday hurt locker.

I took advantage of the time and sent out as many Christmas cards as I could. I was so grateful just to be alive and signing my own name. Despite everything that was still not yet on track in my life, I did my best to soak in every moment of feeling good that I could find. I was so happy to have my family around. I could see that it was difficult for them to see me so physically challenged and broken, though. I knew that the new normal that lay ahead wasn't going to be easy for anyone, but I was up for the challenge. My goal from the moment I was told I would never walk again was to make the best of what I had left. I like to think that no matter how bad things are, they could have been worse. I had no movement or feeling below my arms, but what a game-changer it is that they still work.

After I was home for almost three weeks, Gisela drove me to the Kelowna airport. I boarded the plane and was mentally prepared to spend the next six months in Vancouver. Being uncertain of what to expect, I took solace in knowing that stay would be a vital step in my recovery.

Uncle Al's wife, Wendy, and her daughter, Jodi, picked me up at Vancouver airport. When I arrived at GF Strong, I was taken aback by its size and the number of people there. Most of them, like me, were dealing with varying forms of life-changing illnesses and injuries. In my other recovery programs, unity, a sense of belonging, and knowing we were not alone or terminally unique were a huge part of the healing process. The moment I rolled through the doors and up to the admittance desk, I realized just how different my life was going to be.

I was up and down between positive thoughts, and feeling bad for making a human taco of myself on a dirt bike at forty-five years old. It wasn't long though before I had my eyes opened in that facility, realizing that life happens, regardless.

Not long after being admitted, I started to hear other people's stories. One girl was paralyzed from the neck down from abscessed teeth that had metastasized. Another guy was paralyzed from the neck down after a drill fell on his head at work from the twenty-ninth floor of a high-rise job site. Another girl had been shot in that summer's Grand Hotel shooting in Kelowna. These were just a few of the people who I met and began my recovery with. Suddenly, crashing on a dirt bike in London didn't seem like such a bad fate. No matter how bad things are, there is always someone who has it worse.

Many of these people didn't have use of their hands. When dinner was served, they had to be fed by a caregiver. I was one of the lucky ones. Despite my early prognosis, my hand function was back to 100 percent. I had many tests done at GF Strong. It was determined early on that I was a T-3-and-below compete paraplegic, complete meaning that barring some kind of divine medical cure, I would never walk again. I also learned that the spinal cord contains the only cells in the human body that don't regenerate after being injured. Spinal cord damage is permanent and irreversible. Many advances have been made recently with stem cell research, but these treatments have only been found to be successful if given quickly after an injury is diagnosed. I am hopeful that one day science will get us there. However, the realist in me tells me that I best be nice to my current vessel.

Spinal cord injuries have no mercy. Being a "T-3 complete" means that when I sit upright in a chair, the muscles that used to hold me upright don't work. I had to be outfitted with a special seat that was moulded to my rear end and lower back to hold me upright. We actually had to fly someone in from Colorado for that incredible seating system. Fortunately, the wheelchair was funded. However, the $6,500 Custom RIDE Cushion, which I have now bought two of, were not. Much like buying a motorcycle with the intention of racing it, numerous tweaks, adjustments, and aftermarket parts are required. Simply put, nothing stays the same for long living like that. Just when I solve one problem, four more arise. Such is life, though I hate to think of it that way. A positive mindset is required daily! I would rather think of it like I did when I was racing dirt bikes, programming a mindset of always being prepared and race ready.

My friend and mechanic in the sport, "Donk" (Scott Donkersgoed), had a signature saying on MX-Forum: "Luck is the residue of preparation." I can't argue that one. Writing that down puts a huge smile on my face. It reminds me of something that one of my first motocross idols, Larry Mackenzie, used to say on race days. When asked why his White Factory OW Yamaha was so clean, he would always reply, "A clean bike is a happy bike, a happy bike is a fast bike, and a fast bike always wins." Larry, you were faster than lightning in your day, old friend, thanks for the great memories. No, you're not responsible for my OCD; I am. I couldn't have been more than eight years old when I first heard Larry's podium pontification. Like most of the incredible memories and fortitude that the sport of motocross has instilled in me, it stayed with me and aided in my survival. I did everything I could to keep my eye on the bouncing ball as far as protocol went at GF Strong. I needed to learn so many things about my condition. I had hawk-like focus, and always picked the brains of the other inmates (patients).

My first couple of nights were on the weekend, so not much was happening. When Monday rolled around, it was almost like being back in school. We were scheduled in segmented blocks of group and individual lessons and therapy sessions. Physiotherapy, wheelchair skills (I still didn't even have one of my own), social worker, psychologist, bowel and bladder tutorials, skin care, looking at equipment for home, you name it. Miraculously, I retained most of what came my way. I have been fortunate that way, even with all the brain trauma from hits to the head and years of alcohol abuse. That in itself is a miracle, because I was so preoccupied with getting the $30,000 medical bill overturned. I didn't realize it, but Gisela, her mother, and her sister were contacting everyone under the sun to try and get that bill reversed. There were news crews at the rehabilitation centre, and they aired my story on the 6:00 news on three separate networks. BC's health minister, Mike de Jong, even took to the air saying how an imposed bill like that would cripple almost anyone financially. We still had no resolution over the next three months. The *Toronto Sun* even printed a story on the matter.

Knowing that I was confronted with spending the rest of my life in a wheel-chair, getting a new one was high on my priority list. A company that serviced the area came in and let me use one that I liked. Then they ordered me one of my own, which I picked up back in Vernon in the spring.

Friends, there is nothing glorious about spinal cord injury. I can only speak for myself, but due to the long list of broken bones and internal damage I had, I have paid a huge physical price every day since my injury. I often think back to that fateful day at Walton and wonder why I sacrificed so much for that podium. I guess the simple answer is I wanted to recapture a small piece of a bright future in a sport that I had thrown away. The only person who I can blame for that is me. I was young, I was broken, and I was lost when I left motocross years ago. I still wish I had never done that or that someone would have taken me aside and helped me out. Then again, I likely would have rejected it. My wish is that other young riders never give up on their motocross dreams. I hope that by me sharing my story, it prevents even one person from experiencing the kind of anguish that I went through most of my life without motocross.

It was tough to be so far from Gisela. I know it was difficult for her, too. Several of my friends from the coastal area came out of the woodwork to visit. I thank you all so much. In a situation like that, left to my own devices, historically speaking, I have not done well. So many of you made such a difference. I was lost at times but always did the best I could, given my situation.

Many of my friends were anxious to take me on outings, which was awesome. One night, Wayne and George even drove in from Chilliwack and brought me up to the Future West Arenacross. Another friend I worked with at the Park Board, Greg did the same thing another weekend. It was so good to be back at the track. Future West was still owned and operated by John and Jamie Hellam. I can't thank the Hellams enough for the love and support they have always shown me. I believe the unconditional love from so many people has saved my life.

A few weeks into my stay at GF Strong, I discovered the Handy Dart. I wasn't sure where the heck I was going to go, but I was happy I could get out if I wanted to. I came up with the brilliant idea that I could even board one such bus and head to the Hasting Park Thoroughbred Race Track. If I was lucky enough, I could pay off the medical bill, or at least that was my rationale. No live races were scheduled, but they had a slew of simulcast races that would be the perfect fit for me to bury my head in the sand of pari-mutuel tickets. When I told Gisela what I was up to, I could tell she wasn't impressed, but I got in the Handy Dart, and off I went.

I spent an entire Saturday at the track. After about a dozen Budweisers, and being down a few hundred dollars, I begrudgingly and drunkenly summoned my Handy Dart ride back to GF Strong. Keep in mind that I was also on a 150 cc fentanyl patch. I was pretty hammered but managed to get myself back inside the rehab facility. When I got to my room, I stopped at the foot of my roommate's bed. After telling him what I had been up to, I fell face first onto the floor. The next thing I remember, I was waking up Sunday morning with the worst hangover I had ever had. I guess you could say I deserved it.

As time wore on, Gisela was able to come out and stay, because I was granted weekend passes. We would rent rooms in Vancouver's downtown core. I loved going for drives out to Stanley Park, Jericho Beach, and places where I had worked when I was with the Vancouver Park Board. The entire time, I was trying to get a sense of what life would be like once I was out of the safety net of rehab.

One weekend before heading back to GF Strong, we stopped at White Spot and grabbed a burger. Then we headed back down to Jericho Beach to look at the pristine view of the city as we ate. We weren't there more than a minute or two when my right leg started jumping up and down as if it was jiving to the beat of a good song. My heart rate also began to accelerate. In no time flat, I was sweating profusely. I had no idea what was happening. I thought I was having a heart attack. I threw my burger out the window to the flock of seagulls that had gathered, and we rushed back to GF Strong.

Not saying a word to anyone, once in my room, I launched out of my chair and onto my bed. The first thing Gisela grabbed was my right shoe to pull it off my jumpy leg. When the shoe came off, we were dumbfounded! I was wearing a pair of nice dress shoes that Gisela had brought me and helped me put on that morning before we left our hotel. What happened next still wigs me out. A full-sized shoe horn that had been used to put on my shoes fell out. My sock was wet with blood and sweat. I was afraid to even take it off and look at my foot. When the sock finally came off, two of my smallest toes were cut to the bone. I felt absolutely nothing. That was one of my best lessons in autonomic dysreflexia, a syndrome where in someone with a spinal cord injury that the body tries send you signals that something is wrong. Anxiety, apprehension, irregular heartbeat, high blood pressure, a pounding headache, flushing of the skin, profuse sweating, and light-headedness are all signals of autonomic dysreflexia. The condition can be the result of too much sun exposure, skin pressure issues, bowels, bladder, you name it. So many things are associated with these types of injuries that extend beyond the use of body parts that have been lost or compromised.

Speaking of body parts that have been lost or compromised, due to my motocross-related injuries, I have one piece of equipment that is dear to my heart. Before I get into it, I would like to share a story about a rider who came into GF Strong for a visit just after his best Supercross up to that point in the 2012 season. My visitor was none other than Kyle Beaton. Kyle, as I mentioned earlier, is the son of my long-time friend Brian. Kyle, who had won the last chance qualifier the week before in San Diego, came in to visit, and he had something for me. One of the fundraiser auctions at MX-Forums on my behalf was Kyle's race-worn jersey. I'm not sure who the winning bid went to, but the winner was kind enough to ask Kyle to bring it to me. Very cool, fellas. Your legacy as quality human beings will be with me forever. In a roundabout way, I dragged Kyle into that safety equipment conversation, because I knew he was one of the first professional racers in our country to wear the brand-new Atlas Brace, which was launched that year. The favourite piece of equipment that I alluded to was my downhill unicycle. I gave it to Kyle, because I figured it would be a great training device for him. Unfortunately, Kyle suffered a serious leg injury a couple of years later and had to retire. Thanks for everything, "Beats."

Around that same time, my old friend Rick Sheren of R&M Motocross Specialties (who brought factory motocross to Canada, in my opinion) called. It was so good to hear from friends, new and old. Rick was like many others who saw the success, promise, potential, and future that I had when I was younger. He is also one of many who had no idea what happened to me for the twenty-five years that I was AWOL from motocross. Having the man I had so much respect for when I was young call me with such genuine concern was pretty powerful. Rick had even holeshotted the Hangtown motocross pro national a few years earlier. Just a few though, right Rick?

Rick's son, Brady, was in the process of launching a brand-new motocross safety neck brace company called Atlas Brace Technologies. We talked at great length about my injury and what kind of permanent damage I was left with.

I was excited to hear that their product would or likely could help to prevent injuries like the ones I had. Shortly after that, I got another call from another new Atlas employee, Brad Maclean. It was moving, because he told me that new company was going to donate $5 from every brace sold that year in Canada to my recovery fund. Absolutely incredible. With the money, I ended up purchasing my hand cycle, which I still ride when I am well enough to. That piece of equipment is the last connection I have with going fast on wheels on my own terms. It is an incredibly freeing experience to be paralyzed from the arms down and still be able to ride a bicycle. From the moment I climbed onto one at GF Strong, I knew it would play a huge part in keeping my future somewhat sane—that and the cardio vascular benefits. I can't thank the good people at Atlas Brace enough for helping me in a time of need and for keeping all riders who choose to wear their great products as safe as possible.

I managed to get out of GF Strong one weekend for the Vancouver Motorcycle Show. It was such a good feeling to be around two wheels and good friends like Hammertime, Marco Dube, George Imada, and Wally Levy, my kind of people, "old time motocrossers." Something happened at the show that didn't sit well with me though, or at least, it started there.

I was introduced to a group that advocated on behalf of injured motorcyclists. One of my friends who was with the CMRC's sanctioning body in the west pointed them out to me. I knew I needed help. Maybe they could even help me with my $30,000 medical bill. I arranged for the guy I met there to come and see me the following week at GF Strong.

The day of the meeting, he sat across from me in the cafeteria and encouraged me to sue Walton Raceway. He even asked what kind of insurance they had. How the hell did I know? The last thing I would ever do is sue a motocross track. To me, when I signed the waiver, that meant they were not responsible or liable in any way. That will never change in my mind, ever! Remember my dream? To me that was fate, and I got a glimpse of it long before it happened. That meeting lasted less than fifteen minutes. Then he gave me a card and said that if I ever changed my mind to call him. You know what, fella? Your heart may have been in the right place, but my blood still boils as I write this.

When March 1 arrived, I was sick and tired of being in the rehabilitation centre. It wasn't so much the protocol and life there, but the helplessness of not being able to resolve my medical bill problem. I did the best I could to focus, but it was a losing battle. That was about to change though.

My mother-in-law had contacted Linda Steele at CTV News, who did a segment each night on the 6:00 news called *Steele On Your Side*. Her segment was used to show people's stories, like mine, where people felt they had a wrong that needed to be made right. I had no problem with it. The staff were not fond of cameras inside the centre, but it was the only chance I had. I didn't realize it, but at the same time in the east, a London-based group was also advocating to have the bill overturned.

The day after the *Steele On Your Side* story aired, I got a phone call from the London Health Sciences Centre stating that my bills had been overturned. I was quoted on the radio, saying that, "It felt as if a huge medicine ball had been lifted off of my chest." I added that I was happy that they had followed through on their original promise. By then, it was March 3, 2012.

Seven days later, Uncle Al picked me up and drove me back home to Vernon to begin what I soon hoped would be a "new normal." I knew it would take a while, but I was ready to get started.

Picking up a drink while I was in rehab was a huge mistake. From that moment on, all I craved was alcohol. As I've said, for people like me, the first drink is the one to avoid. Always! It's the first one that sets up the craving for the next one and the next one and so on. The formula is simple: don't pick up one drink, and you will not get drunk.

Sara was still living at home with us, and I know it gutted her to see her father that way. I thought drinking only a bottle or two of red wine a day made it okay. It was anything but okay. My body had a host of other demons and signals to overcome with its many limited functions. Everyone in my family, Gisela included, did what they had always done, which is let me find my own way. I can't thank them enough for that. When it comes to matters of the heart and soul or personal struggles, if the individual does not have an honest desire to change, success is unattainable.

The weekend after the Seattle Supercross, which we attended and enjoyed thoroughly with friends, I fell out of my chair twice at home, drunker than a skunk. Gisela was at work, and Sara helped me up the first time. The second time was in our bathroom, and it was a full-on yard sale. Somewhere along the line, I had decided, in my infinite wisdom, that red wine wasn't enough. I had rolled in my chair to our local liquor store and bought a bottle of vodka. That

403

week I had been nipping at that here and there as a form of self-medication. The bottom line for me now was that there was no in-between. It was first drink to full-on drunkenness in no time flat.

Once the invisible line is crossed pertaining to alcoholism, there is no such thing as normal or responsible drinking. I had it put to me this way by an old-timer at one of my meetings way back: "Son when you have a cucumber, and it's pickled, that pickle can never become a cucumber again." Today, I know full well that if I ever take a drink, I will likely not be here for long. At that time, though, I so desperately wanted to control it, but I knew there was only one answer. The answer was to never give up on trying to achieve my sobriety. I was down on myself for a bit, but that began to change once my mind was again clear of craving alcohol.

Shortly after seeing me drunk again, Sara moved out. It was hard enough for her to get her head around me being paralyzed. Never discount how your life trauma can affect those who love and care for you. Spinal cord injury has decimated many individuals and families. Even though my "sobriety train" was temporarily derailed, I was determined not to lose it again, one day at a time. I have not had a drink since.

We had many things to confront at home in the way of making things accessible. First off, we needed to purchase an elevator or lift, so I could get in and out. Sixteen stairs on the outside of the building was the only way in or out. Having just bought that home, we knew full well that if we sold it, it would almost be impossible to get another mortgage. Luckily, my new occupational therapist, Brenda, told us about a new government grant. I got a quote from an elevator company in Kelowna, Hybrid Elevator, which turned out to be a perfect fit for us. The owner had recently bought the company and told us that one of his family members also had a disability. When he sized it up, and gave me the quote of over $30,000, I thought there was no way it would get funded. Four months later, we had an answer that put a smile on our faces. It was approved, but it would not be ready for use until the spring of 2013. My incredibly strong and wonderful wife Gisela, with all her loving might, bumped me up and down daily until then. Your name doesn't have to be Eminem to have a house with an elevator in it, right, Gord?

In the spring of 2013, Jamie Hellam of Future West Productions called me again. He wanted to know if I was interested in announcing for Future West Moto for the upcoming outdoor racing season. I had been back to the track a few times prior to that. The Kamloops National in 2012 was one of them. Once again, I can't thank the likes of the Watchell boys, Willie and Jimmy, enough, for taking care of me. Events like that were great, as they allowed me to extend a personal thanks to the many people who had stepped up for me.

Hammertime had mentioned my name as a potential announcer. Just a couple of weeks before that, he had picked me up in Vernon, and taken me out to the Kelowna track's opening practice day to watch. It was a full three hours out of his way, round trip, to do that. But Hammer, who had been in a similar predicament himself years before, knew that the track was a good place for me. Hammer and I had pretty much parted ways since childhood, until my injury. I'm so thankful that I got to spend some of the best years of my life with you, Rick. And yes, friends, they were long before he was ever known as an "Internet Assassin" with MX-Forum in regard to motocross. I should also note that, now married, Hammertime has a much more professional approach to his current profession as a top-selling Kelowna and Okanagan-area realtor. If you are ever fortunate enough to be looking for a new home in the area, look up Re-Max Kelowna's Team Hamer-Jackson. His much-tougher brother, Brad, is his partner. They are a chip off of their dad Jack's good stock solid block. How many guys can say they raced with the son of a real Jack Hammer? I'm thankful I can.

Having gone so many years without motocross in my life, I wasn't about to let that injury take it from me. It felt so good to be trackside again, breathing it all in. Dust, WD-40, race fuel, grips, grease, or anything dirt bike-related, it has always made my heart sing like nothing else. I wanted to give back, to be involved. I was motivated and passionately charged for all of the right reasons. The perfect storm was now brewing inside, racing toward motocross.

When the time came to go to the first race and announce, I was excited to get there. As a kid, I always called the games and races as I played along or watched. I even seriously considered broadcasting as a career when I was in Calgary, but my alcoholism and bouts with depression prevented it from materializing. Announcing was different though. It was informal, and no one had any expectations. At least if they did, I didn't hear about them. I was going to the Kelowna race to watch anyway, so I figured I might as well help the club and Future West Moto. I want to thank Chris Hannah for the awesome job that he and his dad and the Kelowna Dirt Bike Club did building the track's brand-new tower, which saw its first official use the first day I announced.

We did a few more outdoor races that season for the Hellams and my friends at Future West Moto. It was an extra-special feel-good moment to be part of their Chilliwack Fair Race. Being back in my hometown at a motocross track with a microphone in my hand was proof enough for me that it was never too late in life for anything. It was a miracle, and I loved every minute of it. Gisela and I sat together on a scissor lift, above the action. At day's end when I looked in the mirror, I laughed at myself. I swear my face was dirtier on that day than it was any day that I raced.

Living a new normal like that or even today comes with hefty physical and financial price tags. Let's face it, I'm not a young man anymore. After a lifetime of living the way I had, just being alive was a miracle in itself. The fact that I cared enough about living enough to be able to take advantage of the narrow opening of willingness to change was certainly another. It seems that the longer one is afflicted, the longer the odds of seeing the willingness become. Physically, I still had the blood clot. I also had and continue to have numerous bladder infections. For the first few years, it was back and forth to the spinal cord clinic at Vancouver's General Hospital. MRIs, ultrasounds, urodynamics, I honestly didn't know if they were checking on me or their investments inside of me in terms of titanium and other aftermarket parts. When I said they could build a Smart Car out of the amount of hardware in my body, I mean it.

Today my bladder is my worst enemy and a real nightmare. I had to get part of it removed in 2017, because it was discovered that I had two urethra channels. I had been unsuccessfully introducing a catheter into an opening with only a fifty-fifty chance of hitting the right spot or damaging tissue. That damaged tissue eventually made its way into my bladder once the catheter was inserted. Whenever I got resistance, I just pushed harder, only to find my leg bag filling with bright-red blood-stained urine.

These are not the kinds of things that I'm proud of. However, I feel that it's important to illustrate the complete picture of what paralysis is like. Today I'm used to not having the use of my legs or anything below my chest, but I will never get used to the torment of trying to pass oatmeal-sized chunks in excruciating pain while fighting a fever from chronic bladder infections. Making things worse is having to run a cycle of the same medication that is used to kill anthrax as a cure. It's horrible, because it kills every ounce of bacteria in the body, good and bad. It makes bowel movements almost impossible for days at a time. Probiotics are not an option either, because they weaken the medication's potency. I have had my fill of infections, and they have caused many other problems. Over time the meds have also depleted my body's ability to block out ultraviolet rays. I mentioned that I was diagnosed with skin cancer in 2003. In 2016 and 2019, I had to have topical radiation treatments. It's just another pain in the ass to deal with that is part of getting old, I guess. I wear sunscreen every single day now, even if I'm not going outside.

Through all the many tests, the doctors have discovered that the rate of velocity I'm voiding (urinating) at is way too high and dangerous. You would think it would be a good thing and help to flush out my bladder. On the contrary, the high-velocity voiding causes a backdraft effect, of sorts. It even sucks the urine sediment back up into my kidneys. To treat that my urologist has to inject my bladder with Botox every three months to prevent the spasms that cause it. In a sense, the treatment is like putting my bladder to sleep. Knowing all that now, I'm so thankful I didn't get hurt like that thirty years earlier. Most of that state-of-the-art medical technology in regard to spinal cord injuries was not available back then. Doctor Schultz and his crew in the operating room at the Vernon hospital are amazing. Even though it was super cool to sit in Vancouver General Hospital with Rick Hansen and tell him face to face about that day in Chilliwack when he passed through during the Man In Motion tour, I'm so thankful that we have that treatment right here at home.

In the fall of 2013, I was lucky enough to be able to launch what eventually became the *Canadian Moto Show*. On September 26, 2013, the first episode of what became four years of live broadcasting aired from my home studio. On Wednesday nights at 6:00 p.m., we were on the air, with some shows lasting over three hours. The show's goal was to interview a broad and all-inclusive cast of motocross racers, enthusiasts, family members, supporters, and industry experts. It was a great way to connect with the human side of the sport. The show wasn't always about racing, but more often than not, we talked about the great two-wheeled journey that we were all on together. Big, small, young and old, new rider, or veteran, the *Canadian Moto Show* provided a great platform for all to enjoy. When the gate dropped on the first episode, I had no idea what to expect. I was as nervous as I had ever been when the seconds counted down to the first live show.

My heart was in it one hundred percent, and I did everything I could to make it as good as possible for everyone. As stressful as it was to learn the many things I needed to know in short course, I don't think I have ever had so much fun learning. Yes, it was stressful, but I was determined to make it work. The equipment, platform, and resources required were not cheap. I even hired a guy from our local radio station to help with many things. Over the course of the 137 episodes and numerous one-off podcasts, I believe I learned more than throughout my school years. I had many backers and supporters, continent-wide. I can't thank you all enough. Without that, none of it would have ever happened. I was motivated and that show was the perfect fit for our sport in Canada at the time.

I picked on some riders a little more than others for certain episodes. One such rider who I would like to extend a personal thanks to is Ryan Lockhart. Ryan, who worked for Atlas Brace Technologies, was a regular on the show, and we talked a lot about safety. I don't think it can be talked about or emphasized enough. We even ran a weekly segment at one point called "Lockhart's Locker." It was an opportunity for listeners to send their questions for me to ask Ryan on the show. That was a great fit, because Ryan was teamed up with show supporters Maple Ridge Motorsports. Troy and Sandra, the owners, are great people. Yes, it's a business, and their goal is to make money, but I support them and encourage you to support people like that, too, because I have seen them do so many good things to make our sport better that they didn't have to do to. Ryan, for obvious reasons, also has a highly-regarded following nationwide. Many of our young riders at Future West Moto have looked up to Ryan since meeting him. He was also one of those riders that I noticed straight off the bat at the Edmonton Pro National in 2008. The first time I shook his hand, I couldn't help but think back to the days in the 1980s I spent with his dad, as Scotty's teammate. I will add that it is only because of Scotty that I know where legendary Canadian Singer Anne Murray is from. The Lockharts, along with Anne, hail from Spring Hill, Nova Scotia. As I have said before, we are all products of our environment. Thanks to you, Ryan, I too have not "stopped believing."

That fall, I teamed up with Future West Moto again, and announced their Arenacross series in BC's Lower Mainland. It was another incredible feeling to be trackside at an indoor race on the special platform that Elmer Niezen from Chilliwack's Ironside Designs had built. As a kid growing up in Chilliwack, friends and I would go into Ironside to get free stickers for our bicycles. That was definitely another full-circle, feel-good moment. Being involved at the races, announcing and doing the weekly radio show kept my finger pressed tightly to the pulse of my passion. Also around that time, Jamie Hellam had a new business partner in Future West Moto—Lesley Reid. Within a fairly short time, Lesley took over as sole owner of that grassroots, family fun, and professionally run, west coast motocross endeavour. Lesley, I speak for many when I say that you have done an incredible job. Our sport is better for your efforts. More important than any of the great work you have done with your team of hard-working warriors, is the feeling one has at those events. From everything I have experienced over the years in motocross, both good and bad, that tenure here in the west is the best that I have seen. I have been around long enough to have seen the good, the bad, and the ugly side of this sport. When I decided I wanted to live and change my evil ways, I promised myself that I would always stick with winners. In that regard, Future West Moto will always be number one in my books. Thank you for everything, Jamie and Lesley. Gisela and I are both thankful to have you as friends.

Early in 2014, things continued to flow well for us. The show was gaining traction, and Canadian motocross fans were getting set to welcome Mike Alessi to Canada. I did the announcing at our local races, but for the 2014 pro nationals, I got to sit across from Brian Koster as part of the CMRC's live radio broadcast. That was an honour. Being at those races as a spectator is cool, but when you add in a gig like that, with a great mechanical viewing advantage—it couldn't have been better. This is as good as place as any to thank my old friend, Mark Stallybrass. Mark and I had raced together many years prior. When I got involved in the sport again in 2008, it was great to see what he had done with CMRC as the main sanctioning body for motocross. Back in our era, it was all CMA-sanctioned racing. Mark, I hope you're enjoying your retirement from motocross and your latest endeavours. I appreciate all the opportunities that you provided for my family and me.

We did a few rounds of the nationals in the west that summer. Then we flew back to the Gopher Dunes race in July, and Walton in August. That year was my first trip to Gopher Dunes. What an incredible facility. While there I was able to meet the medics who saved my life, Carol Henderson and Ron Cameron. It was a powerful moment on top of the Gopher Dunes Honda truck. Thanks to the Schuster family for their great hospitality. The Gopher Dunes National needs to be on every motocross race fan's bucket list. It is one of the most physically demanding sand-based motocross tracks in the world. The racing that day was incredible, too. I will never forget the look of despair, and the conversations with my friend Tony Alessi that day after his son, Mike, ran out of gas in the first moto. Colton Facciotti went on to win the 2014 Canadian MX-1 title. To Colton, Mike, and every other rider that took the time out of their busy racing and training schedules to be on the *Canadian Moto Show*, I thank you.

I wasn't sure how I was going to feel when I got back to Walton for the first time since my crash in 2011. In my mind, the damage was done, and life was about moving forward. Yes, I was still dealing with a lot of garbage medically. It never went away, and a lot of it was silently getting worse. But being passionately driven by not wanting to lose that sport again, it made things that were awkward tolerable.

When we arrived, we were treated like gold by the Lee family and the entire moto community. It was three years since I had fallen from the Huron County hamlet's sky. I never went out of my way to ask anyone about what they remembered about that fateful day. For me, the desire to know or view what happened that day left the moment Gisela told me what she had seen, and that she never wanted to see it again. Out of the love and respect I have for her, the desire to know what happened disappeared. However, some people offered bits and pieces of what they saw during my race and crash. Some even called out other riders who failed to slow down when I was lying there. All I can say is that if you're going by a downed rider, see caution or red cross flags, slow the hell down. None of us wants or needs to be there. Now I realize there's much more to life than achieving a podium finish in a motocross race. I know it's almost useless trying to tell a racer something like that in the heat of the battle, but don't forget, when certain invisible lines are crossed, there's no going back.

Our travels with motocross took us many places over the next four race seasons. In 2014 I also started as a senior writer for *MXP* (*Motocross Performance*) magazine. That was a perfect fit. I love motocross, and I love to write about it. Now there are articles in the magazine written by yours truly. I also penned a weekly blog on their website called "Friday Flight," because, somehow, I had picked up the nickname "Airmail."

Reconnecting with old friends seemed to increase as we became more involved. At our local races, I was excited to reconnect with a friend named Kevin Lefebvre, who I raced with in the 1980s. Kevin, who lives only a couple of hours away in Penticton, was the main man behind launching our *Canadian Moto Show* magazine. See what I mean? Things were crazy in terms of how wide-open, busy, and fun our lives were during that stretch. Kevin, I can't thank you enough for all your efforts to help showcase our great sport and the *Canadian Moto Show*.

I was hired by Walton Raceway to come back the next two years to host their live video broadcast of our country's biggest event. Some of those moments rank up there with the best in my life. At those events I was also able to work with my old friend and photographer Bill Petro. Bill, who is one of our country's best and most legendary photographers, has spearheaded a project called the Legends of Canadian Motocross. His mandate is to preserve our sport's rich and vibrant photo history though a database that can travel to races and be shared globally on the web. To be a part of that project and shake hands with the fans and riders, new and old, at the display will stay with me forever. I can't tell you enough what an honour it is to have my name on a Legends of Canadian Motocross T-shirt. On the *Canadian Moto Show*, I aired a Legends of Canadian Motocross segment most weeks. It was cool to interview some of my former heroes and riders that I raced with, including Rollerball, Jim Holley, Stan Currington, Wayne Jones, Mike Harnden, and Doug Hoover. He was on the show just before he was honoured at the Toronto Supercross with the Legends and Heroes tour. Doug, the night I had you on the show, it was so cool to talk about how much has changed in terms of what can be done on a motorcycle. Bill, I look forward to hearing more news in regard to your Legends of Canadian Motocross project.

The action was fast and furious. Weeks and months flew by. My family life with my father, children, and grandkids was pretty minimal, but I was caught up in my job, and it was all-consuming. I loved every minute of it, but much like when I raced, my body hated it. I swear that my next body X-ray will likely show one solid calcified lump of arthritis. I guess one could argue that the silver lining in all of that is that that my screws will never come loose. On second thought, maybe it's too late for that one.

During a few race seasons, we went to twenty-five or more races a year. From the first day of announcing in 2013 until I shut everything down to write this book in 2017, I was doing moto-related activities from morning to night. Everything continued to mushroom positively pertaining to motocross. More and more opportunities were coming my way. Four years in a row, we were able to spend four to six weeks in the southern California sun. We went to Supercross races and frequented the practice tracks with the racers. Once again, motocross had become a way of life for us. I think that is a great way to put it. Motocross is not just a sport, but a way of life.

On one of those trips to the Lake Elsinore practice track, our friend, the "Seven Deuce Deuce" Adam Enticknap, a professional racer, crashed and broke his femur. We had planned to meet up with Adam, because I was writing an article on him for the magazine. Even though it was a huge bummer for Adam, in a selfish way, it felt good to be able to give back to an injured rider by driving his truck and dog back to his home in Huntington Beach. One of the funniest things about that whole deal was the look his dog, Champagne Frenchie, gave us when we pulled into the Lake Elsinore Veterinary Hospital by mistake. When we finally got to Adam, he was gutted and knew even before the X-ray that his femur was broken. It had been many years before, but I knew that feeling of despair all too well.

The following year Gisela and I got to sit in on the *Pulp MX Show* with Steve Matthes. On that trip at the San Diego Supercross, I also got to sit down and have a long chat with Ron Lechien about some of our races together at the World Mini, among other things. I always love talking with the riders I was in the trenches with years before. Dogger, I'm sure you were late for the press conference after our bench-racing session.

Steve Matthes had also gotten some riders to donate jerseys to be auctioned off when I was injured. His radio show is based in Las Vegas and is the best one that our sport has. Yes, even better than the *Canadian Moto Show*. I can only credit being there, to the generosity of a good friend from our northern areas, Peace Motocross Association's Loni Shevkenek. We had been up to the Peace Motocross's PMA and done some announcing at their Dawson Creek track. It was such an overwhelming experience, because Dawson Creek is Gisela's childhood home. So many good people up there went above and beyond to make our race experience as good as it could be. They even put a new raised subfloor in their tower, so I could announce completely unobstructed. On a sad note, I hope they eventually caught up with the SOB who torched it two years later. I was honoured to be able to pen an article in *MXP* on one of our country's true hidden motocross gems, the Peace Motocross Association. Special thanks to Reed LePine, Wayne Jones, and the gang.

No matter where we went in our sport, we were surrounded by great people. Loni had won the trip to the *Pulp-MX Show* in a Team Canada Motocross of

Nations fundraiser. I can't thank you enough for that, Loni. As for Matthes and his wife, Pookie, great hospitality and radio, bro!

I should also add that, through a fateful meeting with an old friend that weekend in Las Vegas, I was able to spend fifteen minutes one-on-one with Mike Tyson. It was incredible, because Mike was pure gold. I even managed to get some footage of the experience and pieced together a YouTube video. Check it out on the *Canadian Moto Show's* channel. Many of our escapades are there captured in living colour, including a visit to Evel Knievel's ill-fated Snake River Canyon jump site. It was so insane to be able to sit on the mound that his X-2 Sky Cycle launched from in Twin Falls, Idaho. It was also a cool moment to have Mike Tyson tell everyone to "tune in and listen to Brent and the Canadian Moto Show." Thanks, Mike. You went over and above on that day, my friend.

Looking back now, it's easy to see why, when I set out to write this book in 2017 that I was so worn out. I had my hands on so many different things and loved them all. Somewhere along the line though, I had lost the ability to say no to any moto-related media requests, among other things racing-related. I didn't want to say no, because I loved it all—the sport, the people, the travel, the radio show, and the spotlight of being an open and honest writer with *MXP*. But at the pace I was going, it was like crashing on a dirt bike. I knew it was going to happen sooner or later, but I just blocked it out of my mind, and focused on the fun.

Everything was starting to fall apart with my health, my medical needs, my equipment, and even our home. I know a few people who are in wheelchairs will read this. If so, I'm sure you understand the time and commitment it takes do even the most mundane task. If you are one of the many who wonder how I did everything that I did so quickly after my injury, the only answer is another one of my miracles. I'm so thankful that I have been able to make peace with what I thought I had left behind. This time around I gave it everything I had for as long as I could. When I was a kid, I could never say that.

Back when I was injured and shortly after my life-saving operation in London, Gisela was told that my life expectancy would be five to ten years, given the nature of my trauma and known complications. I was also told that it would likely take five years to get everything dialled in and comfortable. That came from my group of Para Peers here in Vernon. I hated hearing it and wanted no part of that, but joining the Para Peer group was one of the best things that I ever did. Having others provide a visual of how they were doing things like transferring in and out of their vehicles was a game-changer. A couple of them have even become Paralympic gold medalists.

I was retrained to drive by Lars Taylor, who is also a paraplegic, in Vernon. He has a driving academy for folks like me. It was quite a process, and I'm thankful I passed on my first road test. We traded my truck in on a Mazda 5 and had it outfitted with hand controls. The Mazda is perfect for us, and when we travel, even down south, we always drive. I had one titanium chair destroyed on an airplane coming home from Walton in 2015. We also have to take a ridiculous amount of stuff, including a pressure-relief air mattress that I have to sleep on to avoid pressure sores. That, coupled with enough medical supplies to make our vehicle resemble a medical supplies store on wheels, means the first question customs officials usually ask when they see the contents is, "How long are you going away for?"

In the spring of 2017, two of my racing friends in British Columbia suffered spinal cord injuries. It was a horrible feeling to see them newly injured. I not only knew the pain firsthand, but I also knew what most on the outside looking in didn't. After getting involved again with a couple of fundraisers for these individuals, for the first time since my injury, I became gravely depressed. My psychologist believes it was post-traumatic stress that precipitated it. After reinventing myself in the moto community after my own near-death and out-of-body experience, I became a go-to guy when someone was injured like that.

I loved helping my friends and giving back as much as I could, but it came at a huge price physically. I was torn. It felt so good to be giving back, but I knew I had to remove myself to be able to write this book. I also knew I needed to address the depression I had been suffering from. I hated that word for the longest time, but I no longer do. God does not make garbage. He challenges people to get the best out of them. Hopefully, one day I will cross over to the other side with a passing grade.

One of the things that I wanted to do as a fundraiser for another injured rider was a motocross trading-card project. I got that rolling, but soon I realized that to save my own life and write this book, I would have to step back from it. I owe a huge thanks to my good friend from Quebec, Jesse Leduc. Jesse, I look forward to mixing it up again real soon, my friend.

Who knows? Maybe one day something like that can materialize. I think it's a great way to promote and grow our sport. I would also like to find a place of employment in the motocross media world. I have some ideas for the *Canadian Moto Show* but may lean back on writing. Who knows? Podcasting, writing, solving world peace—we can all work on that last one together.

I said it before, and I will say it again, I love this sport with all my heart. But the reality today is that my physical being is a lot more limited than it was even a year or two prior to starting this book. I take comfort in knowing that I'm one of the luckiest people alive. I have a wonderful loving wife and a caring family. Gisela, you have seen all of me, the good and the bad. I'm so thankful I saved the best portion of my life to share with you. I love you so much, and I am blown away by the history we have created in our first seventeen years together. As far as my family goes, I love them all and always will, no matter what, though I don't have the greatest relationships with most of them. I understand that. It is not my place to play God, and tell anyone that their feelings don't matter. We all deal with and get over things in our own time frame. At the end of the day, we are all only human beings, and thankfully, no two of us are alike.

My son, Nolan, is with his mom in England, and I hope I get to see him again someday. Sonu and Sara are still here in Vernon, which makes me happy. My dad recently married a wonderful lady named Doreen. I went to school with Doreen's kids in Chilliwack. I'm happy that my father has someone to share his journey with. Dad, I love you more than ever and am so thankful that we are friends today.

On a sad and tragic note, the mother of my girls, Seema, was killed in a car crash in Fiji on December 9, 2018. Even though we had been separated for over twenty years, her death gutted me with sadness. Having lost my own mother in 2004, I know my girls will eventually heal and make their mother proud. Rest in peace, Seema.

After spending the better part of two years penning my story, I realized that for most of my life I never liked myself. I felt entirely responsible for the wreckage of my past. Today I have taken responsibility for my part in it. Being able to look in the mirror and not be repulsed by the reflection is another miracle. That miracle was only made possible by being able to let it all out. I once heard someone say, "Write it down, and make it real." Sharing my story with you is my way of letting go. My motive, however, is twofold. I hope that maybe someone reading can identify with and be spared some of the grief that I endured and put others through. I have learned along the way that it is okay to be flawed. In my wayward days, I always had the bar set way too high. Disappointment was a comfort zone that I used as an excuse to stay active in my addictions. Today it's safe to say that I strive for progress rather than unattainable perfection. I know it's a cliché, but the only thing of any value is what I do today. Why? Because it's always today.

In 2016, after being able to put my life back in order while pledging allegiance to my passion of motocross, something cool happened. One of the moms in our motocross community (Terry Greenough) nominated me for a Coast Mental Health "Courage to Come Back Award," given to those who overcome physical trauma and addiction. I didn't win, but as competitive as I am, the most important aspect was merely being recognized. It was a kind thing to do, so I want to give a big thanks to Terry and our extended motocross family. Anyone who has the courage to face who they are and their adversity in the process of amending their ways is a winner in my book. Trust me, it's not as easy as it sounds. I was incapable of any of that until I made a concerted effort to surround myself with winners. Sadly, many people are not so fortunate.

In the end it's important to note that I only wrote this book after I was approached by three separate individuals to do so. Not one of them were family members. The three I'm talking about know who they are. I thank you now; however, I do emphasize the "now." I had no idea how painstaking and physically and mentally draining the process of writing a book would be. I never intended to write this book to show the world that I was a hero in any way, shape, or form. I simply wanted to put the facts together and tell my story myself. This is the real me—how I see, how I feel, and how I interpret the collective karma of my life. I hope this book will serve my grandkids and future generations.

Whoever you are, I would like to thank you for reading this. I also want to extend a shout-out to my colleagues at *MXP*. In 2014 Mike McGill, one of our senior writers (and the guy who ran me over in the Vet clas race at the Walton TransCanada in 2009) wrote an in-depth article in the magazine called "Motocross Saved My Life, The Brent Worrall story." Today I'm so thankful that each and every one of you knows exactly how motocross did save my life. Who knows, maybe one day it will save yours too!

#LifeIsGold.

Brent "Airmail" Worrall

About the Author

Brent Worrall is a multiple trauma and brain injury survivor, avid sports enthusiast, and former top-level motocross racer and hockey player.

He collected many colourful achievements in his younger years, including being nominated for his hometown's athlete of the year, along with finishing tenth in the world motocross championship for his age group. He spent many dark years in places that he is not proud of and credits many of his painful life lessons to his current resolve. He hosted the *Canadian Moto Show* for four years while reinventing his life following his spinal cord injuries. Throughout this process, he also maintained a position as a senior writer at *Motocross Performance Magazine*. In 2017, he shut down everything to write this book as a final gift to the motocross community. He currently devotes his life to a number of causes and activities, all of which are aimed at sharing his love of sports and motocross while also encouraging anyone who is facing adversity that it is never too late to turn your life around and make it count. He currently lives in Vernon, BC.

CPSIA information can be obtained
at www.ICGtesting.com
Printed in the USA
LVHW072003151119
637062LV00018B/49/P